The
CARPENTERS

ALSO BY RAY COLEMAN

The

CARPENTERS

The Untold Story

An Authorized Biography

Ray Coleman

B🌿XTREE

*For those who cherish
beautiful music.
And to the memory of an
irreplaceable voice.*

First published in Great Britain in 1994 by Boxtree Limited, Broadwall House, 21 Broadwall, London SE1 9PL

Copyright © Ray Coleman 1994

The rights of Ray Coleman to be identified as Author of this Work have been asserted by him in accordance with the Copyright, Designs and Patents Act 1988

10 9 8 7 6 5 4 3 2 1

Typeset by SX Composing, Rayleigh, Essex
Printed and bound in Great Britain by
Butler and Tanner Ltd, Frome, Somerset

Jacket design by Robert Updegraff

A CIP catalogue entry for this book is available from the British Library

ISBN 1-85283-553-2

CONTENTS

PROLOGUE

This is a triumphant and tragic story. It is the first biography of Karen and Richard Carpenter, whose music, begun a quarter of a century ago, is now an indelible part of the landscape of popular song.

Their golden sound sped around the world on a nonstop run of hits including "Close to You," "We've Only Just Begun," "Top of the World," "Yesterday Once More," and "Rainy Days and Mondays." It was a sound built to last.

But the fairy-tale story had a bittersweet aspect. After a seven-year battle against what was then a little-known eating disorder, Karen Carpenter died on February 4, 1983. For years, her relatives and friends thought she had been following a well-trodden female path, slimming conscientiously.

Dieting became Karen's obsession, however; she careered out of control, and despite treatment she died from heart failure brought about by anorexia nervosa, the eating disorder that was then surfacing as a major female problem.

She was thirty-two, unhappily married, loved her work, and was a millionairess. With her brother, Richard, as musical director and songwriter, Karen's voice, aching with melancholic emotion, extolled songs of troubled love and romance that often sounded autobiographical: "I Need to Be in Love," "Hurting Each Other," "Goodbye to Love," and "Solitaire."

Carpenters music has proved perennially popular, perhaps immortal, but they had to overcome obstacles to achieve success. When they began, they were annihilated by critics as "wimpish," "squeaky clean," and "sexless"; they were castigated for their bland appearance as well as music described as "saccharine."

With the contemporary rock air of the early 1970s thick with the textures and attitudes of Led Zeppelin, Elton John, David Bowie, and Sly Stone together with the arrival of disco, a brother-sister act who struck no poses but sang melodic popular music was ostracized. And anyone admitting to be an aficionado could be treated as a leper in "aware" society.

Twenty years later, while many of the artists who jeered at them have burned out, their music has grown in stature. It is heard on planes and in restaurants, in bookshops and supermarkets, on radio stations. Their CD sales are booming. Soundalike and look-alike acts perpetuate them in sell-out concert tours, performing Carpenters hits for all age groups in the United States, Britain, and Japan.

Karen and Richard Carpenter's craft is now admired openly— particularly by a young audience that even considers it "cool" to admit it, pointing out the beauty of that voice and the quality of those songs and arrangements.

If they were not particularly timely when they began, the 1990s have confirmed their appeal as timeless.

Their soft, reassuring music came upon us as an antidote to the crises of Vietnam and Watergate. Amid the drug culture of those years, Richard and Karen seemed to epitomize what many saw as a new American Dream. Wholesome, gifted, family oriented, and absorbed in the work ethic, they were embraced by President Richard Nixon. Describing them as "young America at its best," he had them play at the White House on a state occasion.

Visually, they had little impact. Karen stood out front, pleasing but hardly riveting, while Richard played the straight guy at the piano. Their repertoire, however, was rich in love songs, and their appeal was clinched by Karen's unique gift. Her haunting, some-what sad vocals carried perfect pitch and such a distinctive timbre that many of her contemporaries regard her as one of the greatest female singers.

It was a battle fought and won with music. Yet fate has decreed that the Carpenters name will also be remembered with an under-current of sadness. For Karen was the first celebrity to die after battling against anorexia nervosa, one of the eating disorders that now afflicts some eight million sufferers in the United States. In

Britain, at least sixty thousand people are known to have anorexia or bulimia; the actual figure is probably more than twice that.

She punished her body for years while maintaining a rigorous work schedule, during which, astonishingly, her natural voice never faltered. Her personality remained ebullient; her friends were life-long admirers of her continual thoughtfulness and her humor. Two and a half years before she died, she had married. She said she craved motherhood, but her marriage quickly ran into trouble, adding to her psychological malaise.

But she had no death wish and wanted to go on making music, and perhaps expanding her talent into other fields of entertainment, throughout her life. She was a traditional show business trouper.

So what killed Karen Carpenter? Was it plain obstinacy in the form of a dieting obsession?

Was it a craving for the attention that her skeletal shape would attract from anyone whose eyes fell on her?

Was it her need to make a statement of control through the fork-to-mouth action that nobody can ultimately dictate to the anorexic?

Was it a deep-seated psychological problem, which many theorize about sufferers—a blurred signal to a parent with whom there might be a relationship problem?

Was it, in this case, an ugly and deadly "equalizer" for attention alongside her older brother, who was treated as the "senior" by their mother—and without whom Karen knew she would have no career?

Or, since Karen never considered herself truly pretty enough to stand on a stage, was her starvation aimed at correcting her lack of self-esteem?

These are just some of the questions addressed in this biography. Since Karen's art must have been to a large degree the product of her soul, many interviewees have remarked on her psyche and the quality of her voice which evoked her loneliness. Over a dozen albums, the Carpenters produced a substantial body of work cherished by millions. Karen, like her brother, was a workaholic who enjoyed her success and fame, but did not live to witness their longevity—in Britain, for example, not a day passes without their music being heard on the radio; typically, on April 16, 1993, on national Radio 2, after playing a Carpenters track, disc jockey Sarah

Kennedy remarked, "I don't know what we would *do* on Radio 2 without the Carpenters!"

The trauma of living with the memory of his sister's decline, followed by her death and then the aftermath, has haunted Richard Carpenter since that shocking day in 1983.

Exhilarated by their achievements together, he is forever saddened and puzzled by the loss of his sister; he continues to marvel at the quality of her voice and reflects on their great times together as well as on the tragic circumstances of her death.

He and I had discussed a biography for some fifteen years. It was never the "right" time. Either it was too early, or the Carpenters were busy on the road or in the studios, or Karen was very ill, or he was despairing about his own problem (in the late 1970s he survived a dangerous period of overdosing with sleeping pills). And then, when Karen died, he needed time to recover and place his recollections into perspective.

In the late 1980s I urged him during our regular meetings in Hollywood to consider helping with the assembly of the story. New generations were discovering their music, and the importance of the two contrasting aspects of their lives—the creation of their sound, and Karen's tragedy—needed to be recorded.

Richard was unsure about a book for a long time. Too many heartaches, he said; could he really face opening the door yet again to such a troubled past? He took some persuading, but ultimately his pride in their achievements coupled with a desire for the truth, particularly with the benefit of hindsight, prevailed. He remains acutely aware that Karen's death will forever be regarded as a pointer, a linchpin, for anorexia nervosa and its sufferers, mainly because she was a celebrity whose problem was played out in public upon her death. Many times during our conversations, Richard and I said that if this project saves one victim, it will have been worthwhile.

This, then, is a cautionary tale. Richard and Karen's story was a typical middle-American dream that came true: a Connecticut brother and sister who fell in love with music, migrated to California, reached for the stars, and achieved precisely what they wanted. They had a ball; there is abundant joy in their story. They admired each other's artistry but became too possessive of each other's life. Both fell victim to excesses, Richard to pill popping, Karen to dieting.

Talking to Richard Carpenter, his family, friends, and professional colleagues, I grew to understand why he had guarded the story so zealously.

For this exhilarating journey to a summit in show business has its shocking end with the price a young woman paid for hating what she saw in the mirror.

Interviewing nearly a hundred people on the trail of the truth about Karen's obsession, obduracy, and inner torment, and of Richard's pill popping that nearly destroyed him, too, I saw tears of rage at the appalling, premature ending of a life.

Equally, there remains sheer wonder at the quality and quantity of peerless music, at Karen's matchless voice. Hardly surprisingly, not a day passes without Richard thinking of his sister with a combination of love for her partnership and seething frustration at losing her.

Revisiting this story has been often tortuous for Richard but to attempt to tell it without his enthusiastic cooperation would have been impossible. I thank him warmly for his unremitting candour and help in attempting to provide answers to tough questions, every step of the way. At the end of this book, I acknowledge the many patient people in the United States and Britain who aided my research.

I knew Karen in her good and bad years. Her star shone too briefly, but as it did, her gaiety, sincerity, and natural oeuvre touched all who looked and listened. She loved music deeply. As the sound of the Carpenters becomes legendary with the passing years, her creative legacy grows. She would have loved that.

Ray Coleman

FOREWORD

BY HERB ALPERT

After listening to thirty seconds of the Carpenters' demo tape in 1969, I knew I was experiencing two extraordinarily talented people. Karen's intimate voice sounded like it was singing just for me, and Richard's original flair for vocal arranging and keyboard work made for a very special sound.

Karen's gift was formidable. Her voice rang out like a bell that was clear and friendly; soothing, musical, and honest. And to make things even more interesting, the tape that I heard at times sounded as though many musicians and back-up singers were performing, but it was actually Richard and Karen playing all the parts. Karen was playing drums and singing all the background vocals with Richard.

Although Karen and I were very close, I didn't know to what extent she was suffering with her emotional problems until she was hospitalized. I knew she had a constant struggle with her weight, but never connected it with anorexia nervosa.

Karen was a little "girl-woman" who was always looking for something or someone to fill her life beyond hit records, and seemed very lonely and very innocent in her pursuit.

Although their first album, *Ticket to Ride,* did not take off like a rocket, I knew that it was just a matter of time. Their records were spotless.

Richard always made sure that every sonic detail was just to his liking. The combination of Richard's extraordinary abilities to recognize or write a great song, arrange the material, produce the records, and Karen's magical God-given voice, gave the world a sound that will always be remembered. The Carpenters.

PART ONE

NEW YORK CITY, 1982

TEARS AND FEARS

Anorexia Nervosa:

A psychological illness, most common in female adolescents, in which the patients have no desire to eat; eating may, in fact, be abhorrent to them. The problem often starts with a simple desire to lose weight, which then becomes an obsession. The result is severe loss of weight and sometimes even death from starvation. The underlying cause of the illness is complicated—problems in the family and rejection of adult sexuality are often factors involved. Patients must usually be treated by psychotherapy.

—*Concise Medical Dictionary* (Oxford Medical Publications) (Britain)

A psychological and endocrine disorder primarily of young women in their teens that is characterized especially by a pathological fear of weight gain leading to faulty eating patterns, malnutrition, and usually excessive weight loss.

—*Webster's Ninth New Collegiate Dictionary* (USA)

An eating disorder primarily affecting adolescent girls and young women characterized by pathological fear of becoming fat, distorted body image, excess dieting and emaciation.

—*Random House Unabridged Dictionary* (USA)

K aren needs a hug and needs to be told that she's loved."
The psychotherapist to Karen Carpenter spoke softly and
tapped the bottom of her mother's shoe as she sat opposite
her daughter in his New York office.

It was a risk, and he knew it. Dealing head-on with family sensibilities was treacherous, and this situation was particularly difficult. Parental relationships are often considered to be at the root
of eating disorders, but neither Karen nor her parents believed
there was any central problem that could not be cured. Yet at age
thirty-two, she had left it rather late to be pulled back from the
precipice of disaster, and everyone around her was rallying to support her in her treatment for anorexia nervosa.

Agnes Carpenter did not believe that psychotherapy was the
answer to her daughter's illness, but with Karen's father, Harold,
she had flown from California to attend a ninety-minute "family
therapy session" suggested by therapist Steven Levenkron.

In her seventh year of battling anorexia, Karen now knew she
was in deep trouble. Sobbing uncontrollably in the presence of her
parents, she confronted and finally released some of the emotions
she had been holding in check for years: how badly she felt about
herself; how much she wanted to apologize for ruining her family's
life and causing distress to her friends; how her feeling of degrada-
tion had threatened her career and ruined her personal life. Could
she ever recover?

"In one sense," Levenkron says, "what Karen was saying didn't
matter, but what was *happening* between the people in the room
was paramount. Karen wanted to explain who she was to her par-

ents. She was saying, 'Be my mommy, I'm crying to you.'" At that moment, Levenkron tapped Agnes's foot.

Willingly, Agnes rose from her armchair, walked over to Karen seated on a sofa, and put her arms around her. The emotional electricity was so strong, so private, that both Karen's father and Levenkron had to turn away. "This was a very important, sweet moment," Levenkron recalls. "I felt relieved for Karen. I know she *needed* that. It might have felt awkward for Mom because it wasn't a thing that came easily for her. But we got the hug for Karen."

Karen's problems that had manifested in a physically threatening disease were multilayered and complex. Often, she had bemoaned to her therapist that she faced lifelong misery because the price of success as a hardworking singer, combined with celebrity status, was unhappiness in love. She feared that she would never achieve what she truly craved: a strong marriage and motherhood. That factor alone caused her deep distress.

A wide spectrum of psychological problems plagued Karen as she confronted her problem with characteristic determination. At that moment of her embrace with her mother, perhaps the darkest of all her difficulties was surfacing: though she was loved by so many close friends, and admired by millions for her unique talent, she had lost much of her self-respect. This loss stemmed from her basic worry that while she had a wonderful voice, she did not have natural beauty or a body she was proud of.

Her self-doubt was a deficiency her psychotherapist recognized clearly as he witnessed her breakdown in front of her parents. Silver haired and silver tongued, the forty-one-year-old with piercing blue eyes had a fine pedigree as a counsellor of young women with eating disorders. Karen had submitted herself to a year's treatment by Levenkron, which entailed moving from her California home to New York where he was based. And now, after his initial six weeks of exploring her psyche, Levenkron invited her parents to his office for some interaction with their daughter.

Loving, loyal, and proud, Agnes and Harold were undemonstrative. The Carpenters were never a touching, hugging, or kissing family. Agnes believed that such physicality did not necessarily equate with care, concern, or affection. Harold went along with his wife's forceful view. "This family did not go into depth about feelings," Levenkron says. "Many families don't, but Karen needed depth."

Agnes was a zealously protective mother. Her values were straight-talking common sense, hard work, practicality, and all-around morality. She shunned what she considered the shallow world of show business with its phony fast talkers full of cheap embraces and endless bonhomie. She did not need, she would tell anyone who asked, to touch her children to demonstrate that she loved them. And she instinctively distrusted psychological theories, which the likes of Levenkron might bring to the table when discussing her daughter's anorexia nervosa. As far as Agnes was concerned, Karen was simply dieting stubbornly and stupidly, the way millions of young women do—and she needed to get some common sense without wasting time and money on theoretical mumbo jumbo from "experts."

But the monster that had enveloped Karen in the years when anorexia nervosa was a little-known illness was visible to Levenkron from their first meetings. And what he found in Karen Carpenter was "a terrified, scared little girl." His relationship with her may have been complicated because, in his view, her parents resented him, viewing him as a "competing parent ... I was taking their little girl away from them. The mother kept saying to Karen: 'So when are you coming home? When is all this being fixed up?' Basically, the mother was saying: 'When can I have you back?'"

All his twenty-two patients were different, but Karen—stubborn, wily, confrontational but with a central core of extreme vulnerability—had somehow quickly won Levenkron's heart as well as his head. For so many years, Karen had eloped from her crisis. She didn't want to die, she insisted. She loved her life, her career, her family, and particularly her fame; yet here she sat with her parents, three thousand miles from home, with the tears flowing. What troubled her, and some of those around her who did not dare express their doubts so plainly, was a nagging fear that she may have waited too long to seriously address her crisis. Karen had gone to New York to find a solution to her physical problem. The dilemma she and others found much harder to solve was whether it was symptomatic of a troubled soul and, if it was, how that soul might be reached.

Karen Carpenter's route from her balmy, cushioned world in California to a whole year in New York devoted to therapy was, like most major turning points in her life, circuitous.

By 1978, after three and a half years of continual dieting which had reduced her weight at times to seventy-nine pounds, those around her knew that urgent and immediate action was necessary to stop her wasting away. Talking to Karen about the problem had proved fruitless: like all anorexia sufferers, she was a plausible liar, a schemer who assured everyone that she knew the dangers and had her life under control. Just give her time, she kept saying to her family and friends, and she would get better. Meanwhile, kindly let her make music, which she adored.

But Jerry Weintraub did not believe her. As Hollywood's most influential manager and concert promoter, with a roster that included Elvis Presley, Frank Sinatra, Neil Diamond, Judy Garland, Bob Dylan, and John Denver, he had taken over direction of the Carpenters' career in 1976.

It was a turbulent time. Karen's health was declining in tandem with the Carpenters' record sales. Planning a new strategy for their career came naturally to such a heavyweight manager with enormous influence in the entertainment industry. He had a platonic affection, too, for Karen. But as this "bag of bones," as he sadly recalls her now, curled up on his lap during business meetings in his office, he decided that saving her life was his priority.

"You're gonna die, Karen," he told her so many times. "There's no way you can *live* like this." She had fooled scores of well-wishers with the confidence and trickery that were the hallmark of the anorexic. But Weintraub's genuine affection for his artist was matched by a hardheaded determination to deal tangibly with the crisis, which psychiatrists and doctors had failed to penetrate.

Watching a television talk show one night, Weintraub saw Steven Levenkron talking about anorexia nervosa. He was promoting his novel about "the obsession that kills." *The Best Little Girl in the World* would go on to become a best-seller and form the basis of a two-hour television film. The book had quickly become a word-of-mouth success among those with eating disorders, since it carried the stamp of authority of a therapist who knew his subject intuitively. Karen Carpenter had become absorbed by the book but told nobody about it at this stage.

Impressed by the persuasive tones of this expert, Weintraub checked with friends, who confirmed what Weintraub had not realized: that this "new" disease was, indeed, partly psychological and

that Karen could benefit from treatment by someone such as the
television authority he had just witnessed.

With his book flying out of the stores, Levenkron had become
a media star. His answering machine was permanently stacked with
messages, mostly from distraught, pleading parents whose daughters needed to see him "immediately." So a request for him to
return a call to Jerry Weintraub in Los Angeles meant nothing. It
joined the waiting line. Returning the call after three days, Levenkron got past three secretaries to reach Weintraub, who lost no
time in assuring him that he was a show business VIP. "We're very
worried about Karen Carpenter," Weintraub said. "We've sent her
to people out here, and she's not making any progress. We really
are afraid for her health." Levenkron had scarcely heard of the
Carpenters, but he remembered seeing Karen once on television
and saying to himself, "Boy, that woman has anorexia."

Karen's follow-up phone call from Los Angeles to New York
came quickly. On March 27, 1979, sitting on the couch with
Richard in Weintraub's office, she finally agreed to make contact
with that man in New York who might help her. Walking across
Weintraub's office, she made sure that as she placed the call she
was out of earshot of her manager and of Richard.

Telling Levenkron that Weintraub was "a very nice man who
loves me dearly," she insisted that he was simply misinformed. She
suffered, she continued, from "GI"—a gastrointestinal problem
that caused colitis: "Everything I eat just flows right out of me,
and that's why I'm skinny." Her work was stressful, but she
declared that she did not have anorexia; her manager was well-
intentioned but misguided. With all the conversational force she
could muster, Karen persuaded Levenkron that wires had become
crossed and that people were setting off alarms unnecessarily.

"Well, then," Levenkron said to Karen, "don't hop on a plane
and come to see me here in New York if all you have is colitis."
Not looking for business, and uncomfortable about taking responsibility for someone apparently reluctant to move three thousand
miles to be in treatment, he added: "Well, go see a GI specialist.
And good luck to you."

As anorexics are apt to do, Karen then lied. Returning to
Richard at the couch, she said: "Well, I don't have anorexia. He
can tell just from talking to me." Richard believed that Levenkron
should have detected a lying anorexic on the phone, but he and

Weintraub were now disarmed if still puzzled and worried. At least, they told each other, she had made that important phone call—and silenced them.

Karen and Levenkron forgot about each other. But as she deteriorated, her brother led a chorus demanding that she seek help.

Under pressure, Karen felt the need to look for independent guidance. Her occasional "date," record boss Mike Curb, had been producing for the Boone family—singer Pat Boone and his daughters, Cherry and Debby. Cherry, then relocated from California to Seattle, Washington, had survived anorexia and was happily married to Dan O'Neill. They had a one-year-old daughter. To Karen, news of such a triumph over the problem, especially the fact that Cherry had gone on to become a mother, was inspirational. Tortured by a treadmill she could not conquer, Karen phoned Cherry to describe her condition. "The public really didn't know much about anorexia or bulimia then," Cherry recalls. "There were no role models or support groups, or even many doctors who knew how to deal with it. When Karen spoke by phone with my family and found out how well I was doing, she felt that maybe I could guide her, throw her a lifeline."[1]

Cherry's advice to Karen stressed the need for professional help, preferably out of Los Angeles so that she could cast aside all pressures of work and family. Karen's straightforward style of describing her difficulties surprised Cherry; Karen described her problem as "a real bitch to try to deal with."

"I remember thinking about her angelic voice and the contrast with the way she talked to me on the phone. She pulled no punches, came across as a real pal, as if we'd been friends for a long time."

The advice to devote all her time to getting better confirmed Karen's underlying view, which she had been resisting. She was, Cherry Boone O'Neill avers, "frustrated by the fact that this was something so all-consuming and she didn't seem to have the power to just grit her teeth and be done with it." For anything or anyone to have complete control over her was unacceptable to Karen; that factor alone would have conditioned her attitude toward an expert, especially on her health.

---

1. Cherry Boone O'Neill was completing her autobiography at the time Karen phoned her. Dealing extensively with her eating disorder, the book, *Starving for Attention,* became a bestseller, and Cherry went on to write other books on the subject.

*   *   *

Two and a half years passed after her abortive conversation by phone with Steven Levenkron. Karen astounded, infuriated, and frightened her huge circle of friends, colleagues in the entertainment world, and her relatives. As her weight hovered around eighty pounds and her eyes became sunken, her arms showed more bones than flesh. She wore multilayered clothing to hide the reality of her skeletal body but her voice remained amazingly intact. Working conscientiously and enthusiastically with her brother, she was able to summon an inner conviction to sing almost as well as ever. She was as punctual for her work as she had always been and in good spirits in the studios. But, significantly, she lacked stamina. It was doubtful whether she would pull through without specialist therapeutic treatment, and everyone told her exactly that; after five years of fighting it alone, it was time to confront "that dieting problem."

And so, in October 1981, with Karen's consent, her best girlfriend in New York phoned Steven Levenkron. Karen Ramone found it hard to share first names so became known as Itchy, an abbreviation of her maiden name of Itchyumi. Married to the eminent record producer Phil Ramone, she had become very close to Karen during the singer's sojourns in New York.

Itchy informed Levenkron that she was calling on behalf of an anonymous famous person who was suffering from anorexia nervosa. Her conspiratorial tone irritated him. "I really don't talk about phantoms," he snapped. "I can't discuss with you the *possibility* of talking to a famous person. I've had famous people here before, and they've come and gone, and no one has ever known it. I get all kinds of strange calls every day. Please tell your unnamed famous person to call me direct."

"Well, it's Karen Carpenter," Itchy said.

"Oh my God, then she lied to me a year ago when she called here and assured me that she had nothing wrong with her?"

"Yes, she did," Itchy continued. "She knows she lied to you, and now she wants to see you."

It was a very different Karen on the phone from Los Angeles to Levenkron the next day. Gone was the apologist for her overprotective manager. Instead, she was bold, decisive, organized.

"I'm coming to see you on Saturday," she began to Levenkron. Karen could be bossy and commanding when it suited her, but such a style from a potential patient did not sit well with Levenkron.

"I beg your pardon?" he said.

"I'm coming to see you on Saturday, and I'd like to see you for three hours."

"And what do you think that will do?"

"I don't know, but I'm coming to see you. . . . I'll just take a little while."

Levenkron, replying that he did not have Saturday hours, says he felt like a heel when Karen then burst into tears, spluttering, "You won't treat me because I'm famous." She was impatient, adding her insistence that "this will only take you a couple of hours."

Rebutting her theory that she would be curable after such a quick consultation, he told her: "Oh no, you won't. You won't take a *little* time at all. You're going to be a big job to fix up." Famous people, he added as a warning, often got the worst care "because they control their care, and they contaminate and undermine it."

Karen's apparent ploy was to agree to see him so that her critics would again be silenced and she could then revert to her shell.

Levenkron, used to such fencing with clients in the early stages, told her: "You know, you are really asking for the worst care possible! You're assuming something permanent will come out of seeing me for a couple of hours! Nothing permanent will come of it."

Karen rasped, "I've already bought a plane ticket."

Levenkron tried reason. "I'm sorry you bought a plane ticket, but I don't see people on Saturdays. I'm a family person. And I don't see people on the run. I *will* block out three hours when you can come and see me, but let's give you a straight appointment and the same kind of care that I would give to someone who isn't a star."

Karen began crying, but Levenkron persisted. "You think this thing is over with one phone call and a three-hour appointment. I'm not going to have you come and see me once and think you've been treated for this illness. It's dopey. You sit down and think about whether you really want to fight this thing or not. And if you do, I'll help you fight it."

The conversation ended abruptly and neutrally, Karen saying

she would consider his words carefully. She hung up and called Itchy. This guy Levenkron had upset her, she wept into the phone. He said there was no quick solution, that it was a long process to recovery. Itchy advised her to think positively and move to New York for a while to go under Levenkron's baton. He was, after all, endorsed by so many people. Privately, Itchy felt, as did Cherry Boone O'Neill, that Karen would benefit from relocating from California, shedding temporarily at least the suffocating routine of daily phone calls and regular dinners with her parents, weekly trips to the bowling alley with her brother, Richard, and the relentless recording schedules which Karen could never bring herself to postpone. Karen needed breathing space, a change of environment, and Itchy was not the only friend who believed that.

When Itchy called Levenkron to berate him for upsetting Karen, he stuck to his speech that either Karen dealt with the problem sensibly or he could not get involved.

Three hours after her first call, Karen phoned Levenkron again. She would move to New York for a long period, but he would have to see her every day for five days every week—"because you'll be the only reason I'll be living there." He agreed. Without telling anyone, Karen had decided to take the plunge for six months if she warmed to his treatment.

Karen Carpenter's submission for the whole of 1982 to treatment by Steven Levenkron was more than a crie de coeur from an anorexic to an expert. It was the crucial statement to her family and friends and the music people around her that after so many years of hiding and nursing her problem alone, she would divest herself of all that was familiar to her, and put her career "on hold," to challenge and defeat the relentless disease that threatened her.

Geographically, too, it was a giant step. Moving to the East Coast in winter was anathema to someone who so enjoyed the climate in California.

Flying in to New York in November 1981 for a series of preliminary discussions to determine whether she could get along with Levenkron for a prolonged period, Karen began a long walking routine, which she would continue nearly every day for the following year.

Logically, she should have taken a limousine from the Regency Hotel on Park Avenue to Levenkron's office at East Seventy-ninth Street and Madison Avenue. But Karen always walked the nineteen blocks—in order to lose more calories. And she walked quickly to increase that use of energy.

Sometimes she was stopped on the street, and Karen delighted in talking to people about her music and signing autographs. Levenkron's wife, Abby, who had not yet met Karen, was shocked to see from a distance her "teeny little face on top of a blue, very lightweight, puffy down coat" turning into the winter wind of Madison Avenue after an early therapy session. "It was before she was able to make any weight gains. I'm sure she needed to bundle up in the New York cold."

The cushion of a hotel suite came expensively to someone as frugal as Karen. She told friends the bill was six thousand dollars a month before food and phones, but she needed the comfort, she explained. She was not alone; Itchy Ramone moved into a room next door to ensure that Karen had company and spiritual support.

Every morning, Itchy and Karen would eat the same breakfast together in Karen's suite: orange juice, two eggs over easy, bacon, white or rye toast, coffee. Superficially, it looked normal, but years of slavery to her diet meant that all those calories had to go. Itchy became used to Karen's habitual visit to the bathroom right after she'd eaten, to rid herself of the food by swallowing huge quantities of Dulcolax laxative tablets. Around her suite, she would rarely sit for long spells because standing brought movement, and that meant losing weight.

Levenkron's normal fee was eighty dollars for a forty-five-minute session, but Karen requested an hour, for which he charged her a hundred dollars. She stipulated five daily sessions per week, mostly mornings, and sipped coffee (black, no sugar) or drank her favourite, iced tea. Sometimes she chewed ice cubes—a regular habit for anorexics since they give an illusion of eating but have no calories.

In April 1982 Karen flew home for a break from her treatment. Richard, who never believed the method of daily outpatient treatment was going to be adequate, thought that she looked appalling. By November, Karen decided irrevocably to call a halt to the treatment, announcing by phone to her lawyer, Werner Wolfen, that she was coming home permanently in time for Thanksgiving.

"Well, it doesn't seem like the best idea to me," he said, echoing the view of the Carpenter family.

"I don't care. I'm coming home. I'm cured. That's it."

Agnes and Harold flew in to accompany their daughter back to Los Angeles. With her twenty-two pieces of luggage, she needed physical help in packing as well as her parents' moral support. When they went to meet her as she left Levenkron for the last time, Karen again insisted on walking back to the hotel despite having a sprained foot. "Why in the name of heaven are we walking with you limping like that?" her mother asked as they tramped down Madison Avenue. "Oh, that's all right, I can stand it," she insisted. Back in her suite, she soaked her feet and said her foot hurt. "She wouldn't listen," Agnes reflects. "She walked; we walked with her."

As she prepared to leave, her friend Olivia Newton-John called to see her in her hotel suite. Karen was confident about her physical condition. Olivia was happy to see her in better shape, and they looked forward to getting together regularly when they were both back on the West Coast.

Cheered by Karen's smiles and her gain of about thirty pounds, Agnes and Harold stepped with her into the limousine for the airport. They were in a buoyant mood. Seven years of being plagued by a mysterious eating disorder were about to end, and her parents were relieved at the prospect of her return to normality. As the car left midtown, they mused that Karen and Richard could now resume the career that had been hampered by health problems in the past few years.

When they checked in at Kennedy airport, Karen asked, as was her custom, what type of aircraft would be flying them to California. Told it was a DC10, she became jittery. "I'm not going to get on that plane," she told Agnes and Harold firmly. In recent years, DC10s had experienced problems, and both she and Richard avoided the plane as much as possible.

Her mother pointed out that they could hardly sit waiting for eight hours for another flight, and eventually a nervous Karen reluctantly got on board.

She took a window seat in the first-class cabin, and as the flight got under way, Agnes began to worry. Despite the tasty food offered, Karen ate nothing and only drank water. For most of the five-hour flight she dozed into her pillow.

Agnes did not say much; she knew better than to try to persuade Karen to eat, and she was, after all, returning home at a respectable 108 pounds.

But something bothered Agnes. The way in which Karen ignored all that food didn't seem right. Her mother said nothing but thought plenty. Was *this* a return to normal eating?

DOWNEY, CALIFORNIA, 1983

I knew this was gonna happen.
I knew she didn't look well.

—RICHARD, ON HEARING OF KAREN'S COLLAPSE

T he doorbell at Karen's home in Century City chimed the first six notes of "We've Only Just Begun." Inside, it was spacious and luxurious, with a panoramic view of the Los Angeles skyline. Karen had always been wary of show biz glitz, but she never had any problem about coming to terms with fame and enjoying some of its fruits. She revelled in the splendour and the status of her $750,000 apartment at 2222 Avenue of the Stars.

Yet there was something unsettled about her when she was in residence there. Was it, some friends wondered, her true home or merely a wonderful address? A mass of contradictions, Karen was basically a homey person. But though she was suspicious of jet-set values, she enjoyed sampling them; indeed, she had been hectored by some friends into accepting that to grasp her true identity, she should generate a lot more pizzazz than was evident. Unlike many celebrities, she had never changed her name in her bid for recognition, but some friends felt she should work on her persona. Show business, they told her, bestowed certain obligations upon a star of her stature.

Part of Karen battled with any such transformation. Despite her pride in her condominium in Century City, she had never mentally left Downey. The conservative commuter suburb, twenty miles along the freeway from Hollywood, represented the roots she had known since junior high school. And while Karen and Richard had physically "left the nest," their relationships with their parents were as intertwined as ever. Agnes and Harold maintained the framework of a uniquely strong family unit: fully furnished bedrooms were left as they had been for both Karen and Richard at the Carpenter homestead at 9828 Newville Avenue, Downey.

Since buying her own apartment in 1976, Karen had immersed herself into the Beverly Hills set, acquiring close and trusted friends who wanted her to shed the claustrophobic confines of suburbia—mentally and physically. They wanted her to live in a more sophisticated manner that supposedly represented her life as a singing star. She was far too parsimonious, they implied; she should enjoy her money and spend more freely. Working to combat Karen's lifelong stubbornness and her love of simple values, they tried to psyche her into becoming an "uptown girl."

Karen had been a visitor to Beverly Hills, shopping at such stores as Gucci, for years but had never allowed herself to be sucked into its life-style. Nor had she allowed herself to be overtaken by its materialistic excesses. Her new friends believed she had erected a barrier to enjoyment because she was "overprotected," a description with which her brother agreed. Now, her friends decided, she needed finally to be shown where to shop and how to spend on herself, and taken around the spots on Rodeo Drive where she could develop that indefinable quality, style. Eventually, Karen agreed and spent more time in that glistening locality; the Polo Lounge of the Beverly Hills Hotel became her rendezvous.

Such a change in outlook and stance never rang true with Karen's parents or her brother. The antithesis of the jet set, they saw no reason why millionaire status should change their unswerving ethics. Karen had been raised in moderation, unpretentiousness, and solid family values, and though they didn't say much to irritate her, they worried that she wasn't being exactly true to herself. Karen was virtually leading two lives, and though little was said, her mother viewed her daughter's upward mobility, and her daughter's friends, with suspicion.

Deep down, Karen retained all her root feelings. And she seemed to revel in the exceptionally tightly knit family unit, facing up to her responsibilities within it conscientiously. And so there was a "pull"; while she enjoyed being recognized during walking and shopping expeditions to Beverly Hills, she was drawn back continually to Downey for its familiarity, its security, and its simplicity.

A natural comedienne who enjoyed a self-deprecating laugh, she would join in the mocking of Downey as "hicksville" by her more urban pals. "Downey! What's from Downey? Who lives in Downey? Yeah, I know!" she would say.

But for all those japes, and despite the fact that she railed against her mother's authority, she went back to Downey and "home," as she continued to call it, most weeks. And she often stayed overnight.

Early in the afternoon of Thursday, February 3, 1983, a distraught Karen was on the phone to Richard from her condominium to his home in Lubec Street, Downey. Their mom had just given her a hard time, she said. Karen wanted to plan a weekend with Olivia Newton-John, but her mother's view was that she was not fit enough to be running around as much as she had been doing, and she should rest. When Richard asked how she felt, Karen admitted that she had been yawning a lot, but said she felt OK. "She was griping about how Mom was trying to tell her to do everything, but then Mom had said about the visit to Olivia, 'So go!'—and that put Karen in a spot."

Karen said, "What am I gonna do?"

Richard instinctively registered that nothing had changed and that even after treatment, she seemed neither calm nor psychologically improved. "This was the same kind of thing I'd been hearing from Karen for years."

They spoke about a new video cassette recorder which she needed and then Karen said she would have to decide whether to go to Olivia's home for the weekend or appease Mom.

Whatever she decided to do for the weekend, she evidently felt she needed to mend fences in Downey first. And so, about two hours after that conversation with Richard, Karen's red Jaguar swept into her parents' driveway without the customary advance phone call to her mother to say that she was on her way.

Agnes was surprised but delighted to greet her. It quickly became evident that Karen had a practical, as well as a social, reason for the visit.

At her apartment, Karen's washer/dryer had broken, and she needed a new one, she told Agnes. Most artists of her means would lift the phone for instant delivery, but Karen still preferred what she called "normal" behaviour like this to a pampered life-style. And her practicality had never left her. The best place to buy a new washing machine, she told Mom, was still Gemco, the general store Karen often described jokingly as "the Gucci of Downey."

And there was another shopping outing on her agenda for the days ahead. Triumphantly telling everyone around her that she had maintained her new weight of 108 pounds, Karen said to her mother that she needed a new wardrobe. Those skinny-size dresses—at one stage she was down to anything from a size two to a zero in certain styles—were getting too tight.

Agnes told her that Downey was the wrong place to buy a washing machine since the space reserved for one at her apartment called for a small and vertical model—and Gemco would surely stock only regular sizes. As ever, Karen was not to be deterred. She knew and trusted all those assistants at Gemco, she said. She had known them for many years, and they would order anything for her. Here were two lifelong characteristics of Karen encapsulated into the mundane act of replacing a washing machine: Whenever possible, she sought the security of dealing with people she knew. And she would have her own way.

For Agnes Carpenter, her daughter's impromptu visit was welcome enough for she truly doted on her children. It merely brought the problem of what to provide for dinner. The fridge was rather empty that night, and discussing a menu with Karen was not the simplest of tasks. To Agnes's surprise, Karen said she fancied a shrimp salad so why didn't they go to a favourite local chain restaurant, Bob's Big Boy? Harold happily drove them there.

As he and Agnes enjoyed their chicken, they could scarcely absorb the sight of Karen heartily tucking into a particularly huge portion of shrimp salad. Karen asked for an extra portion of salad and tackled that voraciously.

Agnes was both astonished and delighted. After all those years worrying about her daughter's infinitesimal food intake, it was an enormous relief to see her eating enthusiastically. As the plates were cleared, Agnes pondered to herself that the dieting problem may well have been conquered, despite her scepticism.

In recent weeks, Karen's appetite had veered to spicy foods. Leaving the restaurant, she spotted a taco place next door and asked her parents to wait momentarily while she went inside and bought a take-out meal. "I almost passed out," Agnes says. "I couldn't believe that she'd want a taco." Impulsively, Karen continued her upbeat mood when she came back to them, asking if she might have the treat of driving her dad's Cadillac home.

That done, she went to the kitchen counter, devoured the spicy taco with hot sauce, and pronounced to her baffled but smiling mother, "Boy, that was good."

By nine o'clock, Karen seemed tired. She had complained lately by phone to Steven Levenkron of a lack of energy, but as she moved to the living room to rest on the couch, Agnes again thought there was evidence that her appearance had improved.

Her face seemed slightly chubbier, her body more formed, since she had returned three months earlier from that full year of therapy in New York. Agnes had told Richard so, but he disagreed.

While he acknowledged that she had gained weight, he could not ignore those pouches under her eyes—though she did her best to hide them. "And even now, when I look at the pictures of her in that period, it's clear from her eyes that she was really not well. Now, of course, I wish I had been even more of a bear on her."

Karen and her parents settled down to watch a television favorite, Richard Chamberlain in *Shogun*. Just after ten, as it ended, Agnes answered the phone. Quietly, she suggested that since Karen seemed tired, perhaps the caller, Frenda Leffler, could phone back the next day. But when Karen heard it was her friend on the line, her soporific position on the couch ended. She jumped up and took the phone, almost reprovingly, from her shielding, well-meaning mother.

Agnes was miffed. She reasoned that Frenda and Karen saw plenty of each other in Beverly Hills. Clearly weary, Karen needed the restorative power of a good night's sleep more than the stimulation of yet another long phone chat.

A mother's instinct that her daughter needed rest may have been correct, but Karen rarely heeded advice about her health from any quarter, particularly now. She was telling everyone that she had recently devoted a full year to kicking anorexia—and even though she admitted to Frenda that she was seeing spots before her eyes, Karen felt in better shape than when she started on that slippery road seven years earlier.

She spread her proof of her recovery adroitly: Agnes noted

with delight Karen's passion in recent weeks for chili and prepared cups of it, which Karen took back to her apartment to store in the freezer. What few people knew was that the freezer and refrigerator were invariably empty.

Yet despite simmering fears about her condition by her brother and others, Karen was restructuring her life. "I've got a lot of living to do," she had recently told one friend, Dionne Warwick. Her pride in her appearance was good, and she planned to have her brunette hair streaked blonde. Her career was in renewal, her relationship with her family more stabilized now that those dark days had apparently gone and she had made that effort in New York.

So it was a contented Karen who turned in for bed eventually, leaving her parents to watch "Knots Landing" on television. She didn't care for the programme so she decided to lie in bed and watch a video of "Magnum p.i." in the room once used by Richard. In recent weeks she had often slept there rather than in her own room, since she enjoyed watching a video and there was no equipment in her bedroom.

Friday morning for Agnes meant a ritualistic visit to her hairdresser. Karen was planning to go and order the new washing machine before driving back to Century City. At 8:45, Agnes rose. As she did so, she heard the sliding rumble of the door to Richard's closet. "Gee, Karen's up," Agnes said to Harold. "I'll go out and start some hot cereal and fix the coffee."

In the kitchen, Agnes discovered the percolator was hooked up, ready to be switched on—Karen had obviously been down to fix it. Preparing the cereal, Agnes called "Karen" twice. There was no reply. "I went to the top of the steps, saw the closet door was open, rushed in to the closet, and there she was, face down on the floor. Her eyes were open, but she didn't seem to be breathing." Karen was lying straight, as if she had become tired and lay down, only four feet away from the bathrobe she was clearly heading for. She had not hit anything in going to the floor.

Agnes screamed for Harold and Florine Elie, their housekeeper, to call the paramedics and an ambulance. They dialed 911. Then Agnes called Richard, who lived two miles away.

Morning was never a time to phone the home of night-owl Richard Carpenter. He was asleep when the 8:55 A.M. call from his hysterical-sounding mother jolted him. "Karen. . . I found her on the floor. . . . I tried to get her up, called her name. . . . Her eyes had rolled back. . . . We called the ambulance." As his mom's words tumbled out, Richard feared the worst.

Slipping on contact lenses, jeans, and a T-shirt, he raced his black Jaguar XJS through the overcast Downey streets. With his fast, immaculate driving, it was a mere five-minute trip but long enough for an avalanche of emotions to torment this normally phlegmatic, pragmatic man.

Hoping against the odds that she had simply collapsed, he said to himself as he drove: "I *knew* this was gonna happen. I *knew* she didn't look well. Maybe she's just in a bad way; she was weak; maybe they can revive her; maybe this will finally drive home to her just how serious her health problem is." Alone, he had maintained that even after that year of therapy, she was not right. His heart pumped faster as his car neared the house. Deep down, he just knew his sister was dead.

Rounding the corner into Newville Avenue, he saw a fire truck, then an ambulance. He began to cry. He raced into the house, but Karen and her mother had already been put into the ambulance. A fireman, noting Richard's distraught state, advised him to drive very carefully if he planned to follow that ambulance. At Downey Community Hospital, he joined his parents in a conference room while surgeons tried resuscitation. The news came after twenty minutes when a doctor walked in to say, "I'm sorry, but Karen is dead."

It was February 4, 1983. Agnes and Harold wept, but Richard was overtaken with numbness and anger. Glorious years, raging frustration, and embattled times with his sister and partner had ended in appalling tragedy. His main feeling was silent fury at being robbed. The tears would flow later.

The autopsy report ascribed Karen's death to emetine cardiotoxicity due to, or as a consequence of, anorexia nervosa. In the anatomical summary, the first item was pulmonary edema (heart failure) with anorexia as the second. The third finding was cachexia, which a medical dictionary defines as a condition of abnormally low weight and weakness and general bodily decline associated with chronic disease.

Emetine poisoning implies the use by Karen of ipecac syrup, which some anorexics and bulimics use to force themselves to vomit. Available from any pharmacy in the United States, this very powerful emetic, which originates from a Brazilian shrub, is often given to children if they have accidentally swallowed something poisonous. The pharmacy label states: "To cause vomiting in case of poisoning. Before using call physician, poison control centre or hospital emergency room for advice." The dose is one tablespoonful followed by one or two glasses of water.

After Karen's death, the fear that public awareness might alert those with eating disorders to use ipecac provoked a campaign by some health workers to make it more difficult to obtain this emetic. This campaign failed. Public health authorities ruled that its benefits outweighed its danger.

The autopsy finding confused Richard and his parents. Pointing out that "gagging," part of the vomiting ritual, might well have affected Karen's vocal abilities, Richard emphasizes that her voice was never less than perfect when she sang, right to the end. And she cherished its quality so was hardly likely to take such risks with it. He discounts the ipecac theory. So does Agnes, who says Karen would not have been able to disguise from her bathroom the pervading smell of vomit had she been a regular user of emetics. And she never smelled it.

Steven Levenkron says he has no knowledge of Karen having used ipecac; he believes she would have told him, had she done so. He adds that even if had known of her use of it, "there is little I could have done, because ipecac does its stuff."

A mystery surrounds the official citation of emetine cardiotoxicity as the cause of Karen's death. [Emetine is a constituent of syrup of ipecac.]

Close inspection of the only documentary evidence available, and given to Karen's next of kin—a fifteen-page autopsy and case report—shows no medical entry of any trace of emetine having been found in her body. The Los Angeles Coroner's office, confirming this absence of written evidence, told me they had no further papers available and referred me to Dr. Ronald N. Kornblum, M.D., who signed the autopsy report dated February 28, 1983, in his position at that time of Acting Chief Medical Examiner-Coroner. (He is now in the private sector.)

After reviewing the autopsy report at my request, Dr. Kornblum said it did not state what I was seeking to establish, namely the level of emetine in Karen's body. "Emetine is not a routine drug that you test ordinarily," Dr. Kornblum said, "so when you test it, we have to send it out." The papers Richard Carpenter had passed to me included a toxicology report. "That was a toxicological report from our lab," Dr. Kornblum said. "The emetine was done by an outside laboratory." Therefore there would have been a separate report.

Richard and Agnes Carpenter have never seen any such report.

The only drug recorded on the toxicological report was a small amount of Butalbital (a barbiturate) which had been prescribed for a colon problem.

When I took the postmortem and analytical papers to Dr. Allister Vale, one of Britain's most eminent toxicologists and head of the National Poisons Information Service in Birmingham, he concluded after inspection that the cause of death as given was in his view "unsustained on the basis that there is no histological or analytical evidence to support it." By histological, he explained: "That means that when you look at the tissues under a microscope, you should see certain changes, including cell deaths."

If Karen had been self-administering emetics, particularly in substantial quantities, "very definite changes" would have been caused to both the heart muscle and ordinary muscles, Dr. Vale said. And none of those was present in the heart, which had been inspected "extremely carefully" in the postmortem.

How long, I asked, would ipecac reside in her system if she had been an occasional user? Would it be measurable if, for example, she had stopped ingesting it three months before she died? No, Dr. Vale stated. "If you used the standard techniques of analysis, you wouldn't have been able to measure any emetine in her body." But the effects *would* be present in the heart muscle if she had been taking vast amounts of ipecac.

The changes would be transient, Dr. Vale said, unless massive doses were taken regularly: "It's a cumulative poison." Since no changes in Karen's heart were registered in the autopsy report, Dr. Vale concluded that "There is no evidence at all that emetine was involved in her death."

Ipecac syrup is more freely accessible in the U.S. than in Britain where it is used primarily in hospital casualty departments for the treatment of poisoning. Although there is no legal restriction on its sale in Britain, a pharmacist told me that no responsible chemist would dispense it freely, particularly to a regular purchaser, without inquiring of the need for it. There would be suspicion particularly if a thin girl repeatedly asked for syrup of ipecac.

Purgatives used mainly in Britain by anorexics are the traditional laxatives Ex Lax and Senokot.

Based on what is known and unconfirmed, no tangible evidence has emerged to show that Karen Carpenter used ipecac excessively, or that ipecac abuse was the cause of her death. It seems odd, to Richard Carpenter and me, that the very document that should have supported the cause of death as stated—if it existed at all—was missing from the sheaf of papers given to him.

Cherry Boone O'Neill says Karen told her she did not use ipecac but relied on laxatives. But Itchy Ramone says Karen began using ipecac after August 1980. As Richard agrees, a fastidious person can clean up afterwards.

Theories grew about what led to her death. One was that her electrolytes were out of balance from not having enough potassium as the result of her diet. Another is that the heart could not stand the sudden gain in weight that had recently occurred. Steven Levenkron's concern is that her use of thyroid tablets may have worn away the heart muscle.

"In addition to not knowing how she got anorexia nervosa," Richard says sadly, "I don't think they're sure what the hell actually killed her. It's very easy to say it's the mother, it's the career, it's a failed marriage. But ultimately something vital lets go. All of this is a mystery."

Karen certainly had no suicide wish. "That I know for a fact," Richard says, and his mother agrees. "As troubled in some areas as Karen obviously was, I know she was still a very cheerful person. She didn't take drugs or drink; she had a good time. She was never moody or moping, even though she was temperamental.

"A person who's going to commit suicide doesn't go out buying a new wardrobe and then a new washing machine. She had no idea how serious this was. I just know that. I have a horrible feeling that if she knew she was going, she'd say: 'Oh my God, what the hell have I done?' She never really believed it was life threatening."

Like so many of us, Richard adds, "she wanted it all. . . . In addition to all that was going for her, she wanted to be thin."

*   *   *

Karen Carpenter died a married woman. Two days before her death she had gone to the office of her lawyer, Werner Wolfen, close to her home on Avenue of the Stars; she had expected to sign divorce documents. "Well, did you get the better of him?" she asked impishly, inquiring of the financial settlement with the lawyer she addressed as "W."

Wolfen told her there was a late technical hitch to be clarified. He recalls that she "desperately" wanted to resolve the matter. She agreed to return on Friday afternoon.

Her datebook shows that forty-eight hours later, after a noon date with her pal Frenda Leffler for a manicure, she was due to return to Wolfen's office to finally sign divorce papers. She died six hours before that appointment.

"Mom, I hate the idea of getting divorced," she said with remorse so often. "It's not something that runs in the Carpenter family." Agnes, knowing that the marriage was proving unsuccessful, reassured her that times had changed and there was no stigma in separation. Her mother's attitude seemed to settle it for Karen. Since returning from New York three months earlier, two vital declarations had marked her attitude to her future: "I want to get better," and "I want a divorce."

While battling against anorexia, Karen had been devastated by her floundering marriage to Tom Burris—both throughout her year away in New York and since her return to the West Coast. Her sobbing telephone calls to him from her Regency Hotel suite appalled her visitors, anxious that the trauma would accelerate her physical difficulties.

She had been thirty when she married Tom. He was thirty-nine, debonair, a real estate developer, divorced with an eighteen-year-old son. They had married on August 31, 1980, in a glittering ceremony in the Crystal Room of the Beverly Hills Hotel.

For Karen, that wedding could not come quickly enough. All her adult life she had yearned for something beyond her fame and fortune, a stable, loving relationship, a re-creation of the caring home life from which she came. And, crucially, she wanted children. She doted on those of her friends and was the proud and active godmother to Andrew and Ashley, the son and daughter twins of Frenda and Ed Leffler, to whom she was especially close.

Karen's articulacy with songs from the heart contrasted vividly with her naïveté about her own love life. For about five years before she met Tom—almost from the onset of anorexia—she had been telling friends it was time she found the right man to plan marriage and a family.

She had precise ideas on what kind of man she was looking for, and with Itchy Ramone she had compiled a "checklist." She faced the usual dilemma for a rich young woman in show business: did the men she dated want her for herself or for her money? A major requirement was that her man should be self-supporting with a successful and absorbing career of his own. It need not be in show business. He would also need to be handsome and caring.

Karen's love life in all its phases—when it was warm or cold, or when she was unsure of a man she'd met—was of genuine concern to her girlfriends. In true anorexic fashion, she had built a wall around herself so that it was difficult to penetrate her emotional defences. All that was clear to them was that she was craving "Mister Right" at the very time she was beginning her long battle for life itself.

PART TWO

A MIDDLE-AMERICAN DREAM

I tried to get Richard to fight back, but he wouldn't. He wasn't that type.

—AGNES CARPENTER, THEIR MOTHER,
   ON SCHOOL BATTLES

The music and public image of Richard and Karen Carpenter, stretching from their birthplace in Connecticut to their success in California, epitomized the youthful exuberance of Middle America. But for a brother and sister whose values were steeped in the optimism, patriotism, and opportunity in America that followed their births just after the Second World War, their family lineage was extraordinarily international.

Their father, Harold Bertram Carpenter, was born in Wuchow, China, on November, 8, 1908, of a British father and an American-born mother. Harold would travel the world before reaching America to meet Agnes Reuwer Tatum, who became his wife. Richard and Karen were their only children.

Richard and Karen's paternal grandfather, George Bertram Carpenter, was born in London, England, in 1882 and led a colorful life with extensive travel. After schooling, at age fourteen he was apprenticed to an electrical engineering firm, but the company went bankrupt. Seeking work, he went to Glasgow to a forge company constructing castings for battleships. When George met a Scotsman who fancied sailing to New York to try his luck, the idea intrigued George so much that he saved enough money to join him.

Arriving in New York in 1900, the eighteen-year-old had a tough time finding work, not being a U.S. citizen. Yet George was reluctant to give up British citizenship. Finally, through his interest in the YMCA, he found a job on the maintenance staff of the Western Electric Company in New York.

Eventually he applied for U.S. citizenship and quickly developed an abiding interest in religion, which became so consuming that he decided to become a missionary, entering a training college at Nyack, New York.

At college, romance blossomed. He became engaged to another student, Nellie Jane Lynn. With her unusual reddish gold hair down to her waist and wound in plaits around her head, she was a beautiful young woman with a strong singing voice. By the rules of the Missionary Society, George left for China a year before Nellie, and after she joined him there to marry him, they had two children, a son, Harold Bertram, and a daughter, Esther, both born in Wuchow. By the time their third child, a son Richard,[1] was born, both George and Nellie had left the missionary field for Hong Kong, where George worked as a harbour engineer before moving a thousand miles away to Yunnanfu. There, he was the prime force in the opening of a large merchant firm in China, with branches in London, New York, and Japan.

In 1917, with an eye to the education of her children, Nellie decided to head for England, leaving George behind to work. The risks of a long journey by sea in these troubled times of the Russian Revolution and the First World War were so great that she traveled by train on the Great Siberian Railway, halfway around the world, to reach Europe. Nellie and her three children finally reached Liverpool after a nightmarish trip. They continued to England's south coast, where Harold and Esther were enrolled in boarding schools while Richard went to a foster mother. Confident that her children were in good hands, Nellie returned to her husband in China where in 1919 a fourth child, Geraldine, was born.

In England, German zeppelins and bombers left devastation, and young Harold spent many nights watching from his window the zeppelins illuminated by British searchlights. By day, his schoolmaster took the class for walks to view the areas where bombs had landed.

In 1921 George requested a furlough from his head office so that he could vacation in England. There was a happy reunion for

---

1. Richard Lynn Carpenter—uncle of Karen and Richard, and his namesake—was born on March 14, 1913, and has lived virtually all his life in England, mostly London, with his wife, Mary. He was born with a hearing and vision handicap, which worsened into total blindness and near-total deafness as he grew older. He and his wife attended Karen's wedding; after a period living and working in Devon, they now live in London.

George and Nellie when their family was reunited in St. Leonards on Sea, where the children had been staying.

George and Nellie bought a house in that Sussex town, later moving to Hendon, northwest London. Harold continued his formal education at a boys school, Tenterden Hall, where he excelled at Latin.

The family remained in Hendon until late 1921 when George's furlough ended and he had to return to his job in China. Nellie joined him there shortly afterwards and their fifth child, Guinevere, was born in Kowloon. But with his wife and babies now in China, George was no longer free to travel for the engineering companies, so lost his job. Once again the family headed for England, settling in Golders Green, northwest London.

Shortly afterward, while he continued to look for work, he agreed that Nellie should return to the United States and take the children with her. She went to live with relatives near Wellsville, New York State.

When George and Nellie had married, U.S. law decreed that a woman would forfeit her U.S. citizenship if she married a foreigner (this law has since changed). So Nellie was now a British subject. The children, all born in China, were designated Chinese whites— so when Nellie and the children finally returned to the United States, they were obliged, like all other immigrants, to enter Ellis Island in order to be granted entry.

They stayed on the island for several months until paperwork was processed. Then Harold, as a fourteen-year-old high school student in Wellsville, began the ethic of hard work that would mark his life and later that of his children, Karen and Richard. He rose at 5:00 A.M. every day to deliver newspapers before attending school and did a similar round after school. In summer, he bicycled on the paper route, but in winter he walked. For an extra dollar a week, he checked coats at a dance hall on Saturday nights.

His mother defied an illness to travel to England so that she could be reunited with George. But shortly after her arrival in London, she and George separated and she took a flat at 45a, Granville Gardens, Shepherds Bush, west London, where she died from pleurisy on March 27, 1927, at the age of forty-four.

There was a bonus for Harold from his world travels: the education he had acquired in England was equivalent to a high school education in the United States. Even though he wished to continue his education, at age sixteen he quit school to seek work to help support the family. His uncle Frank Stoddard was superintendent of a paper box company in Middletown, Ohio, and he put Harold to work there feeding the gluer. Later, when his uncle took a job with the Paper Package Company in Indianapolis, Harold went with them, again working with his uncle.

Still living with his Uncle Frank and Aunt Gertrude, Harold moved with them to Catonsville, near Baltimore, Maryland, where Frank and young Harold found work in a printing firm. Becoming friendly with his foreman, Harold would sometimes visit him and his wife at their home. During one such visit, Harold was introduced to the Tatum family a few doors away.

Three of the four Tatum sisters, sixteen-year-old Agnes, twelve-year-old Audrey, and Bernice, age nine, were riding in a coaster wagon when they were stopped to be introduced to Harold.[2] A few days later, while Agnes and Audrey were waiting for a bus, Harold, then twenty-three, offered to drive them to their friend's house in his Chevrolet.

Thus began a four-year courtship for Harold and Agnes, which ended in marriage. Agnes Reuwer Tatum was born in Baltimore on March, 5, 1915, one of four daughters born to George and Annie Tatum. She had been schooled in hard work by her father, who ran a wholesale underwear business. An excellent seamstress, Agnes made her own wedding outfit, and her blue veil concealed a black eye, which she had accidentally suffered when she and Harold were carrying a bed upstairs shortly before the wedding day.

After the wedding in Baltimore on April 9, 1935,[3] the couple went to the movies. Times were hard. The Depression had not yet ended, and so they had neither wedding cake nor honeymoon. Their only gift was an electric iron from Agnes's Aunt Myrtle and Uncle Arthur, who worked for the General Electric Company.

Harold and Agnes lived initially in the Tatum family house but soon followed Harold's uncle and aunt to Richmond, Virginia, where both Harold and Frank worked at a paper company. The

2. Agnes's sister Jenny was eight years older than her.
3. Harold and Agnes were married for fifty-three years. He died in Downey, California, on October 15, 1988.

first real home for the newlyweds was a five-dollar-a-week furnished apartment consisting of kitchen, living room, and bedroom.
The bathroom was shared. Agnes practised thrift and cleanliness,
the hallmark of her life which she would instill in Karen and
Richard. She spent all day cleaning and painting her small apartment until it was immaculate; she made new curtains and helped
clean the rest of the house with her landlady.

After a year the couple moved to another furnished apartment
at 2911 Fendall Avenue in the heart of Richmond's residential
area. Again, Agnes's characteristic of keeping a pristine house was
in evidence. Her landlady was a compulsive collector of plates who
received them from pen pals around the world. She displayed the
plates on a narrow ledge that ran from wall to wall around her
living room, just below the ceiling. The thick layers of dust the
plates harbored irritated Agnes so much that she volunteered to
help clean them. Such meticulousness would become the core of
her life as a wife and mother.

When Agnes's older sister, Jenny Tyrell, decided that she
would like her second daughter to go and live with Harold and
Agnes permanently, it precipitated another move, this time to
Mechanicsville, Virginia. The baby, Joanie Tyrell, was a mere
eighteen months old when she was taken there by Aunt Agnes and
Uncle Harold, and they became her surrogate parents.[4]

Harold was a lover of beautiful cars, and to make extra money,
he and Agnes washed vehicles at their home. They made a forceful
team, taking pride in their work, offering a pickup-and-delivery
service. Harold worked at the Kratz Paper Company in Richmond
for five years until he and Agnes moved to East Haven, Connecticut. Most of their years there, 1940–46, were war years. Harold
took a job at the New Haven Pulp and Board Company, makers of
paper and cardboard. His pay was one dollar an hour compared
with seventy-five cents an hour back in Richmond; his work pros-
pered as he became adept on the colour printing machinery.

Agnes contributed to the war effort, working at a defense plant,
the Mettler Brothers Manufacturing Corporation, builders of motor
mounts and vibration dampers for Pratt and Whitney engines. For

---

4. Jenny, separated from her husband, George, did not feel she could give Joanie the stability
Agnes and Harold could offer.

four years she worked an eight-hour shift six or seven days a week, keeping three thread grinders running continually.

A tenacious and valued worker, Agnes continued to do her own housework and prepare meals for a family of four: she and Harold, baby Joanie and Joanie's mother, Jenny, who lived with them until 1943. Initially they rented an apartment on Sydney Street, but at the war's end Harold and Agnes made plans to buy their own house. The pleasant environment they chose would significantly shape the lives of the future Carpenter family. New houses were being built on Hall Street, a wide road with ample space for solid, detached, large-roomed properties with twin lawns at the front, spacious garden at the rear, and a garage.

Hall Street straddled East Haven and Morris Cove, a serene and desirable part of New Haven where the huge Italian immigrant population would provide the city with an unrivalled reputation for pizza restaurants. With Lighthouse Point nearby, this was an idyllic spot in which to plan a family in postwar America—and Agnes was pregnant as they negotiated the purchase of 55 Hall Street.

By then, after several homes and jobs, the personalities of Harold and Agnes were delineated: he was passive, warm, friendly, and noncombative, whereas Agnes commanded respect for her iron determination, willpower, and an insistence on morality, justice, and fair play.

With typical savvy, she took a firm grip on the builders of their new home, who, after the deal had been signed and a deposit paid, tried to renege by saying Harold was not a war veteran. Since no such clause in the contract debarred them from purchasing the house, Agnes declared that she would report them to the Federal Housing Association. They backed off. But with servicemen returning from the war in 1946, ripe for exploitation, the builders then upped their price by $1,000 to $9,900. Agnes argued that this action was unethical. They were unjustifiably raising their earlier quotation. They relented, and she therefore "saved" a then-substantial $1,000. Agnes later discovered that the builders had used the same ruse on all her potential neighbors and a few had meekly taken back their deposits, enabling the builders to sell at a higher price.

The couple moved into their new home on August 27, 1946, and within six weeks, on October 15, Agnes gave birth to their

first child in Grace-New Haven Hospital. He was named Richard
Lynn after Harold's only brother. The arrival did not affect their
protective feelings toward their niece-in-residence, Joanie, who
was ten years old at the time of Richard's birth.

In these pre-rock 'n' roll years, Harold was fond of melodic
popular music, the sounds of the big bands and light classical
music. He began collecting 78 rpm records and listened to music
on the radio constantly. He and Agnes loved the vocal purity of
Bing Crosby and Perry Como, the swinging band sounds of Harry
James and Freddy Martin, the Dixieland jazz of Red Nichols and
the novelty recordings of Spike Jones and His City Slickers. These
were the sounds that would have a major impact on their baby
son's musical education. The highly popular wartime sound of
Glenn Miller was less welcome with Harold and Agnes; it
reminded them of when they lived above a café where Miller's
anthem, "In the Mood," had blared at them night and day.

With her pleasant voice, Agnes would sing around the house;
like Harold, she had studied piano but gave it up. He was, however, an aficionado of romantic music and an avid listener. "Certain
songs would bring tears to his eyes," Richard recalls.

By the time his sister, Karen Anne, was born on March 2,
1950, three-and-a-half-year-old Richard was beginning to show a
precociousness in music. In the basement, Harold hooked up
swings for his children's pleasure and bought a child's record
player shaped as a jukebox, endorsed by Bing Crosby's name. Even
though Harold and Agnes had resumed their car washing to boost
income, the family budget was tight. Immensely house proud,
Agnes instituted an exhaustive spring-cleaning including changes
of curtains and rugs, and for years she and Harold painted their
new property personally. "We'd all get crabby about the spring
clean," Joanie says, "because this totally disrupted the house for
weeks. But in this area, Agnes pretty much ran the house, and
Harold, a very loving person, would comply out of love for her."

Few records could be afforded, but Richard remembers his
early favorite from an oddball assortment was the music from the
World War I marching song "Over There," by Fred Waring and
The Pennsylvanians. "I wore the hole out in that record," he says.
Orchestral and choral sounds attracted him; he admired the David
Rose arrangements for the Army Air Corps show, "Winged Vic-
tory."

At a mere four years old, his interest in music became obsessive, his memory and fast-growing knowledge of it encyclopedic. The sounds around him at home gave him an eclectic taste as he listened to the Firehouse Five Plus Two, Red Nichols, Tchaikovsky's First Piano Concerto, "and Spike Jones until I was blue in the face."

Family vacations were often spent driving to stay at the Baltimore home of Agnes's sister, Bernice. On one visit, Karen and Richard were fooling around on a homemade trapeze in the garden when Karen, age four, was badly hurt. She was hanging on the trapeze upside down when her shirt covered her face and Richard tickled her and made her laugh. Falling from the bar, she seriously injured her bottom lip. The impact was so strong that she needed stitches in the hospital, both inside and outside her mouth. "It was a real mess, and boy, did I get hell for making her laugh and fall," Richard recalls.

Four-year-old Karen took ballet and tap dancing lessons, and excelled in acrobatics. Joining Richard in the basement at home, she showed just a passing interest in the music that now commanded his attention. Although he recalls her constantly drumming her fingers to the beat of the songs, it was not seen as an indicator of her future prowess.

On Hall Street the Carpenters struck a friendship with neighbors at number 77 that would mark the lives of both families. The Vaiuso family had everything in common with them: Like Harold, Carl Vaiuso was solid and proud, a hardworking farmer, while his wife, Theresa, had precisely the same ideals as Agnes. Both mothers were staunch disciplinarians, and though Agnes would never hit her children, a threatening visit by Harold to collect the yardstick was enough to stop Richard and Karen in their tracks. Theresa occasionally whacked their children with a wooden cooking spoon if they stepped out of line. Both women ran immaculately clean and tidy houses; both had a son and a daughter. As the women became soul mates, the families were quickly as one.

Though they attended different schools, Richard and Joe Vaiuso, two years younger, developed a friendship as "opposites." Quiet, studious, artistic, Richard did not mix with most of the boys in the district. Some considered him wimpish, and he was set upon by fighting bullies. One, Joe Bredeau, saw the slender Richard as an easy target and regularly sought him out for a punching. The muscular Joe Vaiuso enjoyed defending him.

"When I walked with Richard to and from school, we never seemed to have a problem," Joe recalls with a smile. "I was always a tough guy."

Karen, too, was a "scrapper" when necessary. "She'd take up for Richard," cousin Joanie recalls. And Agnes says that when Richard was set upon by other kids, "I tried to get Richard to fight back, but he wouldn't. He wasn't that type."

In awe of his natural ability as she saw him practising diligently on the piano, the contrasting Karen was, by her own description, a tomboy, enjoying softball, baseball, and badminton in the street and on the big lawn of her home with Joe, Debbie, and the other children. A rugged player with a keen eye, she was nicknamed "Butterball" by her friends because of her smooth handling of the ball.

At Nathan Hale School Karen was known as a fine basketball player. She showed no musical inclination. Bright and extroverted but not ambitious, she was the sort of girl Joe Vaiuso expected to become a nurse. That was, he believed, a caring profession for which she would be suited perfectly. Her kindness struck him when, throughout the summer that he had a broken arm, she visited his home every day to keep him company him and play Monopoly.

Recalling her childhood once she became a globe-trotting singer, Karen said: "While Richard was listening to music in the basement, I was out playing baseball and football, and playing with my machine gun! I was very tomboyish, quite a character, I hear! I remember I wanted to be a commercial artist, or a nurse, or an airline stewardess!" And that was funny, she said, because "one, I can't stand the sight of blood; two, if I fly one more mile . . . !"

Their shared taste in music was explained simply by Karen: "I idolized him so much and we were so close, even though we were three years apart, that if he listened to music, I did. I did everything he did. Thusly, every record we've ever listened to is embedded in my mind."

Riding her bike, Karen delivered the local newspaper, the *New Haven Register*, around the neighbourhood, occasionally helped by Richard. "She was different, an iconoclast," he says of her pursuits in those years when very few girls would deliver papers. For extra dollars, she also delivered on weekends. In what would become a lifelong friendship, Karen became close to Joe's sister Debra, two years younger than her.

"Those four kids simply lived in each other's houses," says her mother. "Debbie and Joe practically called Agnes Mom." Debbie, like Karen, preferred outdoor games to the more traditional "teatime with dolls" favoured by other girls nearby.

On Fort Hale Park, the four would unite for snowballing and sleigh rides, and year-round roller-skating and ball games. Every afternoon they would gather around the black-and-white TV set to watch "The Mickey Mouse Club," which appealed to Karen's wacky sense of humour.

Neither family had enough money for expensive vacations. But in the postwar spirit of neighbourly goodwill, all pulling together, Agnes, Theresa, and another neighbour, Marion Connellan, became a sisterhood. Their trust was implicit as they made inter-house visits on an hourly basis.

Of Agnes's reputation for bossiness, Theresa declares: "She was more protective than domineering. I didn't see her as bossy. Agnes is a great person who spoke from the heart all the time, and the kids were smart enough to listen to her." Had it not been for Agnes's strength of character, Theresa believes, Richard and Karen would not have begun to climb the ladder to success.

Everyone who knew Agnes in her Hall Street years testifies to her character—stern, strong-willed, well-intentioned, strong on discipline and manners. She dedicated herself to the job of raising two children with firm morality and an ethic of "deal-with-people-direct." Harold had the same goals but was less assertive. "Agnes was always ready to help anybody, especially an underdog," says Marion Connellan, who lived at number 60. "They were just a nice, decent family."

Long before Elvis Presley ignited the rock 'n' roll explosion to white ears in 1956, Richard Carpenter's ears were wide open to anything tunefully strong.

Born a natural musician, he quickly developed an addict's ability to predict hits. When he wasn't glued to the radio listening to the hip New York station WINS, he was playing his dad's records—"so many times that the holes were worn larger from wear. We had to buy those metal clips to substitute for the holes in the middle." The first 78 rpm record Richard asked his parents to buy, in 1949, was Frankie Laine's "Mule Train," followed by a 45 rpm of Teresa Brewer's "Music, Music, Music." The ice bucket in which his mother systematically filed incoming bills showed that money was too tight to consider going to concerts, and Harold and Agnes believed that to buy records was the wiser investment. A solitary child, Richard remembers putting on a stack of 78 rpm records, or 45 rpm singles, and swaying to the music in the basement on the swing his father had constructed—"hour after hour, month after month, year after year." Analyzing every record, he was in heaven. Too young to read the record labels, he chose the records from the racks by feeling the edge of each one, and he got to know by "feel" which one he was selecting. Al Jolson was another big favorite.

"Boy, did I drive my parents nuts!" says Richard, remembering his years as a boy. "I would hear records on the radio and really haunt them until they bought them." At the onset of rock, Richard's Aunt Esther bought a portable record player that came with a choice of twenty-five free records. Richard, then studying the hit parade charts, was attuned to the music played on WINS by the disc jockey credited with inventing the phrase "rock 'n' roll," Alan Freed. As Richard heard such innovative records as "At the Hop" by Danny and the Juniors and "Sh-Boom" by the Crew Cuts, diversifying his taste from straight popular music into the fresh sounds of the day, it was obvious to his family that music was not merely his pastime but an obsession. He studied the nuance of every record's arrangement.

Always inclined to follow Richard's lead, by the time she was about four and he seven, Karen joined him regularly in the basement for record sessions. It was there that their future craftsmanship as musicians was forged. They sang along together to the records, studying the arrangements in detail.

Like Richard, Karen developed an interest in the structure of a sound. "She knew everything musically that I picked up from those years," Richard says. "I obviously didn't know it at the time, but I was becoming a musical arranger. I listened especially for the little 'answer lines' in a record that were sometimes as catchy as the tune itself." They were both enthralled by the revolutionary sound on "How High the Moon," multitracked by guitarist and sound pioneer Les Paul with his wife Mary Ford's voice. "Karen got to know every solo Les Paul took," Richard says, "and she could sing, note for note, every Red Nichols solo."

At the age of four, Richard had taken accordion lessons but

showed little interest in the instrument. His enthusiasm to make music went on hold for a few years. When he was eight, his teenage cousin Joanie bought a piano for the Carpenter house and began lessons with a local teacher. Richard's interest in the piano was the. sparked and Agnes found him a teacher, but her rigid teaching methods and refusal to let Richard improvise bored the boy.

Mrs. Florence June taught strictly from books, with no deviation allowed. This frustrated Richard's fast-flowering imagination. After a year with her, he told his mother he should quit, and Mrs. June agreed. She did not think he had what it took to be a pianist, "and at that time I have to believe she was right," Richard reflects.

Several years later, seeing him drift toward the piano so often, Agnes was sure he needed serious encouragement. She inquired at Goldie's music shop in New Haven about a good teacher and was assured that Henry Will was indeed the best.

Soon Will was visiting the Carpenter home every week. At twenty-eight, he was quiet, responsive to modern pop and jazz sounds, and dedicated to encouraging talented pupils. Seeing his rapport with Richard, Agnes asked Will to give Karen accordion lessons. Within months he was a family friend more than a visiting teacher; he began a romance with Joanie, and they married in 1963.

While Karen's lessons fizzled through her disinterest, her brother's gathered a natural momentum. "Richard had a firm idea even at that age what he wanted to do," Henry Will remembers. "He didn't want to be bothered by dry tuition books, which he reckoned were superfluous. He wanted to do his own thing. He was exceptional. He didn't want to learn a piece just to master the reading aspect of music, and he liked to use his own chords. He became creative and even wrote some songs." Richard recalls enjoying the scales and studying the piano exercises of Hanon and Czerny.

Eventually, seeing Richard's progress, Agnes and Harold invested in a new piano for him, a black Baldwin Acrosonic. They were all aware of the music in Richard's soul. "You just grew up with that music, morning, noon, and night, coming through the air and through the window screen when we were playing hula hoops in the street," Debbie Vaiuso says. "This was advanced music, not just scales and practising," Joe Vaiuso says. "He was about twelve. The whole neighbourhood knew that he was on his way to becoming a professional musician, even then."

Meeting Henry Will at the door of the Carpenter house every week, Harold would bemoan his son's lack of practice. But Richard would play his set piece perfectly to silence any such criticism. Repeatedly, Will found he had to select more challenging work for the youngster. As for Agnes, Will declares that "She was the matriarch, highly ambitious for Richard and Karen."

This was no traditional teacher-pupil situation, for there was no privacy as Agnes and Harold chimed in with their views. If they didn't like something Richard played, either parent would holler from the kitchen, "He played that better yesterday, and he knows that, Hank!" Will says: "Everybody was involved in those lessons—Karen was walking around, commenting, too. Richard would get frustrated by these remarks, and I often wondered how I was going to contend with all these different opinions."

Such pressure on Hank Will brought an enormous compensation as well as his integration into the family. In three years as Richard's teacher, he decided that Richard was not merely his star pupil. He was a prodigy. "He thought about little else but music, music, music." Believing he had taken him as far as he could, and also that he was getting on too-friendly terms with the whole family to be effective, Will suggested that Richard go for an audition at the nearby Yale Music School. Sailing through the test, Richard went under the tutelage of Professor Seymour Fink for weekly classes. Richard was not enamoured of the professor's apparent preoccupation with coffee and cigarettes. But his level of playing was increasing so dramatically that formal instruction was only a discipline. "Whatever was put in front of him he would play to hell," avers Hank Will.

By thirteen, Richard was certain he was heading for a life in music. "I was in love with it, writing these little tunes which didn't amount to anything, but I figured I was probably going to be a pops pianist like Peter Nero or Roger Williams. And I didn't excel in much else."

Karen, meanwhile, was still tinkering. At Nathan Hale School, she was persuaded to learn the flute so that she could join the school orchestra. Again, Agnes and Harold's encouragement came through: they got her a flute to practise with, but her playing of this went nowhere. Her interest in music was dormant as she watched her brilliant brother with awe. A slightly chubby girl, she was still more attuned to physical pursuits, enjoyed cycling, and had a normal and healthy appetite. Her bubbly personality made her a local favourite—but she was hurt when, as a ten-year-old, she was the object of teasing by other kids because of her tendency to chubbiness. She pointed out to them that because of her athletic interests, she had developed stronger muscles than they had.

Her physical education teacher at Nathan Hale, Rudy Canelli, remembers her as highly energetic. She stood out as someone who respected discipline and regimentation: "She never wanted to flunk." Both Karen and Richard struck the staff as "nice kids, above average in their application and sincerity."

Karen's puberty occurred at age twelve or thirteen—an important consideration for anyone trying to analyze the onset of anorexia nervosa according to Professor Arthur Crisp in London. "It is a disorder psychopathologically of weight and not of eating," he explains.[5]

The only way to regulate weight is to regulate shape, and sensitivity about shape is prompted by puberty. "And it's to do with body fat," says Professor Crisp. "It's not to do with a fear of being obese—that's something most people share—but a sense of alienation in relation to, and a rejection of, pubertal development. In a biological sense, puberty has to do with sexuality that in the human condition prompts a whole new series of tasks: of peer relationships, of identity, of coming to terms with one's biological gender, of separation from the family and renegotiation of relationships, of attitudes to sexuality which have to do with parental value systems—and with, indeed, whether one suddenly discovers that one is the gender one wants to be anyway." All these issues, the professor states, are inescapable with the onset of puberty.

For those reasons, and the fact that female fatness of a pubertal sense is highly sexual, "the majority of teenage females become very sensitive about it," states Professor Crisp, and strive to diet and to regulate themselves and get their acts together as adolescents in those terms.

"And anorexia spills out of that process in those whose conflicts at that point in time, in relation to these issues, are insoluble,

5. Acknowledged as one of the world's experts on anorexia nervosa, Professor Crisp is professor of psychiatry at the department of mental health sciences, St. George's Hospital Medical School, London.

overwhelming, and with a need to be avoided." Dieting becomes effortless, low weight is achieved, "and the pubertal process has been abolished. And anorexia is about reversing the pubertal development and holding it at bay" with a whole battery of defences against the impulse to eat.

Anyone trying to comprehend anorexia, states Professor Crisp, needs to understand the developmental crisis that preceded it and which is no longer there—and which may never have been articulated.

Karen's anorexia, which was not to begin for twelve years from her puberty, might have been lying dormant from this part of her life, for she was certainly prone to weightiness. Richard and Agnes Carpenter say that at twelve or thirteen it just didn't bother her. She never mentioned it and accepted any teasings about it cheerfully.

While Debbie and Joe Vaiuso went to the Catholic school, Saint Bernadette's, Karen at Nathan Hale began a special friendship with Frank Bonito, who lived at number 83 Hall Street. En route to school, Frank would call for Karen most days, and he recalls a "very bright student" sitting alongside him in class: "We were separated because we would fool around a lot. We'd study for exams together, prepare and test each other." Karen and Frank's friendship was strengthened on the walks to and from their homes at lunchtime, since there was no catering facility at the school. They became inseparable but with no romantic overtones.

"Richard was different from other kids," Bonito says. "He was not well liked. He wasn't good in sports, was interested in things other kids weren't, and I don't think he did that well in school. He was on another level, interested in music. That really was his niche. Bully kids didn't like him; he had problems."

Bonito saw Agnes as an exceptionally strong-minded woman "functioning at a very high anxiety level." Determined for her children to do well, she was known by all the local people to have orchestrated Richard's career in music—and now there was talk of a move to California to lift Richard's career to a new level. As for his friend Karen, Bonito observes now: "I think she always felt she was unattractive. Especially when she became a woman she had large hips. No matter how thin she got on top, her hips were always big."

*   *   *

At Wilbur Cross High School, Richard assembled a small group comprising saxophone, bass, and drums to join him in school musical events. "He was a tremendous piano player, even at that age," recalls Jim Squeglia, the drummer. "It was a very rare talent. He could play *anything*." The group practised often, but they were too young to play the clubs. Richard, though, looked mature for a fifteen-year-old, and word spread among the city's musicians, who sought him to play in various groups.

His first appearance was at that age at an unsalubrious licensed pizza café, Patty's Pizza on the Boston Post Road outside New Haven. The musicians he accompanied were twenty-three and twenty-four; because of the way he styled his hair and wore glasses, Richard was able to pretend he was older than his years.

As Harold and Agnes waited in their car one night to collect him, he ran out to tell them anxiously that a nasty fight had broken out inside—and he simply had to return there because he had left behind in the club his musicians' "fake book," which enabled a player of his level to meet audience requests for standard songs if the basic chords were known. It was a vital "prop." Relieved when he returned unscathed, his parents told him to put aside such dangerous appearances until he was older.

Though he was a quiet boy, Richard seemed to strike a rapport with the extrovert Jim Squeglia, who soon visited the Carpenter home to practice with him. Karen often sat behind him, watching him, in what seemed to have been the starting point for her own interest in becoming a drummer. "She would always kid, laugh and joke with me," Squeglia says. "Now I see that she was watching how I played. All the time."

At sixteen, Richard was featured on a record for the first time. A New Haven vocal group, the Barries, pulled him and Squeglia into a recording session for Josie Records, where they cut a single, "Write Me a Letter." Recorded in Manhattan, the record did not succeed nationally, but the young Carpenter made his mark with a Jerry Lee Lewis flourish at the keyboard. He was on his way.

This was how Karen saw her life at age thirteen, when she was a schoolgirl in New Haven, Connecticut. Anticipating the Carpenter family's move to settle in California, she writes that she "hopes to study nursing or become an artist"; she had a talent for drawing.

My Autobiography.

For a long time my parents had been waiting for a daughter. Finally, on March 2, 1950, my mother gave birth to a girl, that, of course, being me. I was born in Grace New Haven Hospital located in New Haven, Connecticut.

There are five members in my family. First there is my father, Harold. His occupation is a printing pressman. He works at the New Haven Board + Carton on a five-color press. My mother, Agnes, is a normal housewife. My cousin, Joan, has lived with us since birth. Next comes my brother Richard, who is 16 years old and attends Wilbur Cross High School. He is a talented pianist.

The fun in my life began when I began to walk. I took my first steps at 8 mths. I received my first tooth at 7 months and learned of my misery during my teething period. I opened my mouth which never closed since, and said my first words, those being "bye-bye" and "stop-it."

I took one trip to Baltimore, Maryland, one which I will never forget. It happened on a Saturday afternoon when I was approximately two years old. My cousin had encouraged me to hang up side down on a trapeze; not knowing any better, I did. Suddenly my brother got an urge to tickle me; the result being a severe cut lip. As I fell to the ground my front teeth went clear through my lower lip. Other than being bitten by a dog my childhood life was not unusual.

Along with my family I took trips to Canada, Baltimore and other eastern states. I do not remember any of my experiences at these locations other than a pleasant and enjoyable visit.

I began my school life at the age of four at Nathan Hale, this being the school I now attend. During the nine years of attendance I have enjoyed all of my teachers and had much fun.

My hobbies are popular dancing, collecting records, and drawing. I like them all very much although I never get much chance to do them. In the year 1962 I won a reward or certificate for a poster I had drawn.

During my life we had many pets.

At this time I have one pet, that being a dog named Snoopy. He is a Beagle or is supposed to be one, but anyway he has had quite a life. When he was a puppy of 2 months he was hit by a car. At this certain time none in my family was home, so I was brought to the veternarian's office by a neighbor. The outlook for his recovery was very bad but after a long week of tension he was released. When he came home the outlook still remained bad. Within a month Snoopy had completely recovered.

I can not be certain on the outlook of my future. In June I know for certain we are moving to California. From there I hope to study nursing or become an artist. *

She accepted that she'd been a pudgy kid and she
kept trying to get rid of the hips.

—GARY SIMS, KAREN'S FORMER BOYFRIEND

Harold Carpenter hated the freezing Connecticut winters. In 1955, with two young children, he began to yearn for an improved quality of life. As he sat watching television showing the sun beating down on California, and particularly the Rose Bowl parades, he told Agnes that he'd love to live out there. Finances were a problem, and when all the money he had saved was spent on an operation for his mastoid problem, his dream of a move could not be realized at that time.

Five years later, he was still determined and took Agnes and Richard for a drive across country during his vacation to have a look at California, staying with a former work colleague. Karen, at ten a poor traveler, could not face such a drive and so went to stay with her Aunt Bernice and Uncle Paul in Baltimore. Finally, in 1962, Harold sat down his family and told them he was certain they would have a better life if they moved out west. Karen was not convinced. Richard, at sixteen, was enthusiastic when, in June 1963, they finally left New Haven. Harold was fifty-six, Agnes forty-nine, hardly ages at which couples lightly change routes. But better prospects for Richard's burgeoning career as a musician were also in his parents' thoughts as they made their plans.

The Hall Street house was put up for sale, but most of the contents were left in it since they did not have enough money to move them.

There was nothing especially glamorous about the move. Such a geographical switch might be a statement, by some, of a desire to build a fresh and dramatic new life. But Mr. and Mrs. Carpenter were far too earthy to consider it anything beyond a chance to propel Richard into a strong career in music, enjoy the better weather, and improve their standard of living. The Carpenter family were the opposite of the jet set of their day, and a move to Los Angeles did not represent a spiritual move to the home of show business.

Harold's new job took him to Vernon, an industrial city not far from Downey. Through his New Haven employer, he had secured similar work as a skilled pressman at a printer specializing in food containers. Agnes soon found a job in the stockroom at the North American Aviation Company, Downey's chief source of employment and the birthplace of the Sabre jet and in later years the Apollo spacecraft.

If Los Angeles was where thousands migrated in order to reinvent themselves, it was certain that sedate Downey, on the edge of conservative Orange County, would provide no impetus for change. A commuter suburb, it had a population of 100,000. Bland and characterless, it was as divorced from the fleshpots of Hollywood as New Haven was from Manhattan. Here, the unfettered values of Middle America would continue to shape their sixteen-year-old son and thirteen-year-old daughter. In Downey, the Carpenter family felt safe, unthreatened by urban life.

Karen had been sad to move such a distance, leaving behind such friends as Debbie Vaiuso, but she was intrigued by the possibility of having more space out west, where she thought she might even be able to keep a horse. Her illusion was squashed when the family moved initially into one of the modest apartments at the Shoji complex on Downey Avenue.

Their first eight months in Downey were particularly tough. It was a struggle to pay the rent there as well as continue the mortgage payments on the New Haven house. There were several offers from potential renters, but Agnes was reluctant to accept; she did not want strangers using their furniture, particularly Richard's beloved piano.

When the New Haven house was finally sold, a year after their arrival in California, Harold and Agnes had enough cash to find a more permanent home. In November 1964 they moved into a small, three-bedroom house with a den at 13024 Fidler Avenue, where Karen settled for a dog and a cat. The house was, however, in South Downey, the least desirable part of town, and friends warned Agnes that people who settled there, "on the wrong side of the tracks," were rarely able to cross town to the better properties.

But for these remarkably hardworking parents, sheer grit and survival counted more than posturing. Agnes quickly established her reputation for tenacity in her demanding work, while Harold plodded successfully in his printing job. The sunny weather, a major attraction for him, was compensation for the fact that finances were still tight. Harold and Agnes counted every dollar and instilled a sense of thrift in their children. All household bills were paid by Agnes as soon as they arrived.

A smiling but rather weighty thirteen-year-old as she arrived in Downey, Karen devoured chocolate, waffles, ice cream, and any candy that came her way. She was so bursting with energy that her mother considered any surplus weight to be "puppy fat," which would surely disappear with school games and swimming as Karen began at South Junior High School. But her enjoyment of physical pursuits became submerged once she left New Haven, perhaps because of the change of friendships caused by the move.

Richard, meanwhile, was at Downey High School. Academically he was average in most subjects, but before long he would make his mark in music. Shortly after their arrival in California, one Sunday afternoon, playing piano at a talent show in Furman Park, Downey, Richard was spotted by Vance Hayes, music director at the local Methodist Church. He needed an organist and immediately gave the impressive teenager the role. Richard said he had never played a pipe organ and knew no organ music, but Hayes persuaded him to try. For the next year, Richard delighted the congregations with improvisations to some of the hymns, even daring to slide in recognizable parts of melodies from a new group called the Beatles, who were making waves in 1964. At these moments, Vance Hayes would give him a knowing wink, but he wasn't too pleased to hear Carpenter playing "In a Monastery Garden."

Though church music was a distance from the sounds and styles he would eventually embrace, the experience strengthened Richard's wide sweep of knowledge of music in all its forms, from classical through jazz to pop. His interest in the piano was all-consuming.

Abhorring physical education, he looked for a way to replace that class requirement and pleaded for a role in the school marching band, which could be substituted for it. When the teacher, Bruce Gifford, pointed out that he could hardly march as a pianist, Richard claimed he could play trumpet—a wild exaggeration. Luckily for Richard, Gifford was also persuaded to listen to his piano playing. Impressed, he nominated the boy as chief featured musician for a school project that year of *Rhapsody in Blue*. Richard was off the hook and never even had to take that trumpet (which he'd bought for four dollars at a garage sale) out of its case.

"He'd conned his way into the band," says Gifford, who quickly realized that Richard was a brilliant young player. "He would get frustrated with us average folk. He just couldn't understand why we couldn't do what he could on the piano. There wasn't really anything I could teach him." Still only seventeen, Richard had an insatiable hunger for making music. "He'd play for anything that came along," Gifford says. "If someone wanted to sing 'Auld Lang Syne' and needed an accompanist, Richard would play. And *everyone* wanted Richard to back them."

Karen seemed to be so intimidated by her brother's natural talent that for her to enter music was to invite comparison. Though she now loved music, especially the Beatles, how could she get close to his level of expertise? He was streaking ahead, playing at church, playing in Bruce Gifford's jazz group at various clubs, dabbling in all manner of casual bands. It was a question of when, rather than whether, he would become a full-time musician.

While Richard was good in history and English, Karen was "just about average in everything," says Jim Allgood, who taught her government studies. He recalls Karen as "a plump little girl, rather quiet, who really did not excel academically" as she moved into Downey High School.

As the sounds of the Beatles and the Beach Boys filled the airwaves and Karen and Richard bought their records, she gradually became as attracted to the idea of making music. Back east, her family had hardly noticed her drumming her fingers to the beat of anything she heard, but now in Downey in the fall of 1964 she was developing a strong interest in rhythm. Although she enjoyed school games like volleyball, she hated physical education, particularly early morning swimming. She asked Richard to try to get her a position like his in the school band. "I wanted also to get out of geometry 'cos I flunked it," she said later.

Richard duly told his friendly teacher Bruce Gifford: "She can read music. Why don't you give her a glockenspiel and let her march with the band?"

It proved a turning point. Inside the band she admired the drumming of young Frankie Chavez and quickly asked her parents for a set of drums. Agnes and Harold were astonished. "Here we were," Richard says, "trying to make a go of it in California, and Karen's accordion and flute playing had gone nowhere—and my parents didn't really think the drums were natural for a girl of fourteen."

Nor did they have $300 to spare, Agnes recalls. "But Karen did have some savings to contribute, so we took her one Sunday a very long distance to a music teacher who sold drums on the side." The kit was a Ludwig, then used by two drummers she admired, Joe Morello in the Dave Brubeck Quartet and Ringo Starr in the Beatles. Immediately, Karen demonstrated to her family through hours of laborious practice that this was to be no passing fad. She taught herself the rhythmically challenging beat of the Brubeck records "Take Five" and "It's a Raggy Waltz" and began a love affair with the drums that would last all her life.

"Boy, could she play 'em!" exclaims Richard. "She and Frankie Chavez must have worked down the rudiments, the cadences, and the press-rolls for hours. By the time she got those drums she could knock it all off. It was no novelty."

The piano-playing brother, meanwhile, was getting work in restaurants and bars and had to dress older than his years to be allowed in to some venues. At the Sierra Room in Downey, Richard kept his head down to the piano, fearful that his youthful look might mean ejection.

Within two months, Karen had persuaded her parents to buy her a more sophisticated set of drums. When these arrived, she could barely see over the edge of the highest tom-tom, but she plunged into perfecting her skills every morning and night, to the delight of her brother. "When I went to high school," Karen would reflect later, "I had no idea that I could do a blasted thing. I just kinda hung around and watched him [Richard] be good!" Then, she said, she "fell in love" with the drums. At home, her practical mother stood by with an endless supply of Band-Aids to put on Karen's fingers, sore from practice.

*   *   *

The American mood was one of profound change as seventeen-year-old Richard Carpenter began his studies as a music major in the fall of 1964 at California State University, Long Beach. President John F. Kennedy had been assassinated the previous November, and as the Beatles made their first visit to the United States in February, their spirit was exploding into the national consciousness, heralding new attitudes among youth—plus new fashions and long hair.

With his horn-rimmed black glasses, slicked-back, parted short hair, and conservative clothes, Richard was hardly in the vanguard of change. Retiring and quiet, he sprang to life only when making or talking music or automobiles. He drove to college in a Plymouth Satellite convertible bought by his parents.

At year's end, when some students had to write and perform their own composition, he produced "In My Dreams." His melody was pretty, the lyrics corny. Karen, still in high school, went along to sing it for Richard. Another student had written something jazzy, which featured a double bass and tuba player named Wes Jacobs. This performance grabbed Richard's attention. "I was impressed and introduced myself to Wes Jacobs, and we hit it off immediately." He told Jacobs that his sister was predominantly a drummer, not a singer (which was Karen's belief too). "Maybe you could come over, and we'd work out a few things," Richard added tentatively.

Jacobs had little to occupy his leisure hours that summer. When he went to the Carpenter home to form a casual trio, the electricity was good. Richard had developed arrangements, and when Karen was urged to sing she sang in an almost country-and-western style. Most of their music was jazzy, including the difficult Duke Ellington classic "Caravan," and Karen sang on the Henry Mancini song "The Sweetheart Tree," a slow, ballad version of the Beatles' "I Want to Hold Your Hand," and the powerful ballad "I Who Have Nothing." Hearing her own voice on a tape recorder for the first time was traumatic. She disliked her vocals and returned to the refuge of her beloved drums.

"Richard was very easy to get along with, but when it came to music he was absolutely uncompromising," Jacobs says. "He had a vision of how a particular song or arrangement should be, and he wouldn't bend until he got exactly what he wanted. They both had tremendous driving force, and their mother especially gave them a lot of push." Jacobs also detected a commercial streak in Richard, who wanted to ensure that when a song had reached its peak of performance, it must be heard by as many people as possible. That commercial edge would shape the future for him and Karen.

The Richard Carpenter Trio worked at weddings and dances, all the time polishing their sound in the living room of the small Carpenter home at Fidler Avenue. "Karen could sing and play drums at the same time, quite remarkably," Jacobs says. But she still regarded herself as a drummer primarily.

Back at Downey High School, Bruce Gifford heard about the trio and saw the changes in Karen's musical approach. Intuitively he guessed that Richard was moulding Karen. "She was never a solo singer here in school, but Richard saw the talent that was in her and brought it out of her. After Richard encouraged her, she sang with our group periodically. She was not really impressive at first, but Richard saw her potential and she'd do everything he said. And that's what Richard needed . . . someone to do what he wanted them to do."

By 1966 the Richard Carpenter Trio was rehearsing frequently and for a short time acquired a regular weekend spot at the Jolly Knight Steak House in Garden Grove, Orange County. There they backed a singer, Ed Sulzer, who would later figure importantly in their search for a big break.

The pop revolution in full swing, there were hundreds of talented players, and the "new music" had spawned songwriting guitarists whose emphasis was on the beat allied to an often rebellious image. Though Richard and Karen loved the new music, they felt detached from that trend. None of the new groups featured such fully-fledged musicians as Richard; only a few had women—and a female drummer who sang was rare indeed. Richard's trio offered old-style traditional popular music, some distance from the musical mood of the mid-1960s. It was going to be difficult for them to get breaks: not only was their sound unaligned, but in the parlance of that period, they looked "real square."

In their stepping stones to success, however, Richard and Karen were lucky to meet people with just the right chemistry to enable them to develop their sound. Before leaving high school for the university, Richard went one day to the campus at Long Beach to accompany his new friend Dennis Heath, who was studying voice. They came under the scrutiny of the head of choral studies, Frank Pooler. "Heath had a nice voice," Pooler recalls, "but I was tremendously interested in this young man playing for him. I gave him an on-the-spot vocal audition, and his ear, one of the best I'd ever heard, absolutely astounded me." Pooler told Carpenter that he should be sure to join the college choir.

Meanwhile, as the Richard Carpenter Trio played for parties and at venues like the Hyatt House in nearby Commerce and the International Hotel in Los Angeles, it was clear that Karen wanted to concentrate on drums. And since she wasn't easily persuaded to sing, Richard recruited for a short period Margaret Shanor to do the vocal work.[1] He had stylish red-on-white business cards printed: "The Richard Carpenter Trio. Karen Carpenter drums, Richard Carpenter piano, Wes Jacobs bass. Featuring Margaret Shanor, song stylist. Music for any occasion."

At sixteen, Karen acquired her first boyfriend. Jerry Vance, who attended Downey High School with her, was her age, a tall, slim all-American teenager who dated Karen regularly. They went to school proms and Valentine's Day dances. He was very keen on her, she on him if slightly less so—but he faced the impossible competition of her new devotion to music. Hooked on mastering drums and watching her brother develop the trio, Karen was too absorbed to devote much time to romance.

Although she was still in high school, Richard wanted to continually encourage his sister's vocal interest in singing so he took her on Saturday mornings to Pooler for instruction. Pooler soon realized that while Richard had vocal talent, he didn't have the capacity to be a soloist [which Richard knew]—but his sister certainly did.

Later, for a recital before the "jury" of professors at California State University, Karen was persuaded by Pooler to repeat her imitation of a hair-lipped singer, which had amused him. "The vocal department chairman who was on the jury just cracked up. He'd never heard anything so funny at an audition." The sense of crackpot humour that would always endear her to friends was evident as early as age fifteen.

---

1. Margaret Shanor was known to Richard as a member of Vance Hayes's group of artists at Downey Methodist Church. She worked with Dennis Heath in a popular group called The Young Americans. Beginning in 1965, Margaret was to appear with Richard's trio as singer for a year.

Soon Richard was gigging as many nights as possible in greasy spoon cafés, bars, and restaurants, and being talked about as a unique talent among the twenty-five thousand students at California State University. Karen was the only female drummer on the campus, and Richard was that guy with the astonishing natural ear and keyboard technique. "I thought of her as a drummer who sang," says Lee Vail, a fellow member of the choir. "Her voice was real loud when she sang solos from the choir, but it was true and right on."[2]

With his black horn-rimmed glasses and lanky gait, six-footer Richard presented a "very hyper, very intense" image on the campus, observed Brent Pierce, who was working alongside him for a Bachelor's degree in composition.[3] Although Karen was clearly talented and developing, Pierce considered Richard "the real genius" and Karen his protégé, "a singer who played drums."

The power of being able to control rhythm is what excited Karen about the drums, Pierce believes. Describing her "wonderful, rhythmic inner drive," he believes that her early work on the drums helped her later with her phrasing as a singer.

As for Richard: he had no misgivings about his future, says Pierce. "He was *driven*. He was probably born that way. He felt he had a destiny, and he was going to find it. And he did." Out of the fifty-five people in the choir, perhaps three stood out as heading for a career in music, and Richard was certainly among them. Karen, the little sister who tagged along, liked to play touch football and wrestle, was in these college years not many people's idea of a future star. Had Richard decided not to go into music with such determination, Karen would not have done so, Pierce believes. "He had a great belief in her."

Richard and Karen now unconsciously consolidated the roles that would determine their still-unpredictable future. He was the consummate, sight-reading musician; she was the nontechnician with the blooming, natural voice. He was diligent and comprehen-

2. Richard attended university at Long Beach from the fall of 1964 and Karen joined him there three years later. Both were studying for Bachelor's degrees in music but by the time Karen arrived there, their minds were set on a recording career.
3. Brent Pierce, who in late 1950s played trumpet in bands supporting Sammy Davis, Jr., and Mel Torme, now teaches vocal jazz and music composition and theory at Fullerton College, California.

sive, dedicated to improving his skills at notation, whereas she quickly tired of anything academic. "So much about the music department bored her," Frank Pooler remembers. "She knew she was never going to be a music teacher, so she had no reason to notate. She was a singer with enormous love and respect for Richard . . . who saw her potential."

But beyond music, her work was poor, and she showed such disinterest in any other subjects that she was suspended. Richard and Karen and the group were getting invited to so many auditions that he was often going in to her classes to "yank her out so she could come somewhere and perform with me."

Agnes knew Karen's work at the university was not good, but both she and Harold were angry about the suspension. Her father, who had a knack for writing good letters, sent one to the university saying she would improve—and that they should be proud to have such a wonderful singer studying there.

Frank Pooler proved a strong ally. He told his colleagues that "there are two kinds of music students. Those who have talent and those who don't. There's a difference between having talent and not having to work so hard, and having no talent and having to work your butt off." Karen was a natural, he stated, and he argued against any system that judged students' weaknesses in some subjects against their real strengths—and then penalized them. In Pooler's unqualified support, Karen and Richard had found an inspirational mentor who would emerge as a lifelong friend.

The suspension was lifted after two days of lobbying. It was spring 1968. Nobody could have predicted that within only a year, the Carpenters' glittering record career would be launched.

Crackling with ambition, Richard was constantly looking for a commercial lynchpin from which to jump ahead. And in early 1966, he got lucky. Through a friend, Dan Friberg in the university choir, he found an unexpected and important link to Joe Osborn, the most prominent, highly rated studio bass player in West Coast pop. The path to their meeting was convoluted: Friberg had met a man in church, Don Zacklin, who wanted to break into show business. Joe Osborn and Zacklin had become joint partners in the formation of a small record label, Magic Lamp, Osborn having met Zacklin through singer Johnny Burnette.

When Dan Friberg secured an audition as a singer for the label, he asked Richard to accompany him. The eager Carpenter agreed, and they worked out arrangements for Dan's big voice to sing ballads such as "Ebb Tide" and "Unchained Melody." Karen was not involved in this operation, but she and Richard were now going everywhere together in the music territory. As the evening for the audition approached, it was natural for him to say to her: "Do you wanna go to a recording studio, hear this audition?" "Sure," she replied immediately.

It was for a midnight audition/recording session in May 1966 that they headed toward the garage studio of Joe Osborn at 7935 Ethel Avenue, North Hollywood. Everyone inside music on the West Coast knew of Osborn as the bassist nonpareil, playing with such major acts as the Mamas and the Papas.

Dabbling in studio work of his own with a four-track recorder, he was experimenting with new talent, but he initially regarded the arrival of a tall, nineteen-year-old youth and his "chubby little girl" sister, as he recalls her, with disinterest. Karen certainly did not expect to perform; she was there simply as Richard's soul mate. As the night wore on, that situation changed.

Their arrival together confused everyone, and it soon transpired that both Osborn and Zacklin expected to hear Karen sing—because Zacklin had asked Friberg if any of his schoolmates were talented enough to audition for the label. "Neither Karen nor I knew anything about this," Richard says. "Karen was just turned sixteen and as nervous as hell. She sang a current ballad and of course they loved her.

"When I heard the playback in the booth I just flipped because Karen's voice had recorded so well. When I heard it come out of those speakers, I thought: 'My God!' She had her *sound*, much like the Karen we all knew later."

The audition of Dan that followed was anticlimactic. "Karen's voice was wonderful from that first moment I heard her," Joe Osborn remembers. Richard would always look back on that significant moment, one midnight, when his love of Karen as a pal and as his sister caused him to invite her to his session . . . and when, in a primitive garage studio lined with egg boxes and cork to help acoustics, their future was shaped.

A fast friendship developed with Osborn. Richard, Karen, and Wes Jacobs spent evenings after school and weekends hanging out at his studio, refining their sound. "I was the engineer, but Richard called all the shots as far as material was concerned," Osborn says. "We all experimented, learning how to stack vocal parts on the four-track." Karen recalled later how they would all study particularly the Beach Boys' "Good Vibrations" and the Beatles' "Eleanor Rigby."

Jacobs remembers that even in those embryonic days, he "did not doubt that Richard and Karen would become very famous, very successful." Not only had Richard grasped what sounds would be commercial but "he had this great knack for doing both arrangements and original compositions."

To Agnes, listening with interest to their progress, it seemed natural that Karen should add a girl's voice to the sound that was still basically an instrumental trio. "When Wes came over for those rehearsals, I'd say to Richard: 'Why don't you let Karen sing?' He finally did, but they played so loudly that I said: 'Karen can't sing above what you're playing!' Well, that didn't go over so big, I'll tell you!"

Within a couple of weeks, Karen was signed as a solo singer to Osborn's Magic Lamp record label. From several songs cut, two written by Richard but named as Karen Carpenter solo records were issued as a single, "Looking for Love" and "I'll Be Yours." Though basic and uninspired, the songs provided a vehicle for her tentative style.

It was a start, but it went nowhere. The small label had no machinery for distribution and promotion, and it folded within a year. The single became a collector's item, with only five hundred copies pressed.[4]

What happened next was every young act's dream. The Richard Carpenter Trio had reached the finals of the prestigious amateur talent contest "The Battle of the Bands" at the Hollywood Bowl on June 24, 1966—and triumphed. Iced tea was the favorite drink of Karen and Richard, and he composed an ambitious instrumental with that title that was a showcase for Wes Jacobs's tuba and Karen's drumming. The group's originality impressed the judges.

---

4. A fire at Joe Osborn's home destroyed most of the tapes made there by Richard and Karen. Osborn went on to record with the Carpenters as bass guitarist on many of their albums.

Their other song was a dazzling instrumental version of the bossa nova classic "The Girl from Ipanema," popularized by Astrud Gilberto with Stan Getz. A multi-time signature rendition arranged by Richard drew applause from the judges—and the trio took three awards including best combo, outstanding instrumentalist (Richard), and the sweepstakes trophy for the highest score of any act in the whole contest. Their victories were the talk of the Hollywood Bowl.

Reviewing the show in the *Los Angeles Times,* Leonard Feather wrote: "The musical surprise of the evening was the Trio of Richard Carpenter, a remarkably original soloist who won awards as the best instrumentalist and leader of the best combo. Flanking his piano were Karen Carpenter, his talented sixteen year old sister, at the drums, and bassist Wes Jacobs who doubled amusingly and confidently on tuba."

As Richard walked with Karen to the parking lot, a man walked over to congratulate them and inquire whether they might like to make test records. "I was nineteen, smug, full of myself, and we'd just won," Richard says. "I told him we already had a contract. He said to give him a call if things changed, and gave me his card." This card gave his name as Neely Plumb, the prominent West Coast manager of pop with the giant RCA Records. Pulling his foot from his mouth, Richard gathered himself quickly and said that although his sister was signed to a small company, he was not. (Richard was signed only as a songwriter to Light-Up Music, the publishing arm of Magic Lamp Records.) Plumb said he was interested in their instrumental sound, and a test at RCA followed. It transpired that Plumb wanted to develop a "rock tuba" sound by emphasizing the uniqueness of Wes Jacobs. In September, the trio signed with RCA and quickly cut eleven tracks, including "Strangers in the Night," the Beatles' "Every Little Thing," and "Flat Baroque" which eventually became a popular Carpenters track. But the RCA committee voted against them all. With psychedelia dawning, they saw no commercial potential in a jazzy trio. Losing confidence in getting themselves established with RCA, Richard and Karen accepted the company's offer of a few hundred dollars to end the contract.

Fresh momentum was needed, and it came, as always, from the company Richard kept. At California State University he met the partner who would help him chart a path to fame. John Bettis was a true hippie with long fair hair down to his shoulders, an old green coat, jeans, cowboy boots. He was exactly the same age as Richard, a political science major whose hobby was playing and singing folk music. A hip music man of his time, he echoed the sounds of Bob Dylan, Peter, Paul, and Mary, and the Kingston Trio. There was a distinct edge and arrogance in his character; when Frank Pooler heard of his prowess and asked Bettis if he would perform something with the choir, the reply came: "Not unless I write it."

Pooler shot back with "OK"—and Bettis was flummoxed.

In the college practice room, Bettis on his fashionable Martin guitar quickly demonstrated a lyrical slant which fascinated Richard. Then, meeting Pooler's challenge, Bettis set about composing a corny song with Richard called "Acapella Music," which debunked the college music department, choral music, and Pooler's ego. Bettis's motive was to get himself kicked out of the "boring" choir. But everyone loved it.

Developing their friendship, Bettis was surprised to find that the staid appearance of Richard did not match his inner self. "His sense of humour and wit, his outlook on life, his image, is the farthest thing from the way people perceive Richard," Bettis says. He identified a strong streak of irreverence.

Richard told Bettis he had a sister who played drums and sang; they had just won the Battle of the Bands, he continued, and he had an idea for a new sound, which Richard described as "a choral approach to pop." Bettis, who had been flunking out of political science classes and needed a creative lifeline, was immediately interested in discussing this idea further.

So began a partnership that would write multimillion-selling songs, a string of Carpenters hits that would stand forever and which within the twelve years that followed would make both men millionaires. Their union would provide Karen with that platform for the voice and style that was fast emerging.

For all that he was a rebel, Bettis soon displayed a strong romanticism that worked handsomely within Richard's orchestral instincts. "He brought colours out in me as a lyricist," Bettis says. "It was the psychedelic era, so the images on the radio were fantastic and I was imitating them." Their first serious collaboration, "Another Song," was hardly pop but three or four sections of different-style sounds bonded together. Shortly after this foray,

Richard invited Bettis over to his house on Fidler Avenue, where he was introduced to Karen.

He found the sixteen-year-old sitting with curlers in her hair, "very old for her years, a mothering sort of soul. I was obviously a little crazy, and she liked me right from the start," says Bettis. The formality of Agnes Carpenter threw Bettis off guard. Karen explained her mother's idiosyncrasies to John, warning him that his scruffy demeanor might irritate her. "Had I been Mrs. Carpenter and seen me coming through the door, I probably would have been a little hesitant," he smiles now. Karen said she liked the music he was beginning with her brother.

As the weeks passed, a rapport developed between them. A strong romantic sweep surfaced in Bettis's lyrics and as they both talked about "making it," their joint goal was not a load of money but the thrill of hearing their new songs on the radio and tearing up the national charts. An extraordinary bonding occurred between the twenty-year-olds: Bettis "desperately wanted to know more about the musical genius and imagination of Richard," whom he would later describe as "touched by God"; Richard was attracted by the freewheeling life-style of his new friend. Polar opposites on the surface, both intuitively felt that their contrast would produce creative sparks. Whereas Richard wanted to discover what it was like to metaphorically "jump off cliffs" as Bettis did, John was mesmerized by the natural musical brain of an obvious genius. A powerful friendship developed very quickly. They were virtually stepbrothers from the start.

Any comparison with the titanic talent and partnership of John Lennon and Paul McCartney seems gratuitous at best, but in terms of contrasting personalities meshing brilliantly, there is a parallel. Lennon was a rebellious poet and wordsmith for whom music was mostly a vehicle to communicate his thoughts, but he fully understood it as a medium. His ideas and words came to him before the tune. McCartney's fertile musicianship, and more orthodox approach to life, are augmented by a true "feel" for the spirit of rock music. They needed each other to generate the creative collaboration that was to prove unrepeatable with any other partner. Ten years after Lennon and McCartney were (in Paul's words) "mining gold," Bettis and Carpenter made their impact— from an utterly different vantage point, musically, but driven by similar human chemistry.

*   *   *

A chain of events and contacts among musicians and friends had brought Richard into contact with the man who would eventually become his group's first manager. In 1963, not long after arriving in California, Richard had been tapped by a local musician named Larry Black to play clubs including the Roaring Twenties lounge in Downey and Leo's in Gardena. Black's group's bassist had a day job alongside a friend who sang, and Black asked Richard if he would accompany him on the piano one night. This turned out to be Ed Sulzer, a talented New York-born ballad singer whom Richard was happy to accompany at various gigs. By early 1967, when Richard told him of his plans to get a new group together, Sulzer said, "When you get your tapes, do you mind if I pump 'em around for you?" This marked the start of a tenacious period of management by Sulzer of an act that was in its developmental stage.

Galvanized by his new friendship with Bettis, Richard knew his jazzy trio had been an artistic success but a commercial failure. It needed to be replaced by something more popular in its appeal. Remembering a talented guitarist he'd met through Vance Hayes at Downey High School, Richard took Bettis to see Gary Sims appearing at a café. "Hell, yes, get *him!*" said Bettis, impressed. Sims, a science major at their college, had known Richard casually from singing in the local church choir when Richard played the organ. Sims had always wanted to add music to his college studies and told Richard so on the campus one day; at that point, Richard informed him of the group he planned to assemble with Bettis.

Sims had precisely the ability to slot into the sound Richard and Bettis heard in their heads. So did Danny Woodhams, another school friend who played violin and sang tenor. With a natural talent, he decided to teach himself bass guitar to join them. To strengthen the vocal sound he believed crucial, Richard brought in Leslie Johnston, a young woman they had met in the college choir, and so was formed a group called first Summerchimes, then briefly Spectra, and finally Spectrum. They went into five-nights-a-week rehearsal at Fidler Avenue and around the piano in the front room.

"Karen and I blended great, and we all teamed together very fast," Leslie Johnston says. Richard had the vocal harmony sound of the Beach Boys, the Association, and Les Paul and Mary Ford firmly in his mind. "It was real tight harmony stuff, and we were good," Leslie remembers. It was, she says, nearly the same sound that the Carpenters later gave the world—but it was to prove a little too early for anyone to take a chance on music that could not be classified.

At Joe Osborn's studio they made some tapes, but when they sent them around to the record companies and attended a few auditions, Spectrum was rejected.

The sound was attractive enough, they were told, but hopelessly unfashionable, neither synchronized with the rock 'n' roll age nor a valid contrast. And it would never sell!

Their appearance was condemned, too. Successful vocal harmony groups like the Association and the Buckinghams looked staid, but there was a fine line not to be crossed, and Richard and Karen and their cohorts were on the wrong side of it. Looking like the antithesis of young pop people, they were dismissed as "square." One record executive told Ed Sulzer: "They're wearing turtleneck sweaters, *blue velvet* suits; they have *short* hair; and they're singing words that we *can understand!* It's sophisticated— but we don't want to take a chance on it." Bettis and Carpenter, as the architects, were livid at so many rejections. In their hearts they knew they had the seed of something commercial even if it might need a little encouragement before it flowered.

If Richard was the prime mover, he was now joined by an equally zealous sister. Her personality was "caustic," says Leslie Johnston, who enjoyed a good rapport. "She was *so* serious about her music I don't think she had time for other things. She wasn't antisocial; she was a fun gal. She just had her head into her music. I was five and a half years older, and I think she thought of me in a sisterly way." At college and inside Spectrum, "she was a Levi's person, not into clothes or particularly caring whether she was real feminine. Yeah, I think you could call her a tomboy; she changed as she got older."

As Spectrum battled in vain for recognition, "we were really gung ho, traipsing around Los Angeles trying to find a place to perform—and I'd spend the night with her and sleep in her bed," Leslie says. With the idealism of youth, they were unshakable in their determination. "College classes went in the toilet," Bettis recalls. "We all started singing as a group, Richard teaching us all the parts, and there seemed a natural blend to it. We were confident, but those rejections were shattering us." They believed they had a better sound than some of those heard on the radio.

Richard was also listening carefully to the bell-like clarity of Karen's voice. Her style was becoming focused, her sound so natural that it would surely need to be featured more in the present setup. For the moment, though, such an intuitive feeling was fanciful and had to be shelved as they lived from day to day.[5]

In the long college vacation of summer, 1967, Richard Carpenter and John Bettis landed a bizarre residency as a duo playing at Disneyland, Anaheim. They received the fabulous union salary of $180 a week each. This substantial sum would help them buy better instruments and amplification. For Bettis, more used to fifty-dollar club dates as a folk singer, it was a fortune.

At Coke Corner, a Main Street, USA, turn-of-the-century leisure spot, they wore straw hats and brocade vests. John struggled along on six-string banjo while Richard played ragtime piano without authenticity; neither of them, especially John, excelled in the style demanded by the location. Booked to play American traditional songs that were appropriate for the backdrop, they played as well as they could, such songs as "A Bicycle Built for Two" and "Somebody Stole My Gal" (which the irreverent Bettis converted into "Somebody Rolled My Gal"). Bored with the pretence, they threw in some hits of the day including the Beatles' "A Day in the Life" and Simon and Garfunkel's "Cloudy"—to the irritation of the conservative talent supervisor Vic Guder. "John and I were completely out of order," Richard recalls. "Vic Guder was absolutely right to take the view he did."

Nor did Guder accept their demeanour. While Richard's hair was slicked back (he looked more like a bank clerk than a musician), Bettis's fair hair was longer than acceptable. When Guder berated them about their appearance and their defiant behavior, they wrote a song taunting him. (The jaunty "Mr. Guder" appeared on the *Close to You* album and became a popular track with their audience. Later, Richard regretted recording it, considering it a cheap jibe.)

5. Wes Jacobs left the group in 1967 to study music at Juilliard. In 1970 he became the tuba player with the Detroit Symphony Orchestra, where he remains.

With eyes for all passing girls, they also wrote "Candy" about a pretty waitress; later retitled "One Love," it would also become a Carpenters recording.

To play at Coke Corner, Carpenter and Bettis had to join the American Federation of Musicians, and though there was a "leader scale" in union rules, Richard had decided to divide their pay equally. This angered Richard's mother, who pointed out to her son that he was carrying the musical load. Bettis, a pure "folkie," needed instruction from Richard from "fake books" in the basement at Coke Corner between their sets.

The matter of their income remained thorny to Agnes, but it became academic when, after a bumpy five-month residency for which they had been ill-suited, they were fired. It was, Richard reflects, four months longer than they deserved to survive.

In the evenings, Agnes had been driving Karen to join Richard, John, Gary Sims, and Danny Woodhams for rehearsals in the sanctuary of a church in Orange County where Danny was employed as choral director. Richard was continuing church organ stints, and he continued to study piano under the tutelage of Julian Musafia at California State University, Long Beach.

At home, with help from his parents, he had bought his first grand piano in 1964, and to help with the instalment payments, he taught piano extensively throughout the Downey area. Though he never put a card up to advertise his services, through word of mouth he had about thirty pupils and drove from house to house, juggling appointments with the club dates that were coming in for him as a solo pianist.

Bookings for Spectrum were in short supply, but Ed Sulzer secured them some useful dates; at the Blue Law in Torrance, they opened for the major group Steppenwolf, a considerable breakthrough. They were also booked for three nights at the prestigious Whiskey A-Gogo on Sunset Boulevard, but they were fired after their first show because their music failed to get people up and dancing.

A little more encouragement awaited them at the famous Troubadour Club on Santa Monica Boulevard. On Mondays at around 4:00 P.M., the Carpenter station wagon would drop off Karen or Richard to wait in line to join the try-out acts at the Troubadour's "Hoot Nights," while the other went back with the rest of the group to get the amplifiers and equipment. "I often stood there talking with kids, along with people like Jackson Browne," Karen remembered.

New talent like theirs found a vital platform on Mondays, but it was basically the territory of folk and rock attitudes, if not strictly all-rock music. So the sight and sound of a harmony group wearing matching velveteen suits drew a crowd response that was initially bewildered. Gradually, though, the quality of their music, and the work they had put into rehearsals, was recognized. "We got standing ovations but still no recording contract," Karen said. "The feeling from the audience," says John Bettis, was "I don't know if that's commercial, but they're good."

Incongruous though their sound seemed among most of the rock fraternity, word-of-mouth enthusiasm was starting to spread for Spectrum. But though he was persistent in his rounds of the record companies, Ed Sulzer still could not transfer this "street" interest to the executives who signed up new artists.

On so many days and nights, Richard Carpenter and John Bettis drove home in tears of anger and bitterness because nobody had the vision to recognize their musical ability. With short fuses, they became livid at a system that would apparently banish them to obscurity—mostly, it seemed, because they stood outside current fashions. "How *dare* these people not sign us?" they echoed to each other.

They wanted to emulate the new-style harmonic strengths being pioneered by the Beatles and the Beach Boys, while projecting the golden voice of Karen via Richard's intricate arrangements. To record companies, this proposal had no category.

Worse, they displayed no sex appeal. They would need an indefinable ingredient as well as a fine song to launch them against such a hostile wall of rejections.

In many groups, female singers are automatically the focal point— because of their gender, their voice, their appearance, their personality. But Karen was still planted firmly behind her drums and, in her perception, "just one of the band." She was a team player, the antithesis of the self-absorbed show business performer, and her physique might have encouraged that stance. She had long been aware of her bulky figure. When she was a child, it had been called "baby fat" by the family; by the time she was nine she was decidedly chubby, as pictures show; and now, weighing 145 pounds (too much for her height of five feet, four inches), she felt that at seventeen years old she had endured it long enough. "The average person would definitely say she was overweight right up to her teenage years," Richard says. This was in spite of her early enthusiasm for such activities as volleyball and biking to deliver newspapers.

Richard teased her as "Fatso"; she responded with "Four eyes," since he had worn horn-rimmed glasses since the age of twelve. It was the level of banter that happens in any house or school playground, but it possibly hit a raw nerve with Karen, who was far removed from the pert, sexually conscious look of 1960s teenagers. With shoulder-length hair and little interest in clothes, she grew to rely for her appeal on her infectious smile and quick-witted personality.

Paying no heed to diet, she had eaten chocolate truffles and junk food freely, but now she told her mother that if she was heading for performing as a career, her weight should be checked. Big hips ran through the Carpenter family tree: Karen's mother, grandmother, and Aunt Bernice had them, and Agnes knew there was no way these could be shifted. But she agreed that Karen needed to lose some bulk and took her to a doctor. He prescribed the Stillman water diet in which she had to drink eight glasses of water a day, avoid all fatty foods, and take some vitamins.

She hated the diet but adopted it rigidly. Meeting Richard and John Bettis after their performances at Disneyland, Karen would go on with them to rehearsals. Following these, the group went to Coco's for milk shakes, onion rings, and burgers—food she normally ate voraciously. But she stood watching them eating and would not be swayed from the task of shedding those pounds. It was a great success: she lost twenty-five pounds during six months in 1967—and stayed at her new weight of around 120 pounds from then until 1973.

Romance beckoned again in 1968 after Karen finished seeing Jerry Vance. Her sweet nature and intelligence had always attracted Gary Sims, the fair-haired sensitive guitarist in Spectrum who had previously been dating that group's singer, Leslie Johnston.

Gary had known Richard and Karen from Downey High School, where she was in the class behind him. And at Downey

Methodist Church, Richard had played organ as the accompanist to Gary's hymn singing. In Gary, Karen found the caring warmth she needed at eighteen. He was outgoing, sincere, bright, and gentle. And they could talk music. Most important to Karen, Richard liked and respected him, and their relationship proceeded affectionately.

In these years long before Karen stepped out to become the spotlighted singer, Sims observed at her home that Richard was cast by Mr. and Mrs. Carpenter as the talented one, who was predicted to be a successful classical pianist in the making. Karen, in Sims's memory, was loved for her zany sense of humour and was the "funny, little bit rotund, tagalong sister." The focus of the teenager he dated had not been set, but their romance bore the sweet innocence of youth. They held hands as they went to the movies to see musicals like *Finian's Rainbow* and *Hello Dolly,* which she loved. They cruised to the beach. Others in Spectrum noticed them "looking at each other differently" when the band got together.

Though Karen and Gary took great care not to parade their association blatantly, Sims remembers the atmosphere as sometimes "slightly awkward." At the Carpenter home, Agnes and Harold liked him, but, like Jerry Vance before him, he became much more intense about Karen than she was about him. A year older than she, Gary was to date her for two years before he went into the army.

"She was probably my first love of any kind of an adult nature," Sims says. He recalls that she "kind of accepted that she'd been a pudgy kid," and she disliked the water diet while conceding that it had been essential. And, Sims says, "She kept trying to get rid of the hips."

Richard, too, paid heed to his appearance at this time, exchanging his studious look with horn-rimmed glasses for contact lenses. He had fought this switch for years, but it took only one sentence from an occasional date to persuade him. The highly attractive Marsha Buehner, studying on a piano scholarship at the university, said he should go for contacts. "That did it! If nothing came out of that relationship, and nothing did, I had a lot to be grateful to Marsha for."

Now their luck in music seemed to change. After months of effort and rejections from almost every record company in town,

two offers came simultaneously in early 1968 from lively indepen-
dents, Uni, where Neil Diamond had recently been signed, and
White Whale, where a group called the Turtles had scored with
"Happy Together." Richard and Ed Sulzer played for time, checking one offer against the other until finally they received a contract
from White Whale—which they disliked and eventually rejected.
By the time they returned to Uni, that company was rightly dis-
pleased at their vacillation.

Realizing it was their "second choice," Uni withdrew the offer.
Shell-shocked amid the turndowns, the strong-minded Bettis
quit. His mood was already low when the final straw came at a
band meeting. Richard announced his plan for dividing what little
money was coming in. He, as the leader, would receive most (as he
should have done at Coke Corner, he mused to himself); Karen
and Bettis would get the next biggest slice; the others would
divide the remainder. Unacceptable, retorted Bettis waspishly. "To
be a leader," he told Richard condescendingly, "you have to have a
book!" (By this, he meant a prepared book of musical arrangements
for the band.)

At this remark, Richard raised the roof. He may not have put
all his music in writing, but he had taught Bettis and the others all
the stuff he had written. "Granted, John had written the lyrics, but
the arrangements were all mine," Richard says. Bettis retorted that
even though Richard was the undisputed leader musically, any new
financial split should be equal from performances since they were a
cooperative unit.

It was a matter of principle rather than significant money, but it
was a bad-tempered departure, with Ed Sulzer trying to smooth it
over. No, Bettis insisted, he was positively out of Spectrum. But he
added a rider. So magically correct were he and Richard for each
other that when it came to songwriting, he would "write with him
until hell freezes over." That rock-solid commitment would provide a key component to the Carpenters' success.

"And that," Richard says, "was just about it for Spectrum."

The taciturn Joe Osborn was the pivot of the group's next move.
Though he didn't care for Richard, Osborn had a soft spot for
Karen and took her around town to see him play bass on studio
sessions.

With Richard now believing that his arranging skills and his sister's singing style were the twin keys to their future, Joe suggested they return to his studio. There, recording all the vocals themselves, they cut three tracks, a new composition by Richard, "Don't Be Afraid," and Carpenter-Bettis compositions "Your Wonderful Parade" and the a capella "Invocation." The texture, and its simplicity, was "terrific," Richard decided after this session. They had hit a winning groove.

"Karen's sound was there. It was just a matter of the right song, and we were getting close." He decided boldly that he and Karen would form a new sound of their own, and to hell with fancy names. They would be Carpenters, without *the* as a prefix, since Richard felt it sounded hipper and in the same style as Buffalo Springfield and Jefferson Airplane.

Although Karen still considered herself primarily a drummer who sang, Richard sensed there was a lot more potential in her vocals. There were to be a number of bumps on their new route to success, but as they now pulled away from the concept of a band sound, luck was to smile on them.

After two years of battling for a breakthrough, the summer of 1968 came with a flurry of activity that brought them an escalator to success.

It was the height of the Vietnam War, and Richard, heavily draftable, had been granted a student deferment, which meant he could stay at the university at Long Beach. There he heard of a new national TV programme, "Your All American College Show," for which talent scouts auditioned acts on campuses. Those selected went to Hollywood to tape the show before a celebrity judging panel. Broadcast nationally, the much-vaunted show was sponsored by Colgate-Palmolive and produced by the prominent radio and commercial announcer Wendell Niles. If they succeeded in getting on that show, the publicity value would be enormous.

With Karen at the drums, Richard at the piano, and a talented bassist, Bill Sissyoev, recruited specially, they auditioned at the Hollywood Video Center in summer 1968 with a short medley of "Dancing in the Street" and "The Shadow of Your Smile." Featuring technically difficult piano solos interjected by Richard to show off his ability, along with Karen's singing talent and drum solo, they easily outstripped the other acts. They were accepted by "Your All American College Show," appearing three times that year and over a period of a year and a half in total. In all, the trio

won $3,500, Richard won $3,500 for his subsequent solo performances, and the public exposure was a valuable fillip.

Another triumph followed quickly. What was at that time still
the subculture of rock and pop music was beginning to be projected in television commercials. Richard was phoned by John
Bahler, who, with his brother Tom, had a group called the Love
Generation. The Bahler brothers had seen Karen and Richard on
"Your All American College Show" and had been hired by the
advertising agency J. Walter Thompson. That firm's client, the
Ford Motor Company, wanted to augment the Bahler brothers'
group it had already hired (by now called The Going Thing) to
help generate interest in Ford and also to promote an upcoming
new car, the Maverick.

Auditioning about two hundred acts in New York and another
two hundred at Sunset Sound in Hollywood, the Bahlers were
impressed with the energy and musicality of Richard and Karen—
and in early 1969 they were signed to a contract worth initially a
gigantic fifty thousand dollars each annually plus a special Mustang
car each.

Richard and Karen were elated at the prospect of this windfall.
At last, it seemed, their worth was being recognized.

Still, a record deal eluded them, and for all their talent and activity,
the only real recognition as popular artists would come from seeing and hearing their music tearing up the best-selling record
charts. That was the only real yardstick of success.

Despite all their achievements elsewhere, their failure to land a
deal deflated Richard. He asked Ed Sulzer in late 1968 to begin
anew the rounds of the record companies. Since an earlier "round"
of the labels had brought only misery to Spectrum, too, Richard
and Karen were not optimistic. A component of luck was going to
be vital.

As Sulzer encountered yet more rejects from giant labels such
as Capitol and Warner Brothers, Karen and Richard felt doomed.
Finally, there appeared on the horizon the vaguest prospect of at
least being given a new hearing. A friend of Sulzer's who worked
with him at Autonetics (a division of North American where Agnes
Carpenter and many Carpenter family friends worked) mentioned
to Sulzer that he knew Jack Daugherty, who had been a trumpeter
with Woody Herman's band.

Daugherty, it was said, was now in public relations work at North American, but he had a passport to a potentially golden introduction. He actually knew John Pisano, who was the guitarist with the hugely successful band the Tijuana Brass—whose leader was Herb Alpert. And so Richard and Karen's tape might well find its way to that influential figure in the music industry.

The chances of this protracted chain working as predicted were clearly remote. When Ed Sulzer told Richard Carpenter of the possibility of getting the tape on its way to such a prominent person via such a tortuous route, Richard laughed sceptically. "Oh *sure,* Herb Alpert's going to hear of *this!*"

As Ed Sulzer touted the new tape with its three songs to record executives, their hopes went sky-high when two key names expressed interest. Kenny Rogers, later to emerge as a major solo star but then leading the First Edition, was seeking a new female singer, and Richard encouraged Karen to audition. He was confident she would sail into this fast-rising group. "Karen, you have to do it—and when they tell you that you're it, you've gotta take it," Richard urged her. "I was more interested in Karen's future as an artist than my own," Richard says. "And I thought that when they heard her, that would be the end for Karen and me as far as the Carpenters were concerned. Because she was so damned good." With nothing on the horizon for them as a recording duo, he felt she had to sail away independently with that voice.

But she was rejected. When she broke the news to him, Richard could not believe it. "She sounded like Karen right there and then." He had fully expected his sister would become the First Edition's lead singer. That group was already successful, and with Karen on lead vocals its popularity would have been lifted enormously, he was certain. "Thank God they didn't sign her," he smiles now.

Next, Bones Howe, riding high as producer-engineer with the popular Association and the Fifth Dimension, was enthusiastic. But when Richard and Karen met him, he said that regretfully he would not have enough time to devote to them. "We were crestfallen," Richard remembers. "Ordinarily, we took all this with a grain of salt, but this had been presented to us as a done deal."

It was as if these negative responses were happening to ensure that when the giant break that awaited them came, just one week later, they would be free to accept a welcome to their haven for the next two decades.

In 1969, the contemporary music scene was on the cusp of a new era. The euphoria of the Beatles revolution had subsided as Lennon and McCartney headed inexorably for a split. The Beatles had not been merely hugely talented performers; they had begun the swing to self-written new pop music. Cream, led by the rock guitar ace Eric Clapton, had broken up after eighteen months of virtuoso rock, while in America Simon and Garfunkel sang "The Boxer." Frank Zappa (curiously, strongly admired by Richard) had introduced the Mothers of Invention two years earlier, and the jazz-rock sounds of Blood, Sweat, and Tears contrasted with the Fifth Dimension singing of the age of "Aquarius." As the Moody Blues sang "On the Threshold of a Dream," pioneering "concept albums" were beginning, with battalions of young musicians like Crosby, Stills, and Nash eager to unleash fresh, vibrant sounds to a generation that was starting to rename pop as rock to identify its different nuance.

Simple pop music was therefore being relegated to the second division. Albums had been outstripping singles in sales, and creative emphasis had slowly been switching to thematic works, enabling ambitious composers to stretch beyond three-minute singles. Straight love songs were having a hard time getting through, except in the hands of unstoppable future giants like Elton John. "Progressive rock" was the hip ticket. It was into this hostile environment that Karen and Richard Carpenter pitched themselves with their smooth songs of romance.

Two singers who exhibited a vocal purity were particularly significant influences on Karen and Richard: American vocalist Patti Page, who had a string of hits in the 1950s; and British singer Matt Monro, whose impact in the early 1960s stemmed from his unique interpretation of his idol, Frank Sinatra.

By chance, when a Los Angeles teenager named Herb Alpert was at high school, he, too, had been stunned by a Patti Page recording of "You Belong to Me." Unwittingly, he was sharing a taste in music with Richard and Karen Carpenter, whom he had never met.

By 1969, Alpert was the world-famous trumpeter and leader of the hugely successful Tijuana Brass. He was also the *A* in the lively record company A&M. As he played one of the hundreds of tapes that landed on his desk every week from hopeful artists, one that featured Karen Carpenter's voice struck an emotional chord: it reminded him of his high school teens, of Patti Page singing down to him from speakers in the trees in a garden when he was visiting Lake Arrowhead, California. "I remember staring up at the speakers thinking Patti Page's voice was in my lap. It had so much *presence*.

"The first note I heard from this tape was Karen's voice. And I had that same feeling. My mind went back to the speaker system on that tree. It felt like her voice was on the couch, like she was sitting next to me. It was full and round, and it was ... *amazing*." Although it appeared to be an unprofessionally unrecorded tape, it intrigued him. "This voice was buzzing into my body, and it was the way they presented it."

With his partner, Jerry Moss, Alpert had begun A&M with two parallels to the Carpenters' route to his door. He had begun the Tijuana Brass in his makeshift garage studio, just as they had experienced with Joe Osborn; and, like Karen and Richard, Alpert had once been signed unsuccessfully to RCA Records—in his case, as a singer. His suggestion that he play trumpet for the label was rejected. These coincidences were not known to either party as the tape wended its circuitous way to Alpert's desk in early 1969.

The performing career of Alpert had recently taken a new twist. After four years of triumph with his Tijuana Brass, who sold some thirty million albums, Alpert had scored a worldwide solo hit the previous year with a smoochy vocal solo on the ballad "This Guy's in Love with You."

Renowned for his exceptional ear for hit songs and sounds, Alpert had doubled his performing talent with a search for new acts to help his company grow. When Jerry Moss attended the epochal Monterey Pop Festival in 1967, he realized that A&M was adrift in its roster of artists: "We didn't have anybody on the bill, and it bothered me." After the Tijuana Brass success, A&M's roll call included Mexican sounds from Julius Wechter and His Baja Marimba Band, the Sandpipers, singers Claudine Longet and Chris Montez, and Sergio Mendes and Brasil '66. To redress the balance in contemporary style, in came Joe Cocker, Cat Stevens, reggae singer Jimmy Cliff, and bands Humble Pie, Procol Harum, the Move, Fairport Convention, and Free under licensing deals with British labels.

As well as heralding new rock sounds, Alpert and Moss valued a backbone of songwriters of pure pop single hits, and two notable Americans were also inside the A&M fold: Burt Bacharach, who with his partner, Hal David, composed a string of golden hits for singer Dionne Warwick; and Paul Williams, an introspective writer who sang his own lovelorn material. Alpert and Moss had thus created a highly individualistic label. It was not challenging such giants as Capitol and Warner Brothers, but it had panache. And it had an asset at the helm which all the musicians respected: Alpert, a natural trumpeter and performer who empathized with the artistic temperament.

The Carpenters tape that he heard had the tentative, homespun sound achieved by Richard and Karen in Osborn's garage studio. The three songs featured, "Your Wonderful Parade," "Don't Be Afraid," and "Invocation," represented not trendy rock but straight forward popular music. Alpert, fortunately, always had an ear for talent beyond what he called "the beat of the week." In love with the voice, the harmonies, and the arrangements, he decided immediately to offer them a deal.

On April 22, 1969, Richard and Karen went to the office of Jerry Moss to sign the contract. Since Karen was at nineteen legally under age, her parents had to countersign for her.

Moss, who dealt with the business aspects of the company more than his artist-partner, offered the Carpenters a standard advance payment of ten thousand dollars with a 7 percent royalty on record sales. Jack Daugherty was given responsibilities for their production and additionally gained a personal production contract with A&M.

After pleasantries were exchanged, the somewhat shy Alpert popped in to say to them, "Well, let's hope you have some hits." Richard, a car enthusiast, went out immediately and spent his half of their advance money on a Chrysler Imperial. And that marked the end of their full-time university studies. Amid the excitement, they managed to complete the college year, Richard successfully sitting a biology exam, but they left without their degrees in music. For all the pleasures and friendships they had enjoyed as students, nothing could rival the offer of a strong record deal.

Karen was particularly thrilled to be joining a company led by Alpert, whose records she collected. Later he invited Karen and Richard to the final concert of his Tijuana Brass at the Inglewood Forum. Alpert remembers that she was rather star-struck, "hovering over the ground some place, and probably the same for Richard." So they scarcely connected on a human level. But Alpert loved their "innocence," and a firm rapport between the trio developed quickly.

Over the moon with excitement at a record deal, they now faced one worrying hurdle—that signed contract with Ford to tour the United States to hammer across "The Going Thing" commercials. Giving up fifty thousand dollars each plus a car was not palatable, but a disc career promised longevity and there was no serious choice. There would be no time to tour *and* launch a record career. With some persuasion from Tom Bahler, Ford let them out of the pact, to Richard's surprise, relief and appreciation.

Elated though they were, they remained pragmatic, and their thoughts turned to their friends in Spectrum. Though the group had dissolved, Richard and Karen felt a keen loyalty. Late one night they went to Gary Sims's house in Downey, scratched on the screen of his bedroom window to get his attention, and told him: "We gotta deal! A&M has signed us!" Richard explained that though they had been signed as a duo, they would still have to form a group to perform their music live. "We can't sing six parts! Would you like to come back?"

Sims, by then a music major at California State University, had joined the Army Reserves. He was trying to defer his liability to be drafted as a full-time soldier in these Vietnam days. The reserve scheme meant he would be absent intermittently for months at summer camps, he told them. Richard and Karen assured him he need not worry; they would work something out.

Now the mocking began. Around Hollywood and inside his record company, Alpert commanded respect for his taste and for his uncanny ear for commercial sounds. But in this age of gritty rock music and assertive life-style, he began to be ridiculed behind his back.

There was incredulity and laughter at his enthusiasm for a brother-sister act whose entire stance reflected the challenged, staid values of Middle America. Here was A&M trying to align itself with the counterculture and its music—and Herb had gone and signed a *duo* who sang corny, old-fashioned love songs, didn't smoke cigarettes or do dope, and fostered a preppy image. They would tarnish A&M's standing among the hip! As the sixties drew to a close, choice of music was seen as a badge, an article of faith, a declaration of attitude. It would be uncool to belong to a record label that gave refuge to the Carpenters. When Richard and Karen began dropping in to the A&M studio, smiling enthusiastically at their future, some of the staff treated them as lepers.

Undaunted, and encouraged by Alpert, who told them not to hurry, they set to work tenaciously on their first album. For Richard, such sudden freedom of hours in a studio was stimulating as he worked to refine their sound for their all-important debut. They worked all day and into the night, slipping into a routine that would punctuate the next few years, visiting Pink's hot dog stand at the corner of Melrose Avenue and La Brea Avenue around midnight when they were recording.

Karen had ceased the rigid Stillman water diet of two years earlier and had settled at a fairly constant 120 pounds. She seemed to burn up the calories, for she ate normally. It was Richard who was putting on weight at this stage, even though he had worked the clubs as well as spending nights in the studio.

With their back-up musicians they would break also for visits to the deli counter at the Safeway store at the corner of Sunset Boulevard and La Brea, hard by A&M; then they would wander down to McDonald's. So high was Richard and Karen's consumption of Big Macs that Alpert joked one Christmas that he would inquire into whether McDonald's made a credit card, which might be a perfect gift for the Carpenters.

Loading up there or at Pink's with the fast food they both enjoyed, their menu was similar most nights: Michelob beers for Richard, Pepsi for Karen, chili dogs, and fries. Karen, very much "one of the gang," traded jokes, enjoyed the lively banter of musicians, and was at a peak of ambition.

Though she played drums and sang well, the dichotomy of Karen's positioning blurred their impact, according to some admirers. Even at this early stage, Henry Mancini, the respected pianist, arranger, and composer of such movie classics as "Moon River," "Charade," and "The Days of Wine and Roses," was among the early sceptics about her dual role.

As a judge on "Your All American College Show" in September 1969, he had been outnumbered when he voted for Karen as she played drums and sang solo on "For Once in My Life." When Richard had appealed to her to step out from the drums and just sing, she said no. Richard also asked the producers, but with Karen unwilling, they could not force the change. Richard believed she would appear almost as a novelty act—that unusual sight, a female drummer! And that was precisely how she was perceived. "Even the way they staged her was a novelty," Richard says. "Initially they had a tight shot of her; the TV audience could not see the drum set, but there was just Karen singing the first verse of 'For Once in My Life' to a piano accompaniment. And then, for the up-tempo rhythm entering the second verse, the shot went wide, revealing a singing and drumming Karen." Upon watching the monitors, the audience chuckled. As a result of this strange presentation, she did not win on that occasion.

Mancini's perception of Karen on that TV stage had been of someone hiding behind a security blanket. As he watched her, he said to himself, "Get outta there, get out from behind those drums!" They were, he decided, her protection, and though playing piano for oneself was fine, a woman playing drums for herself was unorthodox. "You might say, 'Why not?'" Mancini says, "but I have rarely heard of a man sitting behind the drums and singing."

Analyzing her in retrospect, Mancini believes that playing drums gave her something to do with her hands, for one thing. "What you do with your hands as a singer is very important, so she did not want to have to deal with the fact that she was going to have to give up her drumsticks and use her hands as part of the expression of the song."

Herb Alpert points out, too, that Karen "was not born in a trunk and didn't have that Judy Garland quality. She was a little bit withdrawn, a little bit uncomfortable with herself at times, for her own personal reasons, and so I think she needed this barricade, this drum in front of her."

There was, of course, a good reason for such bashfulness. As Richard states: "She never had any coaching in any area of presentation. It's not like young acts today, who are often trained in such techniques as how to use a microphone, how to address an audience. She was completely untutored, so it's no surprise that she kept to what she knew about, the drums." Refuting this theory about Karen feeling insecure, he says now: "Karen had started singing and drumming at the same time, from scratch. It would have nothing to do with insecurity because to sing and drum at the same time was totally natural for her."

Behind those drums, Mancini continues, "she probably felt secure. My supposition is that she probably didn't like getting out alone in front of a big crowd, just her and a mike." As for her ability as a musician, Mancini reflects: "It's a strange thing, I can't remember if she was a good drummer or not. I just blocked out the drums. In person, she had *it,* and that's all I was interested in. I didn't check out her playing. She could have been Buddy Rich sitting back there, but with that voice, I didn't care."

A rewarding friendship between Richard and Henry Mancini would develop later. The "All American College Show" came at a time when their recording sessions offered them the chance to define their sound, and the issue of a singing drummer was not on their minds.

Within six months of their signing with A&M, a reasonable collection of songs was ready to launch their debut album. Unimaginatively called *Offering,* this album was released on October 9, 1969, with a cover picture that still makes Richard shudder: an unsmiling Karen and he are seen holding a sunflower. "We were so in awe of everything, in line for our first album, that when Herbie took us into the art department and we all looked through slides for the cover, he said, 'I like that one'—and that was it! We were kids. We weren't going to disagree with Herb Alpert!"

They looked boring, precisely the word applied to them by the self-appointed hipsters of Hollywood and some staff at A&M. "There *were* a couple of sniggers in the crowd," says Jerry Moss, "because everybody was trying to break bands like Spooky Tooth." That first cover was terrible, he reflects, and it was a kind of jeer by the design team. "I don't think they knew how to market us, being brother and sister, and musically they didn't much care for our stuff anyway," Richard says.

Their music was patchy but passable, yet their form was certainly there, Karen's voice at nineteen already showing poignancy and vulnerability, particularly on love ballads like the Carpenter-Bettis "Someday" and "Eve." "Love is a groovy thing/It fills up your life with sunshine and joy," she sang on "Don't Be Afraid," words that mirrored the optimism and superficiality of the time. On two tracks, "All of My Life" and "Eve," Karen was adept enough to play bass guitar (she had been taught the rudiments of that instrument by Joe Osborn).

The best track on the album, an inspired and slow ballad interpretation arranged by Richard of the Beatles song "Ticket to Ride," was released as a single. This sold modestly, peaking at number fifty-four on *Billboard* magazine's Hot One Hundred chart. It was not exactly a smash, but it was the only A&M single on the charts in that period, and to have such an impact with a debut was creditable. The album, however, got a lukewarm reception from critics. Though it contained several decent tracks, it lacked overall potency and carried no real pointer to their innate talent. The signal was clear that this slightly dated sound might not have a viable record-buying audience.

Although it seemed innocuous at the time, the *Offering* LP carried the credit line: "Produced by Jack Daugherty." Richard let it pass. There was enough friction in the camp because Daugherty and Sulzer, two valued aides, did not get along. But that production credit rankled and would later surface in a bitter confrontation.

It was no big deal for a record company to be faced with a release that "stiffed." The Carpenters had been a gamble, Alpert's indulgence, and it was assumed around the A&M "lot" that they would be dropped immediately. But while they shored up their confidence as an opening act, Alpert made a prescient decision against all the dismissive remarks. "One more time," he told his colleagues defiantly. "We'll give them one more chance." What he knew, he recalls now, was that somewhere in there was quality musicianship fronted by a wonderful voice, the combination he would later describe as "a seductive delicacy." As a player himself, he felt they deserved and needed patience ... and the right song.

Beyond the rock 'n' roll terrain, a buzz began to circulate in Hollywood about this strange, "square" act that A&M was touting in contrast with all the hip trends. Alpert and Moss firmly believed in spreading "good vibes" and secured the Carpenters engagements to play at important film premieres, first for *Goodbye Mister Chips* and then for *Hello Dolly* in December 1969.

A star-studded audience of more than a thousand, including Sammy Davis, Jr., Steve McQueen, Gregory Peck, Richard Attenborough, and Quincy Jones, gathered at a party to celebrate the musical remake of *Goodbye Mister Chips,* and Karen and Richard were there to provide the cabaret.

"That girl's amazing," exclaimed Leslie Bricusse, who had

written the movie's musical score. As he circled the celebrity throng and Karen sang out from behind her drums, Bricusse echoed the view of hundreds of others present. "Listen to that phenomenal voice," he told everyone he spoke to. Petula Clark walked up to the bandstand to congratulate the Carpenters. Karen and Richard considered this high praise from a singer whom they admired and who was also the costar of the movie.

Karen and Richard were highly visible, set on a raised dais in the center of the room. That night and for months afterward, Bricusse repeatedly said to friends around Los Angeles how he had been "attracted to the great natural gift of Karen Carpenter's God-given voice."

"I was simply wiped out how good she was, and I wasn't the only one," he recalls now. Few people at the party knew they were brother and sister. "How would we know? She was dark, brown, and average height; he was blond and tall. He had a nice presence, but she was such an unusual sight—a girl at the drums singing beautifully. She was certainly the talking point of the night."

Later, as Bricusse met Karen at parties at Anthony Newley's house on Lloydcrest Drive, he would contemplate the "wistful, quiet, sweet girl who had an inner sadness about her."

As the reality sank in that their debut album had been merely the first salvo, their next lucky break, essential for a big commercial impact, came quickly. Burt Bacharach, the respected songwriter who had given Alpert his hit song "This Guy's in Love With You," heard "Ticket to Ride" on the radio. When Bacharach told Jerry Moss he admired the originality of the Carpenters' treatment Moss informed him that it was by a new A&M act unknown to Bacharach. And by chance, Moss continued, Richard's and Karen's favourite music was by the three *B*'s—the Beatles, the Beach Boys, and Bacharach. Burt then suggested they open the show at a benefit concert he was giving on February 27, 1970, for the Reiss-Davis child study centre to aid emotionally disturbed children. And perhaps the Carpenters would like to do a medley of his music?

Flattered by such a chance, Richard began researching for some lesser-known Bacharach material for Karen and his performance, in order to impress the maestro.

As Herb Alpert heard the Carpenters rehearsing their medley on the A&M sound stage, the biggest turning point in their young career occurred. When he had been looking for a follow-up to his own solo hit, Alpert had been asking Hal David, Bacharach's songwriting partner, if he had a song "tucked away in a drawer," or could think of something that had perhaps already been performed that might also suit his style.

Hal David's response was to send Alpert a copy of a seven-year-old Dionne Warwick album, drawing Herb's attention to a track called "They Long to Be Close to You." When Alpert played it, he was not keen on reworking it. He was particularly uncomfortable with a line in the lyric that went: "so they sprinkled moondust in your hair." Too syrupy, too corny, perhaps. He just couldn't hear himself singing that.

Meeting Richard on the A&M lot, Alpert asked if he had heard of the song and gave him the lead sheet, suggesting they include it in their Bacharach medley for the concert. Richard duly worked up an arrangement, but he wasn't sold on it. Risking the wrath of his recording mentor, he decided to exclude it from the medley. It was not a particularly significant episode to him, and he expected it to pass without further word.

Back in the studio a few days later, word reached a surprised Richard and Karen: "Herb really wants you to *record* that song." Reluctantly they got down to it, but Karen initially overworked the lyrics. "On our first cut," Richard remembers, "she distorted the emphasis in the lyrics, intentionally and with a fatal result. She sang it like Harry Nilsson might have done, accenting the word *you*, which sounded too contrived for Karen's style. And Herb *hated* that."

"It was very light," Alpert remembers. "It felt to me like it needed more beef. It didn't feel like a competitive record; too middle-of-the-road, as they said in those days. Where was the meat? I felt it needed to come from the bass and drums."

Alpert's theory about the overall sound was that, as Richard explains now, "we needed studio musicians to work with us on this and on our next album, to build up the sound somewhat. Because Herb considered that Karen being a woman of slight build was not really laying into the drums." Richard agreed that for recording, but not for concerts, more muscle would be beneficial.

For the second attempt at "Close to You," Alpert asked Daugherty to bring in two of the best West Coast musicians, drummer Hal Blaine and pianist Larry Knechtel in addition to Joe

Osborn. But for his arrangement, Richard believed Larry's robust style lacked the finesse needed for the sensitivity of the song. It was still not quite right. And even though he still wasn't crazy about the song, it had to be perfect. For the third recording, Richard returned to the piano, bringing with him the song's decorous trademark, and Karen relaxed enough to sing in a more natural manner.

The multi tracked trumpet of Chuck Findley, another prominent local musician, gave the sound a crispness—and Alpert had insisted on leaving in the delicate five-note twists of piano at the end of the first "bridge" featured in Bacharach's original arrangement, and which he had firmly instructed Richard to follow. Alpert regarded that as a clinching hook for the song.

Word-of-mouth excitement about this exceptional session by the unfashionable Carpenters soon spread around the studio. "People came in during the recording and the mixing, which they weren't supposed to do, saying they'd never heard anything like it," Richard says. "They thought it was absolutely terrific. And Herb was so taken with it that he got on the phone to Bacharach, said 'Listen to this,' and played it down the phone to him. We all thought it was some record."

Alpert turned to Richard and asked how he thought the single would sell. "I knew it wouldn't linger around fifty-four in the charts like 'Ticket to Ride.' I replied that it would either go to number one or be one of the biggest stiffs ever. It was so *soft*, so *slow*. That was what worried me. I couldn't picture teenagers listening to it in their cars."

The record label's executives were uncertain, too. A&M's promotion men sent the single to disc jockeys as a "double A side," their cautious message being that programme directors could take their pick of whether to air "Close to You" or the flipside, "I Kept on Loving You." Rather presumptuously, Richard took it upon himself to put the opening four words of the song title, "They Long to Be," in parentheses and make it simply "Close to You." It was too long, he insisted, to have impact as a title in its full form.

The choice by the radio programmers was immediate: they loved the purity of the sound, the hammy, almost vaudevillian part of the song that gave disc jockeys a chance to join in and sing "Whaaaaaaaaa, close to You." Romance was back! It contrasted with the rock 'n' roll of the time, records like Edwin Starr's "War."

But there was strong competition from Neil Diamond's "Cracklin' Rosie," Bread's love ballad "Make It with You," and Bobby Bloom's reggae-rhythm hit "Montego Bay."

Neither Richard nor Karen had been enamoured of the song at first. They felt they knew of far stronger Bacharach compositions. But when they contemplated the overall production, their pride surfaced and they believed they had achieved near-perfection. "Even then," Richard says now, "it didn't stand up to me and say, as a song, 'I'm a hit.'" But what did touch his emotion (as well as Karen's vocal reading) was the string "pad" near the end of the record; that sound gave him the all-important "chill factor" that would define his requirement in their work in the years ahead.

While he was a precision technician in his approach to music, Richard had always sought the "goosebump reaction" that came, somewhat indefinably, from a certain blend of touching lyric and haunting instrumental work. The chill at the nape of the neck that hit him, with such songs he named as Simon and Garfunkel's "Bridge over Troubled Water," the Eagles' "Desperado," Mick Jagger and Keith Richards' "As Tears Go By," John Lennon's "Imagine," and Led Zeppelin's "Stairway to Heaven," provided the moments he cherished in music. He wasn't so steeped in musical technicalities to miss the need for sounds to reach people on that human level. And he knew now that if he could find the "chill" songs for Karen's voice, the Carpenters' imprimatur on popular music would be secure.

While they played a three-week cabaret engagement at north Lake Tahoe, "Close to You" arrived in the Hot One Hundred chart in *Billboard* magazine at fifty-six with a "bullet" to indicate a rapid mover. It was the highest debut record of the week. And then it moved up week by week ... to thirty-seven, fourteen, seven, and three, on its way to the top.

Their music was now all over the airwaves, forming a sharp contrast with the general gloom of the period. By the early 1970s, the Vietnam War had torn the fabric of the United States apart. In music, the Beatles-led musical optimism of the 1960s was being replaced by the brooding of Jim Morrison and the Doors and the threatening sounds of heavy metal rock. Politically, the buildup to the Watergate hearings which challenged the president added to the somber mood.

As often happens in wartime, romantic and nostalgic music was a soothing antidote. Karen and Richard's "Close to You" was being beamed out as a reassuring soundtrack as American B-52 bombers were on their missions over Vietnam.

Drugs, too, were changing. The psychedelic sensibilities of the 1960s (marijuana and LSD) were switching into the more egotistical cocaine, and depression was so pervasive in the United States that the "mood elevator" of the Carpenters' music was in sharp contrast with the introspection that dominated the nation.

While they watched their record's progress, Richard and Karen and their band, playing three shows each night in Tahoe, were buying peanut butter from the local store to make sandwiches. Their record-making future looked secure, but there was still very little money being generated.

Returning to Los Angeles, they were thrilled to hear "Close to You" on their car radio. Then Richard realized part of its appeal: it was a perfect summer record, exuding happiness.

Within weeks, the single had sold 300,000 copies, and by July 22, 1970, it had reached the top of the national best-sellers—and it quickly sold a million. "We're number one, Weeeeeee! Congratulations and love, Herb," said Alpert's exultant note to his two most controversial artists. His label had not scored a number one since his own two years earlier with "This Guy's in Love with You."

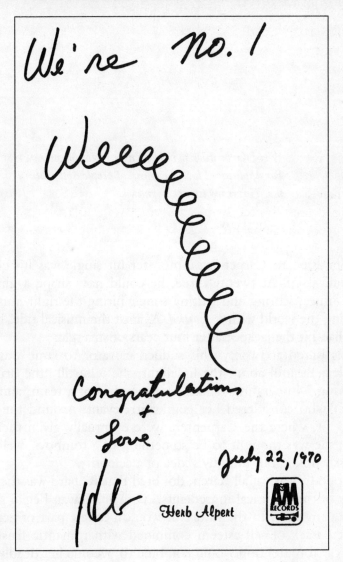

We're no. 1

Wllllllll

Congratulations + Love

July 22, 1970

Herb Alpert

A&M RECORDS

Karen and Richard went "giddy with excitement," as Richard recalls. Around that time, Bacharach began arguing with Dionne Warwick about future material. She had sung a string of his compositions, but their relationship was becoming difficult. Signaling the end of their run of international hits, he asked her, "Who will be the voice of my songs now?" Dionne's curt reply was "Karen Carpenter."

Why DO we work so hard, Karen? Not for money.
For applause. I love the sound of people applauding
me. This is my life, performing.

—RICHARD

For Richard Carpenter, a monster hit single was his elixir of life itself. At twenty-three, he could now shape a glittering future, scoring and writing songs, hiring the right musicians, traveling the world with *his sound*. Against the musical tide, his formula had hit the jackpot after four years of struggle.

For Karen at twenty, this sudden elevator to fame was more complex. Bashful about the limelight, she was still "the drummer who sang," integrating herself as a member of a team, almost an antistar who considered her gender irrelevant. Around the A&M studio lot, where the Carpenters were eventually given their own office, she was thought to be something of a tomboy—well liked, endlessly polite, but nobody's idea of a celebrity.

Nobody, least of all Karen, doubted that Richard was the prime mover of their musical ingredients. As their caravan began rolling, it was a strength. In the future, it would become part of her inner conflict. Lack of self-esteem combined with romantic frustration and a cry for attention would combine to become her deadly cocktail.

While she was content to leave the mastery of their career's architecture to Richard, Karen was meticulous about other aspects of their work. She kept a precise appointment datebook, reminded Richard and the band about pickup times, attended management meetings, and was dedicated to all the logistics of their career. Punctual and pernickety about their schedules as their success grew, she took an inquiring interest in the Carpenters' economy that went well beyond the level adopted by most artists. She gained a reputation for parsimony.

When "Ticket to Ride" had charted and they sought more concert bookings, some of the top agents in Los Angeles went to A&M's sound stage to tout for the group's representation. They eventually signed with Creative Management Associates, whose Dan Cleary became their booking agent. The band needed funding while rehearsing, and CMA had come forward to "front" them with fifty dollars for each member per week.

Soon, though, Cleary confirmed what Richard and Karen had been told from other quarters: that they should drop Ed Sulzer and hire a more experienced manager. With their career poised to go into orbit, they needed a hard-nosed and experienced professional, they were advised. This was a tough call; both Karen and Richard were fond of Ed. They remembered gratefully how he had been there, with his energetic enthusiasm and use of his garage for rehearsals, in their formative days. But they also knew that with success imminent, they had to bite this bullet.

Richard developed a rash at the mere thought of sitting down with Sulzer for the crunch meeting. Karen, though not happy about such a difficult move, confronted the problem head-on when it needed to be dealt with. Often in these situations, the practical Karen would urge the prevaricating Richard to deal with the hard matters immediately.

For an act whose music was so smooth, the "family tree" of their management became extended as allies came and went, not always harmoniously. Firings also upset the emotional side of Karen's makeup. Loyalty was an inherent part of her character, and she preferred stability to friction, particularly inside the team. But once a decision had been made, she wanted swift action. Richard tended to stew for weeks when a colleague had to be let go.

The parting was acrimonious, as Karen and Richard faced Sulzer and his wife, June, in early 1970 in Agnes and Harold's home. Feeling guilty, Richard offered Sulzer the consolation of becoming road manager. With a tilt at them for dumping him just as they began their ascent, the Sulzers stormed out.[1]

For a brief spell they were managed by a man named Harvey

---

1. In late 1972, the Carpenters rehired Ed Sulzer as their liaison man at their office on the A&M Records lot. His new job was to meet song publishers and writers, and screen songs being submitted to the Carpenters. He stayed in that role until 1979.

Shotz, who called Richard after seeing them appear at a film pre-miere party. That association ended when he wanted too much autonomy, which Karen and Richard refused. As Alpert realized the act would have longevity, he brought in the manager of his Tijuana Brass to also manage them. Sherwin Bash was experienced, assertive, and savvy. Ten years their senior, he had the benevolent air of a doctor or dentist rather than a show business hustler. He quickly won Karen and Richard's confidence and stamped his authority on their working pattern out of the studio.

The Carpenters' number-one record was bittersweet news for one close friend from their early years. Gary Sims had joined the U.S Army Reserves three months before Karen and Richard hit the top. As he lay in his barrack room listening to their sweet sound on the radio, a letter arrived from Karen ending their romance. She had met someone else, she wrote, and she "didn't think it would work between us any more." Sims was shattered. His insecurity was heightened by a lack of a guitar in the army—and the belief that his diminished abilities would mean that when he returned, he would have missed out in every way on the Carpenters' journey to the top. He reckoned without Richard's loyalty; he would later join Karen and Richard's touring band first as guitarist and vocal-ist, later as sound engineer.

As they began a blitzkreig touring schedule of the United States, the pattern of Karen's romantic life for several years was set. Her new man after Gary Sims was another "insider," their road manager, Jerry Luby, a gregarious, neat, well-organized guy who had done similar touring work with Julius Wechter's band. "Watch out for the management" was Jerry Luby's cynical regular word to the Carpenters touring party. "They're gonna keep you on the road, man, making money!"

Karen enjoyed Jerry's keen sense of fun and his commitment to work. The safety of a romance with someone within the "family unit"—and, importantly, whom Richard liked also—combined with the speed of life on the road and work in the studio, hemmed her in: there seemed to be few chances elsewhere of getting dates. Jerry would be the first in a succession of romances within the Carpenters' entourage.

*   *   *

The Carpenters' image was perceived as bland and uninteresting as they became talked about internationally as hot new record stars. They received no help from any quarter in any attempt to counter the whispering campaign that labelled them as boring, "squeaky clean" "whitebread" kids. And their appearance was worrying both Sherwin Bash and Gil Friesen, then the vice president of A&M. They suggested that for the photo session for the next album, both Karen and Richard should get new clothes. They wheeled him into Mr. Guy, an expensive Beverly Hills store; but his physique proved a problem. He was tall with broad shoulders and a relatively slim waist, and overweight, especially at the stomach. He weighed 185 pounds. Friesen rushed him into grey slacks and a Cashmere blazer, which his mother had to "take in" to fit just in time for their first photo session. Whatever Richard's weight, he could never wear an off-the-rack coat.

Karen was bought a neat white polka-dot dress. Friesen, who would go on to become president of A&M in 1977, portrays the Carpenters as "very committed, absorbed, maybe obsessed" by their career. Karen was "personable and bubbly, real competitive, often doing most of the talking in meetings," with Richard "more quiet, anxious, a very intense young man." But like all who encountered them, the record boss was struck by their "sincerity and perfectionist" qualities.

But such was their youth and junior status at that stage that Karen and Richard could hardly compete with the alienation they began to feel inside A&M. Richard reflects, "I think we were looked down upon by a number of people, and not much attention was paid to us."

While the boom in album sales concentrated the minds of most record companies on megabucks and quantity, Herb Alpert and Jerry Moss operated on a "less is more" principle. Alpert's innate feel for and love of musicianship and songs was the core of A&M's policy, and with a staff of around seventy-five, he and the canny Moss strove to build a family atmosphere.

Alpert's creative timing was always impeccable. A&M had recruited two resident songwriters to its team. Paul Williams and Roger Nichols, both age twenty-nine, had been writing frustratedly together for about three years without any major commercial success. Nichols had two groups on A&M Records, his "Trio" and "A Small Circle of Friends." But as a songwriting team, he and

Williams had done work mostly for album tracks; they yearned for a big break.

Williams, the lyricist, was a hippie with long blond hair, tie-dyed pants, and a purple hat, whereas Nichols, more conservative in manner, was a consummate arranger, pianist, and tunesmith. When a pianist friend of Nichols broke his arm and could not play to meet an assignment, he handed to Nichols a songwriting task that evolved beautifully for Nichols, Williams—and the Carpenters.

The Crocker Citizen's Bank in California was launching a television campaign to attract customers among young married couples. The theme was to be: "You've got a long way to go. We'd like to help you get there."

Nichols's melody came quickly at the piano, and as he was finishing the tune, Williams walked into their office. Nichols urged him to write the words there and then, so they could deliver the song. The result, written in about ten minutes, was "We've Only Just Begun." The advertising agency and the bank loved it. Williams sang for the television commercial, with Nichols at the piano, as a newlywed couple were shown setting off happily into their lives.

Sitting at home watching television, Richard Carpenter's ear for a haunting melody and a moving lyric did not deceive him. "It sounded like it had been crafted especially for Karen," he remembers.

As soon as he heard the voice, he guessed it was Williams. He also knew that though Nichols and Williams were prolific writers, they had yet to score their big commercial break. The next day, on the A&M lot, he stopped Paul to say he'd heard his "bank commercial." Richard had heard only a sixty-second, two-verse part of the song and wanted to know if there was a total song in existence.

Williams told Richard that there was, indeed, an extended lyric and melody. The song, Richard discovered, struck the perfect tone for the lachrymose timbre in Karen's voice. At her most potent when singing about emotional yearning, she invested the theme with a sincerity essential for its target audience of newlyweds. If there was one moment when the rich pattern of Karen's future was set, it was that day in May 1970 when just before the release of "Close to You," she recorded "We've Only Just Begun" to stamp her voice on the international map.

Thousands of young couples on the threshold of marriage

adopted the song as their anthem. Among those touched by it were Paul and Linda McCartney. They had married in 1969, and as they embarked on one of the most stable of show business partnerships, the optimism and sentimentality of the lyrics struck a chord. "Linda and I were just starting out; we kind of identified with 'We've Only Just Begun,'" Paul remembers.

Released a mere three months after "Close to You," "We've Only Just Begun" roared to the top as the Carpenters' second consecutive smash and was a gold record soon afterward. A hundred and fifty artists were to record it eventually, but Karen and Richard's would remain the classic version and their signature song.

The words were as deceptively simple and powerful as all the best compositions:

> We've only just begun to live
> White lace and promises
> A kiss for luck and we're on our way
>
> Before the rising sun we fly
> So many roads to choose
> We start out walking and learn to run
> And yes, we've just begun

"They had a frightening amount of musical talent drooling off them," remarks Roger Nichols of the earliest encounters he and Paul Williams had with Karen and Richard.

Williams says, "They handed me my career with that start to a run of hits."

Their career now moved with lightning speed. Under pressure from all sides to complete their second album quickly to capitalize on the success of "Close to You," they were in the studio day and night, a typical working day lasting between twelve and fifteen hours.

Their debut, *Offering,* had been repackaged under the new

title *Ticket to Ride* but met with a slow response. They had few tracks in the "can" to offer the album that would inevitably be called *Close to You*. Stylistically this was a patchy album, but two tracks, "Maybe It's You" and "Baby It's You," began to capture Karen's ability to weave heartache into songs about loving relationships. She displayed a strong country-and-western tinge on the Tim Hardin classic "Reason to Believe," and Richard returned to the Beatles for a brilliant arrangement of "Help," with lively harmonies. "Mr. Guder" was in there, but elsewhere two uneventful Carpenter-Bettis compositions, "Crescent Noon" and "Another Song," were baled out by Karen's voice.

The strengths of the album far outweighed its weaknesses, however, and it flew out of the stores. As it did so, only one thing jarred with a jubilant Richard and Karen: again, they had been let down by an appalling cover design. It was as if there was a conspiracy to make them look dull, to underscore their difficult public image. For the photograph, they had been taken to the beach and pictured against waves hitting the rocks, with water sloshing all around them. Their attire was truly bizarre for a beach picture session. He wore a Cashmere coat, she a full-length gown! Far from portraying them as "outdoor California types," the effect was to present them as unkempt. Their hair was clearly soaking, and Karen's stockings were visibly falling down.

Having suffered the ignominy of the *Offering* cover, they decided, when presented with this cover before the album's release, to make a stand this time. "I don't like it," Richard told A&M's Friesen. "Learn to love it," retorted the record boss. "And that," reflects Richard now, "was the whole attitude of the time. These were the things that went to make up our image. That album's still out there with that cover. And it still stinks!"

It took some time before Richard felt he could stamp his authority on how they were presented. When a picture of himself and Karen cheek to cheek was used as a sticker on the cover to promote the fact that the album *A Song For You* contained the hits "Hurting Each Other" and "Goodbye to Love," Richard blew his top again at A&M. "It looks like a goddamned Valentine's card, and we are *brother and sister!*" he protested. His complaint fell on deaf ears. Karen and he should not, anyway, have had to battle over such matters, he believes now, but should have been represented more forcefully by their management.

There was joy, by contrast, with the public response. Released simultaneously with the album *Close to You*, "We've Only Just Begun" began to dominate the radio playlists in late August 1970. Fan mail began to pour in, typically from a teenager who wrote, "Yours is the only music that my parents and I agree on." A twelve-year-old girl wrote to Karen and Richard, "When I hear your beautiful music, I cry."

For all the pressure of production and creative aggravation, the album was the Carpenters' true moment of arrival, ultimately selling nearly five million copies to achieve multiplatinum sales status, contributing to six Grammy nominations, including the categories Record of the Year (for the "Close to You" single) and Album of the Year (for the LP of that title).

Karen and Richard won Grammy awards as Best New Artist and Best Contemporary Vocal Group. They had exploded on to the music scene not just commercially but in the eyes of their peers, who recognized the craftsmanship of their productions, the timelessness of the songs, and the purity and natural beauty of Karen's voice.

Herb Alpert was vindicated. And for all that he adored Karen's voice, he believed, then as now, that Richard was "the absolute key to the Carpenters' success. He knew how to surround her voice with the right tapestry, the songs that would work best for her. And he wouldn't settle for anything less than what he thought was right." As for his own contribution to their success, Alpert is proud to have found them their vital song "Close to You," but he adds: "I was not Big Daddy to them. I was just their friend, and my heart was with them. They saw the runway, and I flagged them down."

In Britain, the Carpenters' straight popular music bucked all the trends. The end of the sixties was symbolized as Paul McCartney began High Court proceedings to finally wind up the Beatles. Guitarist Jimmy Page had conceived Led Zeppelin, progenitor of rock's heavy metal movement. And a new genre of music was being born: "campus rock," high on abstruse lyrics and indulgent musicianship. As in their native land, it was an alien environment for the Carpenters to enter—but Britain became a crucial centre of their success.

Ironically, at their record company, they faced a rerun of the enmity they had encountered in Los Angeles. Derek Green, a twenty-seven-year-old Londoner—shrewd, feisty, enthusiastic for the rock life-style—inherited a mixed bag of commercial acts as he became A&M's British managing director: Supertramp, Humble Pie, Gallagher and Lyle, the Strawbs, and Stealers Wheel. The accent was on rock with a real contemporary edge. To a label trying to sculpt an image, the arrival of the Carpenters signalled death.

They were also contrary to his true taste in music. "I had my hair down nearly to my knees and my whole sense of my own self that I was a new breed of record executive, tied to the progressive marketplace, who did every kind of illegal substance that any of my acts cared to do," Green recalls. "And so if Karen and Richard had been free to pick, I don't suppose they'd have picked Derek Green as the managing director of the company representing them. I wasn't their kind of image."

Their relationship wasn't much of a problem, though: Green, a song lover, admired their quality if not their bag. "My God, Karen's *voice!* People have got to dislike *music* to dislike those Carpenters records," he says now. But back then, it was certainly uncool to like them. "Record company staffs are young, and young people want to be hip. Those in the company who did like the music were very much in the closet."

Cynical about the Carpenters in private, Green was a bright enough operator to use their strengths to aid his company strategy. Income from their record sales enabled him to sign and nurture promising rock acts. "I used to make that point very aggressively to the new British acts," Green admits. The burgeoning band Supertramp went on an expensive, risky concert tour. "We paid for the halls and put them before an audience, and the only way we had the money to do it was from the money we were making from the Carpenters. I literally told Supertramp backstage 'Every night, I'd like you to turn east or where ever you turn, and thank the Carpenters for the opportunity *they* gave you.'"

Soon after the success of "We've Only Just Begun", Herb Alpert's brother Dave, the Los Angeles studio director of operations, took Richard and Karen to meet one of the company's lawyers who might benefit their career, particularly in the accounting and tax area. "I didn't like them," recalls Werner Wolfen. "I thought they were very impressed with themselves and with what they were doing. And they didn't seem to be interested in advice." A cockiness had surfaced in Richard and Karen as they consolidated their early success with sell-out concerts and the formation of a fan club (run by their father) that gathered ten thousand members.

Bluntly, the acerbic Werner Wolfen told them that if he was ever to be involved with them, he had to run his territory just as they ran theirs as celebrities and musicians. "And when you get ready, why don't you come and see me—if that ever happens?"

Richard and Karen reacted negatively at first. It was a stony meeting. They left. In fact, the stern Wolfen had scared them.

But by early 1972, their career pattern then strong, Jerry Moss asked Wolfen to go and meet the Carpenters a second time. "Why would I want to do that?" Wolfen asked testily. "I don't even like them!" Moss said Richard and Karen now wanted Wolfen to take over their affairs. Wolfen, skeptical, thought there could be a conflict with A&M. To represent a record company and additionally one of its acts might present difficulties.

"The only reason I would do it," Wolfen told Moss, "is because you guys are my best clients and have asked me to do that."

"Well," responded Moss dryly, "that may just have to be enough." It was a protective move by Moss. Although in some areas of their record company operation he and Herb Alpert had to delegate to less interested or committed staff, Richard and Karen would later have cause to realize appreciatively that on the really important issues, Alpert and Moss were always "there" for them.

It transpired that Karen had worked herself into a nervous state worrying about their income, which was pouring in quickly from record royalties and appearances. Agnes Carpenter had worked alongside two accountants recommended by Daugherty. But the pension plan and investments had run into a problem. A check had bounced, and Karen believed it was time they had new professional advice since her mother was hardly equipped to deal with the scale of assets that were building up.

Wolfen says he inherited "a big, big mess." As a typical example, "you had the wonderful situation where Richard and Karen had upon advice acquired a shopping centre out of income they hadn't paid taxes on." There were many parallel problems, and if the situation had continued, it would have been "disastrous."

Wading in to analyze the situation and present them with solutions, the lawyer came up against the indomitable presence of Agnes. She had supervised the income and its disbursement from its humblest beginnings when her children would return home from small clubs with twenty-five dollars stuffed in the back pockets of their jeans. Now, even though the figures were in the thousands, a stranger's intrusion was unwelcome.

"Agnes took me on in a big way," Wolfen says, "because the more bad things I said about the way it was being handled, the more she felt under attack." In the first meeting with Wolfen at Downey, she left the table, refused to speak to him, and communicated with notes. Wolfen then laid it on the line to Karen and Richard: to avoid major financial crises, they must inform their mother that her management role would have to be chopped; "You've got to make it clear she's not in charge."

He recognized Agnes as a very smart woman who meant well, but sophisticated financial management of hundreds of thousands of dollars was not her forte. The books she had been keeping mixed individual and corporate funds, and any incoming accountant already faced a Byzantine muddle.

Slowly, surely, but always with an element of suspicion about anyone she construed as an intruder, Agnes let go of the financial reins. Wolfen began making investments for Karen and Richard, starting with the purchase of two large apartment houses in Texas and Georgia. Against Wolfen's instinct and advice, they later loaned some cash to Sherwin Bash, who protested at the interest rate set by Werner Wolfen. "You're putting me on!" the lawyer said to the manager. "You don't like the interest? Pay off the loan!"

With fame and fortune came extensive touring and pressure. Their manager, Sherwin Bash, observed "two separate people—Karen was nineteen looking like she was thirteen, very unsophisticated, let's go bowling, grab a Coke and a hot dog, put the car top down and go cruising." Richard was intense, pushed by his mother to become the greatest that he could possibly be. Bash recalls that when he first saw Richard, the musician was "extremely nervous, under an enormous amount of tension. As for ambition, Richard did not seem to want wealth and fame as much as musical and creative recognition." (Richard disagrees: "Being human, I wanted it *all*, creative success and the financial rewards! When you're making a record, you make it for yourself, and if it strikes a lot of people, that's even better.") "And Karen," Bash adds, "seemed to want success mostly for Richard's sake." (Rejecting this view, Richard asserts: "Karen was *every bit* as driven as I was, if not *more so*. I liked to take time off now and then, but Karen—never! She was much more of a workaholic than me and definitely driven.")

As for being pushed by his mother, he replies: "I didn't need to be pushed by anyone. I was into my career all by myself. It was what I lived for."

Did he resent Karen's burgeoning role as the star? "I was definitely running the show musically. But I never thought for a minute that I was going to be the star of the duo, nor did I care about that. I just knew that if Karen was the lead singer, that was it! Even before she stepped out in front, she was the obvious centre of attention—not just when she began singing leads on those records. Contrasted with a girl singing and playing at the drums— come on, some guy playing electric piano is not going to be the star! All I wanted was a little respect. That's all; I never, ever thought twice that I was going to be the star of this thing."

Karen, he recalls, was slow to carry herself confidently into the role of the focal point. At the Grammy awards for the first time in 1971, she had been shy and retiring, not even holding her head straight but looking coy. "But she was very young, and it was all happening mighty quickly. I definitely knew what I wanted us to record, and Karen and I shared the same musical tastes. She had no qualms. So when we were making a record, I knew I wanted *this* and *that*, and it could be interpreted wrongly because it was very exciting to have our dream come true. And Karen did *this* and *that* because she knew it was good and right most of the time. Maybe that's what Sherwin interpreted as Karen wanting success more for me. But in her heart of hearts and in her soul, she was very much into success for herself—as I was."

As they travelled the United States on the concert trail in November 1970, "We've Only Just Begun" still riding high, Richard started worrying about finding the right song to follow two big hits. During some shows alongside singer Engelbert Humperdinck in Toronto and Chicago, Karen, too, told Sherwin that they were agitated about the hurdle facing them. Bash suggested they relax, perhaps by seeing a movie called *Lovers and Other Strangers*. As they watched a wedding scene in the movie, they were captivated by a ballad called "For All We Know," and sent a message back to Los Angeles that they wanted to record it immediately. They moved rapidly. By early January, it was released and within two months, at the start of a new decade, became their third gold, million-selling single. Yet again, a powerful love theme gave Karen a vehicle for acting out an entanglement:

Love, look at the two of us
Strangers in many ways
We've got a lifetime to share
So much to say, and as we go from day to day
I'll feel you close to me
But time alone will tell

Let's take a lifetime to say
"I knew you well"
For only time will tell us so
And love may grow
For all we know.

Words and music by Robb Wilson/Fred Karlin/Arthur James.
© 1970 MCA Music Publishing, a division of MCA Inc.
Reproduced by kind permission of MCA Music Ltd.

A decision that marked Karen's life came next. Richard realized that her profile was much stronger than that of a drummer—she was the *voice*, their vehicle for songs that were now entering the public consciousness. With a big recording career and sell-out concerts, Karen could no longer be submerged behind her huge battery of equipment. "We'd had three hits, and I knew damned well that people did not want to see her singing these great love songs with her beautiful voice from behind this big drum set. You couldn't see much of her on stage."

Driving with her in June 1971 to Baltimore and New Haven for a vacation with family and friends, Richard told her face-to-face what others like Sherwin Bash had been trying to gently persuade her to accept. "Look, Karen," her brother began, "the time has come when you're going to have to go out in front of the group."

Karen was not keen. She loved playing drums, knew her ability on them was good, and considered her singing to be almost a bonus. Many great natural singers had been heading for a life at center stage since childhood, but Karen had never considered it. She was not prepared psychologically for such a spotlight. But Richard was joined by everyone around in insisting that her vocals were their strength, their passport.

He told her he knew the importance of his abilities, too, as musician, arranger, and composer—but he wasn't naive enough to think that the public heard a song and said, "Wow, that's a great *arrangement!*" No, he assured Karen, they're listening to your voice on those records, "and we've simply got to present you properly."

Insecurity, no belief yet in her role as a star, and a need to stick to her comfortable roots conflicted with Karen's realization that Richard's judgment was right. She was not relaxed about the decision so suggested a compromise: how about splitting the drumming and her out-front position? Richard thought carefully and found the perfect solution. For the important love songs, which formed the heart of their repertoire, Karen should go out to centre-stage as their focus. For the more rhythmic material like "Jambalaya" and "Mr. Guder," she could revert to singing from behind her drum stack.

The uneasy truce was set, and Richard had a brainwave. While they were in New Haven, he went to recruit as second drummer, his old buddy Jim Squeglia, who had played with Richard in his high school band, the Sceptres.

Squeglia, a streetwise, nonconformist rebel whose personality contrasted with the conservatism of the Carpenters, jumped at the chance. They flew him to Downey for intensive rehearsals at their home. He was staggered at Karen's ability as he learned their requirements from Karen to "shadow" her work precisely on every song they played together. Karen's drum technique had improved since she studied the technique of the maestro Buddy Rich.

An even bigger surprise awaited Squeglia when he joined the Carpenters' touring band. Richard insisted there would be no improvisation, that to please the record buyers in the audience every song performed should match, note for note, their records.

He had no truck with ad-libbing, however clever, and the whole band adhered to his rule. This caused a problem with the maverick Squeglia, who could not resist the occasional flourish. Richard would pounce on him after a show: "Jimmy, I don't care if the audience is screaming and yelling with enthusiasm, we have a record out there, and our stage performance *must match it*. When it calls for a certain type of drum break, *do not change it*. The audience gets the same sound as on the record."

Certain classic "breaks" from the guitar and drums were sacrosanct to Richard because he remembered how such sounds hooked him when he was a record-hungry child. There was freedom for the musicians to improvise sometimes, but never on the trademark instrumental breaks in such songs as "Close to You" which were embedded in the public's mind as part of the records. It was a firm demand on his musicians.

Squeglia answered that when they were on the road for months, playing six nights a week, he had an artistic need to breathe: "I don't wanna be doing the same break every night." But Richard's rule was rigid. Squeglia fell in line to keep his four-hundred-dollar-a-week job.

The departure of Jerry Luby in late 1970 from the job of road manager began a new chapter for the Carpenters and ended his short romance with Karen. His successor, Paul White, was at thirty-four more mature than anyone else on the road and soon assumed the role of father figure to her.

She was unsure of herself as the upfront singer, slightly wooden, nervous about facing the audience, and her announcements were at best uninspiring, hardly surprising in view of the lack of training.

"Pulling her out from behind the drums was a big deal, very hard for Karen to do," John Bettis says. What might eventually have bothered Karen, he felt, was that she had not gone to Richard with an independent image of herself in their earliest days. "Karen's whole view of show business grew up with Richard standing right there beside her. It was very indicative that she played drums because they are very loud and you can hit them very hard and they're very physical, and Karen was always very physical, so that was no surprise. She was doing something she was born to do."

Chatting into the early hours in hotel rooms with Paul White, she unburdened herself; he suggested to her that she prepared her appearance, and dresses, carefully, ready for the time when she stepped out front as the singer primarily. In White she found a confidante, choosing to often travel with him in the truck rather than go by car when their journeys were confined to the road.

There were sideways glances from the rest of the party as they became social as well as professional friends, since she had finished her romance with Jerry Luby. Liaisons with the entourage were becoming habitual; when would Karen step outside?

Early signs of concern about her figure were heard by White as they travelled the country: "My jeans are too tight," she would say. But the next day she would join the band eating burgers at McDonald's. And as she tucked into a Big Mac and a milk shake, she made the statement that became a standing joke among them all: "Oh, I gotta diet—tomorrow!"

Protective of Karen, White stood at the side of the stage admiring her work, for which, he said, she got too little recognition from the touring party in these early days: "It was kinda taken for granted. She used to hit the notes like radar. Some singers hit them a little under and slide up or down. Karen was pure."

By late 1971 a power struggle had developed between Paul White and Sherwin Bash, who finally decided to exert his management control. He went to the Carpenters' home to make a pithy statement: "There can be long meetings and there can be short meetings. I'd like this to be a short meeting. I want to fire Paul White."

For Bash, White's closeness to Karen had been one of several difficult issues. Richard, too, had been uneasy about White's assumed role, though he valued the energy and attention White gave to his work. Reluctantly he faced up to the decision. Karen, fond of Paul, was visibly upset for some time about such an abrupt dismissal. As a cushion to help her over the episode, her family bought her a gift of a new Mercedes 350 SL.[2]

As Richard and Karen returned from "the road" to Hollywood for late-night recording sessions, the hits continued to pour out. The routine of intensive performing, songwriting demands, and studio sessions was gruelling, yet they were both on a "high," rev-

2. Paul White went on to become the tour manager for Burt Bacharach.

eling in the pace of their meteoric career.

Introspection was again the theme as Paul Williams and Roger Nichols served up the melodically powerful "Rainy Days and Mondays," a song Richard jumped at recording after listening only twice to a demonstration. Immediately upon its release, it became a perennial radio play and remains to this day one of the Carpenters' most popular tracks. Though it was held off the number-one spot by Carole King's "It's Too Late," it became Richard and Karen's fourth million seller.

Karen's voice is at its most intimate on a song that continues to touch millions:-

> Talkin' to myself and feelin' old
> Sometimes I'd like to quit
> Nothing ever seems to fit
> Hangin' around, nothing to do but frown
> Rainy days and Mondays always get me down.
>
> What I've got they used to call the blues
> Nothin' is really wrong
> Feelin' like I don't belong
> Walkin' around, some kind of lonely clown
> Rainy days and Mondays always get me down.
>
> Funny but it seems I always wind up here with you
> Nice to know somebody loves me
> Funny but it seems that it's the only thing to do
> Run and find the one who loves me.
>
> What I feel has come and gone before
> No need to talk it out, we know what it's all about
> Hangin' around, nothin' to do but frown
> Rainy days and Mondays always get me down.

Music International.

With hits that would perpetuate their name, 1971 was already a sizzling year. Richard's uncanny ear and Karen's soulful voice would make it one of their vintage periods. After "For All We Know" and "Rainy Days and Mondays," in August came the song many of their keenest followers would consider their finest, most ambitious performance.

Richard would sometimes return home early enough from the studio to catch Johnny Carson on "The Tonight Show." One evening, he sat mesmerized by the sight, but more especially by the sound, of rising singer Bette Midler. With more than a dash of Mae West's style, Midler was singing a song called "Superstar," a beautifully crafted melody with a lyric that carried a groupie girl's lament to a rock star passing through her life. Excited, Richard steered Karen into the studio to try it, but she wasn't enthusiastic.

The song, by Leon Russell and Bonnie Bramlett, had already been recorded by Rita Coolidge on the *Mad Dogs and Englishmen* album. Karen disliked the "feel" of it and didn't care for the words—until Richard persuaded her that with a new arrangement by him it could be a potential scorcher.

Richard did, however, have some reservations about its sexually implicit lyric. The groupie's message to her rock star idol, "I can hardly wait to *sleep* with you again," had been changed for Karen's vocal to "... wait to *be* with you again." Richard felt the original was too blatant for the Carpenters, even at the onset of the decade of women's liberation.

"Even with that change," he says, "I was starting to get cold feet as the time came for release. Singing about groupies didn't seem quite right for us, even though I loved the song." They bounced between "Superstar" and a Nichols-Williams composition, "Let Me Be the One."

The decision to plump for a "Superstar" release on August 12, 1971, was made by Jerry Moss. Richard and Karen were worrying needlessly, he told them. "This song is what you think it is. Go for it."

The recorded version was the first time she ever sang it. Still slightly reluctant about its connotation, she read the lyrics Richard had scribbled on a napkin. Her doleful interpretation was thought by Richard to be so unrepeatable that he released that "first take." Though the album with Coolidge's version had already sold a million by the time the Carpenters' single was in the stores, they secured a gold record within eight weeks. Richard would eventually consider it one of their best recorded works. And the song became inextricably identified with Karen's haunting vocal.

That performance was "our first real glimpse of where Karen's voice was heading," observes John Bettis. "Just having her sing things in the room to you was getting to be almost a religious experience. Because Richard now really had the vocal range and placement down. He always *knew* about the lower register being Karen's hit voice, but he had really gotten it by this point. He had recorded her so much that he had a tonal memory of her. So when he composed, he could plug that singing voice in, in his mind; he knew what it would sound like. It was fabulous to watch him do that because I knew he could hear her in a way I couldn't when I was writing."

Sudden fame hurled them under the microscope for their looks. Again the sceptics blasted them, and here they had a point. Twenty-year-old Karen paid little heed to clothes, wearing T-shirt and jeans or cut-off shorts. But in rethinking his appearance, pudgy Richard knew he had the bigger problem. On stage in his three-piece suit, he looked overweight, and when he dressed casually he looked more like a Pat Boone of the 1970s: black or white boots that he'd bought from Beau Gentry in Hollywood, black flared trousers, and a fringed leather jacket. He gave his critics easy ammunition.

After seeing some pictures taken for their third album, a hefty Richard went on a crash diet in mid-1971. He dropped all his junk-food eating habits and shed twenty pounds within a few months, reaching his "normal" weight of 165 pounds. Karen remarked that it suited him, but at this stage she was not particularly concerned with a diet. Their career was uppermost in her mind.

There was a thirst for new songs to be written—and fast. At this stage, Richard did not have a lyric-writing partner. Jack Daugherty, who was technically named as producer of the albums thus far, suggested that Richard enlist Paul Williams. But Richard wanted to get back together with John Bettis, to whom he had not spoken since the disintegration of Spectrum (and Bettis's angry walkout) two years earlier. Richard knew that they had a special alchemy. Daugherty found Bettis, and he returned happily to the team. To mark their reunion, he and Richard began reshaping lyrics for a song they'd written at Coke Corner.

*   *   *

The plaudits for their work continued to pour in as they released the *Carpenters* album, and this time there was no shortage of winning material. "Rainy Days" jostled with "Superstar" and "For All We Know" for public and radio attention; there was a flashback to John and Richard's Disneyland stint with "One Love," an ode to a waitress there whom they had both ogled, and a medley of Bacharach and David hits that Dionne Warwick (by then a friend and admirer of the Carpenters) had recorded.

"Sometimes," the heart-rending song that closed the album, came from the pen of Henry Mancini, whose daughter Felice, while at college, had sent the words to Mancini and his wife, Ginny. He was so touched that he wrote a melody to the prose, and then, hearing that the Carpenters were preparing a new album, he called Jack Daugherty. When news reached Richard, he was in awe of the offer of a song from the maestro; he went to meet Mancini and confirmed that he and Karen would do the song just as Mancini had offered it: vocal and piano.

With the vocal density that marked out a Karen Carpenter interpretation, the words sounded perfectly tailored for her:

> Sometimes, not often enough
> We reflect on the good things and those thoughts always
>   centre around those we love
> And I think about those people who mean so much to me
> And for so many years have made me so very happy
> And I count the times I have forgotten to say thank you
> And just how much I love them.

Lyrics of "Sometimes" reproduced by kind permission of Henry Mancini and Felice Mancini and All Nations Music Publishing Ltd.

"It was the definitive recording," Henry Mancini says. "It was like having Sinatra do your song. You know it's going to be done as well as it can be done." As a result of the Carpenters' "marvelous record," the song has become something of a "cult" among people about to get married or looking for a song to mark a special occasion.

"Karen had a quality about her that was so vulnerable, so exposed that she just demanded attention," Mancini says. "Whatever she sang came right from the heart. They didn't do too many rhythm songs; she loved those ballads that took advantage of that great low end of her voice. I'm sure Richard had a lot to do with it, always making sure that she got into that 'fat' part, songs that took advantage of the 'money' part of her voice."

The *Carpenters* album continued their march, going gold and winning a 1971 Grammy award plus three nominations.

As Karen became youth chairman of the American National Cancer Society and the Carpenters donated profits that would eventually top $100,000 from their concert programmes to aid research, their music and personalities fell under the eye of President Nixon. He saw them as the ideal totems of the kind of American youth he wanted to encourage: apparently against drugs and perpetuating the middle-American ethic.

In September 1972, they were invited to the White House, where Nixon presented Richard with a set of golf balls and cuff links and Karen with a gold powder compact, all bearing the presidential seal.

Karen told me she and Richard had given their image "an enormous amount of thought . . . it ended up as goody two-shoes, and because we came out in the middle of the hard-rock thing, we didn't dress funny, and we smiled, we ended up with titles like 'Vitamin-swallowing, Colgate-smiling, bland Middle America'!

"The fact that we took a shower every day was swooped on as symbolic. It's all nonsense. I know a lot of people who take a shower every day. I know a lot of people who smile.

"We're normal. I get up in the morning, eat breakfast in front of the TV, watch games and shows. I don't smoke. If I wanted to smoke, I would smoke. I just don't like smoking, not because of my image. I wouldn't kid myself about it. I mean, we're not lushes or anything; we're very into wine!"

Karen recalled one summer concert sound-check during which the temperature was around ninety-five degrees, "and some people got in to watch the rehearsal and saw the guys in the band with a beer on stage. And we got letters: 'The nerve of you guys, drinking beer!' It seemed the reviewers didn't like the fact that anybody clean was successful. The more successful we got, the more they attacked our image. They never touched our music. We would get critics reviewing our concerts, they'd review the AUDIENCE. They'd say how ridiculous that somebody came to see the Carpenters in a tie!"

Richard weighed in: "I got upset when this whole 'squeaky clean' thing was tagged on to us. I never thought about *standing* for anything! They took 'Close to You' and said: 'Aha, you see that number one? THAT's for the people who believe in apple pie! THAT's for people who believe in the American flag! THAT's for the average middle-American person and his station wagon! The Carpenters stand for that, and I'm taking them to my bosom!' And boom, we got tagged with that label.

"Well, I just don't believe in that. You try to tell those people that I have every Zappa and Mothers of Invention record!" Carpenters music simply did not set out to represent any particular life-style, Richard continued.

People had not known how to respond to a brother-and-sister act. Richard reflected, "There's never been one, since Fred and Adele Astaire!" And Karen added that they had been bracketed with, and presented as, Sonny and Cher or Steve Lawrence and Eydie Gorme.

Privately, if not publicly, they could be forcefully opinionated. At the start of the decade that marked the onset of the women's liberation movement, Karen was succinct in her view: "I'm happy and proud to be a woman," she said when asked her verdict on the "libbers." "I'm happy to be doing what I'm doing, and I don't have a need to prove anything."

I asked Karen if she expected equality in treatment on the road or whether she preferred to claim feminine rights and have her luggage carried.

"For as long as I can remember I was always part of the gang. But at the same time they would open a car door for me and carry my luggage. [In the early days] we packed all our own equipment. I packed my own drums, and then I helped pack the truck. We set up all our own sound systems. Then I'd go in the dressing room and set my hair, then iron all the clothes for the guys. The whole group did everything; we had a ball. I was always more of a loner because it's different for a girl on the road. Also, I'm pretty shy."

PART THREE

LONELY HEARTS

Not one of us had any glimmer of a meaningful relation-ship. Our twenties were not romantic . . . we all felt really empty.

—JOHN BETTIS, RICHARD'S SONGWRITING PARTNER

C aught between Karen's interference and his mother's possessiveness, Richard was in a no-win situation when it came to girlfriends. He was constantly looking for his "Debbie Reynolds type," someone petite, smiling, and blonde.

In a life dominated by cross-country one-night stands and international travel, plus song preparation and recording, the Carpenters at their peak were a nonstop working machine. Some of the band dabbled in the groupie scene, but dating on the run was never in Richard's or Karen's textbook. Not surprisingly, they both turned inward, toward their own coterie of traveling colleagues, for their affairs.

In 1972 the Carpenters hired a hairdresser and wardrobe manager to travel with them. Maria Luisa Galeazzi was a slim, stunning, twenty-seven-year-old northern Italian with blonde hair and blue eyes. At the beauty salon she ran in Downey, she was encouraged by a customer friend of Agnes to pursue a job with the local duo whose records were exploding all over national radio.

Intrigued but not star-struck, she called Karen. Within a week, Maria had joined them for a tour, starting at a wild concert in Houston, Texas, where fans ripped their clothing, jumped on their moving car, and treated them like rock stars. One fan jumped on the stage, started after Karen's drums, and shouted his love for Karen before security men dragged him off. These memories were to be treasured—and soon Maria and Richard decided, at the request of fan club secretary Evelyn Wallace, to record the events of such concerts and send audio tapes back from the tour to Downey, for posterity; these formed the basis of Carpenters newsletters.

Maria's entrée to the Carpenters' bandwagon was friendly and professional, but she was surprised that Karen kept a distance—unexpectedly, since they were the only two women in a group of twelve travelling by car, bus, and plane. Occasionally, to kill boredom, they would needlepoint together in dressing rooms, "but I don't think we became girlfriends," Maria says. She enjoyed her role, reshaping Karen's "thin, soft, baby like hair," making up her "beautiful thin face," tending her wardrobe and fingernails; ensuring also that the guys in the band had buttons on their jackets and looked smart.

She also supervised Richard's hair and appearance, and despite an early rule from him and Karen that she should not date any member of the band, it wasn't long before Maria and Richard were entwined. It was clandestine at first, for Richard feared a backlash from the band for breaking a house rule. Conversely, he resented the fact that he, as one of the stars of this show, was handicapped when it came to dating, while everyone else in the band was having a great time.

His rapport with the ebullient Maria was immediate. She shared his love of cars, fine wines, and gave him an interest in European food, and Richard, with his huge appetite, loved these experiences. An animated Italian, she admired his contrasting gentleness, his precision, his sleek good looks. He dressed well, arriving for each date immaculately groomed. As for his music, Maria considered him a genius. She called him "electric fingers."

She also found Richard fragile when it came to personal confidence, "needing coaxing toward independence of thought." Soon, her persuasive personality persuaded him to break free a little more from the strictures of the Carpenters touring party on the road. Reminding him that he was the boss, she said he should assert himself, and in a daring salvo they broke clear of the touring party for one leg of the 1973 summer tour, by driving his Ferrari from one engagement to another. There was panic at headquarters. Richard was a superb, safe, and speedy driver, but the danger of being late, and exhausted, for a concert was worrying.

"His mom and Sherwin Bash had a lot to do with that," says Maria, criticizing the tautness of the family unit. "They were always pulling him down, never letting him have a field day on his own. I could not bear to see him being suffocated. I encouraged him to be rebellious."

Bath time for Karen
at five months.
*(Richard Carpenter
Collection)*

(Below)
With one-year-old
Richard, 1947.
*(Richard Carpenter
Collection)*

(Right)
August 1955: Karen,
five years, Richard,
nine, at their New
Haven home.
*(Richard Carpenter
Collection)*

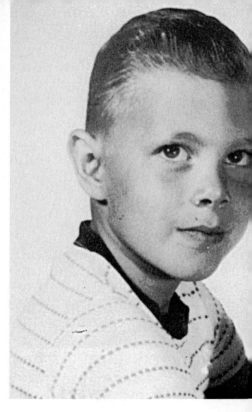

Richard, Karen in 1954:
Richard, eight, Karen, four.
*(Richard Carpenter
Collection)*

On a fishing expedition
with Dad.
*(Richard Carpenter
Collection)*

Karen ready for tap
dancing lessons,
age five.
*(Richard Carpenter
Collection)*

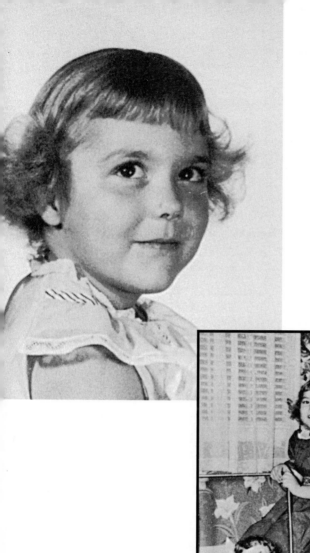

Richard, enthusiastic
at the piano at age
eight.
*(Richard Carpenter
Collection)*

Christmas, 1957, at
New Haven,
seven-year-old Karen
and eleven-year-old
Richard.
*(Richard Carpenter
Collection)*

(Opposite)
With Agnes, 1959,
Richard at thirteen
and Karen nine.
*(Richard Carpenter
Collection)*

(Below)
Karen with guitarist
Gary Sims before the
Carpenters opened a
Burt Bacharach con-
cert for a children's
charity, February 27,
1970.
*(Richard Carpenter
Collection)*

Portrait of Karen at
seventeen.
*(Richard Carpenter
Collection)*

(Opposite)
The teenagers
photographed at
Downey Methodist
Church a year after
settling in California.
*(Richard Carpenter
Collection)*

They'd only just begun:
Richard and Karen in 1975.
*(Richard Carpenter
Collection)*

With promotional gifts for
disc jockeys to launch their
debut album, *Offering,* in
October 1969: a golden
hammer, and a makeup kit for
disc jockeys' wives.
(Agnes Carpenter)

At the Grammy celebrations,
the proud recipients in 1971.
*(Richard Carpenter
Collection)*

Karen, late 1971.
*(Richard Carpenter
Collection)*

Karen during rehearsals for the filming of a video to promote the record "Rainy Days and Mondays" at the Desert Inn, Las Vegas, on April 6, 1971.
(Richard Carpenter Collection)

On TV with Carol Burnett, 1971.
(Richard Carpenter Collection)

Before an Osmonds concert, late 1971; Alan, whom Karen dated, is on her right.
(Richard Carpenter Collection)

Richard
and Karen,
late 1971.
*(Charles
Bush)*

On stage at
London's
Royal Albert
Hall for a
sound check
during their
British tour,
1971.
*(Barry
Plummer)*

After receiving a "Georgie" award for best musical group from the American Guild of Variety Artists in 1971, Richard and Karen are pictured with TV star Ed Sullivan. *(Richard Carpenter Collection)*

Richard on stage, Anaheim Convention Center, January 22, 1972. *(Richard Carpenter Collection)*

Karen studies a lead
sheet for a new song,
1972.
(Richard Carpenter
Collection)

(Below)
With Herb Alpert
backstage after a
concert, Anaheim
Convention Center,
January 22, 1972.
(Richard Carpenter
Collection)

Randy Bash with
Richard, Mike Curb
with Karen, at the
Grammy Awards,
March 1974.
*(Richard Carpenter
Collection)*

(Opposite and above)
The Carpenters in their first
appearance on the Bob Hope TV
special, November 1972.
(Richard Carpenter Collection)

Posing for the cameraman, in this
case Carpenters' personal
assistant David Alley, in the music
room at home, 1973.
(Richard Carpenter Collection)

During their appearance at the White House at a State Occasion to welcome West German Chancellor Willy Brandt on May 1, 1973. From left, Brandt, President Nixon, Karen, Pat Nixon, Richard.

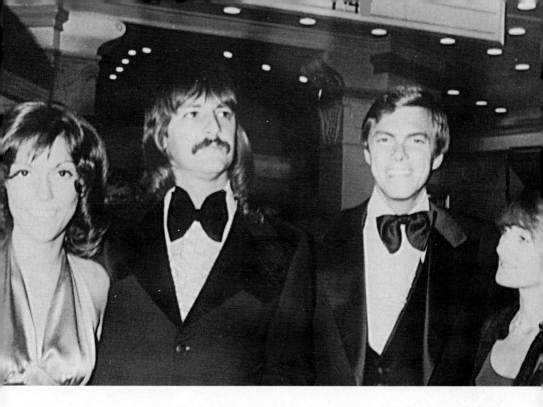

Karen and Richard with their dates: David Alley and Maria Galeazzi. They are at the premiere for the Neil Diamond show "Jonathan Livingston Seagull," in Hollywood on October 29, 1973.
(Peter Borsari)

With Carpenters manager Sherwin Bash, March 4, 1973.
(Richard Carpenter Collection)

Photographed for the *Rolling Stone* interview,
May 22, 1974.
(Annie Leibovitz)

When the tour ended at Detroit and Richard and Maria set off for a leisurely drive home to Los Angeles, the Ferrari broke down in the middle of Oklahoma, forcing them to fly home.

In her constant efforts to make him take chances, she came up against what she called "the system" that blocked change to the Carpenters' status quo. As the months passed, she sensed she was becoming disliked, even though she felt she was doing her job better through her enjoyment of romantic exuberance.

From the start of their affair, Richard had told her, "Don't think this is gonna go anywhere," but she still felt it was a serious love match. "Sometimes," she reflects, "you just ride a relationship for what it is—you don't try to make something out of it that it's not. And that's what I had decided to do." Although she enjoyed the good life with Richard, she says, "I did have a fur coat and a Mercedes before I met him, so that wasn't everything."

What Maria could never have forecast was the simmering fury of Karen, who initially seemed happy at her brother's liaison. "Well, it's the three of us," she would say as they stepped out together to eat when they were on the road. Karen often remarked on the quantity Maria and Richard ate without gaining weight: "Look at you two, eating like mad and losing weight!"

Trouble loomed for the trio, however, when Richard wanted Maria to go car racing with him at the very moment Karen needed Maria to accompany her shopping at Greta, the swank boutique on Beverly Drive.

Slowly it dawned on Karen that the brother she relied on for so much, even doted on, was being pulled away from her—and by her own employee! Their togetherness was hard to take for someone who was still looking for love: "Richard really liked Maria," says an observer with an air of understatement.

And Karen wasn't the only one looking suspiciously at the pretty Italian. When Maria visited the house to fix Karen's hair, Richard would greet her with a hug, an unusual demonstration of affection in the Carpenter household. Agnes would look askance at this. Though she knew Richard and Maria were together, Agnes bristled at such a reminder.

So Agnes began suggesting to Karen that Maria might be getting too close to the family—and it was time she went. Richard says of the romance now: "I did not intend it to happen, but it did. And it certainly wasn't fair to Karen or Maria either."

Karen was not prepared to let the relationship run its course. She began subtle ploys to try to separate them. She suggested he see other women, "and of course," says Maria, "what he needed was me." Maria felt he had a hard time trying to please his mother, his sister, his managers, and also being creative. She hated to see him being manipulated. Karen focused her eyes firmly on her hairdresser's relationship with Richard. Some thought her possessiveness was such that she could not bear to see him seriously involved with *any* woman. "If she had found someone for herself," Maria ruminates, "then the heat would have been off Richard and me."

Although Maria was fond of her boss, she found that Karen rarely released her feelings except when she was angry. The tension that had been brewing came to a head when, during a cabaret stint at Lake Tahoe, Karen snapped at Maria in her dressing room: "Let him *work*"—implying that Maria was luring Richard away from songwriting toward a time-consuming romance.

It was one of their rare frosty exchanges. "Karen," came the reply, "that's not something I can make him do. If he's going to compose songs, he's got to be inspired. The fountain is born somewhere else for creativity."

Karen would, according to Maria, "go half mad" at the thought that Richard's professional discipline might be diluted. "She thought I had more control over him than I did. She gave me too much credit," says Maria. "But that stemmed from fear." She could not recall a time when Karen appeared to be happy other than superficially, such as playing bowling down a hotel corridor. Her anger came through over irritations like catching her skirt in the drums, breaking a nail, or when the stage lights were wrong, and these episodes occurred because Karen kept all her wider emotions inside her. "Richard and I would open up, but not Karen."

Whether it was fear or jealousy, bossiness or tension, or a desire to mother him, Karen was determined to drive a wedge between Richard and his dazzling amour. As with every date he chose, Karen would tell him the woman was "unsuitable" or that his taste was out of line. "It was like some damned game they played," Maria reflects. "She did it to Richard; he did it to her." And Maria was too much in love to realize that her days were numbered.

It was also difficult for Karen to befriend anyone in the touring party without suspicion from all around them that it was something more than platonic. While Karen invariably interfered with his choice of female, Richard says that early on, he remarked only once about a potentially difficult situation for her. On that occasion he had advised his sister not to get involved with a member of the team who was much older than she, and who was married anyway.

Though Richard and Karen and their family were nontactile by nature, there was the occasional hug on the road. Jim Squeglia remembers that he and Karen exchanged an embrace after a show if they had "hit it off" together musically, as dual drummers. This gesture was interpreted by some as meaning they were "an item." When Karen invited Jim as a friend to join her and Richard with his occasional date for dinner, Sherwin Bash raised his eyebrows: "Don't you see enough of him in the show? You have to have him to dinner too?" Eventually, Squeglia says, "Sherwin Bash accused me of not keeping away from her. He said to me: 'If you don't keep away from her, I'm gonna have you fired. So no more dinners, no more hugging, no more meeting her after the show.'"

There were other contretemps with Squeglia, who maintains he was pressured out of the band by Sherwin. But his response jarred with Richard's professionalism. In spring 1973 they were due to resume touring. A few days before, the band were to assemble to "tune up." Squeglia did not arrive and could not be found. Once he was located, back in New Haven, he was fired by phone.

As the Carpenters traversed the United States from coast to coast and flew to Europe, Japan, and Australia, Karen needlepointed away the hours in her hotel suites and dressing rooms. On one return visit home, she presented her parents with a memento: a framed, needlepointed multicolored message shaped as a road leading to a dollar sign, which hangs today in Agnes's home. "You put us on the road," it reads.

It was meant, of course, as a mark of gratitude. In reality, "the road," as any touring musician will testify, is a gruelling pressure, and the Carpenters' itinerary for five years from 1970 was awesome. A typical day began with a wake-up call to their hotel rooms at 6:00 A.M. After breakfast, dressed and packed, they were on their way by early morning, by plane or car, to the next town, arriving around noon. Lunch was often followed by two hours of relaxation; then they went straight to the theatre for a sound check. Snacking in their dressing rooms as the audience arrived, they began the ritual of showering and attending to their hair and wardrobe every night for weeks on end.

After the show and an autographing session, they usually adjourned with the band and crew to a restaurant, but sometimes it was simply back to the hotel for dinner and bed. With the energy of youth, they relished the burden. Eventually, though, the relentlessness of touring while worrying about their next album would be a source of irritation, particularly to Richard as he questioned the strategy of their career.

Winding down from the "high" of artistic effort and audience applause affects performers differently. Richard, the perfectionist, gave vent to his feelings in his nightly analysis of their show. For Karen, who indicated her after-concert emptiness on some occasions in her therapy sessions with Steven Levenkron, the walk away from the stage might have had an effect on her without anyone realizing it.

Dr. Joel Yager[1] has worked with celebrities who explained to him the "emotional shift" they had felt in coming away from a concert where they had experienced "an incredible high." After being aroused emotionally, they suddenly felt alone in a car or in a hotel room. A load of energy and perspiration had been expended so the physiological condition was one of exhaustion, maybe depletion.

Although some rock 'n' roll players used drugs or alcohol, for example, to help them in "coming down" after a concert, the Carpenters were never interested in such things. "We perspired, of course," says Richard, "but I can't say we came off the stage exhausted. A show like ours was hardly like that of, say, the Rolling Stones. Other than the drumming by Karen and our new drummer Cubby O'Brien who replaced Jim Squeglia, there wasn't a great deal of energy used. After most shows, it wasn't a particularly exciting night, that's for sure—either a restaurant or a hotel room." The exhibitionism of some performers was not evident in Karen and Richard, who were fundamentally musicians travelling to re-create on stage their recorded sounds. What pressure there

1. Dr. Yager, professor of psychiatry at the School of Medicine, University of California in Los Angeles, is a respected spokesman on eating disorders and a member of the advisory board of the National Association of Anorexia Nervosa and Associated Disorders.

was seemed limited to ensuring that their sound was impeccable. And yet, Dr. Yager suggests, the "arousal" Karen experienced from the audiences, as does any performer, might, just might, have put her in some kind of conflict.

A well-drilled, inspired group of musicians travelled with them, and they were treated royally. Like Karen and Richard, the band was flown first-class or given limousines. On some tours, when the string of one-night stands was extensive, the party even travelled on two chartered business jets. "With the exception of the roadies who had to get the truck, we took everyone with us on those jets—hairdressers, lighting directors, opening acts," Richard says.

The rented planes freed them from the schedule of having to get up at dawn in small towns to catch normal commercial planes. Such timekeeping was wearing them down. The ability to fly at their own times was a help, but it was financial suicide over a six-week tour. "We thought it was worth the money," Richard says, "and we were never ones to consider ourselves the stars and send the others on commercial flights." In hotel rooms around the world, too, each player ultimately had a separate room, by contrast with many other bands who shared to save money.

Despite Karen and Richard's creative demands on them as their bosses, this was a "family" with unswerving loyalties. There was Doug Strawn, the clarinetist, keyboardist, and fun-loving back-up singer who had known Richard and Karen from college days; Bob Messenger, a quiet, jazz-inflected bassist, flautist, and saxophonist; Danny Woodhams, an extroverted bassist and vocalist; and Gary Sims, who returned to the fold from the Army.

Both Richard and Karen demanded perfection from them on stage every night and berated them for any flaw in their performance. When a note, a song, a routine, an announcement, or a beat was out of step, Richard lost no time after the show in hectoring the culprit. Equally, he and Karen would let fly at each other in such inquests. "Sometimes Karen might take too long on a part, and Richard wanted it to go faster," Doug Strawn says. "She'd persist in doing it her way, continually, say three or four nights in a row, and Richard would be backstage wailing. Toward the end of the song 'Rainy Days and Mondays' she'd take her pause to the maximum, and they'd get into a shouting match."

The whole band knew they'd better get out of their way when

Richard and Karen slammed the door of their dressing room to
beef at each other. But those sparks could never be mistaken for a
serious split. An unbreakable bond took them even beyond a
brother-sister relationship. They were close friends with the same
horizons, similar life-styles, and musical ears. The band reciprocated their intensity. "We wanted to do a good job for Richard and
Karen—to hell with the audience, we wanted to please *them*,"
declares Bob Messenger. "That's exactly how I got rid of my early
stage fright. I was playing for *them*."

By the time the *A Song for You* album was released in June 1972,
the Carpenters had become a prolific hit-making machine. Under
physical and creative pressure as they crisscrossed the United
States, they had produced most of the songs that would guarantee
their sound instant recognition forever.

A *Song for You* contained the attractive Leon Russell composition as a title track, with "Hurting Each Other," yet another paen
to troubled romance, so perfect for Karen, possessing an irresistible melody. (This was to be one of their favourite tracks.) "It's
Going to Take Some Time" and "I Won't Last a Day without
You" were upbeat contrasts to the majestic "Goodbye to Love,"
which also scored as a single to make the album powerful commercially.

The album release, though, marked still more discord in their
ranks. The Carpenters produced music that soothed, and they
were peaceful enough people, but behind the scenes there was
often strife. This time, the problem boiled down to who took the
credit for what was going on.

Richard was immensely proud of *A Song for You,* with its cross-
fading and book-ending. But yet again, as from their very first
album, it bore the credit line: "Produced by Jack Daugherty." And
this credit now gnawed at Richard. He and Karen really liked Jack,
and they recognized that he had been a vital link to their A&M
"home." A popular cheerleader who occasionally offered some
advice during recording sessions, he did the essential job of booking the studios and the musicians. His office conducted production liaison—but a creative producer of the Carpenters he was not,
in Richard's view. That role was unmistakably filled by him. "The
construction of the Carpenters sound was mine and Karen's. I
knew how I wanted the damned records to sound, and for the

recording process, in the ultimate mix, I went through everything with our engineers, Ray Gerhardt and later Roger Young."

So when Richard picked up a copy of *Cashbox* magazine, which opened its review of *A Song for You* with the words "Superb Jack Daugherty production," he let fly.

Travelling on tour, Richard informed Sherwin Bash that future Carpenters records should bear his own name as producer and sometimes Karen's as his associate. That had been the work pattern all along and would continue, he declared. Richard was inflexible. It was time, he insisted, to end this charade.

In addition to his Carpenters income, Daugherty had been earning twenty-five thousand dollars a year, complete with secretary, as an A&M staff producer. And it transpired that Alpert and Moss, who paid his salary, had been wondering why he never seemed to produce anything but his own self-named album. Herb and Jerry were hardly surprised to hear that Richard was no longer prepared to see the credit line of "producer" of his records from the man who acted as liaison and consultant, even if he had been a great morale booster and supporter of Richard and Karen's work.

When Richard returned from the tour, Alpert and Moss told him over lunch at the Hungry Tiger on La Brea Avenue that Daugherty's departure had been implemented.

Daugherty was dismissed by A&M, but he would not go without a fight. For nine years efforts to settle his claim against the company of "destroyed credibility" as a professional music man could not be settled, and finally in 1981 the case went to trial. It was the first time in a courtroom for Richard and Karen, and the first time A&M had been sued. Together with Alpert and Moss, the Carpenters took the stand to testify that Daugherty had not been entitled to the credit line as published, and that Richard was the de facto producer of Carpenters records. For the remake of the "Top of the World" single, Richard had insisted on a production credit line that read: "Produced by Richard and Karen Carpenter and Jack Daugherty." Without that, he stipulated, it should not be released. Even that, said Richard, was a concession to Jack.

The court rejected Daugherty's appeal against unfair dismissal. It was something of a pyrrhic victory, for Jerry Moss says: "We actually won, but what we won basically was nothing. The one thing he didn't get from us was a ton of money, but it cost us something like $350,000 to $400,000 to defend ourselves and a lot of angst time." Another link with the Carpenters' early years had ended in tears.[2]

While their image was still scorned in some quarters, the musicality and attention to detail in performance were incontestable. Their concert at the Greek Theatre in Los Angeles in August 1972 drew praise in the *Hollywood Reporter*. Writing of their sound precision, Jeff Thomas said Richard's "dedication, concern, direction and ability" were visually apparent as he led his band through "a fine blend of instrumental and vocal arrangements and harmonies." Richard was, wrote Thomas, "serious, often to the point of stage-personality restriction, but understandably so. The result is perfection."

Karen, the show's focal interest, added her irreplaceable contribution to the total sound, but, commenting on her dual role as the drummer, the writer noted: "She performs nearly half of the vocal material while playing the drums. ... it is still difficult to accept the ambidextrous delivery of drums and vocals due to the general ungainliness of the instrument contrasting with her crystalline, saccharine, lyrical presentation." However, the reviewer conceded that Karen defeated such difficulties with authority, maintaining femininity.

The *Cleveland Press*, describing Karen's voice as "clear, warm, smooth, soaring," wrote of the same touring performance, "Rarely do you see such a fetching brunette seat herself at the drums and flail away so perfectly." On her appearance, the paper noted that she wore a white blouse with little-girl puff-up sleeves, a pink-and-blue patchwork gown that fastened up high like bib overalls. "The gown had legs for lady-like drumming. And she wore a red ribbon in her hair. She was Miss Innocence personified."

Richard's insistence that their concert sound should reproduce the Carpenters' records was made abundantly clear to the drummer who replaced Jim Squeglia in early 1973. This time there was no problem. The pedigree of Cubby O'Brien was immaculate: he was an experienced player, a former "Mouseketeer" on the "Mickey Mouse Club" show on TV, and a veteran of other shows who

2. Even after such a prolonged battle ending in litigation, Daugherty showed up for Karen's funeral, an act which Richard found moving. Daugherty died during bypass surgery on February 2, 1991.

would go on to work with some of the biggest names in entertainment. His link with the Walt Disney creation was a big hit with Karen, who adored Mickey Mouse and collected as many items of that design as she could find.

In these high-energy years on the road, with irregular mealtimes and stops at all-night diners, it seemed normal for a young woman to be watching her figure. The band regarded her diet dabbling as normal conversation. "Karen was certainly not slim when I joined the band," Cubby O'Brien says. "She got into this cycle of wanting to look thinner. She might have got caught up into thinking that in a society that wanted slimness, she needed to shed weight to stand out front as the solo singer. And I think it just kept on going into some other kind of control thing, where she felt that she could definitely take charge of this part of her life."

The Carpenters were playing a successful season in 1972 at the Riviera in Las Vegas. There Karen began to see Alan Osmond, a singer with the hit Osmond Brothers. Like so many of her attachments, it had little chance to develop when they left the city. The Osmond family lived in Salt Lake City, a ninety-minute flight from Los Angeles. It continued as a strong telephone friendship, and occasionally Alan would fly in to see Karen. But his work, too, was demanding as his group was riding high.

Karen made light of her friendship with Alan Osmond, saying their careers and geographical distance meant it was destined to stay just that: a friendship. On a visit to London, asked in a BBC radio interview whether she looked forward to marriage and children, she replied: "Oh, I love children. When I do get married, I want to be in a position to settle down and have children, and stay home with 'em. I would never have a kid and haul them on the road and give 'em to a maid! I think that's the most absurd thing that anybody could ever do."

She dismissed, too, any suggestion that she might go solo as a singer, splitting from Richard. "It never occurred to us because it's senseless. We're so happy and things have been so lucky. It works so well, we wouldn't touch it with anything." Praising her brother as the undercredited designer of their sound, she said their audience ranged from "crib age" to grandparents, "from three to eighty-three." "Our type of people would like the Fifth Dimension, Elton John, David Gates, Carole King—right down the middle." Karen seemed on a natural high for the interview, enjoying dissecting the Carpenters' popularity and talking about everything from needlepoint to cars.

As they clocked up gold records in Japan and Australia and the world beckoned for tours, Richard and Karen's thoughts turned to strengthening their sound. Their opening act in early 1971 had been a group called Instant Joy, backing the successful singer Mark Lindsay. As they stood watching the band from the wings every night, Richard and Karen were impressed by their guitarist. Twenty-year-old Tony Peluso looked like a hippy rock 'n' roller, but his resonant guitar work demonstrated a broad-based talent. "How come we never heard of you before?" Karen finally said to him as he left the stage one night. "When we get back to Los Angeles, we're gonna call you—and you're gonna play with us." Peluso was flattered; the Carpenters were one of the hottest acts in the world.

Almost a year later, when he'd virtually forgotten about the praise, Peluso's phone rang. Richard told him he had a song that he thought was the perfect vehicle for Peluso's guitar talent. When Tony showed up at Studio B at A&M, Richard was taken aback by the sight. Astonishingly thin, he wore his hair down to his behind. He was hired against the advice of Jack Daugherty, who wanted to use an established session guitarist, but Richard's insistence on bringing Tony in was to prove an artistic breakthrough for their sound.

The song in question was a watershed for the Carpenters. Watching a late-night movie in 1971, Bing Crosby appearing in *Rhythm on the River,* Richard became absorbed by the theme: a songwriter who struggles to the top but then loses his muse. The writer's most famous song in the story was called "Goodbye to Love"—although there was no actual song of that name in the movie. Richard loved the whole idea of it and kept it on his mind as the Carpenters left for a European tour.

In London, Richard wrote the beginning of a haunting melody, and back in California he called John Bettis. They began work on it immediately, with Richard writing the opening lines: "I'll say goodbye to love/no one ever cared if I should live or die."

For the lyrical theme demanded by the title and those first words, a weirdly autobiographical lyric for Karen was born. As Bettis constructed a story to match Richard's developing melody, he reflected on the emotional vacuum that he, Karen, and Richard were experiencing. "Not one of us had any glimmer of a meaningful relationship at that period," Bettis says. "Our twenties were not a good romantic time. And we all felt really empty."

So was launched a searing heartbreaker of a song, tailored subconsciously for Karen's psyche. It would become her toughest song to sing because Richard's demanding, elongated phrasing allowed little time to breathe during certain key parts.

She warmed to it instantly, immersing herself in the density of the story and melody that John Bettis and her brother had created. Giving the record a distinctly human edge at the start, where it began with voice and piano, Richard decided to leave in Karen's audible intake of breath. As Roger Young, their engineer, points out, because Karen sang very softly, very close to the microphone by habit, the "intense presence" of her voice was accentuated, and Richard's instruction to not edit-out the deep breaths on "Goodbye to Love" and on other tracks added a special, unexpected dimension.

"Goodbye to Love" would always be one of her favorite Carpenters tracks. Although it was too early in Karen's life and her career for the words to be accurately identified with her solitude, they assumed a poignancy as the years passed. She was singing words about love passing her by, of making up her mind to live life alone. And she sang of a world in which loneliness and empty days would be her only friend.

I'll say goodbye to love
No one ever cared if I should live or die
Time and time again the chance for love has passed me by
And all I know of love is how to live without it
I just can't seem to find it.

So I've made my mind up I must live my life alone
And though it's not the easy way
I guess I've always known
I'd say goodbye to love.

There are no tomorrows for this heart of mine
Surely time will lose these bitter memories

And I'll find that there is someone to believe in
And to live for, something I could live for.

All the years of useless search have finally reached an end
Loneliness and empty days will be my only friend
From this day love is forgotten, I'll go on as best I can.

What lies in the future is a mystery to us all
No one can predict the wheel of fortune as it falls
There may come a time when I will see that I've been wrong
But for now this is my song.
And it's goodbye to love, I'll say goodbye to love.

Lyrics by John Bettis. Music by Richard Carpenter.
Copyright © 1972 Almo Music Corp. & Hammer and Nails Music (ASCAP).
All Rights Reserved. International copyright secured. Used by permission,
courtesy of Rondor Music International.

As she often did with such evocatively personal lyrics, Karen extracted every ounce of meaning from "Goodbye to Love." Heard now, she sounds almost tearful as she runs through the tapestry of her own emotions.

> *Goodbye to love*
>
> *I'll say goodbye*
> *to love*
> *No one ever cared*
> *If I should*
> *live or die*
> *Always on the outside*
> *lookin' inside.*
> *How I've tried*
> *to hide the*
> *the time I've*
> *cried.*
> *pain I've felt*
> *without it.*
>
> *I've been so long*
> *without it*

This gem of a recording had an unexpected, magical ingredient. Richard had told his raunchy new guitarist Tony Peluso at the session: "For your solo, I want you to play the melody for five bars, then improvise from there." Richard had an inner feeling that something startling might result. And it did. Peluso delivered a bold, inventive, fuzz-guitar solo more akin to Jimi Hendrix in full flight than someone on a sedate Carpenters record.

Karen and Richard and everyone in the studio cheered Peluso's daring break. Richard's ambition for new ground breaking had been matched by an exhilarating solo that would be discussed and celebrated by musicians and record buyers from all aspects of popular music for years.

The song's two guitar solos, which had been completed in several takes lasting a total of fifteen minutes, were later edited by Richard. Immediately worried, Peluso feared that his fiercely rock 'n' roll stamp on the lush Carpenters sound was far too adventurous.

Power ballads in this vein became the norm in later years, but as Peluso recalls, "It seemed way out at that time to be putting rock 'n' roll fuzz-toned guitar on beautiful, mellow music like theirs! I thought: 'My God, is this going to *ruin* them? Maybe I'm going to single-handedly spoil their careers.'" Added to this, he idolized Richard and Karen as consummate musicians and felt very much like the upstart rock 'n' roller infiltrating from a different league. "But they were bouncing off the walls at the solo." It was a pivotal moment in Peluso's life and career: "I've made a million records since with a load of people and never felt the magic I felt that night."

Everyone knew his solo worked strongly inside the passionate context of the song, but, he says, "I liked it musically, and it *was* my first ever session with Richard and Karen. But I wasn't sure how their audience would react." Richard had no doubts about Peluso's startling originality, and he joined the Carpenters' touring band in June 1972, enjoying a featured role on stage as the disc jockey in the "oldies" medley.

They did not have to wait long for audience response to their innovative record. They got some "hate mail." "Goodbye to Love" confused some Carpenters fans, who wrote accusing Richard of abdicating good quality, of "going rock 'n' roll," of playing "devil's music." With its choral ending, Richard had polished the record into a thematic and musical masterpiece, and he was saddened by the charges of "selling out," of "bastardizing" the Carpenters sound. In Britain, the song and the hypnotic guitar solo were critically acclaimed, with even pop cynics applauding its inventiveness. The Carpenters, they now admitted, could be judged outside the dreaded "easy listening" category.

John Bettis, admitting he was self-indulgent with the lyric ("I kinda wrote the truth, and we got away with it"), notes that Richard was "the first person ever to use electric guitar like that in a period when ballads dominated. He was a groundbreaker. To this day, they are copying Richard Carpenter's licks every month."

Though Richard had mixed feelings of pride and hurt about the song, Bettis wept tears of joy when he heard the playback. The single stormed to number seven on the national charts.

But the fans' critical backlash temporarily hit Richard's confidence in extending boundaries, for he now played it safe. The Carpenters' next single, six months later in February 1973, was the lightweight "Sing," a trite sing-along from the TV series "Sesame Street," complete with children's chorus. Though it broke no ground for them musically, the catchy tune safely returned them to million-selling status and won two Grammy nominations.

And then he and Bettis sprang back. They always composed around Richard's prized Baldwin piano at his Downey home, where John was now accepted as "family." The handicap to this location was that there was no privacy for the songwriters, but somehow, amid the mayhem of the Carpenters' family life, with Agnes and Harold coming and going and Karen wandering in with asides, as well as friends and dogs, Richard and John's chemistry was such that they could ignite sparks in each other.

In 1973, pop fans suddenly realized they had a rich heritage that stretched back two decades. Karen and Richard had been performing an oldies medley since the summer of 1972 in their concerts, to great applause. One day early in 1973, driving along Highland Avenue to A&M, Richard "heard" the melody and lyric in his head for a song to reflect the nostalgia. It would become one of their most noted anthems: "When I was young, I would listen to the radio." By the time he reached A&M, he was able to play the chorus to Karen in Studio B. That night, he wrote the first verse and called in John Bettis to complete "Yesterday Once More." It was perfect: Richard had been seeking a song to anchor an album with an oldies theme—and the *Now and Then* album concept was born.

Remembering the construction of "Yesterday Once More," John Bettis says: "We were in the Newville house, which he'd just made into his fantasmagoria with speakers the size of small condominiums! Richy was always more addicted to old records than I was, and he told me he was going to do a whole side of an album of oldies and he wanted an anthem for it." Richard had the opening lines to the song, and when Bettis had completed the lyric, they had a jewel.

Walking into the room to hear the new song, Karen inquired about other material. She was puzzled to find Richard and John scanning discographies for titles of oldies. "We're planning to put some names of old songs in the second verse of 'Yesterday Once More,'" they told her. "What? Oh, I hate that!" she said.

That idea was dumped because it proved too hard to achieve as well as appearing contrived; the lyric was completed as it appeared on the final version. "Nothing was ever finished when we first got together," Bettis says of their songwriting pattern. "It was always search and discovery, totally unscientific, just the two of us playing."

With its mood of nostalgic yearning for "those happy days" of pop's golden period, "Yesterday Once More" was another perfect vehicle for the mournful quality in Karen's voice. When Richard mentioned the idea for the album to his mother—one side of oldies, another more contemporary—she suggested the title *Now and Then*. He then orchestrated an oldies medley to reflect the growing interest of radio stations, and the public, in pop's halcyon years. Karen returned to an old favorite, the Skeeter Davis ballad "The End of the World," while other golden songs like the Crystals' "Da Doo Ron Ron" and the Chiffons' "One Fine Day" rounded out a lively departure, which was presented as a radio programme. The segment, used in their concerts, met with great applause.

The "current" side of the album began with "Sing" before a definitive version of the Leon Russell classic "This Masquerade" and "Heather." The lilting "Jambalaya," which would become a permanent radio play, was followed by yet another song that could be read as a mirror of Karen's soul. In Randy Edelman's "I Can't Make Music," she sang rather obtusely about a writer who had lost his muse:

Same old feeling's come again

So uncertain, hurt and scared

I thought I grew but here I am again

I can't do anything to take me away this time.

This dark song predated Karen's dilemma by a couple of years, but heard now it assumes an awful eeriness. It also stood out as the only item of introspection on an otherwise cheerful album.

It sold a million copies very quickly in the United States and sent their already strong popularity soaring in Japan, where the "Yesterday Once More" single went on to sell an astounding 750,000 copies. With Britain, Japan would be the Carpenters' prime market in the years ahead.

With British sales of Carpenters albums exceeding 300,000, they were the economic foundation of A&M in Britain. In 1973, the country in the grip of an industrial strike by miners which caused a three-day work week, the record industry was badly hit by production problems. The energy crisis brought a severe shortage of vinyl. To cope with the demand, the label's commercial director, John Deacon, had to arrange for Carpenters records to be pressed in Germany, Holland, and any other European cities that could help, and then shipped into London.

While they remained "boring" to some of A&M's musicians and executives, there was also gratitude that they had given the company's London launch such a strong financial boost. "Karen seemed to be a worrier," Deacon recalls. "Richard was very protective of her. Some said he was—well, difficult."

The hit team was now in harness. Richard and John were back within months with the country-tinged "Top of the World," a song that had a long, convoluted journey to the top. After the album called *Carpenters*, Richard wanted to spend more time on choosing material, and on production, since he didn't think that had enough material on it. For their next, what became *A Song for You*, he started to sift songs that came down from A&M's music publishing division, Almo.

Initially, Karen and Richard were lukewarm about the finished version, but in time it would become a Carpenters standard and is now often played on commercial planes on takeoff—a neat parallel with the song's birth, since Bettis first thought of the idea during a flight from Nashville to Los Angeles.

Once finished and on the album, Karen and Richard and John considered it simply nice but uneventful. But an early review said "Top of the World" was a standout track. The Carpenters were very surprised: they put several songs ahead of it, particularly "Goodbye to Love."

Then they introduced it at the Houston concert which began their summer tour in 1972. "We'll do a tune off our new album," Richard said . . . and as they went into "Top of the World," the crowd erupted into applause.

During that tour, as the song continued to get strong crowd reaction, Richard and Karen looked at each other, nonplussed; they had never known an album track to get such a big reception.

Its success gathered momentum before Richard and Karen

could grasp what was happening. "A&M's Japanese affiliate took it upon themselves to cull it as a single, and it went gold there," Richard says. "Then Lynn Anderson recorded it, and it went to the top of the country charts. We were getting letters about the song, and kids were going to the home of our parents asking when it would be released as a small record, meaning a single. Some radio stations were charting it on requests alone."

In their homeland, however, rarely can such a big hit have had such a strange birth. For a year, Richard and Karen watched public interest in the song soar—but it remained an album track. They should have moved faster to pull it off as a single, swelling album sales. But finally, in late 1972, they remixed it and decided to make it a single. In September, they flew to Las Vegas, where they announced it on stage as "our next single."

But hearing of this announcement back at A&M, Gil Friesen had other ideas. When a local Las Vegas radio station played "Top of the World" from the album and announced it as their next projected single, he flew out to Las Vegas specifically to tell the Carpenters in their dressing room that they should not be releasing "Top of the World" as a single. The song may have had some chart potential, but they had put out too many singles from that album already, Friesen added. It was not going to work.

As a result of that conversation, Richard decided not to release it, to the irritation of the disc jockey in Las Vegas who had announced it.

But between June 1972 and September 1973 there were far too many signs that "Top of the World" was an unstoppable winner for Richard to ignore. Public demand was coming into play; Richard now knew it had a lot of potential for them. And anyway, Friesen and others had even questioned "Sing" earlier, he mused, and that had done very well! He would not be discouraged this time by anyone; he would trust his instinct.

Coming off the road, Richard swung into the A&M parking lot. Friesen walked over. "I just want you to know," he said, "that I was obviously wrong about 'Sing.' I loved 'Yesterday Once More.' But anyway, I'm never going to question your choice of single again."

"Good," Richard shot back, "because we are releasing 'Top of the World.'"

Karen was dissatisfied with her original lead vocal, and there were other improvements to be made, so they went in to rework it. Featuring Buddy Emmons on steel guitar and Tony Peluso playing electric guitar, their third version of the song went to the top of the charts, becoming their second number one (after "Close to You"). In Britain, where it went to number five, the song remains one of their most popular radio plays. The upbeat lyric represented different feelings to a wide audience, some even considering it a religious or spiritual song.

TOP OF THE WORLD

SUCH A FEELINGS
COMIN' OVER ME
THERE IS WONDER
IN 'MOST EVERYTHING I SEE.
NOT A CLOUD
IN THE SKY
GOT THE SUN IN
MY EYES
AND I WONT
BE SUPRISED
IF IT'S A DREAM

EVERYTHING I WANT
THE WORLD TO BE;

IS NOW COMING
TRUE ESPECIALLY FOR ME.

~~FROM DARKNESS IS~~
~~CLEAR FEEL~~
AND THE REASON
IS CLEAR
IT'S BECAUSE ~~IT YOU~~
YOU ARE HERE.
~~IS~~ YOURS THE NEAREST
THING TO HEAVEN
THAT I'VE SEEN

CHORUS:

3

I'M ON THE TOP
OF THE WORLD
LOOKIN' ~~ON~~ DOWN ~~IN~~ CREATION
AND TH ~~THE~~ EXPLANATION ~~FIND I~~
I CAN ~~FIND IN~~

~~[scribbled out lines]~~

IS THE LOVE
~~THAT~~ I'VE FOUND
EVER SINCE ~~I HAVE~~ YOU'VE
BEEN AROUND.
YOUR LOVE'S PUT ME
AT THE TOP OF THE WOR

Commercially it would always vie with "Yesterday Once More" as Richard and John's most successful single, to the chagrin of Richard, who always wanted his nostalgic creation to be ahead of the more flippant "Top of the World."[3]

They were slogging around the country in freezing winters as well as very hot summers, and their itinerary was relentless. "We were at the absolute height of our game," declares John Bettis of the early 1970s. "But how Richard was able to put together that hallmark *Song for You* album was an absolute miracle. We got lucky in one two-day period and wrote 'Goodbye to Love' and 'Top of the World'—and 'I Won't Last a Day without You' was there. To have six hits off it bespeaks the fact that he was only in his twenties. We were writing on adrenaline, a spiritual high."

Nobody except Richard and Karen deserved credit for their ability to put that crucial album together. The world touring schedule, as well as the traditional long summer tour of the United States, was too tough, and Bettis is not alone in looking back with the view that someone should have implemented a pause in their schedule and looked at their longevity. "Someone should have said: wait. Karen is out front of the band, there's a wonderful little clown in there, and she's growing into a pretty lady. This is getting pretty good. And Richard may be overworked and bad tempered, but there doesn't seem to be much end to his musical ability. They are both world-class talents."

The people around Richard and Karen "read the trade papers too much," says Bettis. They said to themselves, "Well yeah, maybe there *is* a little bit of truth about these stories of them being goody-four-shoes."

And that lack of vision, Bettis asserts, was a shame "because had there been a few steps taken back, all sorts of wonderful things might have happened. As writers, Richard and I could have done hundreds of things we haven't done yet. As a performer, Karen could have done hundreds of things she'll never be able to do now. And the time to make that decision was back in 1973." He recalls Richard telling him they were going on tour for *A Song for You* and playing as many dates as in the pre-

3. The biggest-selling Carpenters single internationally remains "Please Mr. Postman." In the United States, the biggest seller is "Close to You," and in Britain and Japan "Yesterday Once More."

vious year. "And he was accepting it!" says Bettis incredulously. "And I remember saying: 'I don't know WHY! Nobody in your position would be doing this. It's dumb! A six-week summer tour ending with two weeks in Lake Tahoe and two weeks in Las Vegas, two shows a night? *Excuse me?!* Sure, the money's great, but the money will always be great for you guys, because you're good!'"[4]

The Carpenters grossed about $100,000 a week when on a concert tour and their fee rose from an initial $50,000 to $100,000 a week at Las Vegas (later, after 1976, their Vegas fee rose to $135,000 a week). Setting off their crippling touring expenses against these figures, the tours were not very profitable enterprises. Paying the sound company staff, the opening act, their band, lighting directors, and road managers, and often leasing planes and paying for hotel rooms, the bills soon escalated. "And I, foolishly, was hiring orchestras that the public generally didn't give a damn about," Richard reflects. "We later found out the public was more impressed by the amount of music seven of us in the band made than by any orchestra!"

Sherwin Bash, refuting any suggestion that he overworked them, declares: "I'm not comparing the Carpenters to most people who get up and work nine to five in an office, five days a week for something like fifty weeks a year and have a two-week vacation. But I think a reality check of how much they actually worked during the time I represented them would make most people in this world say: 'What *are* they talking about?'"

Pointing out that twenty years ago the Carpenters were performing during the earliest period of the burgeoning popularity of concerts in their category of music, and made a great deal of money, Bash adds: "I am someone who gets up in the morning and works five days a week, fifty or more weeks a year ... in my vocabulary, these people were retired!"

Emphasizing that he never considered their itineraries to reflect overwork, Bash states that he never heard a complaint or observation from Richard or Karen to that effect. "I never accept engage-

---

4. Since his collaborations for the Carpenters with Richard, John Bettis has written the lyrics for many other successful records, including "One Moment in Time" (recorded by Whitney Houston), "Crazy for You" (Madonna), "Slow Hand" (the Pointer Sisters), and "Human Nature" (recorded by Michael Jackson on his *Thriller* album).

ments for any of my clients that I don't discuss beforehand or get their approval."

Richard, citing the itineraries he has kept, says the Carpenters played 145 concerts in 1971, excluding a European tour and TV shows, plus ten TV appearances on U.S. TV, plus the "Make Your Own kind of Music" series, and recording sessions.

In 1972, they played 174 concerts, excluding a scheduled sixteen cabaret performances at Eden Rock, Miami, which ended up as two due to a contractual dispute. That year, they also did six TV shows and made the album *A Song For You*.

1973 brought 174 concerts again, plus the *Now and Then* album and three TV shows, while the following year brought 203 concerts. That year of 1974, there was no new album "because there was simply no time to make one. Nor was I in the mood." If they had released an album that year, after the hit singles compilation, it would presumably have been a monster seller, Richard believes.

In 1975 there were 118 concerts plus scheduled Japanese and European tours (46 shows) which were postponed into 1976. Additionally in 1975 there was an album, *Horizon*.

"We were keeping up far too hectic a schedule," Richard maintains. "It is evidenced by the fact that I was not finding enough time to write, or to find new material, and by the way Karen looked physically, and by the trouble I got into."

They were, he believes, overbooked rather than overworked, and Richard adds: "As a seasoned, professional manager, I felt Sherwin should have seen that things were not quite right. In 1975, when I was working on the *Horizon* album, I remember Sherwin saying I looked close to a nervous breakdown."

Richard does not blame Sherwin Bash in isolation for their schedule. "He was not autonomous. He did send down lists about what was being proposed." And Richard agrees that neither he nor Karen contested the schedules. "But we were very young, with everything just starting out. We were apprehensive about calling Sherwin on these matters."

And they liked their manager, enjoying his company. As an ambassador for the Carpenters out on the road and in the industry, they felt Sherwin represented them excellently, since he was so well liked as a personality, as well as experienced.

Bash wonders whether Karen or Richard "felt they couldn't

discuss it [their schedule] honestly with me. I discussed every potential offer and they knew what was happening and they accepted it. At no time did Richard Carpenter ever say to me: 'This sounds like too much and this is something we shouldn't be doing.' I never heard that from him." Accepting that, Richard reflects that nobody in the Carpenters circle really confronted the issue of the schedule which has been analyzed with the benefit of hindsight. Many entertainers complain about various business factors around them—the record company, the promotions department, their management, and other decision-makers. But looking back on it, Richard feels that he and Karen were "not just a trendy act that needed to be booked heavily because within a year or so we wouldn't be selling records any more. The act had legs."

One record industry veteran remarks that the Carpenters were unfortunately judged alongside those acts considered to be transitory. "In those years, we were used to acts burning out fast: get a few hits and good-bye. So you felt you had to get the mileage out of them quickly. Pop acts around the world were flogging their butts off, working too hard. It wasn't right, because human beings were treated as cattle, but there was a genuine assumption that most acts would only survive a few years, so management inevitably took a short-term view."

No account seemed to be taken of the fact that Karen was a woman—probably because she seemed as strong as everyone else on the road. And since she had fostered the image of equality, it was understandable that it scarcely occurred to tour organizers that such an exhausting schedule might be too punishing for her.

Werner Wolfen later calculated that they would have had to have performed 150 shows annually before Richard and Karen saw a cent of profit. "It would have been much easier on all of us if Karen and I had just recorded," Richard says now. "We would have had a lot more records out there, and we would have made a lot more money.

"Travelling to Japan and to Britain, well, that was necessary. But to have been flogging around the U.S. like that ... I get mad when I think about it." And they would have been less tired. "I would have been much happier working on records than out on the road. But hindsight is twenty-twenty vision!"

During those years of intensive touring, Bettis joined them on their trail across the United States to see how life was for them inside the goldfish bowl of fame and frenzy. "The white heat around them was very intense. Richard had assumed total responsibility for everything in their career, because he believed that if you wanted something done right, you did it yourself. In addition to their crushing celebrity—they were selling tons of records, implying millions of adoring fans—they couldn't be real people. This was some adjust from the time when Richy and I were bumming around, and that had not been very much earlier. There was always something to worry about, usually five hundred things to worry about." And "since nobody gets that many good ideas in one single day," the pressure on Richard when it came to planning for recording was immense.

And that, Bettis remarks, is one reason why the *Now and Then* album gained its format as a retrospective of Richard's favorite oldies. "He didn't have the time to listen to five hundred demos a year . . . so all he had to do was remember the songs he wanted to record. Richard did honestly love these songs, but they were also a very good by-product of existing hits."

Driving themselves hard toward perfection, squabbling when the slightest blemish appeared in their stage show, Richard and Karen were tough bosses to their band and entourage, which totaled around thirty. "You didn't last in that organization twenty-four hours unless you knew what you were doing," says Tony Peluso. "They insisted on excellence: there was no skating through. You couldn't fake it.

"They were very compassionate, always fair, but very, very demanding, insistent that everyone else came up to their standards." Sometimes it seemed unreasonable, he felt; but this was a brilliant band who genuinely believed they were the best of their kind on the road. They were driven hard but treated well. Peluso states: "From the sound check to the show, when we all took our bows together alongside Karen and Richard, we were never made to feel we were the back-up band.

"If they flew first-class, we did. If they had a limo, we did. If they had a suite, we did. And we were expected to be nothing less than perfect every night—*for them.* 'We're doing it for you—be there for us' was their view. If you made one little mistake, you'd hear about it after the show.

"These two were the most driven professionals in any business I've ever known or seen in my life. Completely committed, morning, noon, and night, every waking hour, to their career and making themselves more excellent. The bigger the show, the bigger the crowd, the more famous they could be, the Grammys, another number-one record, more gold albums, they loved it. Not in a conceited, egotistical way, but through pride. They ate it all up insatiably." Karen and Richard enjoyed the success equally, but she was more commercially ambitious than he.

It would have been preferable, Peluso says, if the Carpenters had made a mistake occasionally, so one of the band could point to it in self-defence. "But they never screwed up! Richard and Karen didn't drop a note, or make a mistake, night after night."

"Half of Richard was trying to do what his audience wanted; the other half was him being his own audience," Peluso says of his old boss. And Karen was "the most dedicated, loyal fan, believer, and champion of Richard in the world. She gave him a 110 percent for any idea he had."

This indestructible clinch that went way beyond their family ties became something of a talking point. When Sherwin Bash mentioned to Peluso that he would not manage groups "because they become famous and then they break up," Peluso challenged him. "But you manage Karen and Richard and the Carpenters. That's a group," said the guitarist.

"That's different," Bash pointed out. "That's not a duo, that's one entity. They're joined at the hip."

When success came, whatever Richard and Karen's intentions, they were lifted into a world separate from their old buddies in the band. Some felt they were being isolated from musicians, causing tension, according to Bob Messenger. Once, when Maria invited the whole band and touring staff back to her house for pasta, excluding Richard, he was miffed. "Well," she explained in her forthright style, "it's obvious that someone has put up a partition, so the guys feel uncomfortable with you being around." To a baffled Richard, she added that things were "not like before … you are getting the same treatment you are giving them."

Karen was less aloof, but the temperature between her and the band went cold when anyone made a mistake. Head down and stony faced, she would stalk to her dressing room in a black mood. She or Richard would berate the musician, and then it would be "on with the show."

Still sitting behind her drums and singing for a considerable part of their act, Karen posed a problem for television in these pre-video years. Planning the films to promote their singles internationally, Clare Baren of A&M decided to look for unique locations to beef up the interest in what critics saw as a boring act. The hippie fashion for long hair meant young people were not always welcome at Disneyland, but for the first time they allowed the Carpenters, a pop group who would hitherto have been shown the door, to make a short film there in 1974 to promote "Please Mr. Postman." Karen and Richard were filmed on the Dumbo ride and other attractions.

And for "Only Yesterday," in 1975, they filmed at Huntington Gardens, a huge private garden complex in San Marino with an art museum and a library that was not easily secured for commercial projects like pop record promotion.

The makers of such promotional film clips, which cost one thousand dollars a minute, faced difficulties presenting the Carpenters. "Karen was getting very pretty," says Clare Baren, "but at the beginning there she was with her legs spread apart behind a drum set. Yet she was also very feminine, and it didn't feel right."

Another problem was the brother-sister relationship on a love song. "You couldn't have Karen and Richard goo-goo eyed, singing to one another. In the studio, Karen had her eyes closed and headphones on, and she wasn't singing to Richard. But suddenly, in the video, there they were, together." It was awkward. Richard agrees; they faced the same dilemma as with the album covers.

Agnes Carpenter loved basking in the glory of her famous daughter and enjoyed seeing Karen recognized on the street or in the stores when they went shopping. But when she saw them on TV, she was often irritated by the focus on her. A glancing shot of Richard followed by his fingers at the piano was just about all he got. It was a reminder that while Richard charted the path, the singer was the star. "They should show Richard more," Agnes would say to the television set.

"*WHAT*? You play guitar in the *CARPENTERS?!*" Members of their band became used to the stigma of admitting they worked with such objects of derision, even if they were proud of their music.

The snide remarks against Karen and Richard because they were not hip rock 'n' rollers had cut them deeply; "Mom's apple pie," "whiter than white," "squeaky clean"—and "goody-four-shoes" had been some of the jibes. These angered them; not, they emphasized, because they couldn't take a knock or didn't sometimes deserve one. But they were honest, moderately right-wing Middle Americans who had eclectic tastes in music. They loved rock 'n' roll and studied it carefully, but their music came from a different framework.

"We're normal people," Karen told me around this time on a visit to London. "Get up in the morning, shower, go to restaurants, argue, go to work. I can't see why we should get criticized so much because we don't seem to fit into some kind of category." Richard pointed to the enormous variety of records in his collection, ranging from Frank Zappa's Mothers of Invention to Irving Berlin. If he had an open mind, he said, others might be more generous to them. "It struck us all so deep when they tore us apart," John Bettis says. "The hypocrisy of it wasn't fun to live with. Humans loved what we did, but the self-appointed arbiters of what humans *should* like hated it. Why, because I'm a white middle-class kid who speaks about life and struggles with it, is that negative? Those who denigrated Richard and Karen sprang from the same background but were in major denial. They didn't want to be that person any more. We committed the arch sin of being ourselves."

"Karen and I were painted as being sexless and viceless wimps," Richard says. "We were, in a way, the Great American Dream, the boy and girl next door who made good, middle-class suburban kids whose dream came true. What I didn't like and rebelled against was when the people writing about us as 'too wholesome' did it because they didn't like our music. It was irresponsible and nasty.

"No one I ever knew had been that perfect. Karen and I were no exception. They described us as 'wholesome' as if it were a dirty word. What was wrong with that? Had we been a hit in the forties or even the late fifties, no one would have said anything. But you know, we loved Elvis, both Karen and I, and yet we also admired Henry Mancini.

"The criticism of us was divisive, making it appear like camps. People who liked us were cast as having no musical sophistication or any idea about what was hip. They could not appreciate Led Zeppelin *and* the Carpenters, and that was wrong. Not so. If someone really likes music, they can tell something done well in any genre."

If the fraternity embracing the rock life-style sought confirmation that the "too clean" Carpenters should be disenfranchised, their evidence came when President Nixon embraced them. It was a shrewd political move to align himself with one of the hottest acts in the United States, white middle-class kids. "He was trying to say," reflects Richard, "that the average person out there supporting the president, the silent majority, don't get their pickets out. Maybe he thought we represented that majority, and maybe we did." Richard is "a moderate Republican," and Karen, disinterested in politics, had similar leanings.

Nixon first invited them to the White House in 1972 for a photo session, and then, proclaiming Richard and Karen publicly as "young America at its best," he feted them by inviting them to play during a state visit by the West German chancellor, Willy Brandt.

The date, on May 1, 1973, came in the middle of a tour, and the entire Carpenters band and entourage were exhausted. "We'd never been so nervous," Richard recalls. "We could play for tens of thousands of people, but to have to play for these statesmen in the East Room of the White House was quite mind-boggling." Karen said it did not hit her until she was "standing there singing 'Superstar' and looking right at President Nixon ... and I was saying to myself, what are you *doing?* I mean, we were afraid to touch anything. I was afraid to even breathe on the drums. I was barely touching 'em because I didn't want to offend anybody." The small size of the room inhibited them. "It was rough to have to play that softly," Richard says. "Whether we were easy listening or not, it was still an amplified sound, electric guitars, electric piano."

Their jitters were perfectly captured when, with their microphone left on accidentally before their performance, Richard could be clearly heard to say, "Who's the babe with Kissinger?" (It was actress Mamie van Doren.)

"Your music is good," Nixon told them each individually as he shook hands with Richard, Karen, and the band. There was no sign that he was beset by problems that were unfolding, precipitating his resignation.[5]

The insularity of life with a band, her dedication to her work and to continuing success, and the reality of living at home in Downey combined to prevent Karen from a significant romantic involvement—even if she had wanted it. And her dedication to her work left her little free time anyway.

It also meant that her eyes focused on the guys in the touring party. Sherwin Bash noticed that she showed interest in 1973 in a mild-mannered, polite Texan who represented the equipment company Showco, which provided the Carpenters with their touring needs. David Alley had been assigned to their tours, and his polite, comforting style met one of Karen's requirements in her men.[6]

When Bash casually mentioned to Alley that Karen liked him, David lost little time in asking her for a date. As he went into all their tours from his hometown of Dallas, Alley—five years her senior—fell passionately in love with Karen.

While he cherished their attachment, Karen tended to consider him a firm friend, but with no serious future in her life. As with Gary Sims, Agnes noted that what Karen should really be seeking in her man was more assertiveness, confidence, and perhaps as proof of those two qualities, more professional success. It began to occur to Karen, particularly, that her potential marriage partner needed to be financially secure and not reliant on her bank balance. David Alley cared deeply for her and she grew fond of him, but his status did not fit and she kept their romance at a safe level. And even though she had occasional dates such as Alley, she was lonely. "It was work, work, work," says Maria Galeazzi. "So who could she meet?"

In 1973, after recording the *Now and Then* album, touring, and the Washington trip, Richard and Karen needed a break. Even that turned out to be an adjunct to work, "though not much of it," adds Richard. Sherwin Bash had an invitation for them to perform

5. When Karen died ten years later, Nixon handwrote a long, eulogistic letter of sympathy to Richard.
6. Becoming wary of the sound quality they were given on the road, Richard and Karen in 1974 formed their own equipment company, Morsound, which Alley ran for them.

for the giant IBM Company at two twenty-minute concerts on suc-
cessive Saturdays in Acapulco. This could be a rare treat, he told
them, a paid-for "holiday" in a beautiful villa overlooking the bay.
Richard and Karen went with their partners, she with David Alley,
he with Maria Galeazzi, and they shared the luxurious main house
in the holiday complex. Bash was there, too, with his wife, Bobby,
and Richard and Karen invited their parents to join them. But when
Agnes found that she and Harold had been given accommodation
in the nearby Acapulco Princess Hotel rather than in the plush
suites occupied by their children, "the balloon went up."

Not amused at the separation from the main party, Agnes criticized Richard and Karen for separating her and Harold. It was not
that their accommodation was inferior, just that they felt shunted
away. At this criticism, Richard's well-known short fuse blew. "I'm
not ten years old any more!" he yelled at his mother as others
looked on, embarrassed. "We all have our own lives to live." There
followed, says one of the party, "one of those terrible family scenes
you shiver about." Richard's volcanic eruption was a release of
pent-up feelings. When the tension subsided, everyone settled into
an enjoyable vacation.

Some months later, Karen decided to confront "the Maria situation." Back from the winter tour, Richard flew out to Great Falls,
Montana, to see a former girlfriend, Mary Saville, who had preceded Maria. That sudden trip was interpreted by Maria as a plot
hatched by Karen to separate her from Richard, to so hurt Maria
that she would finally leave her brother's life. Not so, declares
Richard. "I knew pretty much that this relationship with Maria was
at an end. I had not seen Mary in a while and wanted to. I had
made up my mind [about the split with Maria], and it had nothing
to do with Karen."

"I was crushed," Maria says. "Suddenly he disappeared off the
face of the earth, flying out of Los Angeles into a blizzard to see a
former girlfriend!"

For Karen, this was a tough decision to confront, for Maria
was, as everyone agreed, terrific at her job. She would be hard to
replace: Karen said she had a knack for dealing imaginatively and
speedily with her hair and also Richard's; she was also talented at
manicuring their fingernails and ironing their clothes at a
moment's notice. How could she fire the woman who had
brought her so many compliments on her appearance?

But she stiffened as she gave Maria a straight ultimatum: if she wanted to stay as her traveling hairdresser and wardrobe assistant, the romance with her brother would have to end.

Maria flatly rejected this ultimatum. "How could I pretend?" she asks now. "I had a relationship with him. What was I gonna do, watch him date others while I went away? I said to Karen: 'No, that's it, *finito!*' It was inhuman to ask such a thing."

Maria believes Karen's lack of a deep relationship meant she could not interpret or relate to the strength of feeling between her and Richard. And she thinks the intensity of the Carpenter family unit was what sealed the fate of their romance. "He said he was under too much pressure from Karen, Agnes, and then me. I just could not stay passive any more. They were trying to enclose him. The minute he tried to draw himself to someone, they drew him away."

During Richard's visit to Montana, Maria called the Carpenters office, but she was told not to do so again. And when she saw Karen in his absence, "I got the hint that something was terribly wrong. Karen was very cool about it, but I died inside."

On his return, Maria told Richard that she had been put in an untenable position by Karen. In her apartment, Richard confirmed to her that they would have to stop dating. Analyzing the forcefulness of the Carpenter family, she says she felt like a coat that had been put on and then taken off. "You could not encourage Richard. I can see where I pushed him too far." Within the Carpenter enclave, she felt, "you had to have a personality that did not have an opinion."

Of the intensity of the Carpenter family unit, Maria remarks: "You had to fit into that little spot just perfect, like a puzzle! It was like: this is our family, and no one can infiltrate. And you can see that's why Karen wasn't happy. She was trying to find a perfect guy who was going to penetrate this ten-foot, Plexiglas wall."

Richard, Maria believes, had a hard time trying to please his mother, his sister, the managers, the record company, the fans, and himself.

The finale was tearful. "That last night," Maria says, "we were going to have dinner and then go to the movies, but we just went for a bite to eat at his favorite restaurant, St. Germain on Melrose. He had so much pressure put on him that he just said, 'Hey, that's it.' He got pushed. I couldn't blame him."

The next day Richard phoned to invite her to visit him as Christmas approached. No, she replied. She had too much pride to do that if someone else was already doing her job.

The affair, Richard says, was ill-fated. "Maria worked for Karen, and it just wasn't fair to either of them. Because of the schedule and the work we were doing, I just didn't get out, so it just stood to reason that I would run into people who were in the circle. It led to friction. Maria felt she didn't want to be bending hair, as she put it, whether I asked her out or not. She just didn't like hairdressing. So it didn't sit right for her to be dating one of the team, going to fancy places with me, riding around in the Ferrari, and then have to do Karen's nails."

And he adds that "Karen or no Karen, I couldn't have spent the rest of my life with Maria." Her view is more incisive. She says she did not realize until after their split the degree to which she loved him. "I was too cut up. Until you're out on the shore, you don't realize that you just swam the ocean." The tears and stress at the parting caused her to contract hyperglycemia, with her weight dropping to eighty-six pounds. "I looked like a skeleton. I cared for him so much, I was destroyed physically."[7]

7. In 1979, Maria—who had said she "did not want to be bending hair forever!"—launched her own highly successful pasta factory in Los Angeles, called Pasta Pasta Pasta, supplying hotels and restaurants. She lives in Hollywood with her husband, Ron Cooper, a dentist, and their daughter, Tiana.

Yep, one of us is gonna get married someday.
It'll probably be during a rehearsal.

—KAREN

Between Karen and her mother, I didn't stand a
chance.

—RANDY BASH, RICHARD'S FORMER GIRLFRIEND

I Need to Be in Love," Karen sang—and it was highly significant that this was her very favourite of all the songs she recorded.

As he wrote that lyric in 1976 and considered his other similar themes of emotional bankruptcy, John Bettis realized he was regularly writing lyrics that could later be interpreted as sound tracks of her personal life. Karen, too, felt an intuitive response to the messages in John's lyrics, and though it was too tender a subject to debate, they would exchange a knowing remark.

Karen's melancholia for a song that demanded that quality was always part of her strength, but this song went somewhere else for her. It was an anthem for her lifelong lack of fulfilment, so accurately did it pinpoint her heartache; and she sang it with a poignancy that could only have come from within.

The hardest thing I've ever done is keep believing
There's someone in this crazy world for me
The way that people come and go through temporary lives
My chance could come and I might never know.

I used to say "No promises, let's keep it simple"
But freedom only helps you say goodbye
It took a while for me to learn that nothing comes for free
The price I paid is high enough for me.

I know I need to be in love
I know I've wasted too much time
I know I ask perfection of a quite imperfect world
And fool enough to think that's what I'll find.

So here I am with pockets full of good intentions
But none of them will comfort me tonight
I'm wide awake at 4 A.M. without a friend in sight
I'm hanging on a hope but I'm all right.

"The whole Carpenters experience was a dream come true for us," says Bettis, "but as wonderful as it was, it didn't solve any-thing. Didn't make life easier, didn't make us happy. We shared an absolute obsession with success, quality, and career. And people locked into that end up with lousy personal lives."

She was twenty-six, but Karen had hardly stepped out of the perameters of her parents, her brother, her career. Collecting Mickey Mouse items (hot-water bottles, plates, music boxes) was her passion. When she mentioned her love of stuffed animals on the "This Is Your Life" TV show, fans swamped her with fuzzy cats, dogs, turtles—and a three-foot-tall purple elephant was given to her by Caesars Palace in Las Vegas. She loved her two dogs, Lady, a Belgian Shepherd, and Mush, a Samoyed. Karen's devotion to them was such that when Lady died, she was buried in a satin-lined casket in the pet cemetery in Huntington Beach with a tombstone that read "She truly was a lady"—and Karen bought a second plot next to her for Mush's future resting place. Needing love and cuddles, Karen clung to her animals and toys as life rafts.

Her isolation worried her friends. "Something about Karen touched a part of me, made me want to just grab her and run off with her at times," reflects Paul Williams. "It was like there was something there that wanted to be pulled away from the family, pulled away from Richard . . . break that symbiotic relationship and get out and develop two full lives."

Even on stage, where she visually held sway, she was aware that no matter how strong her voice, the sounds that were being created had been conceived by Richard. That was even truer in the recording studio.

And since Richard was Agnes's favourite—"the apple of her eye," confirms Agnes's sister Bernice, and this view is accepted by Agnes—Karen knew that whatever her achievements, she was never going to be the actual star of the family. "Oh, Agnes loved Karen dearly," Bernice adds, "but I think Richard was her favourite." Others confirm that, to Agnes, "the sun rose and set" with her son.

Karen, however, never bore a grudge against Richard over this favouritism, and the degree to which it affected her will always be a matter of conjecture. It could have been a silent pain in her life; it could have been just a minor factor which—as she was often inclined to do—she cast aside and made light of.

When the issue of favouritism was put to Richard for this biography, he was palpably surprised. It was one thing for an observer to arrive at that conclusion, he said, but very different to be the actual person involved. "I never saw it that way," he said, acknowledging that his mother had conceded the point. "But one thing needs to be made crystal clear. Everything's relative. Karen never wanted for a damned thing. Anything she wanted she got, and my mother was every bit as much behind her as she supported me."

The success of the Carpenters as an entity certainly fueled Agnes's dreams and determination. And perhaps because she saw Richard as its engine, from his childhood, she focused on him.

Describing Karen as "up in a tower looking out of a window," Paul Williams continues: "Part of me wanted to yell at her to throw down her hair—'I'll get you out of there!' Then, I thought it was such an impudent idea, I kept my mouth shut."

He saw her as trapped, imploding. "Part of her needed to run out of there and raise hell, kick the locks off a lot of doors, and then go back and mend them. Part of me wanted to snatch her out of it and say, 'Let's go raise hell, Karen; let's go do something that we'll be horribly embarrassed about in the morning.'" Sentimental and emotional, Williams felt a spiritual rather than a physical attraction to Karen; he considered her voice on his songs "clean yet so sensual."

A fundamental psychological problem plagued Karen. Despite her own natural talents, and despite her priority over Richard in the public eye, she felt the towering presence of two people: her brother and her mother. Increasingly in awe of Richard, she told everyone that he, not she, was the genius responsible for their sound and success.

In an interview with me on this subject, Karen stated: "You know, there's so much in Richard, just so much that hasn't even been touched. He's so talented it just makes me weep that everybody just walks right by him. They never give him any credit, but he does everything. He's the brains behind it.

"And yet I get cracks like, 'Well, what does the brother do?' Or I get the impression that it's really nice that I've brought my brother on the road!

"Look what he's produced! There are sixteen gold records [she was speaking to me in 1975]. He's produced one of the most successful acts in the world, and nobody gives him any credit. He never gets referred to as a producer or as an arranger, and they walk right by him. Richard and John Bettis are terribly overlooked as writers.

"I really get upset for him because he's so good and he never opens his mouth. He just sits back. And because I'm the lead singer, I get all the credit."

Karen added: "They think I did it, and all I do is sing. He's the one that does all the work. There isn't anything I wouldn't do for him to give him the perfection that we both want."

This frustration over recognition for Richard, and her reluctance to accept that, as Richard says, the starring role was hers, never left Karen.

To add to these complexities, Karen's romances by her midtwenties were not as significant to her as they were to her partners. And though she knew the quality of her voice, her low personal self-esteem was underscored by her belief that she was not pretty enough to be a star. This was absurd. Karen was attractive and carried her own vivacity. But jibes from the media did not help her.

She had become supremely confident about her singing. Though she would never boast about it (an endearing characteristic), she knew her intonation was perfect, and her understanding of the lyrics and shape of a song was always immaculate. Her keen musicianship was epitomized by her praise, in the studio, for a good arrangement; she took an interest in Richard's scoring and individual instrumentalists' contribution that was unique for a singing star.

Yet as she looked around at her friends, notably Olivia Newton-John who had progressed to movie stardom in *Grease,* Karen bemoaned to such close friends her own lack of beauty. Those sparkling brown eyes that seemed to conceal a tear, that visibly healthy hair, that strong bone structure, made for a striking young woman. But she felt that in her role as a singer, she was somehow lacking something. Those who knew Karen loved her affectionate personality, her wit, loyalty, strength of character.

Yet it seemed that even with the monumental gift of that superb voice and a career that soared so high, something troubled her and she carried a self-imposed handicap of what *she* considered an inadequate appearance. This problem was illogical; many of the great female singers she admired were just that and were certainly not slaves to the mirror. But this was California in the 1970s, and Karen felt that to be a modern young woman, it was a requirement to be slim and beautiful, talented and assertive, intelligent and independent. In her opinion she held only the last four cards. On the road, her self-effacement and clear vulnerability proved attractive to many in the band. Tony Peluso warmed to her and took her to dinner occasionally, but theirs remained a casual friendship. John Bettis says that once their success began, nobody could be around Karen for any length of time without feeling real affection for her. He remembers attending a concert in New Jersey and, standing in the wings, thinking romantically about her before stopping himself quickly with the reproving thought: "My God, this is bizarre! She's like my sister! What am I thinking?"

Karen was, believes Bettis, bred to be much more of her father's child emotionally—"steadfast, enduring, warm at the core. Richard and his mom are more alike." Disagreeing, Richard says (and Agnes agrees): "I am my father's son, other than with my hot temper, which I got from my mother. But my general demeanour, my love of cars, my love of music, my draggy voice, and the way I will hold things inside me all came from my father. Karen was more like my mother in that if something was bothering her, she would not stew. Mom confronts the problem right away, as Karen used to. With me, to avoid a confrontation, I will simmer and then finally blow. And that's how my dad was. But Karen and I both enjoyed games a lot—cards, bowling, charades, which our parents did not. So we were not identical to either parent. She was, though, more aligned with Mom, I with Dad."

According to Bettis, Karen was better able than Richard to make friends and in that respect was unlike her mother. But on the road, as he points out, there were so few friends to make.

Because she was rich, she felt it essential to eventually find a man whose stature and success matched hers and Richard's. Agnes emphasized to her that she should not accept as permanent any romance born of expediency.

So although she felt warmth for Jerry Luby ("The happiest I ever saw her; she seemed to be enthralled with him," says cousin Joanie), and though she had genuine affection for David Alley, Gary Sims, and, more platonically, Tony Peluso, Karen knew she would probably eventually look outside the Carpenters circle for her man. She had an eye for the handsome Herb Alpert, but he was married. Of her dates with members of the touring team, Maria Galeazzi remarks: "Karen liked David Alley because he was *there*. But it wasn't like: WOW. He was somebody to talk to. It was a convenience, and she should have had more conveniences"—a view echoed by several observers. "In the light of what happened, I wish she *had* ended up with a Gary or a David," Richard reflects.

Ken Black, an employee of the Carpenters' company Morsound, had a crush on her but was too shy to pursue her; she seemed to him too headstrong to be approachable by him even though he believed the real Karen preferred his level of "normality" to the status-conscious man she evidently had cast for herself.

While Karen "hammered on" to David Alley, as he remembers, about Richard's perceived "terrible choice" in women, she ended their relationship abruptly. Though he was devastated, he had the consolation of remaining particularly close to her in his role as Richard and Karen's personal assistant. (Karen was too caring to consider ejecting him from the Carpenters staff.) And their "heart connection" never ended; like so many whom she touched, Alley would never forfeit his absolute love for Karen, unrequited though it seemed to be. He continued to send her red roses on special days. A strong mutual affection remained. "I never quite fully understood that," Alley says.

She was not yet looking for a potential marriage partner. Her life, like her brother's, was frantic in the studio and on the road. "Yep, one of us is going to get married some day. It'll probably be during a rehearsal," Karen joked to me. And networking with her wide circle of friends was a pleasure for her. In her midtwenties and enjoying meteoric success, she had no compelling reason to be contemplating marriage. She seemed content around this time to enjoy occasional dates.

Her next was an Englishman. In 1973 the songwriter Nicky Chinn and his partner, Mike Chapman, were named Songwriters of the Year in Britain's prestigious annual Ivor Novello Awards. Their success came from a string of hits for the groups Sweet and Mud. They went on to produce, via the eminent hitmaker Mickie Most, singer Suzi Quatro before clinching an exceptionally fast launch into success with the group Smokie.

As with the Carpenters, these sounds were unfashionable when contrasted with the heavy-duty rock of the day. And like Karen and Richard, Chinn and Chapman became rattled by their critics.

Visiting London while managing the Osmonds, Ed Leffler met the personable Nicky Chinn at the Tramp nightspot. When Chinn flew to California, he joined Ed and Frenda Leffler, with Karen, for dinner.

Chinn had been a major Carpenters fan since 1970. Attending the wedding of his partner, Mike Chapman, in Bristol, England, they were having a drink in a club the night before the wedding when "Close to You" was played … "and we both looked at each other and said: 'What is THAT? What a smash!'" It began Chinn's lifelong admiration for their music, for Karen's voice and Richard's skills.

In Los Angeles, Nicky and Karen hit it off. They met frequently for lunch at the Polo Lounge of the Beverly Hills Hotel where he stayed; he went to Downey for parties; they dated frequently for dinner, and he called her often from London. Two years older than Karen, he found her "very warm, extremely funny with a great self-deprecating humour, wonderful company, and with a smile that just radiated her face." Though he had romantic aspirations, their friendship panned out as platonic.

Whether they were serious relationships or just strong friends as this one, Karen had a mesmerizing effect on men. Many were attracted to her sense of fun, her sincerity and energy; some felt fiercely protective of her. Chinn saw her as not very strong physically but with a soft, vulnerable side that he now feels, with the benefit of hindsight, hid deeper problems than anyone around her could hope to uncork.

One aspect of her self-perception slightly disturbed Chinn: she seemed mildly dissatisfied with all her work. "I'd say, 'That's a great record, Karen, congratulations'—and she'd say, 'Oh yeah, it's a hit, but maybe I could have done it better.'"

This might seem to be not merely false modesty but a reflection of poor self-worth. But at least two eminent figures I interviewed, from the arts and medicine, offered a less superficial interpretation. Henry Mancini says her voice was "the manifestation of everything within her. Maybe if she had more self-esteem, it wouldn't have been the same voice," a profound observation from a master musician. And Dr. Joel Yager adds to the theme: "A great artist has an internal sense of what greatness is, and isn't going to simply accept your opinion about what's great. It may be that she was better than us at determining what's good—for her."

No matter how much praise her voice attracted or how successful the Carpenters became, her image of herself as strangely inadequate seemed to remain. She was therefore shattered by personal criticism. In Chicago's *Sun-Times* on July 24, 1972, reviewer Dick Saunders wrote positively about their four shows at the city's Arie Crown Theater, but there was a sideswipe at Karen's appearance. "Take hairdo's," he wrote. "Karen, who never really had one before, has added a few curls and looks positively done up. Not gorgeous, but at least she's trying . . . . Karen may look like the girl next door you'd never peek over the fence at, but she really can sing." The writer's praise for "the best sounding pop show I'd heard anywhere . . . I wouldn't have missed it for the world," was lost on Karen in that gratuitous tilt at her look. And for the ten years that followed, such remarks chipped away at her self-image.

She could not handle such taunts—unlike Richard, who became used to tossing aside remarks about his corpulence at one stage, or jibes that he was "gangling and awkward" ("which I am," he laughs now).

Although she ate normally when she stepped out with Nicky Chinn, he saw the beginnings of her obsession about her body shape. "She would go on about her exercises, and I knew she had that electric vibrating belt that was supposed to tone up the butts and thighs. It didn't strike me as anything more than another woman concerned about her shape. I'd say, 'You don't need to lose weight'—but she did talk about it a great deal. And Karen was a very determined lady."

Artists of her calibre and achievement often demonstrate brazen assertiveness and a cockiness, but Karen's self-image tipped the scales for her too far in the opposite direction. An example came when she went to dinner with Nicky Chinn at Le Restaurant, on Melrose Place in Los Angeles. As they were leaving through the pretty restaurant's tree-lined open-air courtyard, John Lennon was walking toward them. As he recognized Karen, he stopped and said to her, "I just want to tell you, love, that I think you've got a fabulous voice"—and then he walked on, having not even introduced himself.

Karen was like a little girl bowled over. As she and Nicky walked toward his car, she was breathless with excitement. "Did you *hear* what he said? *John Lennon!*" She had always loved the Beatles and found it hard to accept such a compliment from one of them. "It was so nice to see someone as big as Karen be so affected by such praise," Chinn reflects. "Lots of stars get blasé, don't give a damn, and wouldn't care much about someone even like Lennon taking the time to say that. Her warmth, innocence, and genuine reaction was amazing."

Emphasizing Karen's modesty, Richard remembers her telling him that she had met Barbra Streisand. "Karen was excited because Streisand had told her she had a 'marvelous instrument.' I said to Karen: 'Well, of *course* Streisand's gonna say that! Streisand has ears!' Karen really admired Streisand, but I asked her why she was getting so excited. Karen was every bit the singer Streisand is. Just a different style. But I don't think Karen realized how phenomenally talented she was. I said to her: 'Don't you understand, you are one of the greatest female vocalists who ever lived, who ever will live? You're every bit as good as Streisand!'"

He does not think Karen ever came to terms with her own level as one of the great singers. Exploring the reasons, he says: "Maybe it's because we didn't tough it out in New York; maybe we were sheltered and then suddenly burst into the big time. As seasoned and as worldly as she became, knowing how to phone this person and that, when it came to running into Johnny Carson or Lennon or Streisand, she seemed sometimes like a teenager *aspiring* to greatness, whereas in fact she was recognized not only as great but world famous. We were behind all these folks chronologically—and suddenly we were meeting artists we'd looked up to. And working with them! Here was Burt Bacharach asking us to open his show; here was Hank Mancini coming by to pitch us a song. And they were unabashed fans. It happened so very quickly, and it may be something that we never got over."

The blips in Karen and Richard's relationship continued to be centered on their choice of partners. Inheriting her mother's possessiveness and watchful eye over Richard, Karen would shrug her shoulders disdainfully or sometimes speak out to their inner circle about what she described as Richard's "dumb" choice of women. Whenever he had a date, Karen would want to know as much as possible about the woman (if she knew nothing of her); and if she did know her, she was always judgmental. Either the woman was beneath Richard's class, or they were plainly unsuited for each other, or she would pick on something the woman had said or done that rendered her unthinkable as his permanent partner.

Sometimes, he admits, his mistakes were politically incorrect. When Sandy Holland, a slim, pretty redhead with long flowing hair, was recruited from a beauty salon to succeed Maria as Karen's hairdresser, Richard decided to bide his time because of the fracas over her predecessor. But eventually he dated Sandy, taking her to formal dates like dinner or the movies. Karen could scarcely believe the incestuousness within the Carpenters unit, but she was hardly blameless for its profusion. Just as Maria had incurred Karen's wrath, so did Sandy. Sharp remarks were exchanged; by now, Karen was experienced at dealing head-on with "staff problems." A rerun of the tension over Maria was not going to be tolerated.

Sandy deduced that if she wanted to keep her job as Karen's assistant, the dating must cease. Less fiery than Maria, more easily persuaded, she capitulated and stayed happily in the job for seven years.

Even before their return from the stormy trip to Acapulco, Richard wanted independence. "We'd stayed at Newville Avenue with our parents mostly to keep my mother happy," he says.

"Mom is definitely possessive and overly protective, and I guess we didn't want to create tension and conflict. Between the studio and the road, we weren't home that much anyway, so we figured we'd stay there for a while." He was twenty-six, Karen twenty-three, ages by which many have left the parental umbrella. But the Carpenter mother, father, brother, and sister were a tight and harmonious family, and no generation gap existed. Agnes and Harold were immersed in their children's music and success, delighting in every new record and stories from their concert travels.

But finally in 1974, Karen and Richard felt it was time to leave. "We'd really stayed there longer than we should," Richard says. Their comings and goings were erratic for continued coexistence to work sweetly. And dating was becoming a drag. One night in 1971 Richard had taken a woman home "and we were listening to records and got into a little petting. And Mom opened the door to see how I was! It was definitely not a good situation!"

Richard and Karen bought a stylish, spacious new home for Harold and Agnes at 8341 Lubec Street, in Downey. A mere five-minute drive away from Newville Avenue, this hardly represented the wanderlust. With its lucky, sound-proofed music room where some hit songs had been born, the Newville house was Karen and Richard's preference, and they expected to stay. But their parents loved it so much, they wanted to remain there. Harold was particularly fond of the Japanese-styled garden. So Karen and Richard made the move to Lubec Street.

Soon their new home became the scene of their most bitter confrontations. "Karen wanted to mother me," Richard says. When he went out for the evening, she would ask what time he would be returning. "Maybe by midnight," Richard answered reluctantly. Karen's retort would infuriate him: "Well, try to make it by midnight, or I'll worry." To Richard, that attitude signalled a doomed future in the house together. "It was my mom all over again."

Scenes that followed over Richard's next serious romance would damage their relationship even more.

Over dinner in January 1974, Sherwin Bash's wife, Bobby, casually mentioned that her young daughter, Randy, had returned home after living away. Richard, who had noticed the pert twenty-one-year-old around her father's office and spoken to her casually, perked up at this news. "And," Bobby Bash continued jocularly, "does anybody know a nice Jewish boy for my daughter?" Richard's response over the dinner table was immediate: "Does he have to be Jewish?"

The next day, Bobby told her daughter that she might get a call from Richard. Randy was excited. When "Close to You" hit, she had been in high school, thrilled that her father had become their manager. She disliked hard rock, adored the Carpenters' strong melodies, and their tapes boomed from her car stereo at all times. She was a true fan.

Within two days, their first evening together was set. On the phone to Sherwin Bash that afternoon, Karen passed Richard a message: "Randy wants you to collect her in your Ferrari." Even though it was yet another romance blooming "within the family," Karen was very fond of Randy and seemed pleased they were getting together. Richard wasn't keen on taking the Ferrari; it had a problem gear shift and was always breaking down. He would have taken the Lincoln but demurred to his date's choice.

Grumbling about it as he arrived at her home in Beverly Hills, Richard pointed to the Ferrari. "So there, I brought it for you." Randy was baffled. She had passed no such message about a car to him, she said.

After dinner at La Scala in Beverly Hills, they went to see the Woody Allen movie *Sleeper*.

Effervescent and thoughtful, Randy had qualities Richard sought, while she found him a stimulating conversationalist. They hit it off instantly and met again two nights later. From then on they were together almost every night, and when they could not meet, they phoned.

So began the most traumatic love affair in their lives. Randy Bash quickly became the victim of a nuclear family. She was vilified, ostracized, banished into the wilderness by Karen and Agnes. "At first, Karen had no problem," Richard says, "but soon, as with every girl I dated, it developed into one." He was harangued by Agnes and Karen almost every day to drop her. With determination laced with anger, Randy and Richard were to stay together for an intense eighteen-month affair. But the pressure about to bear down on them both was sheer hell.

"Within about three weeks of our going out," Randy says, "Richard told me his mother disliked me." She had done something of which Agnes disapproved. "You've gotta be kidding?" Randy queried Richard. No, Richard replied, his mother was not one to mince words or leave people confused.

Soon it was clear to Richard that Karen would have nothing to do with his new girlfriend, either. And while Agnes's condemnation was difficult enough, she was at least back in Downey; Karen was his sister and partner, with him most hours of the day, on the road and in the studio. And Randy was now by Richard's side day and night, too.

Following her mother's lead, Karen quickly denounced Randy to Richard as unsuitable. It didn't stop there. As Randy joined the Carpenters' European tour in February, Karen snubbed her every step of the way: backstage, in hotels, in cars. What Randy hoped might break some ice—that the two women might go shopping, have lunch, and be pals when surrounded by the Carpenters' male entourage—proved a daydream. Karen's active dislike became plain. "Hello" and "Good night" was about all she could bring herself to intone to her brother's girlfriend as the tour proceeded through Britain, Scandinavia, and Germany.

"I'd have had to be a total idiot not to know I wasn't liked," Randy says. "Karen just didn't *want* to like me. I was in the way. If Karen had been seeing someone at that time, she probably wouldn't have felt as threatened. Richard and Karen were so close to each other, I don't think either really wanted someone in the middle."

Richard says Randy's view of the situation is wrong in his case. "I *certainly* wanted someone in the middle—that's why I moved Randy into Lubec Street!" he declares. "*Karen* didn't want anyone in the middle! For me, by that point, it was too stifling. We spent all that time in the recording studios and on the road. I really wanted to live by myself, please myself away from work. I didn't want to live at home, either. But Randy really did suffer from Karen's attitude toward her. It was rough."

Karen's fury reached a crescendo when Richard moved Randy into their house. "I'm not moving all my belongings from Newville until that girl has gone," Karen shouted. When she wanted something important to her and it wasn't easy to get, Karen had a raging determination. Bad enough, she told Richard, that he continued to see "that girl," but to expect his sister to tolerate her under the same roof was appalling. "Here I was, between two women," he says.

He faced little alternative, he says. Randy had to go after a week. "He told me they'd had one of their meetings," she remembers. "What it came down to was: this was their house. So I moved out. But I was there almost every night afterward so it made little difference." Karen had kept on making it plain she did not wish to wake up in her own home and find Randy in residence. Relations between Karen and Richard were at an all-time low.

Their career, meanwhile, continued its parallel course of public acclaim and media resistance. In Britain, where they rapidly secured a loyal and lasting audience, young writers continued to carp that they were an irrelevance, primarily because they were not in the vanguard of rock 'n' roll rebellion. That feeling permeated from the media back to the record company, whose press officers would often feign embarrassment at having to supervise their tour. Charged with the task of making the Carpenters appear hip in the eyes of young critics, press officers mumbled, out of authority's earshot, that this act was hugely embarrassing for A&M's image. The prospect of having to phone reporters and ask them to meet Karen or Richard was daunting, since it was often met with derisive laughter. If a writer admitted a fancy for Carpenters music, he would be scorned, disqualified from the rock 'n' roll club. Bruce Springsteen, Lou Reed, David Bowie—these were the badges of identity to be worn in the early and mid-1970s.

When A&M's press officers complained about the difficulty of marketing the Carpenters, the stiff reply from all the executives was a repetition of their cynical boss from the moment the group had been launched. It was hammered across to the entire staff that the Carpenters paid their salaries.

"There wasn't a great deal of charisma or rock 'n' roll credibility in the Carpenters," admits Brian Southall, one former A&M press officer who toured Britain with them. But when he and his colleagues saw Jerry Moss and others from the United States flying in just to see them on tour, they thought, "God, these people really *are* important."

Karen often shocked with her forcefulness. After a charity show at London's Talk of the Town nightspot on February 24, 1974, near the end of the tour, the band was more spontaneous and relaxed in attitude than they had been in previous concerts over a three-week period. Their stage presence was less regimented, and they missed cues. Karen was furious, berating them on and off stage for what she considered unprofessional behaviour. There was no point in their defence that on this final night in Britain they were allowed to be a little looser. The audience for a charity show had paid the same entrance money as any other, she rasped, and should get the same standard Carpenters performance.

British writers took the view that the pair who made the music were as dull as the music itself. And there were even gratuitous sideswipes at people in their entourage who caught their eye. Randy Bash was described as "resembling nothing more than a dormouse, albeit an attractive dormouse," and her name was the subject of leering jibes. Even the way Sherwin Bash replaced his handkerchief in his pocket after blowing his nose was scorned.

And then there was the music. Reviled as the antithesis of the rock ethos that formed the backdrop of 1970s culture, it was dismissed as "treacle," "drippy easy listening," or even "schlock music."[1]

Inside A&M, staff were shell-shocked at having to justify an act so universally mocked but so central to the record company's economy. In Los Angeles, dealing with requests for interviews was a weeding operation for Doug Haverty and his publicity department colleagues. Richard and Karen's very ordinariness intrigued writers from around the world more accustomed to reporting on exhibitionistic rock stars. A&M flew in writers to meet this strangely normal brother and sister who had succeeded with such a

---

1. By the mid-1980s and particularly at the start of the 1990s, revisionist thinking finally recognized the Carpenters as a quality pop sound. The absurd comparisons with rock were jettisoned in favour of a general admission of Karen's superior voice and Richard's arranging skills. As their music gave them a renaissance with new young fans around the world, there was grudging concession that if the Carpenters' personalities and music were alien two decades earlier, time had been kind to their endurance. In London's *Daily Telegraph*, Chris Heath wrote: "When punk rock appeared and its instigators laid into the old rock and pop gentry, they didn't even bother to criticise the Carpenters. Everybody already knew they were awful . . . to have had a sneaking admiration for the Carpenters has had to be one's darkest secret."

Writing in the *New York Times* on November 3, 1991, Rob Hoerburger, describing the Carpenters, said: "They always dressed as if they were going to church, and they sang sticky songs about love (but never sex). Worst of all, parents loved their music." Hoerburger conceded, though, that twenty years later "the Carpenters acquire something resembling depth—or at least conviction." Noting "similarities" between "We've Only Just Begun" and Barbra Streisand's 1973 hit "The Way We Were," he added that if Karen's illness has legitimized her among the hip, "the sound and image that remain indelible belong to the Karen and Richard of the early 1970s, America's most defiant squares."

traditional musical sound in the age of decibel rock. And some were shocked to find a pair of anti-stars who bought their clothes at department stores, spoke affectionately of their parents, enjoyed hamburgers and shakes, and went bowling. The rock star characteristics—drugs, groupies, loud mouths, and hedonism—were not to be found. Writers looking for their "hidden secret" went away dissatisfied and contented themselves by attacking their music.

With the British tabloid press looking for a scandal, the A&M policy was ultracautious. Nothing was allowed to be officially stated that might puncture their wholesome image, which was seen as a major asset. No matter how much Richard and Karen came on as normal, the press department policy was unequivocal: if the Carpenters were perceived as bland, then they should be projected as bland, because they sold millions of albums and concert tickets and nothing should be done to rock that boat!

It would have been more real, Brian Southall says, to have projected them as "straight" people who dated, who lost their tempers with each other, and who had the emotions of those who made up their audience. Richard says he would have preferred that image of normality to have been advanced. But Southall insists that he was told to erect a wall of candy floss around them in terms of media projection. Consequently, the bland perception of them remained, and any rumours that grew were left unchecked.

As for their image, which had become cast in stone by mid-1974 as "squeaky," "smiley," and "saccharine," and the frequent jibe that they looked like a couple of dummies, Richard reflects: "I was so sick of this that I probably became too sensitive about it. For our picture in *Rolling Stone,* they said that Annie Leibovitz, the photographer, had *not* asked Richard to smile . . . and I didn't!" The problem was that when he didn't smile, he tended to look stern, perhaps even angry. It was an acute case of "no win."

Describing their projection in Britain, Brian Southall reflects with regret: "This was a superficial job of press relations. On tour, we invited twenty journalists to a conference, and the Carpenters sat in front of them and said how good it was to be in Manchester or Nottingham. Richard's life was crafting songs, and he would talk at great length about what project was coming next. I got the feeling that Karen was not much more than the messenger."

In America their press agent Paul Bloch at Rogers and Cowan experienced a more political Karen, forever anxious to ensure that writers and critics recognized her brother as much as her. "Without Richard there is no Carpenter sound," she continually told Bloch to emphasize to magazines, radio, and television people.

"I was wary of Karen," says Southall. "You knew this woman could bite your head off for no apparent reason. She surrounded herself with this aura of being a person who demanded perfection and anything else was not acceptable. And if anything did go wrong, it was raised and dealt with immediately by her. Sherwin Bash spent a lot of time pulling her back from brinkmanship. While we were on tour, the word that went around was that if you were going to cross anyone, don't let it be Karen. She would actually give you a serious mouthful."

At the end of their British tour, though, Richard and Karen annihilated their antiseptic image. They sent to six key record company executives a weird parting gift. Inside a velvet box was a gold ring, inscribed on one side with the word *love* and on the other *fuck*. Everyone chortled at the incongruity of such a present from the "squeaky clean duo."

Karen's tetchiness when anything went even mildly wrong on stage sometimes irritated the band, too. If Tony Peluso or Doug Strawn were caught sharing a joke between songs and Karen saw them, she would castigate them later. For in this show, which ran precisely to the same pattern night after night, with every announcement, pause, and note intended to be the same, nothing was allowed to interfere with its formula. At A&M there were knowing smiles about the realization that few people in the entertainment industry rang to ask for free tickets to see a Carpenters show; there was no "buzz" about them. "If anyone in the business did ring up for tickets, they quickly added that it was for their parents," said one A&M staffer. There was a stigma in even being associated with admiration for them.

As staunch Beatles fans for ten years, Richard and Karen were flattered to be invited in the spring of 1974 to meet Paul McCartney. During their British concert tour word reached Karen and Richard as they arrived in Manchester for their show that Paul was in nearby Stockport, working in Strawberry Studios on an album called *McGear* by his brother Michael.

It was a heady time for the Carpenters, whose album compilation of their hit singles was in the midst of a sixteen-week hold on

the number-one position in the British charts.[2] *Now and Then* was
all over the nation's airwaves at this time, also, and their concerts
drew excellent responses from audiences who would stay uniquely
loyal to the Carpenters long after Karen's passing.

For Richard, the prospect of a handshake with McCartney,
whose work had so inspired him, was warming. As they entered
the studio, Paul greeted them by singing the chorus line to "Top
of the World." He says now, "It was nice to put a face to the
voices."

Michael McCartney recalls Richard and Karen "sitting quietly
in the corner, watching Paul produce. They were obviously Beatle
children and seemed overawed to be in his presence." As much as
the Carpenters were Beatles fans, the McCartney brothers were
admirers of the sister and brother. Had they not been recording a
rock 'n' roll tempo track, "the best female voice in the world,
melodic, tuneful, distinctive," as they rated her, would have been
invited to guest on the album.

It was hardly a summit meeting, more a brief social exchange,
yet there was an unspoken bond. Paul, Richard, and Karen were all
lovers of rock 'n' roll, but they did not operate rigidly inside the
rock framework. By writing beautiful popular songs that were outside the category of rock, they had all faced flak from the critics.
Getting mauled while writing hit love songs was a topic Paul and
the Carpenters had in common, and they talked a little about that,
shrugging their shoulders.

Paul, who was in the throes of re-forming Wings, reflects:
"The essence of why I loved them was Karen. The sheer quality—
musically it was a heck of a voice—was so impressive. And there
were those songs. . . . I knew they were mates with Henry
Mancini, too, so musically that said a lot for them.

"They had nice songs like 'We've Only Just Begun' and 'Close
to You,' and they sang them well. And there's a part of me that
says you don't need to do any more."

Richard had with him a copy of the current Wings album *Band*

---

2. In its astonishing sixteen-week grip on the top position in the best-selling British album
charts compiled by the *Melody Maker,* the Carpenters' *The Singles 1969–1973* reached the top on
February 9 and was deposed on June 1 by Rick Wakeman's album *Journey to the Centre of the
Earth.* Other hot albums around at this time were Elton John's *Goodbye Yellow Brick Road* and
Mike Oldfield's *Tubular Bells.*

on the Run. Paul's autographed dedication on it struck a note of tomfoolery: "To Dickie, from a chum," he signed.

The Beatles were high on Karen's list of favourites; Barbra Streisand was "the best" in her field, she said. But she disliked the Rolling Stones: "Too raucous, not enough melody."

Paul McCartney, pondering the tragedy that was about to engulf the Carpenters soon after he met them, is puzzled. "I never thought Karen was fat."

Touring around Europe, Randy Bash felt uncomfortable sharing a hotel room with Richard while his sister was usually next door, alone. After a while, Randy asked the touring crew to please put Richard's room on a separate floor from Karen's. When this happened, Karen was apoplectic with rage: the working pattern of her life was being changed by that girl, who had no right to interfere! "It was hard enough to have a relationship with someone who's attached to the hip to his sister; this was not a normal brother-sister relationship," Randy says.

"They were together, working, twenty-four hours a day and used to being alone until each one got to the point where they were old enough to find a partner." But even when that day appeared to have arrived, "neither was ever going to find the perfect person whom the other would love and embrace into their family. I hung in there because I really, really liked Richard and just thought: this is *it*. This is the guy for me. But it was hard, really hard. And it was hard on him because he was in the middle of it."

He gave her small consolation, assuring her that the animosity of his mother and his sister wasn't directed at her individually but at almost any woman he might choose. "Don't take it personally; it isn't you," Richard would say. Randy adds: "It was always going to be that way. Between Karen and her mother, I didn't stand a chance."

Forcing Richard to make a decision, Agnes and Karen piled on extraordinary pressure. Most days, Richard would get a phone call from Karen—when she knew he was with Randy—that left Randy in no doubt that she was being discussed negatively. Karen would clearly be saying she had an interesting woman for Richard to meet; Richard replied, irritated, that he "did not want to discuss that now." Often, he would go to see Randy after what he called "one of those meetings" with his mother and sister at which he had yet again been urged to ditch her. When he refused, there had been black moods. Initially, Randy's response was to inwardly reciprocate the hatred to the two Carpenter women who had shown her the door. But as time wore on, Randy grew to consider her boyfriend and his sister as "really unhappy people." Karen could be charming to interviewers and others, then immediately do a 180-degree turn when she came face-to-face with Randy.

Karen's need for a husband and children was paramount, but in Randy's view, the singer was tied to her brother and they were tied to their family, "and they couldn't get away. I'm really close to my family, but when I want time alone, I take it. I don't think they were capable of doing that. They felt guilty about everything— 'what if we don't do this or that?' They felt so *controlled*."

Explaining why there was never a proper discussion between her and Karen, Randy says: "I was intimidated. I wasn't going to be her friend. Richard would tell me what was being said about me, that they really didn't want me around. I don't know that Karen could really dislike me. It wasn't like I was mistreating him.

"And I wasn't a gold digger. My family were not zillionaires, but I wasn't needing anything. I think it's just that they were so close to each other, neither of them wanted someone in the middle."

Since she and Richard never argued, she hung on to the hope that Agnes and Karen would see that "I was really good for him and he really liked me. I wonder how I put up with it. But I was younger, it was a new relationship, and we had a good time which was hard to give up just because the family didn't like me. After a while I realized the family was *it*, and I wasn't going to win."

Independent of spirit, Randy did not attempt to court Karen's friendship. Richard therefore faced a stiff choice—"between his girlfriend, or the three people in his family who were saying 'grrrrrrr' about me every day, and 'she's doing this and that to you.' They thought I influenced every decision he made."

Karen, says Randy, was "silly" about the problem. "Here's someone with her brother, whom he obviously liked, and she couldn't even make an effort to be at least civil! She could have said, 'God, I hate her underneath but I'll *try* ...' But no, she could just about manage 'Good morning' and 'Good night' in the house. So when Richard told me the family wasn't going to like me, I guess maybe I went the other way and said, 'Well screw them, I don't need them.'"

It was a hopeless deadlock. After an agonizing eighteen months which had taken her to Japan as well as Europe, and as his partner across an American tour, Randy told Richard it could not work. And he agreed. "It was very painful for her, really uncomfortable," he reflects. The tension was damaging everyone, and Randy was going to bed every night with shattered nerves. At Los Angeles airport after returning from a Carpenters concert in Baltimore, she and Richard kissed good-bye. As he got into his family's car and she into hers, she knew that was symbolically the end. But it was a fire that neither could fully extinguish: their fondness remained. They would meet often in the years ahead to renew their friendship from a safer distance.

At this time, Karen was articulating to friends her definition of her ideal man. Good looks were a prerequisite, but professional success was crucial, she stipulated repeatedly—because that often came with "urban awareness," which she preferred to the more casual, easygoing types. New York–style confidence in a man attracted her. She dated briefly the successful U.S. TV actor Mark Harmon, later to become a screen sex symbol. Above all else, her man had to be strong in word and deed as well as taking an interest in her career and having a successful one of his own.

"Karen may have seemed simple and homey, but one side of her wasn't," declares Richard, underscoring her sometimes complex makeup. "At heart she, like I, was a middle-class person who enjoyed working but at the end of the day wanted to plop down and watch television with a dinner on a tray."

Another side of her enjoyed sophistication. A problem with several dates, she told her brother, was that "when we got to the restaurant, he didn't seem to take charge." And then, when the maître d' often recognized her, this would detract from her date's need to be nominally "leading" her through the evening. Here was a perfect example of her contradictory nature, for she wanted it both ways. While she loved the recognition, she expected her man to come to terms with it and even to triumph over her high profile.

"She was so bullheaded on certain things," Richard says, "that if someone took charge and she didn't agree with his doing so, it wouldn't work anyway because she would, sure as hell, argue with his decision. She didn't know what the hell she wanted. She really didn't. She wanted it both ways."

Frustrated in love, she turned inward, toward herself.

*   *   *

Slimming and health foods were becoming fashionable in the early 1970s, particularly in image-conscious California. So was the cachet of having a trainer visit private houses to supervise exercises. When Karen saw pictures of herself in concert in Lake Tahoe in August 1973 she was appalled. An unflattering dress revealed her paunch, and she hired a "workout guru" to visit her home. She bought a "hip cycle" and lay on her bed with it every morning and took it on tour. Her "guru" advised her to go on a high carbohydrate intake, and she eliminated most of the known calorie-packed foods from her diet, particularly ice cream which she loved.

None of her friends considered there was anything unusual about a young woman keeping herself in shape, but Karen was obsessive about doing everything right to achieve results. Evelyn Wallace remembers seeing her pedaling furiously, lying on her bed. Combined with her irregular eating and the energy needed for her work as recordings and touring continued apace, it didn't seem right.

Then something happened to truly frighten her. As she stepped up her exercises, instead of losing weight she became muscular. "She definitely began to bulk up. She wasn't too heavy," Richard says, "but the weight was coming on her." This threw her into a muddle and could have been the chrysalis of her problem.

She stopped most of the exercises, which she believed to be too muscle-building, and began what she considered to be a normal diet, nothing remarkable or even noticeable by others. It was just sensible enough, she assured Richard, to shed a few pounds which was necessary. With the benefit of hindsight, he now thinks that the "bulking up" caused by the exercises might have been the turning point that intensified her decision to maintain a strict check on her weight.

On November 13, 1973, the Carpenters guested on Bob Hope's TV special. When Karen saw the video of the show soon afterwards, she remarked to Richard about her fleshy arms and thick butt. Self-consciously unhappy about how she appeared, she assured him she "intended to do something about it." He agreed that she looked heavier than she had. The conversation passed as insignificant.

Despite the myriad pressures on her body through travel,

erratic eating, her appetite for junk food, and a punishing work schedule, Karen had maintained her weight of a 120 pounds from the summer of 1967 all the way through to early 1973.

Nobody can be certain of exactly when her anorexic habits took root, Richard insists—chiefly because Karen had always been conscious about her weight. She remarked often on how much she hated her "hourglass" figure.

As far back as 1970, during their first visit to Japan, when she was certainly not dieting, she had taken with her a rubber contraption to puff up and wrap around her problematic hips. "This was supposed to make her sweat, and we both laughed at this funny-looking weight reducer," Richard says. "She was so concerned about keeping track of her weight, all the time, so the start of her big problem kinda passed us by."

As they scored two more hit singles, "I Won't Last a Day without You" and "Please Mr. Postman," and as they toured extensively, the band noticed that, for the first time, Karen was absent from the meals they usually shared, informally, in hotels. The pounds began to drop away, her arms and buttocks became less fleshy, and she seemed cheered by this, talking about it casually to the band. They all felt it was normal dieting. The year 1974 set no alarm bells ringing, as Karen was seen as one of the many health-aware young women—and since she had a historic reason for weight watching, why should anyone have been surprised? Photographed for the cover of *Rolling Stone* magazine on May 22, 1974, wearing a tank top, a beret, and the upbeat expression that was part of her trademark appeal, she looked radiantly happy and healthy.

It was at a family dinner at Newville Avenue to celebrate Richard's birthday in 1974 that the Carpenter family first noticed her disinterest in eating. A sumptuous feast had been arranged, but no one could miss the amount of food Karen placed on her plate: the tiniest portion of shrimp and salad. "If I'd been on a diet that day, I could not have resisted that food, but she did," says Evelyn Wallace, the Carpenters' personal assistant, who sat near her.

The young woman who loved desserts rejected all the goodies on display that evening. Shortly after that, Karen began serious dieting, switching to Sweet 'n' Low sugar substitute, sugar-free jelly, and having the tiniest scoop of ice cream from the fridge when the craving overtook her. Soon she introduced into the house food tailored to her diet, such as noodle or vegetable soup cubes which she diluted in a cup. They were not very tasty at best. When Karen cut them in half and then added extra water to the recommended amount, they must have carried zero nutrition as well as tastelessness. Agnes, Harold, and Richard considered it simply a female figure-watching trait. By now, she had abandoned her high-neck stage dresses for more sophisticated clothes. Her first choice was a red satin, sleeveless, low-neck dress, which contoured a well-shaped, not particularly bulky, frame. And her new look brought hundreds of complimentary fan letters, which included many proposals of marriage. Several men sent her diamond rings, which she returned.

Within months of that dinner, she had plunged into what Richard believes was the period marking the start of the decline that was to prove deadly. Its seriousness eluded them all, for when she walked into the A&M studio in the autumn of 1974, her attractiveness caught everyone's eye. Gary Sims recalls, "All of the people in the studio one night said how great she looked, from the engineers to Richard, to the whole band."

She was smiling triumphantly as if to say she had won an important battle, but she implied in a few throwaway remarks to the players that it wasn't over yet. "We all said, 'But you don't *need* to lose any more, Karen!'" Sims remembers. If the actual beginning of Karen's descent is difficult to pinpoint for certain, Richard remembers vividly one conversation that reflected her determination to continue losing weight, no matter what he or anyone advised her.

In early 1975, as they continued studio work on the album that would become *Horizon,* they adjourned together for dinner, as they did so often, to a local favourite, Au Petite Café on Vine Street, Hollywood.

"I remember saying to her how good she looked. She had dropped some weight, and she looked just perfect. She said thanks, and she was going to lose a few more pounds. I asked her what her weight was, and she replied, '115 pounds.' I said, 'Why do you want to lose more when you look fine just now?'

"'I want to get to 105,' Karen said." Richard told her he felt that would be too low. There was no need for him to be alarmed, as she was at that stage in fine shape. The conversation passed on, but from that moment she seemed to him and to her family and friends to become obsessed about dieting.

"She had a thin waist, broad shoulders, and some hips, but Karen wanted to be straight up and down," he says. In the months that followed, as he saw his sister begin her baffling slide, his frustration surfaced. First he tried gentle persuasion.

As she ordered small salad portions in restaurants and pushed most of her food to the side of her plate, he told her so many times: "Karen, you're never going to have this up-and-down figure. You've got a classic woman's figure, and you look fine. And why don't you think of everything else you have—a great brain, phenomenal talent, and things that people would give their eye teeth to possess. A good family, fame, wealth, and your voice. You're good to look at, you know."

She ignored him. He felt as if he might as well have been advising an alcoholic not to have another drink. As the pounds continued to drop away during 1975, the first theory that Karen's problem might be a virtually unheard-of disease was voiced by Evelyn Wallace. Reading a magazine article about a twelve-year-old girl who was dieting rigidly with something called anorexia nervosa, she said to Agnes, "I'll bet you anything in the world that this is what Karen has." Agnes read the article but was puzzled. The phrase alone was difficult for a layman to absorb or understand. To her, Karen was simply dieting too much.

In the light of what happened some ten years later, it is easy to see now that Karen's simmering problems (assuming they were present) would have been dwarfed by the Carpenters' frenetic activities. And she was a willing, energetic part of their crazy schedule. One of the most popular acts in music in the world in the early 1970s, they were at a creative peak at a time when her difficulties may have been beginning. They were as passionate about making music and fuelling their popularity as the business machine around them was to capitalize on their impact.

A bad motorcycle accident that injured Richard in early 1973 had no effect on their rigorous work pattern either. He often rode the streets of Downey, but one Sunday, visiting a motorcycle park to taste freedom from traffic lights, he was in a head-on crash. Thrown to the ground, he sustained a broken left leg, a broken left wrist and a sprained right wrist. In the hospital both wrists and leg were put into casts but his work continued even with a left wrist in plaster for five months.

In Japan, where "Yesterday Once More" had hoisted their popularity to dizzy heights, the Carpenters received a phenomenal reception in 1974 from fans, in scenes that recalled the wild days of Beatlemania. Five thousand fans greeted them at the Tokyo airport as they entered a country that became fanatical about their music (and remains so).

Meanwhile, in the United States and in Britain, the anthology of their hit singles that had entered the charts in 1973 would remain there for two years. Though it was a formidable collection, this seemed a strangely premature release so early in their career. But then, they expected many similar hit collections in the years ahead—and there was no hint of the problems on the horizon that would slow down their output of hits. "That singles collection was intended as volume one," Richard says now. Yet, as it turned out, it was a retrospective that would demonstrate their golden moments.

As their star continued to shine and they broke new ground, Richard realized a solo ambition to play the Warsaw Concerto with Arthur Fiedler and the Boston Pops as part of a televised Carpenters appearance with the famed orchestra.

Back at home, Richard gradually began what would develop into a lifelong hobby, collecting rare cars of the 1950s and 1960s. Karen consolidated her collection of stuffed animals, which she had loved since her teenage years. Small animals crowded the glass shelves in the corner of her bedroom at Newville Avenue. A huge purple elephant reached higher than the windowsill, and a five-foot-high Snoopy sat on her king-sized bed. She often went looking for new Mickey Mouse items at an antique shop in Disneyland. There she bought a rocking horse and other items with the Mickey insignia: cookie jar, hot-water bottle, camera, electric toothbrush, records, and one of the first watches. Karen rarely read books, and together with needlepoint, Mickey Mouse was one of her fondest diversions.

You never smile on stage!

—KAREN TO RICHARD, ON HIS SERIOUS PERSONALITY

How can I smile when you look like that?

—RICHARD TO KAREN, ON HER SKELETAL FIGURE

Despite the glorious eruption of her career, those around Karen sensed that she was lacking something or someone. She told friends that her music, brilliantly steered by her brother, was on course for a lifetime's success. But still she gave off to the band and many of her friends a sense of loneliness.

Her suffocating supervision of Richard, her interference in his romances, seemed to point up her own neediness all too clearly. Her dates thus far had been just about that. Perhaps if she found a permanent partner of her own, she would be able to shed the matriarchal role she had adopted with her brother.

As events unfolded and she acquired a serious boyfriend and then a husband, that theory was squashed. Because Karen's mothering of Richard remained. She believed that his genius deserved nothing less than her protection; that his callow, non-show-biz personality needed hoisting in the eyes of their contemporaries. And one of her methods of ensuring that Richard's platinum talent and personality were untarnished was to drive a wedge between him and anyone who she believed did not measure up to his standards ("which of course was nobody!" Richard says).

By the time Richard's partnership with Randy Bash was nearing its finale, Karen had met the man who many believed was perfect from every perspective, and Karen's detailed requirements meant that there were many perspectives.

Terry Ellis seemed correct from every angle for the tender but tough singer.

They met in February 1975 under the aegis of Frenda and Ed Leffler, who had worked alongside Sherwin Bash as part of the

Carpenters' management team. The Lefflers, a sociable Beverly Hills couple, invited Terry to dinner with Karen. It would be interesting, they told her, to meet one of Britain's most prominent personalities in the record industry.

Tall, fair-haired, and confident, Ellis had qualities that Karen found immensely attractive. Highly articulate and intelligent, he was a forceful and opinionated Leo, knew the record industry intuitively, and was well respected.

He was a young meteor of the record world. After studying geology at Newcastle University in England, he had launched with a friend, Chris Wright, a world-beating London-based independent record company which took its name, Chrysalis, from theirs. As well as personally managing the leading rock band Jethro Tull, Ellis planned the record careers of other successful artists including Procol Harum, Leo Sayer, and Ten Years After. His octopus-like organization also promoted concerts for Roxy Music, Cat Stevens, Van Morrison, Yes, and Johnny Cash.[1]

A millionaire at thirty-two, Ellis was living in California to mastermind the expansion of his company.

Soon after that first dinner alongside the Lefflers, Terry and Karen were dating and were considered the ideal couple. By contrast with her attitude toward his recent girlfriend, Richard immediately admired his sister's choice and developed a rapport with Ellis.

Terry loved Karen's warmth, the natural qualities so far removed from the show business clique, while she found in him the commanding authority combined with tenderness that she looked for in her man.

It was a love match. Having known them both before their romance, I met them both together at concerts and in restaurants in Los Angeles. Like many others who observed the clear chemistry between them, I believed their future together was certain.

But with Karen's dieting problem surfacing, Ellis was anxious. A gourmet, his idea of a wonderful evening was a four-hour dinner at a fashionable restaurant, preferably French. He pored over wine lists and considered fine and leisurely dining to be a fruit of his

---

1. Ellis would go on to become chairman of the British Phonographic Institute, the major record industry organization in the United Kingdom. In 1991, having left Chrysalis, he launched a record label based in New York, Imago.

success. In this, there was an early incompatibility with Karen. When I accompanied them to La Serre, one of the best restaurants in southern California, Terry worried about her disinterest in the menu. She picked away at a green salad and drank only a spritzer. But she was in good spirits, talking enthusiastically about her work, and Ellis showed obvious affection for her.

Just as their record company people had distanced themselves from the Carpenters, so Ellis faced mockery as he stepped out with his new date: "You're dating *Karen Carpenter*? Oh, she's so frivolous! And here you are, involved with really heavy, meaningful rock 'n' roll" (as a record industry mogul). With his cool authority, Ellis laughed away the taunts with an assurance that unfortunately "the world has never been allowed to know what she is like as a person." Ellis admired her sense of fun, her talent and dedication to work, her unpretentiousness, her sincerity.

When Karen told Richard that she was moving in to Terry's house, her brother approved—but the move would bring immediate culture shock for both partners. An ideal evening for Karen was a snack at about 6:30 P.M., then on with the television for any light entertainment shows while she needlepointed away. The gregarious Ellis preferred to dress up and drive his Rolls Royce to a dinner, often inviting friends to combine that crucial pleasure with music business conversation. Karen loved the music business, but she felt uneasy in restaurants. She had not yet mastered the rudiments of the anorexic's textbook, which enables those with the disorder to go to restaurants and diet, often undetected.

"She was a strong-minded girl," Ellis reflects. "And in business discussions she was very tough." With his skill in management and his overview of the record industry, it was not long before Ellis was drawn into the Carpenters' affairs.

Late one evening in 1975, the phone rang in the office of the London boss of A&M, Derek Green. On the line from California was Terry Ellis. The two men were friendly competitors, but the conversation was immediately tense for Green as Ellis made it clear that Chris Wright, his London colleague, was listening in on the phone conversation.

"As you know," Ellis began to Green, "I'm dating Karen, and I'm calling you as head of the company to ask you some things about her career."

Uneasy and suspicious, Green asked, "What's your position?" He wondered if Ellis was now something more than Karen's boyfriend. "Well, I'm dating her," Ellis repeated. He followed with a series of pointed questions about activities for the Carpenters in Britain, a prime market for them: Had it been right to tour, as they had just done, all around Britain? Were they playing the correct venues? Was the right record being released?

Green was wary. "I answered as politically deftly as I could, but I felt it was a most awkward call," Green says. "I said, 'Do try and understand, Terry, that you're a competitor to me.' I gave away as little as possible because he had no position as far as I was concerned. I was very unhappy at receiving that call. Man to man we were friends, but imagine how he would have felt if the roles were reversed and I was calling him as the boyfriend of Debbie Harry of Blondie!" (one of Ellis's hot acts on his Chrysalis label).

Replacing the phone, Green said to himself agitatedly, "Phew! You can count the days until Terry's *managing* her." Then he immediately phoned Jerry Moss in California. "Oh my God, here's some bad news," Green began. When he said that Ellis had tried to inveigle information from him, Moss was phlegmatic; in the incestuous world of the Los Angeles record industry it didn't strike him as so lethal. And Moss knew the unique betrothal between Richard, Karen, and his partner, Herb Alpert, was probably invincible.

What irked Ellis was what he construed as passivity on the part of A&M toward their most important act. He sensed that the Carpenters were not being handled with any strategy. The label was not sufficiently *proud* of Richard and Karen's achievements and profitability.[2]

Alpert was the only person there of whom Karen and Richard spoke with any fondness, avers Terry Ellis. "They were aware that despite the millions of records they sold, their company was embarrassed at the image having the Carpenters on the label presented to the competition," Ellis says. "It's an enormous shame,

2. Richard is hurt to this day by the fact that when he walks into the international department of A&M in Los Angeles, "there is not one poster on display of the Carpenters, and heaven knows how much money we have made for A&M internationally. For example, as recently as 1990 in the UK, we had the second biggest selling album of the year. You'd think that might warrant a poster in the international department. It galls the hell out of me."

such a pity nobody had the compassion to take the time to get to know them, and it reflected badly on the company because the three most important entities in an artist's career are himself, his management, and his record company, which should play a major role in development. A record is such a mighty project that if it's not approached with an artist's career in mind, it can do lasting damage. It is quite clear that no one at A&M gave a damn about the Carpenters. They had a girl with the voice of an angel and a guy who was a gifted songwriter and musician. Why was someone not asking what they could do about their career?"

Richard and Karen did indeed feel sore about what they perceived as A&M's lack of care. In six years, their success had contributed such profits to the label that many called the Carpenters "the ship that A&M sailed on." Having overcome early sneers, they now expected serious recognition. Werner Wolfen, confirming the disenchantment, says: "There was a lot of feeling on both their parts that A&M did not treat them as well as they should, given their standing. Herb Alpert thought a lot of them; Jerry Moss was not a great fan of their products. It wasn't hip to like the Carpenters, and on the studio lot they didn't get the same acclaim they thought (a) they were getting elsewhere and (b) they thought they were entitled to. That was down to the fact that they thought they were 'carrying' the label." Wolfen adds that while Richard's loyalty meant he would never leave the label and he had a fine relationship with Alpert, "his relationship with Moss never jelled."

But it was getting late. In the next two years, their lives would be so turbulent that mere irritation with their record company became the least of their difficulties.

Consumed by their record success, Karen and Richard had drifted into their stage act with little planning. Visiting them in concert in 1975 for the first time, Terry Ellis was appalled. Not only was there something of a problem with A&M's corporate attitude, but, he says, "with all their success and money, nobody had taken the trouble to teach Karen the rudiments of stagecraft." Years of travelling as manager with Ian Anderson, the consummate theatrical leader of the rock band Jethro Tull, had given Ellis a professional, demanding vision of concert work, analyzing strengths and weaknesses after each show. "But here was a girl," he says of Karen, "who had *no idea* what to do. She didn't even know about not turning her back to the audience."

At the hotel after one concert, Terry saw Karen alone. "You were terrible," he said firmly, "and you are never going to be that terrible again." This admonishment hit a raw nerve. Critics had been pounding the Carpenters' lack of stagecraft and wooden movements for years, and now her best friend, hardly a man to be argued with, confirmed it. The next day, he took her alone to the theater and gave her some advice.

"Communicate with the audience!" he urged her. "They *love you,* and yet you are frightened of them."

Confessing her shyness, she said: "Should I do that? How?"

She could start, Ellis suggested, by saying "hi" to the people in the front seats. "And wave to the people in the balcony. Communicate with them. They will wave back."

Bashfully, Karen said that would be hard for her—"What if they don't wave back?"—but she'd give it a try that night. It worked.

Richard had been acutely aware of their need to graft some professional theatricality into their stage show. Performance was hardly natural to him, and Karen's valiant attempts to come to terms with being the star still looked stilted.

One difficulty was that they rarely had time to absorb the shows of other acts. Sensing the need for change, with Randy Bash and John Bettis, Richard had driven to Las Vegas in June 1975 to catch the kind of cabaret performances that he and Karen ought to have in mind when restructuring their own production, and he acknowledged the fact that at Vegas and Tahoe, "people did not want to see concerts, but properly planned performances." They hired Ken and Mitzie Welch as their producers. As well as working with such troupers as Carol Burnett, Lena Horne, and Ella Fitzgerald, the Welch's had seen service on a Barbra Streisand TV special. To work with such comparative shyness as that of Karen and Richard would be a stark contrast; but before they could join them, the Carpenters were to go on the road for a watershed touring experience.

Terry Ellis's relationship with Richard Carpenter continued warmly. Both were wine connoisseurs, and they compared restaurants. Both were punctilious workaholics, with a streak of obsessiveness. Thrilled that his sister had at last found an attractive man with status, Richard decided to go to him for personal advice.

Quickly concluding that Richard fundamentally resented Karen's stardom, Ellis discovered an even knottier difficulty facing the brother who felt that to the public, the Carpenters meant Karen, period. Richard had been shocked and angered when, sitting alongside Frank Zappa and Quincy Jones on a record industry seminar sponsored by *Billboard* magazine, he had been introduced as "Richard Carpenter, piano player with the Carpenters." He told Ellis he hadn't known whether to laugh or cry. He was particularly saddened by the lack of identification by people in the music industry. Ellis sympathized because, as he declares now, "as much as she was the voice, he was the genius."

Richard had been losing confidence, too, in Sherwin Bash, since he and Karen needed more scientific career strategy than they felt Bash was providing. A decent, honourable manager of the "old guard," Bash was generally criticized for booking them too heavily, tour after tour, around the United States and the world. It was "dumb," John Bettis says; "they were a pop success working a country band schedule." Bettis felt it was miraculous that songs of the quality of "Goodbye to Love," "Yesterday Once More," and others were created during such crippling concert schedules.

Richard was edgy about his and Karen's future. Bash's contract was coming up for renewal, and Richard was uncertain about automatically re-signing. "What shall I do?" Richard asked Terry Ellis naively about his management. "Fire him and get another one," Ellis answered. "Would you manage us?" Richard asked. Ellis said this was impossible. He was running his own big organization.

Richard was acutely aware that they did not project an exciting live stage show. "How could it be?" he asks now. "No thought had gone into it. A girl and a band go out on stage and sing some love songs!" It wasn't the kind of music, or visual appeal, that brought people to their feet. Their theatricality was minimal. Now after five years of untutored concerts, as Ellis emphasized, their presentational package needed surgery.

That tough truth could not have hit them at a worse time. As they spoke, the human tragedy was taking root.

Richard had an idea for a song title. "It's called 'Only Yesterday,'" he said to John Bettis. "What do you want the song to be about?"

asked his lyricist. As they sat in his music room, Richard turned and grinned. "I want this song to appeal to the average American dollar holder," he said. "OK, I can do that," Bettis said. He gave the haunting Carpenter melody a touch of Neil Diamond gravitas, and with Karen again adopting her melancholic delivery—the song was peppered with words like *sadness, tears, the past,* and of course *yesterday*—it was their most manufactured work.

Because the melody was upbeat, Richard asked John to ensure that the lyrics were not completely sad, so it changed in midstream to become what Bettis describes as "a manipulated, positive song. We wanted it to be positive at the time. So I turned on the technique button. It was a 'construct' song—but easily one of our most commercial." He and Richard, believing it was not a big hit, lost a thousand-dollar bet with their recording engineer, Roger Young, when the song reached the top five in April 1975.

That year, as Karen began her decline, was planned as one of the Carpenters' most grueling. With a new album, stints in Las Vegas and Lake Tahoe, full tours of the United States, Britain, and Japan, Richard was on his knees as they were in the studio making the *Horizon* album. The result was a collection he was never entirely happy about, but which included some gorgeous readings by Karen of songs written by others: her doleful "Solitaire" and "Desperado" and yet another song that sounded lightly self-analytical, "I Can Dream, Can't I?" for which they enlisted the legendary arranger Billy May to help give the old standard a 1940s atmosphere.

Topped off by "Only Yesterday," the *Horizon* album represented a midstream pause for them. It was released in June 1975 when artists as diverse as the Eagles, Barry Manilow, John Denver, and Steely Dan were making waves. Some felt *Horizon* showed the Carpenters' growth with experimental ground-breaking qualities akin to the Beatles' *Sergeant Pepper,* a rock milestone.[3]

One particular song marked out the album's distinctiveness. Capturing yet again the romantic dilemmas that Karen, Richard,

3. A letter congratulating Richard on his production of *Horizon* came from an unexpected source: Jerry Moss. At A&M, where Alpert was manifestly their creative champion, Richard and Karen jokily called Moss "The Principal" because he supervised the business. He visited them in the studio and recognized fully their importance to the label plus their "incredible fixation to be perfect . . . to have that voice on A&M was really a thrill."

and he were experiencing, John Bettis and Richard came up with "(I'm caught between) Goodbye and I Love You." She delivered this song with such soulfulness that it might have been a heartfelt reflection on her break from David Alley:

> I have something to tell you/and I know it won't be easy
> I've been thinking these past few days/it might be time to
>   leave.
> You're like a stranger/then you're a lover
> Never the same, always hard to believe.
>
> I'm caught between goodbye and I love you
> Never knowing quite where I stand
> I'm caught between goodbye and I love you
> Falling both ways, nowhere to land
>
> So constantly stranded/I can't understand it
> This troubled life you've handed me/Is like the devil and
>   the deep blue sea.
>
> If we go on much longer
> If my doubts grow any stronger
> Then I may have to let you go
> If only to survive.
> Give me a reason, why should I stay here
> I've tried so hard just to keep love alive.

The album marked the debut as their recording engineer of Roger Young, whose offbeat sense of humour and flair for the creative process had meshed well with Richard since his role as the assistant sound engineer. He already had experience of being their road engineer for their concerts (most of which Richard recorded for his private collection). Young responded well to Richard's precise instructions, his addiction to perfection, and his intuitive knowledge of how to pitch Karen into her most comfortable milieu in the studio.

From his very first track with them, "Only Yesterday," Young acknowledged the recently built Studio D at A&M to be totally Richard's domain. "Richard knew what he wanted, and Karen trusted him because everything Richard touched turned to gold. She was a musician in that she had a beautiful voice and a great ear, while Richard had such a talent for arrangements. And for the background vocals, being brother and sister, they blended beautifully," Young says.

Richard was firm with his instructions, and when Karen hesitated about a song's range, he would reassure her that he knew for a fact that she could manage the song's extremities, high or low. "And once Richard had told her she could do it, she did it. And Richard is the only person I've ever known who, when he hears a song, hears the whole arrangement in his head, how it should sound before the first note is laid down."

On a difficult reading like "Goodbye to Love," Richard devised precisely the moments when Karen could breathe and advised her, particularly before singing the long passages, and she would interpret his advice successfully. On "Solitaire," an immensely powerful and difficult song, it was the arrangement, Richard's delicate piano work and the richness of the strings, that rounded out the "chill factor" which Young saw Richard striving for so often. "That song sent chills up and down our spines when we just had the bass, piano, drums, and working vocal, before the strings went on," Young says. "It was like Karen was in your lap, singing. She was very aware of its quality and very aware of her singing. Just as Richard knew how he wanted an arrangement to sound, she knew how she wanted to express herself." As a drummer, Karen's timing was impeccable, too: "As solid as a metronome. Richard would give her a tempo; she would count the song; and it would stay locked into that beat"—unlike some major studio drummers who speeded up a tempo toward a song's end, claiming it increased excitement. "Karen never did that."

Creatures of habit, Karen and Richard drank iced tea in the studio, never alcohol. "Every second engineer had to learn from me how to make the correct strength of Lipton's," Young says.

"But we never sliced the lemons." The immaculate touch of Richard was entrusted with that operation.

Even if Karen had been in perfect health, their 1975 schedule was crippling. After completing the *Horizon* album, they were touring America for six weeks, moving on to Lake Tahoe and Las Vegas before Japan and European tours. Normally, Karen loved the whole commotion of touring, the camaraderie, the energy level, even the boring flights, which gave her a chance to needlepoint. But she was now in terrible shape. Richard, too, felt exhausted.

To contrast with their musical textures, their opening act was invariably the comedy duo Skiles and Henderson. But as they set off on their U.S. trail in June 1975, Sherwin Bash had paired them with Neil Sedaka. The veteran singer-songwriter, riding the nostalgia boom, played to the hilt his up-tempo oldies catalog: "Calendar Girl," "Next Door to an Angel," and "Breaking Up Is Hard to Do." And he had a new smash, "Laughter in the Rain."

As opening act to the lackluster Carpenters, Sedaka was dangerous. Those songs and his punchy delivery carried such a big impact that he was getting standing ovations. Standing in the wings night after night, Richard and Karen enjoyed his music but gritted their teeth. He was stealing their show. Although he inspired them to perform more animatedly, his repertoire and communication with the audience were hard to top. The tiring shows—two shows nightly while in Las Vegas—were planned for outdoor theaters that summer, and as the tour wore on Richard became tetchy with Sedaka.

When the tour reached the Oakdale theater outside New Haven, Richard and Karen's home turf, they were riled when Sedaka arrived from his nearby home in his chauffeured Rolls Royce Silver Cloud while they drove to the show in a rental car. What was *this*? they exploded to Sherwin Bash. Who was topping the bill here? Who sold more records? Their manager explained that it was no big deal; the man was rich and owned a Rolls! So? The jumpy Carpenters suffered a bruised ego. Sedaka, however, believed there was no real top of the bill and that, if anything, he was a first among equals.

For some of the tour, Bash was in Europe to set up the Carpenters' trek that would follow, and he appointed an assistant, Rebecca Segal, to go on the road with the Carpenters and Sedaka.

But Richard and Karen were quickly irritated by the focus on Neil. They seethed when, in Warwick, Rhode Island, as Neil began to perspire under the lights, Rebecca met him off stage to pamper him with a towel—while they were ignored. In this prickly atmosphere, such seemingly small episodes sent the temperature soaring.

Gritting their teeth, the Carpenters soldiered on, telling each other that the pairing with Sedaka was disastrous. By the middle of the tour, Karen was firmly in the grip of anorexia nervosa. And although everyone around her knew she was dieting rigidly, the seriousness of her imminent plight was not known.

Amid such tantrums, Richard and Karen became jittery with each other. "You never smile on stage!" Karen scolded Richard. "How can I smile when you look like *that?*" he'd reply. They snapped similarly most nights. One tiny hiccup in the show's routine would start them bickering. Karen's dresses showed too much of her arms and back—and when Richard said she should show more sense than to wear them, she hit back that they looked pretty and her clothes were not his territory. The band knew to walk away from such pre-show battles, but there was no escaping the noise as they continued in their dressing room.

And now her clear physical problem could no longer be disguised. She looked so gaunt that as they walked out each night after the MC said, "Ladies and gentlemen, the Carpenters," the audience applause was followed by the crowd's loud gasp of horror. People could not believe what they saw: as she raised her skeletal arms, her rib cage was visible. "Her skin was literally hanging off her bones," says Debbie Vaiuso. Visiting her backstage, her old schoolmate remembers, "It was like hugging a lampshade."

Although Karen must have been aware of the audible sounds from the audience, Richard does not recall her remarking on this. As he points out, for her to have reacted would have drawn attention to the fact that something was wrong. And since she was in denial of that, she did not react. "She looked like hell," Richard remembers. "It was downhill from then on."

When the tour neared New Haven, their parents flew in to see the "homecoming" show. On the evening of the concert, Theresa Vaiuso called to collect Agnes and Harold from the hotel. "Have you seen Karen lately?" Harold asked her with an uncharacteristic concern in his voice. "Only on television; she looked pretty good to me," Theresa replied. "Well, she's not fooling me," Harold said to her. "That girl's got anorexia nervosa."

Agnes, disinclined to believe this, said Karen was merely too enthusiastic about her diet because of her shape. But Harold insisted. When Theresa inquired about the symptoms of the disorder that was then more obscure in its name to the public than it became in the 1980s and 1990s, she felt sure Harold was right.

Defiantly sweeping aside all the concern and criticism from Richard, the band, and old friends like Debbie whom she met on the road, Karen persisted with her diet. Instead of eating with the others as before, she took to ordering hotel room service to her dressing room, and Richard often noticed it was always a salad that she picked at. Four weeks into the tour, she was in deep physical trouble, down to around eighty pounds according to Richard, yet astounding everyone with her perfect vocal performance. But there was no kidding between the shows. In Las Vegas she could hardly wait to leave the stage and reach the couch in her dressing room, where she lay, or slept, until the second show. And then, as if by magic, she would click into action, change herself, have Sandy Holland attend to her hair and her nails which were now looking suspiciously thin in texture. Walking slowly to the stage, she turned on that infectious smile and sang like an angel.

So robotic and perfect was her performance that it defused some of Richard's alarm and mounting fury with his sister. "Her voice didn't wear out because she sang properly," he says. "You could have awakened Karen up in the middle of the night and said, 'Sing "Superstar,"' and I'm sure she could have sung it perfectly. She was so thoroughly gifted, *nothing* affected her voice. Everything that makes a great singer, Karen had it. She knew immediately if she heard something by anyone that was out of tune."

Flying into some of their concert dates, Terry Ellis found a double crisis. His girlfriend, down to eighty pounds, was clearly ill and needed care, but nobody had a real solution. And she insisted that resting on the sofa was enough to carry her through. Asking her to eat more sensibly met that stonewalling response: "I'm OK."

In August the looming explosion occurred with Neil Sedaka. When Ellis realized that Bash had allowed Sedaka, as the tour opener, to use the orchestra, which the headlining act should get exclusively, he was livid. He lit a fuse under Richard yet again, then had to jet off to Europe on business. Richard was by then irritated at the fact that Sedaka had been using his grand piano and at times breaking off keys.

Before he left, Ellis told Richard he was aghast at the arrangements that allowed Sedaka to score triumphs over the Carpenters from several angles. Ellis, a keen strategist when it came to concert organization, had been staggered to learn that for the forthcoming Japanese tour, Sherwin Bash had guaranteed Sedaka a payment from the Carpenters of fifty thousand dollars to appear.

"Do you realize," an angry Ellis said to Richard, "that the Carpenters are the biggest act in Japan since the Beatles—and for the hundreds of thousands of people you will be performing to, record companies would pay YOU a large sum to just have one of their acts on YOUR BILL, in order to get them the guaranteed exposure to such crowds! And YOU are paying Neil Sedaka? *It can't be done!* You *have* to let him know." The entire fabric of this tour was working against the Carpenters, Ellis insisted. That diagnosis ignited even more anger in Richard.

Accepting Ellis's admonition, Richard phoned Sedaka the next day during their season at the Riviera Hotel, Las Vegas, and played the role of honest fool. Unhappy to be making the kind of tactical call he felt should have gone out from his management, Richard told Neil he had been stealing the show. He was far too strong to be the opening act, Richard continued, and he could not tolerate him as part of the bill with the Carpenters when they went to Japan. Sedaka was distraught.

Then, halfway through the two-week engagement, Richard one evening received the traditional information from the management to artist, detailing which celebrities were in the audience that night—so that Richard could do a little research about their accomplishments before introducing them under the spotlight. It was unwritten show business law that this introduction fell to the top of the bill.

Between shows in his dressing room, Richard was just preparing how he would introduce that night's celebrities in the audience, singer Tom Jones and TV star Dick Clark, when he could not believe what he heard over his speakers. Sedaka was addressing the audience: "We have two people in the audience tonight . . . we have Tom Jones and Dick Clark." This broke all the ethical boundaries of show business, and Richard, already jumpy, now went ballistic. Screaming with anger, he tore into Karen's dressing room. She, too, was furious but too tired between shows to put up much of a fight. It was better that she conserved her energy, and Richard retreated. To compound his problem, there was no Carpenters management figure present that night: Sherwin was in Berlin, his assistant Elliot Abbott in Los Angeles, Terry Ellis in Europe, and their lawyer was out of his home when phoned.

Finally reaching Elliot Abbott in Los Angeles, Richard screeched off a list of complaints—from the orchestra issue to the introduction of celebrities, from the fact that Sedaka had erected his logo outside the venue to rival that of the Carpenters right through to the core problem that a second on the bill considered himself to be at least equal. Abbott flew to Las Vegas immediately, but this gesture did not assuage Richard since it soon became apparent that Abbott leaned toward Sedaka's support in the managerial tussles that were unfolding.[4]

The next day, Sherwin Bash returned Richard's call. "Do you want to fire him?" asked Bash. "You *bet* I want to fire him!" thundered Richard.

By the time Terry Ellis phoned in, it was all over. Told of the brouhaha, Ellis asked quickly, "You didn't *fire* him, did you?" Aghast when it was confirmed to him that Bash had formally fired Sedaka at the insistence of Richard, Ellis remarked on the poor strategy of the decision. "That's the last thing on earth you should have done!" he said. He correctly forecast an outcome that would explode against the Carpenters.

The backlash came quickly and damagingly for Richard and Karen. Sedaka, gleeful at the news, spread his statements quickly to the world's press. The Carpenters had fired him, he announced, because he was too strong to open their show. "He [Richard] knew that I was too good to go to Japan with them, so he fired me straight in the middle." Richard, exhausted, listening to his heart and his short-fused anger rather than his head, had scored an embarrassing "own goal," and Sedaka capitalized in the media for weeks.

Addressing Carpenters fans in their newsletter, Richard wrote

4. Abbott later left Bash's company, and Sedaka signed to Abbott's management.

of the debacle: "It often happens in our business, not only with the Carpenters but with other headliners, that the choice of the opening act proves to be unsuitable for personal or other reasons. Under those circumstances the headliner has no option but to terminate the engagement of the opener. This was the situation with Neil.

"Please be assured that we DID NOT fire Neil for doing too well. In fact we were delighted that he was receiving a nice response from the audience. It was a result of other circumstances of which he is totally aware that made it necessary for us to terminate his engagement . . . . It is a disappointment to us that he has found it necessary to make statements concerning same to the press."

The Sedaka affair brought another Carpenters relationship to the boiling point. Richard felt sore with his manager, for he did not feel that Sherwin Bash should have planted in his mind the thought of personally firing Sedaka. An artist in such a volatile state as Richard should have been told not to behave rashly or immaturely, to go and kick a wall, or yell at his manager, and possibly to bide his time and see the tour through, he now says. Bash should have been taking care of all Carpenters complaints, Richard believes, particularly such a knotty problem as this. Now, finally, Richard had lost confidence in his manager.

Flying into Las Vegas to evaluate the crisis, Werner Wolfen met an agitated Richard, who told him firmly that he wanted to fire Bash and hire Ellis as manager. Experienced and professional though Bash was, Richard felt that Ellis's philosophy and vision had been precisely what the Carpenters had been lacking. Wolfen was wary; he knew about Terry's romance with Karen, and now he was "curious as to what Terry's real intentions were." For some months, gossip columnists had mused that Ellis, with a considerable transatlantic power base, might be en route to managing the Carpenters.

"Is that really wise?" Wolfen asked Richard about his enthusiastic plan. "Why?" asked Richard. "Well," the lawyer said, "he would have to represent both of you, and he's got a separate relationship with Karen. It seems to me that it could lead to big trouble."

"I wanna do it," said Richard emphatically. Normally, on such a big issue, Karen would have been vocal, but she was too exhausted to take part in the debate.

Wolfen went ahead and fired Bash for them. He received a pay-off of $250,000 and paid them back his loan.[5]

Meeting Ellis for "frank discussions," Wolfen voiced his concern. But Ellis again rejected Karen and Richard's request to be their permanent manager. He said he would look after them temporarily until they found a new man who would give fresh impetus to their career.

While Ellis was their temporary manager, Richard's worry about his public profile surfaced again. "I did try to get Richard to develop his role," Ellis says, "because he was so jealous of the attention Karen got from the public. He wanted recognition for his talent and contribution." What about his doing back-up vocals at the front of the stage? Richard asked. No, Ellis said, that wouldn't work; as a model, they should study the Marlene Dietrich-Burt Bacharach stage act. She was always up front, and although he wrote the songs and was the musical mentor, he never came forward, but the public knew his role.

And so Ellis's suggestion was tried. Richard went on first to an announcement: "Ladies and gentlemen, Richard Carpenter." Under a blaze of spotlights, he led the orchestra through an overture. His key role was thus established. "In the minds of that audience," Terry Ellis told him, "you are heavy-duty. It makes people understand your role, that of musical director of the whole operation." Karen then walked out to assert herself, and everybody was happy. It was an object lesson in how to deal pragmatically with sibling rivalry.

If Richard had entered that tour feeling low, he now felt battered. It had ended ignominiously on every level. While the issues of Sedaka and their management had been bruising, Karen's health had now degenerated into a critical issue. Summer 1975 had marked out Karen's difficulty as no longer a diet drifting out of control. It was a mysterious illness.

Her doctor confirmed that she was too exhausted to go on the tours of Japan and Europe that were scheduled to follow the U.S. trek. She was not even in any condition to travel, Richard was told. A September charity concert at Anaheim was also canceled. Terry

---

5. Sherwin Bash continues to operate a successful management company. After he managed the Carpenters, his roster of clients included Neil Diamond (in the 1970s), and, in the 1980s, singers Lou Rawls and Natalie Cole. His current clients include singer Anita Baker.

Ellis accompanied Richard to Tokyo, and John Bettis traveled with him to London to hold press conferences and to explain to promoters and apoplectic A&M executives that because of Karen's general poor health, these tours would have to be postponed until the spring and fall respectively of 1976. In Britain, where *The Singles* album had sold well over a million copies, the Carpenters had been scheduled to play twice nightly in thirteen cities, and tickets had sold out quickly everywhere; additionally, they were looking forward to playing for the Queen at the Royal Variety Performance. In Japan, too, there was disappointment and worry about Karen. Jerry Moss ensured that A&M paid the losses on ticket sales incurred by the promoter, Tats Nagashima.

Rumours spread that Karen had cancer, but this was denied by their official fan club magazine. Coupled with "severe physical and mental exhaustion due to overwork, dieting, and lack of rest, she developed colitis, i.e., inflammation of the colon," Evelyn Wallace wrote to their supporters. "Her collapse was inevitable after the rigorous schedule of the past summer months, and her willing spirit was eventually dominated by Mother Nature, who compelled her to take a well-deserved rest."

While Richard was away in Tokyo and London, Karen went into the Cedars of Sinai Hospital. "They're just going to make sure I put some weight on," she reassured an alarmed Gary Sims who visited her there. But she seemed so unsettled that her physicians decided that she might be better at home following simple instruction: rest, eat, and don't work until the end of October.

Back at Newville Avenue under Agnes's watchful eye, Karen stayed in bed most of the time and ate sensibly. Get-well cards, letters, gifts, and phone calls from fans poured into her home, and Karen was touched by the volume of affection. She gained weight to 104 pounds in six weeks of recuperation.

It turned out that as one problem was being surmounted, another was around the corner for either Karen or Richard or for the Carpenters as an act. During Karen's enforced rest Richard set to work with John Bettis songwriting—but ripples began to occur in her romance with Terry Ellis. Under his temporary management, they decided that their return to work would be from December 27 until January 4 at the Sahara Hotel, Lake Tahoe. Meanwhile, Terry believed she would benefit from a holiday with him at his home in the south of France. Karen felt guilt about this plan because of the consternation of her mother, who preached moral rectitude. But Ellis was deeply worried about Karen's health. As the weeks passed, he remembers someone suggesting to her that she see a psychiatrist. Richard and Karen replied in unison that their mother would never approve of that move. "We don't believe in people like *that!*" was indeed Agnes's response to Terry when he broached the subject.

Ellis had grown to truly love the "wonderful girl," as well as to admire her talent, her sense of humour, her abilities as a mimic, comedienne, and actress, all of which his keen managerial eye saw could be developed if she became healthy again. He told me at that time of his worries that a woman on the road could hardly be expected to stand up to the schedule they had been given. Reflecting now on the situation, he says Karen "*had* to be tough and strong because she was not allowed to be the pampered star of the show. . . . This was the Carpenter family on the road, and the principal role was recognized as Richard's." It was a case, he maintains, of "look after *him,* he's the star." Richard rejects this contention as "nonsense."

Ellis's relationship with Karen was doomed. When she accompanied him for a vacation to his home on Tortola on the Virgin Islands, it again did not sit well with Agnes's principles of propriety, much to Karen's embarrassment since she wanted to appear worldly.

And the confirmation that they would not be able to build a life together finally came when, back in California, she moved into Ellis's house. There it quickly dawned on them both that the gap separating their life-styles was too wide to bridge.

She was forever a true Middle American; he, despite his thorough absorption of American life-styles, was still culturally a European. And Karen's evidently unbreakable habit of preparing herself a "TV tray" for an early evening snack while watching a rerun of something like "I Love Lucy" was absolute anathema to Terry. But that was how she had lived, and she was not comfortable about changing such lifelong habits.

Karen was attracted to his assertiveness, confidence, practicality, and shrewdness, but after only a week together she went back to Downey and tearfully told Richard it was not working.

"I wasn't happy when she came back," says Richard, who liked

Terry and hoped he and his sister were heading for lasting happiness. "But what do you do when your sister shows up, beside herself, in tears? There was that contradiction again; she wanted her man to take charge, but when Terry did so, saying 'you're not going to have a TV tray'—home she came." Ellis's more formal, structured approach to dining and other disagreements meant that "the romance didn't have a prayer," Richard says. "Things like this usually happen after a few years, not after a week. It couldn't have worked. I don't think it would have done so if they had got back together ten times. Their life-styles were too different. And it's a damned shame."

Ellis declares that aside from any differences, Agnes had made it impossible for their relationship to continue—"because I was a threat to her dominance. Karen found herself in an emotional conflict, so the easy way out was to terminate the relationship."

This was no small event in Karen's life, but a negative end to an important love connection. She would always carry a torch for Ellis and deeply regret her loss. Her friend Carol Curb says Karen soon realized how wonderful the relationship had been, "but by then it was too late to revive it." Other friends were bitterly upset at Karen's separation from such an eligible bachelor.

The theme of that song "Goodbye to Love" seemed to have become unnervingly accurate: "Time and time again the chance for love has passed me by/And all I know of love is how to live without it." And yet . . . Karen's sickness during her spell of great happiness with Terry Ellis seemed to indicate that the cause of her illness was rooted in something more than the need for a loving relationship. When it ended, friends told Karen she would find it impossible to replace him as a partner. And Karen knew they were right.

In October 1975 I interviewed Karen and Richard separately. Both spoke candidly about her illness, which had forced the postponement of the British tour. But though the diet was fully discussed, the words *anorexia nervosa* were not mentioned.

"All my strength is not back yet, and that alone gets me upset," Karen said. "I'm not used to being slower than I normally am. Being idle is annoying because I never have been, from working on the road to coming into town and going right into the studio."

Karen made the point that vacations had been in short supply since their record-making and touring schedule had begun five years earlier. In 1971 they had driven to see relatives and friends back east (the journey on which Richard had told Karen that her move from the drums to upfront was essential); and there had been the trip to Acapulco in 1973 which combined business with pleasure. She voiced her feeling of pressure:

"Until in the middle of making the *Horizon* album, I went away for four days and didn't know what to do with myself! And it's stupid. That amount of work turned out to be harmful to me. It's going to be a whole learning process for me to do things in a different way. To really seriously calm down and do things at a slower pace. Because I'm very regimented."

Richard was more specific on her physical condition, which clearly worried him and others. "She called me today, and now she's got the flu on top of her sickness. Her resistance is so low that she picks up just everything that comes along.

"She really isn't, at this part of her life, strong. She's just kept up far too tough a schedule for her and really run herself down. She always wanted to show that she could do just as good as the guys could, and really pushed herself. She would never dream about complaining about work, even if she might've not felt like it, in which case she was prepared to go down. She just took on too much.

"And she went on this huge diet and lost a lot of weight. And when she *would* eat, it would be salad without dressing, and she had everything figured out calorie-wise. No starch, nothing except fish and never with a sauce. I knew eventually that she'd run herself down. I kept talking with her. It did no good."

Her doctor warned her that it would happen, that she should start eating. Karen recalled: "I had been singing straight for three or four years without a break. I finally got so wiped out I got sores on my vocal cords right in the middle of recording the 'A Song For You' album.[6] My doctor said, 'I don't want you to sing for a

---

6. This extremely rare breakdown in Karen's vocal ability occurred during the recording of "I Won't Last a Day Without You." "It was a low point," recalls their engineer Roger Young. "Richard wanted the chorus doubled and Karen, who usually did that with no problem in one or two takes, couldn't match her 'other' voice. We went back and did it over and over again." Richard says that normally, Karen, whose voice was giving her pain, would have completed such a task quickly. While she and Young reworked the segment many times until it was successful, Richard was so frustrated that, uncharacteristically, he sought refuge, as the session stretched into the early hours, in Herb Alpert's office where he watched a sci-fi movie on TV. The track, a Paul Williams-Roger Nichols composition, has become a perennial radio favorite.

month.' I said, 'What do you *mean,* not sing for a month? I'm in the middle of an album!' I was home for two days, then back in the studio."

Richard admitted: "We are very nervous. On top of being too thin and not eating enough food to keep up with the schedule, it lowered her resistance. A cold would come along, and she could not shake it off.

"Also, she gets upset very easily. She's a very tough girl, very strong. When I say tough, I mean resilient, and a persistent personality. The strength of her personality kept driving her on, saying, 'I can do it.' Now, she's even got nerves thinking about the decision to cancel the British tour. It's troubled her all week."

Despite her deteriorating condition, which caused so much alarm in 1975, Karen remained hyperactive as she told me: "I cannot stand to be late. I go to bed at night with a pad by the bed, and the minute I lie down it's the only quiet time of the day. My mind starts going, 'This has gotta be done; you've gotta call this person.' I find myself with a flashlight in bed writing down about fifty things that have to be done by ten o'clock next morning. It's not the best way to be. It's better to hang loose.

"But I'm just not that type of person. 'STOP WORRYING!' they say. That's a riot! You cannot calm down, recording an album. You would get to four or five in the morning, then drive home, and get a couple of hours sleep and be back in the studio by noon. It's going, going, GO."

Emphasizing how Richard's creativity had been definitely thwarted because of their "ridiculous schedule," she continued: "We got to a point where he was not interested in going to a studio and he hadn't written for a while. He was totally exhausted. That upset me. And I said we had to take some time off. So we canceled a tour—and ended up in a studio." She recalled that on their parents' fortieth wedding anniversary, they "worked all day, ran to the anniversary dinner, and then went back to the studio at one in the morning to cut the two things at the beginning and end of the *Horizon* album, 'Aurora' and 'Eventide.'"

Richard had made that album in "the worst state I've ever seen him in. We've always said, 'Hey, I can't wait to get into the studio,' but we got to a point where we didn't want to go. That album just drained everything, every drop of blood out of us. When it was done, we weren't glad it was done; we were upset with the way it turned out. Richard can work unbelievable hours, but this last time it was getting to us. But now it's gotta change. The two of us can't go on like that. The way that things have happened in the last six months, we're just fed up with being treated like two things that the blood spurts out of."

Significantly, Karen spoke candidly about her exhaustion and overwork but did not mention her diet, as Richard did. And while she rightly pointed out that they had been overstretched at work, she would not change her self-discipline in the next seven years. Combating Karen's iron determination to work whenever she was able to physically get to the studio, combined with her allegiance to a diet that proved unyielding, was to prove the impossible battle as the weeks, months, and years went by.

The Carpenters' homespun stage show, which Terry Ellis and Richard had diagnosed as needing surgery, finally came under the scrutiny of Ken and Mitzie Welch in late 1975.

The central difficulty in creating a visual identity for them was that neither was a natural exhibitionist, Ken Welch says. "Richard sprang from the tradition of songwriter/musician/producer and was not very comfortable being the front man." Mitzie Welch is another who observes that Karen was psychologically hiding behind the drums because she found it hard to "show off" as the lead singer. "The show business quality was not there," Mitzie says. "But their minuses were also pluses: people felt they were the kids next door; they were reachable; there was nothing high and mighty about them. We all respond to that kind of honesty; there was no baloney about them. People really *liked* Richard's lack of flash."

Ken and Mitzie deduced that both Karen and Richard needed encouragement in the theatrical area. Particularly Richard: reviewers called him wooden, but "reserved" would be Mitzie Welch's description. "He was a studio man; musicians tend not to want to be out there on stage but are really devoted to their music. What mattered to Richard was the sound." The Welch's devised a routine based on a Spike Jones-style interpretation of "Close to You," and even a Ginger Rogers-Fred Astaire sequence which never appeared in their show. Richard and Karen were game for these visual forays, and Karen's sense of fun made rehearsals enjoyable.

"Karen was interesting," Mitzie Welch says, "because she was the Mommy of us all. We were a lot older, and she always wanted to take care of everybody. She was so caring and did that with Richard all the time. I thought, gee, for a performer she's more interested in others than herself."

As for her weight: "A costume designer had said something to her about her need to lose weight," Mitzie recalls. "Some remark was made that stuck, that she needed to respond to. Her father said to her: 'You're crazy, Karen; you're *thin;* you don't need to lose any weight. You look great up there.'" What nobody could realize was that, faced with such logic, Karen simply was not listening.

After her split from Terry Ellis, several friends close to Karen detected a heavy heart, an inner emptiness. Her lack of "life experience" was a major problem, according to the songwriter Paul Williams. He observed "a longing that used to virtually eat her up." Reflecting on his own problems with drugs and alcohol, he says: "As rotten and as crazy as my life got, I survived; I had something to *recover from.* And I used to think that if Karen had just had a crazier childhood, or raised hell in her twenties, she'd have something to recover from instead of just that emptiness. I would have loved to have seen her fall in love with, say, a rock 'n' roll guitarist, go on the road, get nuts, get her heart broken, drink too much, eat too much . . . and get better."

She came close to that during a British tour in an explosive collision between romance and career.

London A&M chief Derek Green, anxious to cushion his company's biggest-selling act during a European tour, appointed his promotion chief, John Adrian, to personally attend to Karen and Richard. Nicknamed "Softly" because he appeared in a British TV series called "Softly Softly," the debonair Adrian was a thirty-three-year-old former model whose bonhomie equipped him perfectly for the job.

To acquaint himself with the Carpenters before they came to Britain for concerts, Adrian flew to Düsseldorf. Often, promotion men approached such tasks cynically, and in the trend-conscious atmosphere of the mid-1970s, being appointed to marshal the Carpenters was considered by many to be a punishment. But Derek Green had chosen his man carefully. Softly was a true fan of the Carpenters' sound. As he boarded the plane for Germany, he craved a chance to meet the woman whose voice he adored. And as soon as he met her, recalls Softly, "I knew that I was going to have an affair with her."

The introductory meeting in Germany lasted only a few hours, but when Softly welcomed their plane into Glasgow he began a trek around Britain and Europe that went well beyond their professional base. At Karen's insistence, Softly stepped straight into their limousine beside her and Richard to establish a romantic liaison very quickly.

They sneaked away together for a limousine ride around the Scottish moorlands, returning uncomfortably late for that night's Glasgow concert; they wandered around London's Portobello Road buying antiques; into pubs for lunch; and on shopping expeditions around all the cities on the tour. As the relationship blossomed, those who had known of her earlier relationship with Terry Ellis now mused on her penchant for British record industry executives. But while the band treated Softly as one of the gang, Richard remained aloof. He considered Softly simply the promotions guy.

Soon Softly fell in love with the "sweet, sentimental, refreshing, innocent" girl he also found strong-willed but physically frail. She ate chocolate for instant energy, and he had a sweater made for her inscribed with "Snickers," her favorite.

Yet his protective arm had its limits. He believed she was "pushed and bullied by a lot of people. I don't think Karen felt she had any life of her own. She had a problem with eating. I'd never met anyone, before I met Karen, who would *not eat*. She told me it was because she was fat at school."

Karen's liaison with Softly came under the scrutiny of her Beverly Hills pal Frenda Leffler. At a dinner at the fashionable London restaurant September, to mark the Carpenters' tour, Frenda fixed Softly with the straight question: "What would you do with all that money?" He replied that he would be able to handle it OK. Later, he felt that since he was being screened, his reply might have been misconstrued as avaricious. Frenda emphasized to him that Karen was "a normal girl who likes to cook and wear fluffy slippers."

Hoping he had a future with Karen, Softly told Frenda and Derek Green that he genuinely loved her. Those who saw him as a playboy were cynical, but Softly was truly smitten. This was not merely an on-the-road affair for him, and he believed his affection was reciprocated. But shortly after that dinner party to celebrate another triumphant British tour, a time bomb that had been ticking under Softly and Karen exploded.

*   *   *

Only a few months earlier, Derek Green had fielded that intimidating phone call from Terry Ellis. Now came another heavyweight
voice from California. As the Carpenters tour continued around
the British theatres, Derek Green recalls that he lifted the phone to
a call from a member of the Carpenters inner circle.

"Derek, you have a man working for you named Softly . . . he's
got very close with Karen." Green remembers telling the caller
that they were, indeed, out on the road and that Softly, as head of
promotion, was doing a very good job.

That was not the issue. It quickly became apparent that Softly's
character was being scrutinized from California, since Green was
told that Karen seemed "very taken with him"—to the extent of
inviting him to join her in Los Angeles. There was concern from
Los Angeles, says Green, that more needed to be known about
Softly if the romantic affair was to continue. Karen, they felt,
seemed "infatuated."

In an effort to assuage the telephone inquiry, Green portrayed
Softly as a decent guy. He was a lively and animated character but
not a gigolo. Softly had been in the Merchant Navy, was a friend
of Green's as well as an employee, and had a good future at A&M
where he worked well.

On one level, Green says of the telephone conversation, it was
like talking to a concerned parent. On another, he felt a "shiver,
feeling sad for Karen, thinking that a young woman couldn't date
who she liked. And why? Because there was a lot of money
around."

Although Green believed his description of Softly had reassured the caller, when he replaced the phone, the record chief felt
he should attempt to "buy" Softly off the tour. "It seemed the best
way to save a lot of aggravation."

Calling Softly off the road, Green decided to offer him two
free flights for a Caribbean holiday for Softly and a friend, in
exchange for his departure from the Carpenters' travelling show.
Green says now that he couldn't have preplanned the result of that
offer "because I didn't know until I saw him how he would react;
if he truly loved the woman, he would surely have said no."

Facing Softly in his office, Green was blunt to a man whose
work and friendship he valued. Referring to Softly's plan to visit
Karen in Los Angeles for Christmas, Green said: "I know you want

to go, but if you do then when you come back you don't have a job any more. You're my friend, and I'm advising you to go somewhere and relax. Here's an air ticket."

Softly believed this was an elaborate plan by Karen to end their affair surreptitiously. Taking the offer from Green on the chin, he replied: "Forget it, then! If she doesn't want to know, then I don't."

With his friend, disc jockey Tommy Vance, Softly flew off for a holiday. By the time he returned to London, Karen was back in Los Angeles. Telephoning her, Softly oozed diplomacy, believing still that *she* had engineered the split. "Look," he told her, "I don't think this is going to work. I'm sorry you feel like you do, but the truth is that you're Karen Carpenter and I'm a promotions man in London." Karen replied, "Fine, if that's how you feel." She evidently believed Softly was gently ending the affair—just as he felt that Green had given him her message.

Until he received the ultimatum from Green, Softly had expected their romance to escalate naturally with his visit to California. Sadly, he says, it never had a chance to blossom. And although in his job "dating an artist was a definite no-no, this was chemistry and you couldn't stop that. I remember wishing she was a bloody hairdresser from Glasgow. I hated the fact that she was Karen Carpenter because I knew that was a block."

If the romance had continued naturally, he felt they might well have married. "That's what they were scared of, I think, that I was going to be her manager, or something, and take her money. It was the beginning of something that could have been fabulous because we really liked each other." This seems, however, a most unlikely partnership for Karen to have considered serious at that level. Adrian did not meet her stringent checklist on several levels, and they appeared to me to be polar opposites.

The phone call from California and the record chief's decision had in effect torpedoed the relationship, Softly declares, by persuading them both to think there was disinterest by the other: "That was the plan, and it worked! I didn't lose my job because I played into their hands." The episode pinpointed the protection and isolation that contributed to Karen's lack of fulfilment. Genuine relationships were difficult to establish once she became successful, so she seemed doomed never to have a normal, impulsive romance.

It would be a full fifteen years later that Derek Green, no longer with A&M, admitted to Softly that his homily to him had not originated from Karen but was his own response to a call from Carpenters HQ. It was not, Green says now, a conspiracy; the decision to offer the air tickets was his alone. Richard Carpenter, who knew nothing of Karen's fling with Softly, was not a party to the episode in any way. As for Karen—she always believed that her attractive London promotions guy had said farewell to her because he had found somebody else.

PART FOUR

THE SLOPE

I enjoy money. Not enough people in this world are happy. I'm determined to be contented, and having plenty of money from working makes it easier for me.

—KAREN

I wish Karen wouldn't act, sometimes, like a twenty-six-year-old Jewish momma and interfere so much with my personal affairs.

—RICHARD

E v, will you do me a favour?" Karen asked the Carpenters' personal assistant Evelyn Wallace so many times. Always, the reply would be the same from the woman who had worked for them from their earliest days. "Karen, you're my *boss!* Just *tell* me!" Both would laugh at this frequent exchange.

But one particular request surprised the normally unflappable Evelyn. "She wanted me to go to her mother and let her know that she wanted to go and live in a place of her own."

It was Halloween, 1974. Karen had technically moved back to Newville Avenue from the house she shared with Richard in Lubec Street after the contretemps over Randy Bash. But Karen, restless, had plans to get away completely. While she stayed with her parents, she asked Werner Wolfen to begin looking for a condominium for her. Under her mother's roof, she believed she could eventually persuade Agnes that it was healthy for her to leave the Downey nest, but clearly, the ramifications of the first salvo to Mom on such a topic worried her enough to plant a seed.

At twenty-four, Karen might have been expected to cross this bridge herself. She was no child and hardly needed permission, but she reached out to Evelyn for help. She could surely not have guessed that it would take nearly two years, through her personal ordeals, for the plan to become a reality.

"Well, yeah, I'll see what I can do, Karen," Evelyn answered her apprehensively. Although she was close to the family, this seemed almost too private and domestic a matter for her involvement.

The next day Evelyn warily approached Agnes in the office at Newville Avenue. "Now Karen, she kinda wants to be on her own," she began. "She kinda wanted me to ask you how you felt about, you know, her moving on . . ."

POW! The words had scarcely left Evelyn's lips when Agnes jumped up. "She was out of that office, into the kitchen, and she picked up the phone and called Karen (who was visiting Lubec Street).

"She went screaming at her over the phone; she said, 'You're nothing but a traitor,' and she went on and on and on." Embarrassed, Evelyn upped and went home. "I couldn't fight with her any more. I just didn't want to listen."

An uncharacteristically sheepish Karen drove over to her mother's home the following day. She shrugged her shoulders as if to say to Evelyn, well, that didn't work out. Evelyn smiled knowingly but said nothing. Agnes, however, froze Evelyn from conversation for a while, and they conversed only about Carpenters business. A mere cog in this particular wheel, Evelyn reflects, "I was trying to do my boss a favour, and then Agnes jumped down my throat."

During the traumatic year of 1975, when Karen's anorexia seems to have taken root, during her liaison with Terry Ellis, the battle over Neil Sedaka, and the dismissal of Sherwin Bash, the worry about quitting Downey lurked at the back of her mind.

Frenda Leffler told her that until she made that important move from Downey, she would never have a life of her own. It was not merely a physical move but a mental approach that was required—to shed the strictures of suburbia, to behave like a star, to be seen on Rodeo Drive and driving around Beverly Hills. All this played havoc with Karen's conscience. Karen was "very beholden to, and in embrace with, her mother," declares Werner Wolfen. While Karen realized that Agnes exerted dominance, "she was always prepared to go back there and put up with it—and rather loved it," Wolfen adds. "I used to say to her: 'You've got to draw the line, you know, Karen. You can't let Agnes run your life.'"

Then there was the sensitivity of a symbolic break from Richard, a lifelong conservative who was happy to stay in Downey. His seniority and intimidating talent had combined to put her into an emotional checkmate. Though Karen had a competitive streak which perhaps impelled her to equal him, she never wanted to squash him.

Only once in their partnership had there been a true expression of assertiveness from him, in response to frustration from her. During rehearsals for a medley of songs for a Carol Burnett TV show, Karen had remarked that the selection was not as hot as the Burt Bacharach medley they had once done. Richard shot back tartly that she did not know what she was talking about; she should just concentrate on her singing, he added.

"So what am I—just the dumb singer?" drawled Karen.

"Yeah, that's right," retorted a testy Richard, regretting his words even as he spoke. He had been hurt by her questioning, for the first time, of his work as an arranger and of his unerring selection of their material from the start.

Karen started to cry. "Oh Richard . . ." It was, he ruminates, one of those moments a person regrets for the rest of his or her life: "I felt like hell as soon as it had happened—especially since that was obviously not what I believed."

In the opinion of John Bettis, Karen was never "making a snowball to throw at Richard" to overtake him. And Richard adds: "She did not overtake me. She was the star from the word go! What was there to overtake? A guy sitting at a keyboard!"

That desire not to trump her brother extended outside their work. And, bereft of a loving relationship, she needed the foundation of her tight family behind her all the time. This was a conflict for Karen as she sought independence leading to her own family life. "It was traumatic for her," says Wolfen of her decision to get a home of her own. "Her mother was resisting it greatly." Karen often wanted much more than a professional relationship with those who surrounded her, and to some intimates paraded her innermost thoughts. To Werner Wolfen, she confided her need to strike out alone from Downey, about her sex life, about her desperation to be married and have children. Not so simple, Wolfen told her. She was on the road a lot, loved her work, and her search for the right man who didn't want her just for her money would be a recurring problem. With Terry Ellis gone, Karen knew that was true.

Wading into the setting up of her new home with a gusto that belied her slight frame, Karen was excited. Wolfen found for her two apartments, which she agreed should be gutted into one huge condominium on Avenue of the Stars, Century City. High security was crucial for a young woman celebrity: a gate that needed a passkey was augmented by a doorman who checked every arrival.

Karen monitored the construction work regularly and finally moved in in late 1976. The spaciousness of the condominium was almost overpowering, and Karen's love of uncluttered modern lines showed in every detail. Gigantic windows overlooked Century Boulevard, giving the huge living room lots of daylight and a panoramic view of the glittering skyline.

The apartment comprised bedroom, living room, a huge kitchen/dinette with the stove area in the centre in "French country" style, a small den, and two bathrooms. In the living room yellow was the dominant colour, with a typical Karen trademark: an eight-foot-tall stuffed rabbit sat on a love seat. In the bedroom was a movie-size seven-foot-diagonal television projection screen as well as a beautiful rocking horse made of solid teak. Since her frequent mention during interviews of her love for animals, Karen had been sent hundreds of stuffed pets from fans; these now adorned her new home and included dogs, a racoon, cats, and her favourite Mickey Mouse paraphernalia. Agnes's housewarming gift, a collection of leather-bound classic works of literature, was prominently displayed in the room.

Karen was thrilled and proud to have got her ivory tower. Most days she would slip across to Beverly Hills to shower affection and gifts on her godchildren Andrew and Ashley Leffler. And she stepped up her lifelong hobby of sending greetings cards to friends around the country, enthusing about her new home. It should have been her happiest time, but she rarely had visitors and returned to Downey two or three times a week; she clearly felt rootless.

"Now, you order something *substantial* to eat!"

The commanding tone of Agnes Carpenter was hardly to be ignored. Whatever ripples there had been in parent-child relationships down the years, she evoked respect, and invariably Karen and Richard would respond positively and courteously to her in private and in public.

Agnes and Harold first recognized her problem as serious when they visited the condominium. Slipping out, as they often did, for breakfast or an early dinner at the Hamburger Hamlet in Century City, Agnes would plead with her daughter to order a proper meal. But as Karen dug deeper into her diet, she unconsciously began a battle of wits that Agnes could never win. For whereas Agnes was always upfront and unaware that Karen was becoming immune to attempts at persuasion to eat, her daughter was becoming adept at the devious methods of an anorexic.

Strong and persistent though she was, Agnes was no match for Karen's newfound wiliness that employed every trick in the rabid dieter's book.

So Karen always ordered "something substantial"—often a hamburger, always with extra lettuce, and, of course, her favourite iced tea. Into this she would slide extra ice to reduce the already minimal calories.

"Oh, I'm gonna share this with you . . . you take some," she would say to her mother and father in turn. On this and most other visits to restaurants with relatives or friends, she made certain she was the last person to order. That way, she would be sure to order an entrée different from anyone else's, and after each person, so that she could justifiably offer everyone at the table a taste from her unique dish. Another ploy was to surreptitiously slide the meat into a napkin and into her bag, rarely noticed. It would be thrown out later.

At Karen's condominium, her huge fridge, the size of two normal models, was permanently empty. Evelyn Wallace, who visited every Thursday to help the gardener tend Karen's precious indoor potted tree plants, regularly peeped into the fridge hoping the tide had turned and that she would find food. "Nothing, and no food in her cupboards either. . . . No milk, no bread, nothing," muses Evelyn. This lack of supplies was hardly what one would expect in a breathtakingly beautiful condo owned by a millionairess.

Karen had every imaginable kitchen device and a full range of pots and pans and cutlery, which remained largely unused from the moment she moved in right up to her death. "If I'd have had to live there, I'd have starved to death," says Evelyn Wallace.

While Karen amassed a huge collection of Mickey Mouse items, many of them sent in by fans during her illness, Richard went for cars with almost the same degree of obsessiveness that had marked his interest in music. He had studied and loved automobiles all his life, and by 1976 he had the capital to invest in them.

"SONG 4U" was the predictable registration of his red 1972 Ferrari, and he scoured specialist car magazines for rare models from the 1950s and 1960s, particularly Chrysler 300s. His acquisitions included a 1959 Desoto Adventurer, a 1966 Corvette Roadster, a 1957 black Ford Thunderbird, a 1957 Chrysler Imperial, and 1960s models of such cars as a Buick Riviera, a Studebaker Avanti, and a Plymouth Satellite. By 1979, Richard had a prized collection worth hundreds of thousands of dollars. With his characteristic precision, he insisted that in his warehouse, a manager should keep them in pristine cleanliness and full working order.

Karen was happy with her 1979 Jaguar XJS, a 1972 Mercedes 350 SL, and a 1956 Ford Thunderbird convertible.

Their fan club dispersed all such details, while sales of such paraphernalia (bearing the Carpenters logo) as memo pads, pennants, stationery, posters, bracelets, key fobs, T-shirts, playing cards, and needlepoint kits were flourishing.

While 1976 ended with them both finding time for car collecting by Richard and condo building by Karen to enjoy some materialistic pleasures from their success, a fresh crisis erupted to parallel the continual concern over Karen's health. Their record sales began to dip.

Since "Close to You," all their albums had achieved platinum sales status, representing a million copies sold. The *Horizon* album had not been a flop, either artistically or commercially, but it was their first to merely "go gold" in the United States, meaning sales of half a million copies. In Britain, the album made its debut at the top of the charts, following the prolonged success of their hit singles compilation.

By any yardstick, they were still stunningly successful, and judged creatively alongside anything else in popular music, the sheer class of *Horizon* stood any test. They never recorded trash— but they had set themselves extraordinary standards. *Horizon* was as polished as ever and carried such great songs as "Solitaire" and "Desperado," yet it had an indefinable drag, a lack of spark which made Richard unhappy soon after its release. Now, in 1976, came *A Kind of Hush,* and he believed that was inferior. Apart from the aching beauty of Karen singing "I Need to Be in Love," the album marked time.

Herb Alpert, visiting the studio during the making of the

album, asked Richard if he was happy about everything; their record boss was unstinting with such benevolent care, but later it would be plain to Richard that on this occasion he was politely registering that the album was not quite up to their standard. "I didn't know how to react at that time," Richard says. "It wasn't too hot a collection, aside from 'I Need To Be In Love.'" A&M could have held up the album, but when Richard and Karen told Herb they were content, *A Kind of Hush* went forward.

The vapid title track, a hit for the musically lightweight British group Herman's Hermits, was joined with too many inconsequential songs. There was "Sandy" (an ode by John Bettis to Karen's hairdresser Sandy Holland), a pretty enough little song; and an attractive "One More Time," plus a redundant reworking of the Sedaka smash "Breaking Up Is Hard to Do." It "went gold," but *A Kind of Hush* signalled a loss of impetus that matched the crises in their lives.

The bloom, it seemed, was off the rose. Terry Ellis's days as their temporary manager were ending. They needed a fresh injection. Richard was sure their whole career needed examining as he worried simultaneously about Karen's physical state.

In late 1975 he and Werner Wolfen pondered who might be the best person to manage them and steer them into new pastures. What they needed was an influential show business heavyweight who could get them their own TV special. That, Richard was sure, would be a key element in ensuring their longevity, since they had an across-the-board appeal to the generations and were surely the kind of act that was attractive to home viewers.

Like everyone in the music business, Richard was impressed by the reputation of impresario Jerry Weintraub, whose business roster included such names as Frank Sinatra, Elvis Presley, Neil Diamond, the Moody Blues, Bob Dylan, and John Denver. He might be the answer to their problems, Richard said to Werner Wolfen, and maybe they should call him.

They decided that a stronger position, psychologically, would develop if Weintraub got to hear of the Carpenters' need for a manager on the grapevine. And it would be preferable if he called *them*.

Weintraub had admired their music for years, considering Karen "one of the most distinctive voices in history." Though he had a fearsome reputation as a business bulldozer, he had a creative streak and good "ears"—his favourite singer was Peggy Lee and his wife was the singer Jane Morgan who had hits in the 1950s, notably with ballads called "Fascination" and "The Day the Rains Came." Jane named Karen her favourite female vocalist.

As Richard and Werner hoped, Weintraub heard of the management "vacancy" and phoned them. They signed to his management on January 22, 1976, to open a new chapter in their career.

Weintraub approached his task with chutzpah, verve, and hard-dealing music industry muscle. An abrasive and formidable adversary, strong for his artists, he had earned a reputation as a tireless worker.

Inheriting the Carpenters when he knew their career was "in a state of flux," he relished such a challenge. He explained to them, as he had done to so many of his acts, that there came a time when outstanding artists simply stopped selling records at a fast rate. "Nothing to do with talent," he said. "The audience will buy a concert ticket, a movie ticket, watch them on television, but they won't go to a record store [in the same volume as previously]. They just won't do it! I worked with the biggest artists in the world, from Elvis Presley to Judy Garland to Neil Diamond and Sinatra and Bob Dylan and more, and I don't know an artist who doesn't reach that point. Try to explain this to artists, and none will accept it. Their audience grows up—and wants to play their old records and listen to new songs by others."

Examining their six-year career, Weintraub considered, like many others, that they had worked "the road" too hard. A fresh approach was necessary because he felt the Carpenters was an act "to last a lifetime."

Having faced artists in recession before, Weintraub recognized the same problem with Richard and Karen. "All these artists have a lot of money, and they get depressed when they're not selling records," he reflects. "It was my job with such artists not to just find them work but to find new things for them to do, make them want to be creative."

Despite their slipping record sales, one of Weintraub's first forays was to A&M, where he informed Jerry Moss that in his opinion the Carpenters had a "terrible deal." Moss replied dryly that it was not a terrible deal for A&M. "It's not a kibbutz here," he said to Weintraub, "but most artists are on this level. We sign people very early in their careers, and we don't give them big advances."

Moss laughs at the recollection of Weintraub's next thrust to him: "You've got to give me a million dollars because if you don't, I'm gonna print your first deal with them in the paper, and you're gonna be run out of town."

With their exceptional track record, Weintraub persisted, Richard and Karen deserved a considerable "top up" on their first advance, since they had demonstrated long-term profitability for A&M. Weintraub secured them a $750,000 nonrecoupable payment to resign with the label in 1976, together with a better royalty deal for future records.

Of crucial value to Richard, forever the proud custodian of Carpenters music, was an agreement also negotiated by Weintraub that A&M would never release anything by the Carpenters without Richard's permission.

Next, Weintraub turned to their appearances, which had drifted along, artistically and strategically, since they had begun their helter-skelter of roadwork six years earlier. Rationalizing that their old record buyers were probably at home with young children instead of out buying records, Weintraub confirmed to Karen and Richard that they should aim their act toward television. Two Carpenters-hosted TV specials a year would accomplish for them, at this stage in their career, what selling many millions of records had done. It would regenerate a concert audience so that if they wished to, they could tour to their hearts' content, without the necessity for a smash hit album to boost ticket sales.

The Carpenters had always been disappointed that they had failed to secure their own TV special in order to clinch that huge nationwide audience in their homes. The absence of such recognition had been a sore point with Richard and Karen since shortly after they had become established. They were baffled because most artists who enjoyed their level of success, particularly in the arena of adult popular music rather than rock, were given a prime-time TV special.

Richard maintained then, as he does now, that Sherwin Bash should have battled to get them this big break. Bash told me that he had made a conscious decision to keep them away from TV, because in their eight-week 1971 "summer replacement" series "Make Your Own Kind of Music," Richard had "come across as nervous and intense." Mass-audience television might have done them no favours, he says.

Richard disagrees with that theory, saying the series cited by Bash was never their own show but costarred other acts such as Al Hirt, Mark Lindsay, and less prominent artists. It was bad, Richard feels, to have placed the Carpenters, one of America's hottest record sellers, alongside such names as the Doodletown Pipers. Year after year they would guest on the shows of such strong hosts as Johnny Carson, Andy Williams, Johnny Cash, Carol Burnett, Ed Sullivan, and Perry Como. But they believed that the "Make Your Own Kind of Music" series had simply lacked style or commercial impact. And they deserved better.

To Bash's statement that he appeared nervous and intense, Richard says: "Absolutely not! The little time we were on, there was no time to be nervous and intense. At that point Karen and I were having a ball. But the first thing they did on that show was put a Superman outfit on me for a routine with Al Hirt, and I hated that wardrobe and that whole show. It was wrong. It's no wonder we had a bad taste in our mouths and that television felt that way about us regarding the prospect of our own show after that series. Even though it wasn't our own show, it may have been perceived as such because the Carpenters were the biggest name on it."

Refuting Bash's contention that he made a decision to keep them off TV, Richard cites that in addition to their many guest appearances, Sherwin had been in negotiations with Anheuser-Busch concerning sponsorship of a Carpenters TV Special. Believing it to be a done deal, Bash acquiesced to a request by Anheuser-Busch to have the Carpenters fly on January 16, 1973 to Houston to play for a theatre full of the firm's representatives the next day. Taking time off from the recording of the *Now and Then* album, Karen and Richard and their band did just that. "Nothing came of it," Richard says.

There were, Richard emphasizes, a number of things that Sherwin, as a professional, did well. And he and Karen liked him as a person. But the issue of their TV profile and his long-term management philosophy were to prove irreconcilable problems.

The appearances on "Make Your Own Kind of Music" soured other program makers toward them. But when Weintraub came in, he bullishly told Richard, "You are the Perry Comos of today!" Unwittingly aligning Richard with one of his favourite male singers, Weintraub was alluding to Como's huge impact on family audiences. Karen and Richard felt boosted when Weintraub rolled up his sleeves, determined to establish them in that same TV medium. But Weintraub encountered early resistance to the Carpenters because "Make Your Own Kind of Music" had stigmatized them, in the view of producers.

At ABC TV, programme director Fred Silverman was cynical because of their track record, but Weintraub promised him the Carpenters would pull in good ratings. It was no walkover, but Weintraub's offer of John Denver as a special guest, combined with his own assumption of a production role, clinched the deal. On December 8, 1976, their first nationwide television special was aired. It was a smash, arriving at number six on the weekly national ratings list. They were offered more; a new aspect of their career had begun.

Yet while Weintraub had arrived to give their career a surge in the direction they craved, he was, just like Terry Ellis, coming into their lives too late. A kind of neurosis had set in, Bettis believes, from years of travel and a deadly schedule: by then, "Richard and Karen were so used to it that they felt that if they weren't working those dates, their career must be in trouble." They might even have been masochistically proud of their exhaustion: "We did *this* for the last five years! Look at us! We can kill ourselves doing this!"

What they needed, says Bettis, was to be cultivated and nurtured as artists. "I think Jerry wanted to go in and say, 'Well, it's John Denver times two.' And to a certain extent as a commercial piece of machinery, he was right. There was nothing wrong with what he thought in terms of right or wrong. But it was not accurate for Richard and Karen. It was a very cursory view of them as individuals. I don't think Jerry took his marching orders from nurturing and expanding Richard and Karen's talents. I think he took his marching orders from making them successful again."

I asked the analytical Bettis why, since he viewed Richard as in charge of their career, Richard had not applied the brakes or insisted on the intake of breath that Bettis and others felt would have been wise, physically and creatively, for Karen and him.

"When success comes," Bettis replied, "the single hardest thing for any of us to do is believe it's going to last. Because in getting there, you've been told by legions of people that you're not going to get there. So you're going to make the most of it while you've got it."

And then came Richard's role as what Bettis described as "the older child, literally touched by God musically, assuming a responsible role to get the machinery of the Carpenters rolling around him. You're liable to decide: 'Well, let's just keep it moving because if I try to stop it and it breaks, I've just screwed up everything. So if it seems to be rolling, let's not stop—because what if I can't get it started again?'

"The problem with making any decision is that you're trying to predict the future. A hundred times a day, Richard was having to make that decision, unfortunately. Should he record 'Funny Faces' or 'Close to You'? Should they wear this or wear that? Should they tour 250 days a year or not at all? Should Karen get out from behind the drums? And then, once I've made that decision, how do I get her to do it? Because she was as resistant as hell! All those decisions had to be made over and over.

"There's something neat about being right, and if you're on a roll and making right decisions the majority of the time, that's pretty good." And then there was Richard's youth. "Come on, he was a kid running a multimillion-dollar-a-year organization and within the rubrick of that having to be a creative genius, too. It's tough. I mean, look what happened to Brian Wilson. In comparison, Richard made it through with flying colours. So there was a lot of forgiveness in my heart for him."

What Richard needed was the advice of a contemporary of the caliber of Elton John or Paul McCartney, who had travelled a similar helter-skelter route to fame. Coming from Bettis, as his cowriter, any advice might have seemed gratuitous. But he believes he should have said more when he realized the Carpenters' jet was speeding too fast. "One of the guilts I will carry around with me forever is that I felt so insecure with my knowledge. Because it was my first time through; and I was a good friend."

Richard was never bothered by the lack of confidence that ate away at his sister on one level, but others viewing the Carpenters' career were getting jittery. By 1976 they had gone two years since "Please Mr. Postman" had reached the top of the American charts, a position they had never occupied in Britain despite having albums that sold by the million. In their home country, 1975's "Only Yesterday" had reached four, "Solitaire" had gone to seventeen, and "There's a Kind of Hush" had been a number twelve.

These were respectable positions, but some observers expected the Carpenters to keep on producing bigger smashes. Now the word began to pass around A&M that they needed a blood transfusion in the shape of a new producer—because Richard had lost his touch, some said. To the surprise of them all, he agreed that some fresh thinking might well benefit them: "I felt I was doing my job as the arranger and songwriter, so let someone else come in, certainly, and do the production." He was also weary of the general commentary on their performances: "If it became a hit, it was Karen's achievement, and if it didn't, then it was my fault! It was like being the president! No credit when everything was going well, and criticism when it wasn't." Had the Carpenters been perceived as hip, though, the record company team would have been fawning over them.

With manager Weintraub, Richard met several producers with strong track records, but too many seemed in awe of his achievements. Big hits or not in the past couple of years, his level of musicianship and ability seemed to intimidate them. "I think they were aware of the fact that we were starting to be looked down upon by self-appointed hipsters who were programming the radio stations," Richard says. "Acts like the Carpenters and Barry Manilow were becoming tough nuts to crack at that time."

Finally, they thought they had settled on Joe Wissert, who produced Boz Scaggs, but at the eleventh hour Joe called Richard and asked for a meeting at the Hollywood restaurant Musso and Franks. There Wissert announced that he was pulling out because he felt Karen would not respond to him as she had done to Richard in the studio. That unbreakable bond had surfaced to yet another corner of their lives, and so Richard continued after this episode in his role as producer. Weintraub confirmed to him that still more candidates had declined, saying he was too tough an act to follow.

Putting heat on Karen and Richard to sell more records and hit the charts was still more proof that too many people close to them had failed to recognize them as artists with longevity. Even if their career had leveled out and they never had another hit single, they had a strong, loyal audience awaiting their concerts and albums to sustain their popularity (as was to be proved by their record sales for the next two decades). They stood outside the fickle rock territory, and no disgrace should have been attached to their shift to a new level.

What Karen did not need at that stage was the broadside at their career represented by such questioning of Richard's ability. "He was an absolute God to her," says a close friend. "She felt that if it wasn't for him, she would not have made it, and she knew that he was irreplaceable. And because he was *the one* not only in her eyes but in her parents' eyes, her value of herself was much lower than it should have been. Talk to most people, and Karen is *the one* who carries the Carpenters, but that wasn't the case to her whatever anybody told her. So she had a sibling problem."

Since 1970 the Carpenter family had become friendly with the family of Beverly Nogawski, a realtor who had found them most of their Downey properties. Karen now began to date Beverly's son, Steve, but he became discouraged because of Karen's dedication to her work, which always took priority over his ideas for their dates. The Carpenter-Nogawski family friendship remained when Karen and Steve's dates stopped, and Beverly regarded Karen as "like a daughter, very kind, giving, and sweet." Like so many others, she considered her unfulfilled: "The depth of her singing reflected what she wanted to be, with the emotion she showed when she sang. She really wanted to find somebody she could really be happy with."

Karen took more interest in the business side of their career at this stage and related more to Weintraub's gregarious personality than did Richard. As she developed a platonic affection for Weintraub, she enjoyed his droll sense of humor, keen business sense, and his clear fondness for her. At many of their meetings she would curl up on his lap.

In the earliest months of their association, he was unaware of her health problem. "She went through a very long period of fooling us all, and herself, about her sickness." Having admired her work from afar, he quickly became "mad about her as a friend," he says. Pretty soon, like many others, he would soon be mad at her for a different reason as he felt "a bag of bones" hugging him.

"You look like something out of a concentration camp," he told her. "If somebody laid on top of you, he'd break your bones." She smiled at this, regarding it as a funny line—and disregarded its ugly truth.

In direct contrast with his sister's disinterest in food, Richard always had a hearty appetite and maintained it even during her anorexia. In the studio, he was nicknamed "Mister Eat Dinner," since he routinely called for a restaurant visit at 6:00 P.M. every night. Martoni's, a traditional Italian restaurant on Cahuenga Boulevard off Sunset, was a regular haunt. A man of habit, he would invariably choose veal followed by ice cream, preceded by a martini.

It was at Martoni's, during the recording of *A Kind of Hush*, that John Bettis first noticed Karen's "total game" with food. As he remembers: "She would make a big deal out of showing everyone that she was having shrimp on the side and then she would take a roll, and butter the hell out of it for about thirty minutes—and then eat about half a mouthful of it."

She could not have found a more exasperating disease for Richard and John to deal with. "The subtlety of it, the inability to directly attack it, drove Richard and me absolutely nuts. It wasn't like a bad record, where you could listen to each track and find out where the bad note was. It drove Richard sideways. You couldn't browbeat Karen into eating. There was no solution."

Despite all these problems, both Karen and Richard hungered for work; and they wanted to lift themselves to a new stratum. Along with Weintraub, they believed that their stage show needed more surgery. Six winning years into their career, they and most people around them felt that in two areas at least, they had been stagnant.

They had musical credibility and wealth, but their personal images and attention to their stage shows needed still more development and they did not shirk from it.

Their concert routine had survived through the sheer weight of their music. Weintraub told them they needed to inject fresh professional flair into the act. They agreed. What transpired was a demolition of the old, cosy show and a theatrical flirtation with animation and acrobatics that gave them a blood transfusion.

Enter Joe Layton, a high-pedigree Broadway producer friend of Ken and Mitzie Welch. He had worked with Diana Ross, Raquel Welch, Lionel Richie, and Bette Midler and would later go on to work with Barbra Streisand and Cher.

Warming to Richard and particularly to Karen, Layton walked into two psychological problems. He wanted to project Karen visually but found, like many before him, that she "hid behind her drums." Her mentality reminded him of someone who didn't want to be seen in a bathing suit: "She had to hide behind a screen to talk."

Surmounting that barrier of insecurity, Layton came up against one that was bigger and more significant. He drafted in dress designer Bill Whitten, fresh from his success with the Jackson Five, and the suggestion that she start to wear tighter-fitting dresses worried Karen. Like many anorexics, she had come to rely on the principle of wearing multilayered clothes to conceal the reality. Suddenly, with her enforced new look, the truth was going to be visible.

"When we started fittings and designs, she started on about the size of her hips," Layton says. "Richard would say, 'Can we do something to hide those hips?' and their mother and father would say, 'You *sure* you wanna wear that?'"

Every time something like that was said in her presence, Layton says, "it was like a sledgehammer pounding her further down because of her enormous insecurity. So we had enormous problems about clothes, what seemed to be the bone of contention and the bane of her existence.

"Yet she looked wonderful," in Layton's perception. "She was a woman, happened to have big hips, and was a slight girl. But I believe that's called having big hips so you can have babies. That's the way she was built. And they didn't leave it alone."

Those remarks were not intended by Richard to emphasize in particular her shape. He simply felt that "she was so goddamned thin with some of these new outfits that you could see her pelvis. That's what I didn't like. If you look at the photographs of Karen at, say, the London Palladium in 1976, it's the pelvis that's sticking out.

"I'd *never* give Karen the impression that I was harping on her hips."

To Joe Layton and others, Karen's devotion to her parents and to Richard was at once admirable and a self-induced pressure of a kind. Says Layton: "I think that satisfying the family was number one. I think she stayed a little girl. She never broke the ties."

When I went to see the Carpenters in Germany in November 1976 at the start of a European tour, I found dramatically different personalities, on and off stage, from those of two years earlier. They disarmed any criticism of their pristine image with a new openness and self-deprecation. It was not generally known that

Karen had begun her slide into anorexia nervosa or that Richard was addicted to pills; their problems weren't apparent in either of them. Perhaps these difficulties had brought a kind of humility.

On stage, their change was incredible. Gone was the coy and stilted look, replaced by a speedy Joe Layton production routine that accentuated theatrics rather than the songs that had made them famous. In one segment, a spoof on the 1950s, Karen dressed as a busty tart and played the role of a fast woman, while Richard roared on stage on a motorcycle during the song "Greased Lightning." For Carpenters fans of yesteryear, it was a surprising switch in direction. If you went to the London Palladium (which they played on the tour) expecting a graceful rerun of their oldies and a few new love songs, you were in for a shock.

During their classic "We've Only Just Begun," Karen and Richard held hands for a split second, looked into each other's eyes. It was a rare moment in an act never noted for its tactile warmth, in spite of the romantic beauty of their songs.

Later, they explained to me and other writers how it came to pass that they introduced such a segment into the show. "We've never been a touching and kissing family; we're not raised that way," Richard said. And Karen added: "Now, when we're thinking about it, it seems natural and normal. People who came to see the show, close friends and managers, said it was ridiculous that we didn't touch each other throughout. So we put it in."

She said holding hands felt uneasy for a while; Richard, too, fought off the idea on the grounds that they were "not in love that way." Then, in the context of a violent change in their stage act, they agreed to it.

It was only one aspect of a production that steamrollered over their past.

Of their daring transformation, I wrote in the *Melody Maker:* "Richard no longer sits sternly at the piano. He roars on stage in a motorcycle (with Buddy Holly-type spectacles and a leather jacket) and Karen has abandoned that forlorn stance in a sad little red dress which helped to dent their reputation last time."

Their performance of "Close to You" was two or three times its recorded tempo, with the band spoofing it up à la Spike Jones with kazoos and hooters; and during "Sing," Karen actually moved from the stage to walk among the first rows of the audience. Richard's piano peaks began with a fine "Warsaw Concerto" accompanied by a forty-piece orchestra before the medley of hits started, and they ended with the Beach Boys' "Good Vibrations" and—incongruously—"Coming through the Rye."

Cynicism among British newspaper reviewers was beginning to subside in the wake of the Carpenters' sustained achievements and ability to sell out the London Palladium for six nights. In *The Daily Telegraph*, John Coldstream, describing Karen as "angelically voiced," added a rider about a show he admired for its energy: "This week's six full houses may well feel disappointed by such a short, uneven show, especially at £6 a seat." The *Daily Mail*'s Clive Thomas felt that Richard demonstrated that he "could have had a successful career as a concert pianist," and reported that the audience applauded the opening of each of the Carpenters' songs, "something that is seldom heard today." "It is only when the Carpenters appear live and sing medleys of their songs that you realize just how many hits they have had," Thomas wrote.

Writing about the air of desperation that permeated this show, I added: "At least it's a positive effort to blitz the audience with something beyond Carpenters music. The big question is whether they've reversed too far and skated too thinly over their real strengths, the songs. More than anything, the show qualifies them for bravery medals. Less bold stars with millions of record sales would have sat tight and played the old stuff to the 46,000 people they'll attract to British theatres on their tour.

"Now she tears at three sets of drums and a battery of congas, looks kookie in jeans, changes from sharp culotte suit to a beautiful ball gown and acts neatly while dressed as a tart with a bouffant wig in the 1950s sequence."

Layton's Broadway eye had turned the Carpenters' stage act inside out, giving a firm role to Richard who was told that though Karen might be the star, he had to think of his contribution visually as well as musically. "You may think everyone is looking at Karen," Layton told him and the group, "but with thousands of people watching, at any given time someone is looking at *you*. So there will not be any of this schmoozing between songs, and not one of you is going to have a glass of water on that stage."

He insisted that concertgoers wanted the Carpenters to DO something beyond singing their hits. He reasoned that the ticket buyers had their records at home and did not go out for an evening merely to see the songs replicated.

"The positive view of the mind-boggling Carpenters show," I wrote, "would be that they have planted the kiss of life on a two year old corpse and that their audacity has won. Their 1974 show was boring. This 1976 show is over-ambitious.

"The uncharitable would say that they have snatched catastrophe from the jaws of disaster. The truth lies somewhere between those two extremes. Like it or not, the new show forces a reaction. Nobody sleeps during this concert."

This was a stunningly ambitious realignment for an act presenting this kind of music, and Richard was confessional about their professional niche when we spoke before the concert in Munich's Deutsche Museum. He said he thought their musical achievements deserved a chapter in history and he was afraid that if they didn't stand up and declare themselves a little, the Carpenters might well be dismissed and forgotten as "bland, easy listening, middle of the road . . . we've gotta change all that. And I've always been concerned that we've not been accepted in concert as well as on record. It's sure not the fault of Karen's voice because she sings the same anywhere. The group's usually been clean and tight. No, some magic was missing."

He revealed that this concern had worried him after most shows for the previous five years. "Charisma! That's been missing! Guess we're now trying to graft it on to our act. Well, it sure isn't before time." Showing his competitive edge, he added: "There are people out there who don't sing as well as we do, haven't had our amount of hits, who aren't a fraction as well known as us, but they're getting the audiences going. Thus far, we have failed in that direction.

"And when you know you're doing a good concert and not pulling in a response from the audience, it's demoralizing." He agreed that their audiences, who were older than the rock set, were not the types to get animated when they did their hits. "On the other hand, the nice part is that they don't talk throughout our show."

Richard continued to open up about his concern: his manager had told him not to worry, but he had been "worried sick" by the fact that for an act that sold so many records, "there's something wrong when something better isn't happening from that stage." Certainly their manager had been proven correct in his prediction that people would always return to their shows, and, Richard said:

"We kept selling out. Maybe we've just been selling records to quiet people! Anyway, it built up in my mind. It nagged away.

"So here we are with this radical change. Joe Layton says we've been playing the role of good musicians for too long. He says we're too good, that people don't want to concentrate on music so much. If they want the Carpenters sound, they'll stay home with the stereo."

Karen said simply of their new personalities on stage: "We're hams." They were both agitated, but neither showed the physical duress they were clearly under at that time. Richard's face was gaunt, but that was so even before his pill problem, while Karen, wearing a T-shirt with the enigmatic words "Lead Sister" on the front, simply looked like a young woman who had been dieting. Their apocalypse was about to begin, but neither they nor we who knew them could have prophesied its extent.

During the German leg of that European tour, Richard and Karen went their separate ways most of the time apart from a chilling visit together to the site of the concentration camp at Dachau and an evening out to a Charles Aznavour concert. Richard made a point of visiting Steinway Hall, while Karen went shopping in all the cities, Hamburg, Düsseldorf, and Munich. They carried on normally with no signs of the prima donna touches exhibited by so many artists. Their energy level was extraordinarily high in public, even though he was relying on sleeping pills at night and she was eating little. Although Richard's pill-taking habits were about to surface in a self-destructive debacle, there was no visual evidence of this. The public was completely unaware of his private drama that was about to reach a crescendo for the Carpenter family.

When I sat with them for an interview, they were exceptionally frank. I asked both together to name the other's most irritating characteristic. Richard bridled slightly, while Karen came straight out with it: "He'll always stall when we're due to go into the studios and not let me know the title or nature of a song until we get there. I keep saying, for days before, 'What's the song?' and he keeps saying: 'Oh, you'll be OK. It's easy for you.' He doesn't let me know what *my work is!* And I hate that about him."

Richard thought deeply before being pushed to a reply: "If I'm with a girl Karen doesn't like, she gets in her three cents' worth and then doesn't leave it at that. And after a while it starts to get on my nerves and we argue. It's usually not musical. I wish Karen wouldn't act, sometimes, like a twenty-six-year-old Jewish momma and interfere so much with my personal affairs."

Did Richard interfere with her private life, or did Karen accept his role as big brother? It was a sensitive question to ask a thirty-year-old man about his twenty-six-year-old sister, and his reply was honest. Karen sat expressionless, as if she'd heard it all before, when Richard said: "Sometimes I'll offer a view, but I'd never tell her not to date this guy or that. I figure that'd be impertinent. However, Karen seems to see it as her duty to give me advice. I don't like that."

What were their joint worries? I asked. "Staying where we are," they answered in unison. "Maintaining, which is very difficult in the American pop market," Richard said. "Y'know, it seems that if you're in country and western and you make a couple of hit singles, you're there for life. Not in pop. We can go down as quickly as we came up if our records are not selling."

And how vital was it to him and to Karen to keep on achieving those mass sales? More important than their private lives at that moment?

Karen answered that if it came to a choice between privacy and fame, hers would be fame. Her career meant everything to her, she told me candidly. In a sentence, she summarized the person embedded in her psyche: "I gotta sing," she said. "I love that crowd." Because she was so obsessive about her work at that stage, there seemed little time to develop meaningful relationships.

Richard was more equivocal. "Sometimes I think it wrong that we aren't famous enough in person, considering the millions of records we've sold. Sometimes we are not noticed in the street, and that gets to me. Other times, I get hassled in a restaurant and I don't like that, either."

Conversely, he said he wanted to go to the grave having been regarded as a musician rather than a pop star. "You can be a pop star for a week," he said thoughtfully. "I'm gonna be a musician forever."

Both were certain that whatever else they recorded, the song "We've Only Just Begun" would be their epitaph, musically.

"Huge though 'Close to You' was," Karen said, "it didn't have the impact of 'Begun,' and no one song has been so associated with an act so much for a long, long time as that has with us."

College students were beginning to write essays on the theme of the song. "Yep," Richard agreed, "that's the song that's going to remain with us, and if you ask me what song I'll take to the grave, that's the one." I asked him how he wanted to die. "In my sleep." Karen nodded her agreement.

During that European tour, Karen voiced to Norman Weiss, the president of Weintraub's company, her concern about something. She wanted their careers to continue, but she was getting worried that Richard's health was not going to stand up to it. His reliance on sleeping pills was worrying her, and by the time they reached London, Richard was "a stick" (his words)—down to 139 pounds, which for his six-foot frame was spindly. His appetite, normally healthy, was reduced by the pill-popping routine which threatened him.

The London Palladium audience during their week's residency there was as intensely loyal as the British crowds had always been. Richard was able to miraculously draw a veil over his pill dependency and performed the newly designed stage show on autopilot.

Astonishingly, he and Karen were still not work-shy. With two days clear in their schedule before they had to leave London for Europe, Weiss suggested that since it was just before Christmas, they should do a free show for a children's charity. "A Ticket For a Toy" meant that if a fan took a toy to London's Capital Radio studio, the reward was a free ticket to see the Carpenters. The foyer was jammed with children's gifts, and Karen told the concert audiences that since she loved kids, these were among her most satisfying shows.

In Japan, wildly enthusiastic scenes greeted them at all their concerts. Fans showered Karen with gifts from below stage while she was simultaneously singing and holding the mike; this practice became so dangerous that Karen and Richard were told not to shake hands with fans from the stage lest they be pulled over and injured.

Both in their British and Japanese treks, no damage had been suffered from the postponement of their tours from the previous year because of Karen's illness. Even in a wintry Japan with rain and snow for most of their tour, Karen maintained her health and energy level.

As they took in the sights of Japan, visiting a temple, and the homes of Sony and Panasonic, *A Kind of Hush* went to the top of the country's charts, and they were presented with four gold records, bringing the total of Japanese awards at that time to eleven.

Karen had learned enough Japanese to be able to thank fans at each concert for their support and concern during her illness. She even changed the dialect from city to city, with some coaching from their promoter, Tats Nagashima. Her sense of irony surfaced in a card sent home to Downey recounting the language problem when ordering room service at the hotel. "I've just had breakfast. I ordered three scrambled eggs. I got *three orders* of scrambled eggs. I'm very full."

Though she enjoyed dabbling in Beverly Hills glitz, Karen never lost her homespun values and non-show-biz friends remained a central part of her life. She sent an inordinate number of greetings cards on her travels, rarely forgot a birthday, and delighted her friends with impromptu phone calls when they thought they had been forgotten by a "star."

In Chicago on tour, Karen struck a chord with Elizabeth Van Ness, who worked at a local radio station where the Carpenters were interviewed. After a discussion about perfume, Elizabeth sent her a bottle of Touvache, an act which touched Karen. Phone calls and correspondence sealed their rapport.

"It was hard for her to make friends on the road," notes Elizabeth, whose closeness developed when she moved to Los Angeles and got married. Karen enjoyed her "supervisory" role, advising Elizabeth where to shop, which were the best restaurants and doctors.

The two spent a lot of time at the Hamburger Hamlet in Century City, near Karen's apartment, and as Karen became embroiled in the role of a part-time "uptown girl," she wanted Elizabeth to join her coterie. Elizabeth demurred. Nor did she want to visit Downey often, a fact which mystified Agnes since Karen often spoke warmly of her new friend. Elizabeth's kinship with Karen worked on a different level, separate from either show business or family.

Karen's personality bubbled during their shopping sprees. With her slender frame, she was very proud that she could try on any outfit and—to her—look terrific, Elizabeth remembers. On one such trip, their inevitable debate occurred over Karen's weight. "She was trying on clothes and just looked horrible. And she clearly thought she looked great. There wasn't an ounce of flesh on her; she was all bones. She made some reference to it, said she felt she was almost there."

When Elizabeth said she was too thin, Karen responded that Frenda Leffler thought so, too. "But it was clear," says Elizabeth Van Ness, "that she wasn't going to deal with it."

Richard liked to see Karen date—but she continued to watch all his encounters like a hawk. Her "dream match" for him was Olivia Newton-John; she constantly told friends that they would be right together. "Where do you think *that* would have gone?" Richard asks now, "if I had dated Karen's girlfriend!" It seemed that Karen often liked Richard's dates until he started getting serious with them.

The arrival of someone by his side probably triggered her realization of her own emptiness. And she resented their focus on him. Significantly, she bristled with resentment when Maria Galeazzi, after a concert in Valley Forge, Pennsylvania, climbed into the front passenger seat of his Ferrari, consigning Karen to the back. She always expected Richard's prime attention. "She's just like Mom," Richard would say wearily to close friends as he reflected on his smothering mother.

"Karen was against every woman I was ever with," Richard declares. Conversely, when in 1974 Karen began dating Mike Curb, Richard was delighted. The two men struck a fine rapport and over dinner enjoyed trivia quizzes on pop music. Both had an encyclopedic knowledge of obscure records and chart positions down the years, and Curb outstripped Richard most times, a remarkable feat.

The brother of Karen's friend Carol and a prominent figure in the music industry, Mike Curb was the former head of MGM Records. By then running his own company, Curb Records, the striking and confident Mike was a prominent Republican party activist and Ronald Reagan's campaign chairman for California at the time he dated Karen. "She was interested in music, in the world, in children, in people. She was a great, great lady," Curb says. Her vote, however, was more likely to go to a person rather than be politically aligned.

Curb was handsome, thrusting, and successful, but with both his career and the Carpenters' schedule so demanding, their dates were sporadic. Several years later, his label scored a five-million-selling record that stayed at the top of the charts for ten weeks. Mike had played the song "You Light Up My Life" by Debby Boone, earlier to Karen, who declared: "I should have done it!" as the record climbed to the top. She and many others had not registered it as such a potential winner.

When they went for dinner, often to Knotts Berry Farm, he faced the regular speech from Karen: "If I eat too much, it will go to my hips." But in Mike she faced a determination as resolute as her own. "Don't worry about it. You're pretty the way you are. Eat; let's have a good time," he would tell her. She preferred straight "middle-American" cooking such as chicken rather than fancy French cuisine with sauces, Curb recalls; his insistence that she eat properly was always an issue on their dates. "I'd be finished eating, and she would look at her food, and I would say, 'Karen, I'm gonna stay here until you eat because I want you to feel good and be healthy.'" At this she would reiterate that her hips were out of proportion with other parts of her body. Curb says he "waited until she had taken her last bite and then I would make sure she had dessert."

Having faced a similar eating barrier with his sister Carol, he says he had learned to say to such people: "Wait until tomorrow. Enjoy your dinner tonight." And Karen would laugh at that; it was, he says, as if a veil had to be lifted to penetrate her with such common sense. And she also seemed to respond to the truism that he spelled out to her: "A woman's beauty is not in the size of her hips. It's the whole person that's beautiful." It was, he pointed out, the totality of her that was important: from her voice to her personality, from the way she played drums to her appearance.

Though Curb seems to have won through in his insistence that she eat during their dates, the habits of the anorexic continued when they stopped meeting regularly. Their spell together was probably deflected by her dedication to her career. And she gave Mike the impression that Richard was "the most important person in her life, and rightly so," says Curb, describing the Carpenters entity as "geniuses."

He gleaned the feeling from Karen during their year or so of close friendship that she wanted to achieve much more in her career before contemplating marriage. While their fondness and friendship remained, the romance ended with both Karen and Mike pursuing their busy lives.

With the battles that beset them both in 1977, the wonder was that they were in any condition to make a new album. But neither Richard nor Karen would easily be diverted from their work ethic if they could make it to the studio, "home base" to their souls.

By that year, though, Richard's musical goals were becoming blurred by the unclear map reading of others. Even though they had recorded strong songs like "Can't Smile without You" and "I Just Fall in Love Again," radio play eluded them. "Programmers were getting concerned about their image," Richard says, "and the Carpenters were regarded as too square." That was partly why it had been hard to find a producer to succeed him: "No matter what records they turned out by us at that point in time, it was going to be a hard sell."

They entered the studio to record *Passage,* their eighth album, with the knowledge that *A Kind of Hush* had not performed well enough commercially (even though it would eventually go gold); Richard had not been proud of it as an entity.

When he heard the song "Don't Cry for Me Argentina," from the musical *Evita,* Richard knew it would be perfect for Karen. He wanted a symphonic arrangement. Impressed with the abilities of the British conductor and arranger Peter Knight, Richard asked Ed Sulzer (still employed by the Carpenters as production administrator) to phone and ask Knight to fly in for the session. Knight arrived in Los Angeles on May 15, 1977, to begin a musical partnership and friendship with the Carpenters and their family.[1]

Recorded in three months and significantly lacking any Bettis-Carpenter compositions, marking a conscious break from the past, *Passage* pawned the Carpenters' identity in favor of eclecticism. There were but two creative sparks: Karen's stunning reading of "Argentina" and Knight's rich arrangement, plus the haunting

1. A respected arranger for artists from the 1950s onward, Knight had a contemporary edge, working with the Moody Blues on their orchestral-rock album *Days of Future Passed.* He had first worked with Richard on an overture for the Boston Pops project in 1974. Later he collaborated on several key songs, including "Because We Are in Love" (The Wedding Song) which Richard cowrote with John Bettis for Karen's wedding; and many Christmas songs with Karen and Richard. Knight died on July 30, 1985.

"Calling Occupants of Interplanetary Craft," the surreal "recognized anthem of World Contact Day."

The Beatle-ish Canadian group Klaatu had written and recorded this imaginative song about supposed creatures watching over humankind from another planet, and Karen and Richard jumped in with the definitive version of a record that inspires sci-fi students.

In addition to "Argentina" and "Occupants," three songs, "All You Get from Love Is a Love Song," "I Just Fall in Love Again," and "Sweet Sweet Smile" rounded out an average collection.

Jerry Moss believed the Carpenters should never have attempted "Argentina" since it was a "Socialist anthem," but Richard defended his choice stoutly, pointing out that it was a beautiful song, a big hit, perfect for Karen, and he felt that singing it did not constitute a political statement from the Carpenters.

When *Passage* failed to sell well in the United States (it was their first album to fail to achieve gold, 500,000-sales status), Moss suggested the material had been avant-garde. But Richard, who felt the album was a creative success, says: "If someone else had come in to produce us other than me at that time, the resulting record might have been more avant-garde. The new man would have been told that sales were down, and then he would understandably have pointed us in a different direction."

Again, the only person who seemed to accept the Carpenters' record graph as a natural trend was Jerry Weintraub. No artists could sustain the figures achieved at the launch of a career, he repeated.

While some still voiced cynicism, their loyal defenders inside the record company pointed to A&M's "Real Picture Report," an accurate log of sales for each artist that showed the number of units returned from retail outlets as unsold. For seven years, the Carpenters' returns had been minimal; even in these years before Compact Disc repackaging sent all catalogue sales soaring, it was clear that Richard and Karen's work would always sell steadily. As it turned out, their catalogue contributed heftily to the survival and eventual growth that enabled Alpert and Moss to sell their stock in 1990 to Polygram for about $500 million.

"No Carpenters, no A&M," said some. "They built that city." (An overstatement; Richard points out: "Herb's Tijuana Brass was the foundation of the company, but the Carpenters certainly helped sustain it as the Brass wound up.")

Less charitable views persisted from some onlookers in the wake of *Passage,* and soon they would drive a wedge between Karen and Richard.

And tremors about Karen's health persisted. During a visit to their Morsound equipment and rehearsal warehouse in North Hollywood, Karen suffered what she would later describe to Steven Levenkron as "a ministroke."

One side of her face went numb. She called Richard to mention it, but dismissed its significance to him and to Ken Black [a Morsound employee] who was nearby when it happened. Richard believes she went to see a doctor. Since nobody saw it happen, its seriousness cannot be judged, but she considered it important enough to notify her brother. Such was the bounce and determination of Karen that she quickly cast the incident aside and didn't bother to mention it to her close friends.

Karen was always *worrying about Richard.*

—HER FORMER BOYFRIEND TOM BAHLER

Either sit there and kill yourself, or deal with it.

—LAWYER WERNER WOLFEN AND MANAGER JERRY WEIN-
TRAUB TO RICHARD, ON HIS PILL ADDICTION

As anorexia nervosa increased its grip on Karen, their story turned grisly. Richard fell victim in 1976 to an incredible pill-popping addiction that took him close to death.

Karen, busy concealing her difficulties as much as she could, was hardly in a position to hector him, although she did. Agnes and Harold, too, urged him to go and get help. As both Karen and Richard plunged downhill, the scene defied logic: a proud and gifted musician who had come through the 1960s shunning drugs, who drank a little wine but only smoked cigarettes occasionally, now drifted into a life-threatening abyss, seriously damaging the multimillion-dollar career he had steered with such pride.

His habit with pills had innocent beginnings that dated back to 1971. Just after their initial success, he found their schedule punishing, particularly in the studio, which he considered their most important workplace. Their third album, despite spawning the hits "Superstar," "Rainy Days and Mondays," and "For All We Know," shortchanged the public, in Richard's view. It lasted a mere thirty-one minutes. Musicians and friends were surprised at his disenchantment at such quality, but he knew it had been produced hurriedly—"under the gun" to capitalize on their speedy success. And as they went on a European concert and promotional tour in the fall of 1971, the perfectionist inside him grumbled that "quality control" was being overtaken by expediency. There was too much road work, too much clock-watching, and they were not spending enough time in the studio.

"By the time I got back from Europe, I looked like hell through lack of sleep. Mom had just been given by our family doctor the new wonder sleeping pill Quaalude. It said on the label, take one or two, and I said why not, I'm beat! I couldn't sleep, and a good night's rest sounded good."

For about four years he took one steadily and sensibly at bed-time, and all was fine. Then all hell broke loose. The problem began when he took one or two for a different purpose than going to sleep. He found that when he took them and stayed awake, the effect was to make him feel high—and he enjoyed it. At first he found the effects stimulating, then gradually he found himself rely-ing on them. (At one period Quaaludes became a fashionable drug sold on the circuit of trendy parties, where they were displayed in bowls.)

The more his body built up a tolerance, the more he took. He enjoyed the results so much that by 1976 he began to stop eating properly since they worked best on an empty stomach. After break-fast, he ate nothing until a snack at night. His weight dropped by twenty-five pounds to 139, and by late 1976, at the Carpenters' performances at the London Palladium, he looked gaunt.

"It got to the point where at times I got the shakes and couldn't sign my name or play the piano properly on certain songs. In Amsterdam in November 1976, going to the breakfast bar at the hotel in front of the whole group, I remember my hands shak-ing with the orange juice. It was like they say of an alcoholic, all I could think of even when I was on stage was getting back home to take more pills. By late 1978 I was up to around twenty-five a night in doses of six at a time. Take some, go to bed, wake up, take some more."

A year into his problem, on a doctor's advice he checked into Century City Hospital in Los Angeles in November 1977, but this provided no long-term cure since it was solely a detoxification pro-gram. A few months later, the slide continuing, he returned to the hospital for a week, but again the treatment proved temporary. Karen believed Richard would be cured by this programme, but he was cynical about it: short trips would not cure his deep-seated addiction, and he knew it.

By 1978, the drugs took progressively longer to wear off. His speech became slurred at times, and his hands trembled. He could not write even his name properly, and by November had trouble performing. As he watched his sister careening downhill, he was powerless, locked into his own nightmare. One side of him castigated himself for letting her and his parents down and for threatening his own life, while the other convinced him that he could not get by without those pills.

Precise and orderly at home, punctual and immaculate in his work, Richard astonished everyone who knew him by becoming the opposite. His clothes were slung anywhere, and he did not even clean his beloved cars. His unreliability in every department of his life now angered Karen, who, in the face of all her affliction, was soldiering on. "I must have been doing a hell of a good con job," Richard reflects, "because at one time someone asked to sign a programme and my hand was shaking. But I replied that it was from the cold outside."

He became as devious as an anorexic, staying in bed in the mornings, feigning exhaustion—and though Karen sympathized with his physical state, she was also angry and anxious about their future career.

"In late 1977 Karen urged me to go and get treatment. She was concerned about me, but not about her health. I thought she should have been worrying about herself; she thought I should be worrying about myself. I probably told her what she said: that I had it under control; leave me alone."

Though detoxification in the hospital had eliminated the drugs from his system, for the week that he was there, had not confronted his central problem of addiction. And yet against all their physical odds, they were back in the studio to fulfil a plan they had nursed for many years: an album of traditional Christmas songs.

This plan had its roots back in 1970 when they had recorded a single, "Merry Christmas Darling," written by Richard with Frank Pooler. Dissatisfied with her performance on that, Karen in 1978 recut her vocal lead. Karen's vocal warmth seemed the very essence of Christmas, and she and Richard tore into the project with such enthusiasm that they recorded too many tracks for the album that became *Christmas Portrait*. "But then," Richard states, "had Karen lived, we would have made one or two more Christmas albums."

With very little of the Carpenters "overdub" sound, the album was virtually a platform for Karen's solo vocals. "It gave her a chance to stretch and sing some of the standards," Richard says.

Memories of his physical condition during the making of

Christmas Portrait cause Richard regret. He was not mentally strong enough to do much of the arranging, most of which fell to Peter Knight, with input from the veteran Billy May. Seasonal favourites like "The Christmas Song (Chestnuts Roasting on an Open Fire)" and "White Christmas" would make the album, released in October 1978, a hit every yuletide. Yet there was a curious attitude toward its obvious commercial prospects at A&M. It received scant attention, and when Karen flew to Britain, she was baffled that she was not asked to help promote it. All attention was focused on their British 1974–78 singles compilation. Here was another bizarre view of marketing the Carpenters; *Christmas Portrait* assumed its own momentum and has sold more than two million units, demonstrating that when they found their niche, their audience was waiting.[1]

During the recording of the Christmas music, Karen was driving down Highland Avenue toward A&M in heavy traffic one day when she saw a man do a U-turn in his Porsche convertible. Shocked at the speed of his illegal action, she was astonished to see that the driver was Tom Bahler. Ten years earlier, he and his brother, John, had been their mentors for the Ford car commercial deal.

A rapport in music had kept the Bahler brothers friendly with the Carpenters as their careers had lifted off; Tom had coproduced *The Wiz* with Quincy Jones and also the hot group the Brothers Johnson. Richard had asked Tom to help their Christmas album project by assembling a choir.

Karen would later say that the sight of Tom Bahler doing a U-turn in his Porsche had "peaked her interest" in him as a guy, for during that period when they were cutting the Christmas album, they began dating. Dinner dates became frequent, as did lunches, for Karen and Tom. Watching her diet, but powerless to change her habits, Tom decided she was "in denial . . . she would not accept that her thinness was a major problem." One night, as he was going out to dinner with Karen, Tom was implored by

---

1. A second Christmas album, *An Old Fashioned Christmas,* was released in 1984. With Karen gone, it was touching for Richard to reflect that his all-time favourite vocal performance by Karen, "Little Altar Boy," which had not been completed in time for the first collection, was on this set. Additional recording for this "overflow" album was done by Richard at EMI's Abbey Road, London, studios, giving him a kick since the venue was the "birthplace" of the Beatles.

Richard to do his best to make her eat. Tom badgered her to have a chicken entrée, but when they went back to her apartment, she disappeared to the bathroom. "See what happens when I give my body food it doesn't want?" she said. Naive about the anorexic ritual, he became puzzled when they met at a café regularly for lunch.

"She would start out with coffee, and every third cup of coffee she would ask for a fresh pot and drink five or six cups. And I'd say, 'Well, are we going to order?' She would reply usually that she had just eaten, or wasn't hungry, and it was all done in such a perfectly normal manner. She was so in control of her feelings."

Expressing concern, like so many others, for her health, Tom was consistently up against her disarming reply: "I'm perfectly healthy. I'm fine. There's nothing wrong with me."

And it was difficult, sometimes, to argue. Appalled though Tom Bahler was when he caught sight of her bony body on the beach during a holiday in Hawaii, her energy level was high and she swam enthusiastically. They had gone with Richard and Olivia Newton-John and her manager at that time, Lee Kramer. "See, I've got more energy than *you*," the bikini-clad Karen would smile.

And he came up against the formidable reality that her voice remained constant and true. A singer himself, Tom was stunned one day when, as he drove her around Los Angeles, she suddenly started singing in a high-pitched voice. "Wow, where did *that* come from?" he asked her. She told him she had a four-octave range. "Her pitch and control was right there," Bahler remembers, "and I said, 'My God, I had no idea you could sing that high.'"

Her laconic riposte convinced Tom that she had a master plan for her vocal work. "That's because the money's in the basement," Karen said.[2]

A year before his romance had taken off, Tom Bahler had written a haunting autobiographical ballad, "She's Out of My Life," which would become a big hit for Michael Jackson in 1980. When Karen met Tom, she had no inkling that the song mirrored her boyfriend's domestic strife. As their relationship intensified, that

2. Karen's vocal range was from D below middle C to G above high C [using falsetto].

became an issue that brought her up against one of the most tortuous decisions of her love life.

She would regularly tell Tom, as she told others, of her requirements in her man. "She had a whole cupboard she would open," he says. "It was like, Karen's Wedding Ideas!" She was obviously looking for a relationship, but she had stringent rules. Money was a big question: she worried that any suitor might want her for her income rather than her personality. "It wasn't a hurdle for me, but it was a concern for her," Tom Bahler recalls. "I was able to say, 'Karen, I don't need any of your money.'"

They discussed marriage frequently, but as they did so, Tom had to level with her about his background. Divorced in 1975, he also had a teenage daughter by a married woman. As "things were really heating up," he decided to tell her, knowing that the issue of his daughter would make or break their relationship. Already bothered by the social gaffe (as she considered it) of his divorce, Karen spent three weeks hardly sleeping and worrying about a love affair that meant a lot to her.

The news of his daughter had not reached Karen until late in their romance. Finally, they sat together to discuss it in his car at the A&M studios. She was distraught but not tearful. "Tom, I have tried to reconcile this, to see in my heart if I can accept this, but I can't," she began. Tom felt Karen was worrying unduly that his daughter might somehow become a dividing problem between them if they were married. But, acknowledging that she would have to do what she felt right, he said it was more important that she choose the right path than go against her instinct. "Because I care for you very deeply," he added. They drifted apart, but a solid friendship remained. Another important attachment had gone awry for Karen, and she returned her focus on her work and the simmering problem of her brother's health. "She was *always* worrying about Richard," attests Tom Bahler.

By the autumn of 1978, Richard Carpenter, the musician whom many regarded as a genius of popular music, had lost confidence in his ability, particularly to perform "live." He began to ditch from the Carpenters' song selection any material that called on him to play extended or intricate pieces at the piano. "I was in trouble," he recalls. "No two ways about it."

Their nadir came in September 1978 at the MGM Grand in

Las Vegas. Richard had reached the point where every day, he could hardly control his slurred speech until 5:00 P.M.—and he simply could not wait to get back to bed. "I was going through such anxiety, panic attacks, wanting to take these pills, that I was afraid to walk out on stage," he says. He yearned for the moments when the concerts ended and he could hurry off the stage to return to his hotel room for some more pills and sleep, the terrible cycle that now haunted him.

It was so debilitating that he decided he would have to act against all his professional instincts and end their live shows. After telling Karen and Weintraub, who informed the management at the MGM Grand, he suddenly told the band and crew between performances on September 4, 1978: "That's it. I'm not playing another night." Karen, uncharacteristically quiet about it, knew Richard had to deal with his difficulties before they could continue. Scheduled to play twenty-eight shows in a two-week engagement, he was cutting free after one week.

"You could tell he meant it, but it was weird," Tony Peluso says. "This whole giant career ended like that—boom, in the middle of a season. I mean, you'd think when you do your last show that there'd be flowers, a feast, whatever. Richard said, 'That's it,' and we stopped playing."

Returning to Los Angeles on a private jet, Karen commented wryly on the atmosphere they had left behind: "I'm surprised we got out of that without the plane blowing up."

"What I wanted to do was get off the concert cycle at that time," Richard explains. "Never in my wildest dreams did I think that the MGM Grand was going to be our last concert. I meant I was not playing another show *then*. I thought we would pick up again when we got better, and I certainly didn't mean that was the end forever." But as events unfolded, there would be no return to the stage. It became their last professional live engagement, a sad, anticlimactic finale to an illustrious stage career.

For the band, shell-shocked and now rudderless, there was a financial olive branch to augment eight years of happy memories. As well as receiving more than a year of full pay as severance, each received money from a pension plan. Gary Sims, Tony Peluso, and Bob Messenger describe Richard and Karen as "generous and loyal."

If Richard wanted confirmation for himself that he had made

the right decision in disbanding, it came as Christmas 1978 neared. He and Karen were scheduled to perform at a Carpenters Choral Scholarship fund-raiser for their old California State University. As the day drew close, Richard kept calling Karen saying he would not be able to play difficult works like "It's Christmas Time" and "Nutcracker."

"My hands were shaking so much, I knocked that programme down to almost nothing because I knew I wouldn't be able to play most of it," Richard says.

In Britain, where a second "hit singles" album was released at the same period as the 1978 Christmas album, the Carpenters were in big demand at precisely the time Richard was in dire straits. They were booked to appear on the "Bruce Forsyth" TV show, a prospect that horrified Richard. "I knew damned well I couldn't get on a plane and do that show. I was doing nothing but staying home, counting the hours between taking the pills."

He tried to convince Karen that the British album would take care of itself in sales performance and they did not need to visit London to promote it. At this, she erupted.

"What *are* you talking about?" Karen yelled. "We're *going!*"

Here was an ugly and bizarre twist. She was in desperate need of treatment for a diet that had made her look like what Jerry Weintraub calls "a Biafra child," yet Richard was now the bigger threat to their act. "The two of us looked like hell," he says—but it was he who fell to the floor once when he stood to visit the toilet. He severely bruised an eye and needed hospital treatment.

On the day of rehearsals for the British TV show, Karen drove herself from her apartment to their warehouse in North Hollywood. By the appointed hour of noon, the band was there but not Richard.

She phoned him. "Where are you? We're all waiting."

Richard, in bed, told Karen he was in no condition to go to rehearsal or go through with the London date.

Devastated because she believed he was over the worst of his trouble, Karen went to see him later that day. He admitted he was still taking pills. There was no possibility of going to London. "In fact," he said wearily, "I can't do much of anything." He remembers that he had developed a "screwed-up reasoning" that since he was only taking sleeping pills, and only at night, he was not a drug addict. He would not drive a car while under their influence, but his habit was now overpowering. In his hooked condition, he told Karen, he certainly could not travel to Britain for a television show.

It was a crisis Karen could have done without, but if anyone in or out of the Carpenters' camp wanted evidence of her tenacity, she was about to deliver it. She flew to London alone with their band and performed on the TV show. With their British friend Peter Knight as musical director and spiritual supporter, she sang "Please Mr. Postman," "I Need to Be in Love," and "Merry Christmas Darling." It was the immaculate performance of a trouper. She told everyone that Richard had the flu.

During her London visit, her ex-boyfriend Softly was assigned by A&M to look after her. They got along well, both realizing the need to keep a distance. Softly was now married—to someone he had met on the holiday to which he had been banished by A&M to get him away from Karen—and Karen was miffed at his failure to at least acknowledge her wedding gift. "You never said thank you," she chided him. "I sent you a crystal punch bowl and glasses for your wedding." Softly had never received it; it was yet another disappointment that their friendship had apparently been thwarted. Their last moment together was a hug at London airport as Karen returned to Los Angeles, and more problems.

While the public view of them remained aglow, they each now endured a private agony. Innocent desires—one to slim, the other to get to sleep—had turned into human disasters. The brother and sister from New England, so disparagingly labelled as bland and squeaky clean, had arrived at crises that far outstripped the flirtations with dangerous living of their self-appointed "brave" critics.

Bitter exchanges followed Karen's return from London. As he ranted about her physical appearance, she pointed out that he was diving downhill on a different path. "She had every right to be mad at me," Richard says. "Trouble is, she was no example of how to deal with a problem." But at that moment she certainly held the upper hand, for despite all her trials she had never blown a performance or a recording session.

Although his pill popping had been a major drama in the comparatively sedate world of the Carpenters, at his record company it was a yawn. "Is that *all*?" they asked him. "A few Quaaludes? You mean you didn't wreck a car, burn down a house, or throw a television set through a hotel window?" Compared with the antics of some rock stars, Richard was still angelic; but Alpert and Moss were baffled at Karen's figure.

Richard then faced ultimatums from Weintraub and Wolfen. "Either sit there and kill yourself," they warned him in Weintraub's office in Beverly Hills, "or deal with it. It's a simple choice, but if you decide to carry on like this, we don't want to represent you." Richard was spending no time in the recording studios and frightening all his colleagues since his behaviour was so out of character.

"I had enough common sense left in me to say to myself that whether they represented me or not, if I continued to take these pills, I was going to kill myself. So I said, 'OK, find me a place.'" Weintraub did his research; Richard would have to leave California for treatment.

On January 10, 1979, a rented Lear jet whisked Richard from Los Angeles to Topeka, Kansas, for residential treatment. With him was Karen and Werner Wolfen. He was so frightened of what awaited him that he popped ten pills before boarding the plane. "I was a mess," he reflects on his jittery and remorseful state.

Richard was barely able to talk as they arrived at Menninger's, where he went into the chemical dependency unit. Wolfen reassured and cajoled him: "Richard, you're signing in. But nobody's going to do anything to you. You can leave, but I think you ought to stay."

Karen, concerned at the spartan nature of the place, asked, "How can poor Richard cope with these circumstances?" She was shocked that though he had his own room, there was no television or creature comforts.

They stayed in Topeka's Holiday Inn overnight before leaving him to "the darkest days of my life. I was in a dump in the middle of nowhere. It was the dead of winter, and it didn't stop snowing."

Initially he was so despondent that he did not bother to tidy or clean his room, again going against his usual characteristics. For the first three weeks he imploded with anger—at the doctors, the world, and especially at himself for plunging into such an abyss.

Unlike his earlier hospital treatments, which had made him go "cold turkey," the Menninger's programme was a "tapering" process. He was allowed one Quaalude each night for a week to ensure that he did not "seizure" from sudden withdrawal. This

Karen, enjoying success, dressed to the nines, 1974.
(Ed Caraeff)

With Bette Midler at the
Grammys, March 2, 1974.
(William E. Easterbrook)

Karen with Mike Curb, 1974.
*(Richard Carpenter
Collection)*

(Below)
On the road again:
in Las Vegas after a
Riviera concert,
1974.
(Ed Caraeff)

BORDKARTE V
SHOW TICK
BOARDING PAS

(Above)
On a European tour,
1974.
(Richard Carpenter
Collection)

At the Japanese press
conference, 1974.
*(Richard Carpenter
Collection)*

(Left)
Karen at A&M
Records, 1975.
*(Richard Carpenter
Collection)*

At the recording studio
console, 1975.
*(Richard Carpenter
Collection)*

The billboard at the Riviera, Las Vegas, 1975. *(Richard Carpenter Collection)*

The Carpenters touring party, 1975. Front row, from left: sound manager Robert Wellborn, Tony Peluso, Richard, Roger Young, Sandy Holland, Ken Black, lighting director Curt Mercer. Rear, from left: Sherwin Bash, Bob Messenger, Karen, Doug Strawn, Danny Woodhams, Mark Rudolph. *(Bonnie Schiffman)*

In 1975, with Karen ill, Richard flew to Japan with her boyfriend and the Carpenters' temporary manager Terry Ellis to explain to a press conference why their tour would be postponed.
(Richard Carpenter Collection)

Karen and Richard receive gold discs at the rearranged Japanese tour in 1976.
(Richard Carpenter Collection)

(Opposite and above)
At the Sahara Hotel, Lake Tahoe, in July 1976: with their stage show designer Joe Layton *(opposite)*; Ken and Mitzie Welch *(above)*; and with Karen's wardrobe assistant Sandy Holland *(above, right)*.
(Richard Carpenter Collection)

(Below)
From left: Karen, orchestra leader Lawrence Welk, Doug Strawn, Richard, Bob Messenger, Cubby O'Brien, and Tony Peluso.
(Richard Carpenter Collection)

Candid camera portrait,
1976.
(Ed Caraeff)

Discussing their
first TV special
with guest John
Denver, September
1976.
(Bill Harris)

On their eagerly
awaited TV
special for ABC,
"The
Carpenters,"
September 1976.
(Bill Harris)

Behind her beloved
drums, Las Vegas,
1976.
*(Richard Carpenter
Collection)*

At their parents' forty-
second wedding
anniversary party,
April 9, 1977.
*(Richard Carpenter
Collection)*

Karen that same year,
1977.
(Neil Zlozower)

With old friend Wes
Jacobs on the A&M
sound stage, during
the recording of
"Don't Cry for Me,
Argentina," for the
Passage album,
1977.
*(Richard Carpenter
Collection)*

(Right)
Karen singing
"Sweet, Sweet Smile"
on their third TV
special, "Space
Encounters," for
ABC in 1978.
(Yoram Kahana)

(*Above*)
Dining out in style with one of
her best friends,
Olivia Newton-John,
in Beverly Hills, 1978.
(*Peter Borsari*)

(*Below*)
Olivia Newton-John and Karen
with the Bee Gees before their
concert at Dodger Stadium,
Los Angeles, 1979.
(*Richard Carpenter Collection*)

(Left and below) Karen alone, and in the studio with producer Phil Ramone, making her solo album, 1980. *(Bonnie Schiffman)*

Radiant smiles for her wedding rehearsal and dinner: Karen with her friend Karen "Itchy" Ramone, wife of producer Phil. *(Richard Carpenter Collection)*

At the wedding rehearsal dinner: Tom Burris *(left)*; Karen is flanked by Carol Curb and her husband, Tony Scotti. *(Richard Carpenter Collection)*

(Below) With their early hero, guitar pioneer Les Paul, in Studio D at A&M, Los Angeles, November 1980. But Karen looks drawn. *(Richard Carpenter Collection)*

Carpenter family friends at the wedding rehearsal, from left: Theresa Vaiuso, Marion Connellan, Richard, and Debbie Vaiuso, Karen's best friend. *(Richard Carpenter Collection)*

Wedding day happiness: at the Beverly Hills Hotel, Agnes and Harold Carpenter, Karen and her husband Tom Burris, and Richard.
(Peter Borsari)

Mom and Dad visit the studio to hear the strings added to the album *Made in America*, 1981. *(Richard Carpenter Collection)*

(Above)
After this dinner in a Downey Japanese restaurant, Tom and Karen's marriage was doomed; he returned to her parents' home to tell them: "You can keep her," and they never met again. From left: Evelyn Wallace, Tom Burris, Karen.
(Richard Carpenter Collection)

"YOU WIN—I GAIN"—Karen's needle-pointed farewell gift to her New York therapist, Steven Levenkron, in November 1982.
(Steven Levenkron)

Christmas at home, 1982: Karen had recently arrived home in California from her year of treatment in New York. Dennis Heath joins her with Richard at the tree.
(Agnes Carpenter)

(Below)
In their office on the A&M lot, 1981, doing press interviews for their new album *Made in America*.
(Richard Carpenter Collection)

A month before she died, Karen with Evelyn Wallace: "You could see it in her eyes," Richard declares. "They were always big and bright, but here she just doesn't look well."
(Agnes Carpenter)

Frank Pooler, their early music mentor at university, with John Bettis and Richard around the jukebox at Lubec Street, Downey, June 19, 1983. *(Richard Carpenter Collection)*

Richard with Werner Wolfen at the dedication of their Tennessee building to Karen on September 21, 1983. *(Richard Carpenter Collection)*

Richard and Mary Carpenter in September 1984, the year of their marriage. *(Richard Carpenter Collection)*

reduction to a normal intake actually worked more successfully than had his indiscriminate gobbling of pills. He developed a natural nightly sleep.

Outside, in that bleak winter, it was at times twenty degrees below zero. But inside, after his initial anger, Richard realized it was make or break. He had taken his portable cassette player and some compilation tapes, and winced when Karen sent him a collection of their recorded work, hardly what he wanted to listen to as he recovered. But Richard was lucky to soon find a kindred spirit in Menninger's. Don Murphy from Kansas was there to kick a drinking problem when he learned that Richard of the Carpenters, a favourite group, was a fellow patient. They shared similar tastes in music, TV, and the movies, and began a lifelong friendship.

Richard had to combat an early lack of self-respect. But within three weeks, he was integrated, sitting on a committee to complain about the food, regaining his confidence. His weight increased as he ate heavily, having stopped the habit of starving himself to get stronger effects from Quaaludes.

Two weeks after Richard had arrived at the clinic, Karen went to visit him. The bombshell she dropped was as difficult for her to ignite as it was for him to absorb. She was thinking, she said gingerly, of making a solo album.

She could hardly have chosen a worse time to broach the subject. It was a broadside when his spirit was at a low ebb. Her timing was based on inquiries she had made at the clinic, which indicated to her that once a six-week period there had been completed, any patient would need time to readjust. "She probably figured it would be a long time before I was going to be fit to do anything with her again," Richard reflects. "And she was right."

He responded with an impassioned plea to her about her health. "Look, Karen," he began as they sat together in his small room at Menninger's. "I'm in trouble here—but at least I've owned up to all this. I'm getting myself better. Why the hell don't you face up to the fact that you have anorexia nervosa?

"While I'm in here, you go somewhere else and get treatment. Let's *both* clean ourselves up. And we can go into 1980 the way we went into 1970. We'll make a new album, and we'll be better."

She said she'd think about that. Karen knew intuitively that Richard had not taken her "solo album" overture at all well. In her

diary for January 24, 1979, she wrote (as always, in red): "Confrontation about album."

For Karen, this was a tumultuous time. With her brother sick,
the folks at A&M had pointed her toward New York producer Phil
Ramone. That was hard enough for her to confront. And now
Weintraub was increasing his pressure on *her* to get treatment, too.

Her first response to Richard's plea and to Weintraub's iron
determination was to check herself into the Cedars of Sinai Hospital in Los Angeles for a few days of checks and to try to end her
general state of exhaustion. Agnes was shocked to find that Karen
had been given an intravenous drip of food, but at least she was
facing up to her needs. "She still hadn't decided to fix her problem; she'd just got herself too far down," Richard says. "She was
wiped out—and obviously in no condition to commute to New
York."

By February 16 she was on a flight to New York to discuss the
solo album plan with Ramone. Four weeks later, an old problem
with her ear recurred, and she had a minor operation which laid
her low in Downey.[3] The prospect of breaking away from Richard
was now a pressure on her psyche: he had always taken care of
everything, and here she was, about to thrust herself into foreign
terrain. She mentioned her solo plan to her mother, who, with typical directness, told her: "Then do it!" The bonding with Richard
was clearly giving her problems of separation.

Richard, meanwhile, faced up to the clinic experience with his
usual combination of resilience and pragmatism. Once he saw a
horizon of being cleaned up, he dedicated himself to the programme.

Six weeks at the clinic worked. Richard could sleep without any
pills and developed a voracious appetite, particularly for weight-
gaining food like fries and milk shakes. Within a year, his weight
would rise to 185 pounds, causing a television producer to remark
on his "corpulence." And then Richard went on a diet.

Leaving the clinic, he could not face an immediate return
home. He went first to stay with Wes Jacobs, by then settled in

---

3. Karen had suffered a burst eardrum during a flight to Hawaii in February 1977. She rested in
her hotel suite for several days on medical advice.

Detroit, and then visited with his new friend Don Murphy in Topeka, Kansas, before finally returning to Los Angeles. Even then, he could not summon the strength to go back to his former milieu. He took refuge for nearly a year at the Long Beach home of Gary Sims and Dennis Strawn, brother of the band's Doug.

The final plans for Karen's solo project were hatched during Richard's slow journey back to California. All was set for her to fly to New York on May 1 and begin recording sessions the next day. But before she did so, on the night of April 30, she had to square her "confrontation" with Richard.

Telephoning him at Sims's house, she was "beside herself," Richard remembers, asking for his blessing in going ahead to New York. She was going to virtually commute to New York for two-week stints. The emotional intensity of the decision to go was matched by the madness of it—because she was in no physical condition to commit to the rigours of night recording sessions, song selection and preparation, together with a fresh environment.

Hysterical and tearful, she told Richard she needed his OK since she was leaving the next day. "Obviously she did not *need* my blessing," he says. "But she would have known instinctively that I would not want her to do it. What was I going to say? No?"

It crossed his mind that if the album turned out to be fantastic, better than anything she and he had done together in the recent past, that could threaten or undermine his future with her. Putting that aside, but with a heavy heart, he told her: "Karen, you have my blessing. Just do me one favour. Don't do anything disco."

Finally Richard was ready to leave the Sims homestead and get back to Downey. But he cast aside, temporarily, the reality of returning to Lubec Street and moved into the comparative anonymity of one of the apartment blocks that he and Karen had bought as investments in Downey at the start of their success. They were named "Close to You" and "Only Just Begun."

He was to sleep there for the next seven years, throughout Karen's illness, her New York sojourn, her death, and beyond it. Lubec Street would bring with it too many memories, good and bad, and the clinic had recommended he avoid returning to old routines and environments too quickly.

For Richard, the worst period in his life was over. His troubles were hidden from the public, and fans were informed that he had taken 1979 off for "personal reasons."

Karen was still beset by demons and problems, which she, by now a professional anorexic, was able to shuffle aside. In denial of her troubles, she continually assured her family and friends that she was fine.

As she sang as perfectly as ever and some still regarded her as a slave to a crackpot diet rather than the victim of an eating disorder, nobody had a strong enough vision of the situation to argue with her. And if anyone had, she would have been a formidable adversary.

As Richard emerged into his daylight, Karen was certainly not ready to face the reality—that her troubles were much more severe than his had been.

*The more people told her about her slimming too
much, the stronger she got into it, maybe the more
she wanted to lose.*

—SANDY HOLLAND, KAREN'S HAIRDRESSER AND WARDROBE
  ASSISTANT

*If you don't take care of yourself, you won't be
around very much longer.*

—HAROLD CARPENTER TO HIS DAUGHTER

A moment on the lips—a lifetime on the hips." The
anorexic's maxim was tailored perfectly to Karen Carpenter's new obsession. Now she was dealing with those
wretched hips, and nobody would deflect her.

As Agnes saw her daughter get progressively thinner, picking at
her food and drinking mostly water with lemon, she found pleading with her a waste of time. Karen had, her mother says, inherited
her stubbornness. "I don't see how she could have lived," she
reflects sadly on the morsels of salad that she pushed around her
plate. Alone and clearly lonely in her plush apartment, Karen
phoned her mother every day and often asked her and Harold to
drive across and join her for breakfast in a Beverly Hills restaurant.
As a shared meal, it was always a nonevent. "She wouldn't listen to
us," Agnes remembers of those breakfasts. She firmly rejects any
theory that it was a psychological problem. In Agnes's view, Karen
was simply gripped by an iron determination to get very thin and
stay that way.

Many experts on eating disorders, however, submit that there
is a deep-seated psychological cause; "I'm convinced it's psychological," Richard says, "although some people say it's a chemical
imbalance."

"Nobody disliked Karen for having a little bit of weight on,"
Agnes says, thinking back to the years before Karen's dieting. "I
mean, her fans loved her. They didn't want her to be skinny." She
seemed to get a vicarious pleasure from insisting that when she was

out with her parents, they had to order ice cream and eat it, while Karen denied herself this favourite dessert since childhood. "Trying to talk her into eating was a big mistake. She was not a girl who seemed to want to face the fact that she was very ill."

Probing the reasons for Karen's problems throws up a hornet's nest of theories, accusations, and convictions.

One close friend feels that she was so warm, so giving, that it may have been a "front" to command reciprocal feelings, because she felt so starved of attention: "People who don't think much of themselves often give a lot of themselves to others because they think it makes them more attractive." This sounds uncharitable, not even giving Karen the benefit of being remembered as a decent, loving, caring woman. There doesn't have to be a reason for that; it's how she chose to be.

Another cites her poor body image as a manifestation of a much more serious malaise. "The problem was undoubtedly all about her self-worth," says this close-up observer. "If you think your parents don't think as much of you as they do of your brother, there's a solid reason for doubting yourself, however much talent you are showing."

The anorexic therefore starves for attention, to exert complete control of an area that cannot be penetrated easily with logical persuasion. "I may not be in control of anything else [in her case Richard's brilliance and his unquestioned role as captain of the ship], but *I* am in control of my body. *And you are going to notice me.*" It's a negative form of power that inevitably attracts a lot of negative attention.

It's possible that the psychological problems had been embedded since her teenage years—a more likely period for anorexia nervosa to develop than in her twenties—but went "on hold" with the escalation of her career. And since she was attracting adulation and gathering friends from 1970 when she was age twenty, she would have no need then to allow her darker feelings to envelop her. Add to this a frantic working schedule as the Carpenters toured and recorded, made television shows, and gave interviews around the world, and there is a recipe for delaying the inevitable. She probably didn't have *time* to allow any painful feelings to develop.

By 1975, she had theoretically got most of what she wanted in her professional life. Love and marriage and children of her own were to prove elusive, and Karen might have begun wondering why she felt an inner dissatisfaction in spite of the outward evidence that she had triumphed as an artist. Her feelings were now surfacing: she may have expected that all would be wonderful when she scored big hit records and got audience applause at concerts—but it was not so. She had *not* got everything she was looking for, hence her statement to Steven Levenkron that when she left a stage, she felt empty.

In *The Golden Cage: The Enigma of Anorexia Nervosa* by Hilde Bruch, M.D.,[1] the author writes that the puzzling disease is full of contradictions and paradoxes. "These youngsters willingly undergo the ordeal of starvation, even to the point of death. . . . There is something exhibitionistic about anorexia. . . . During therapy many will confess that this cruel dieting was a way of drawing attention to themselves, that they had not felt sure that anybody really cared for them" (p. 3).

By controlling their eating, Bruch writes (pp 4–5), some felt for the first time that there was a core to their personality, that they were in touch with their feelings. It was "amazing, even awe-inspiring" to the onlooker to discover the iron determination with which anorexics pursued their goal of ultimate thinness, not only through food restriction but also through exhausting exercise. Most had been interested in sports before the illness (as was Karen).

One of the enigmas, Hilde Bruch writes, is that on the one hand anorexics declare that they do not see how thin they are, denying the existence of even severe emaciation—but at the same time they take extraordinary pride in it, considering it their supreme achievement (p. 7). "Though anorexics are very reluctant to give direct information on the starvation experience, I have come to the conclusion that the effect on psychological functioning of low food intake is to a large extent responsible for the drawn-out nature of the illness, sustaining it and making recognition and resolution of the precipitating psychological issues difficult, if not impossible. The whole behaviour may be so severely disturbed that it borders on psychotic disorganization" (pp. 11–12).

1. Published by Vintage Books, a division of Random House, New York, 1979. Copyright © 1978 by the President and Fellows of Harvard College.

In Marion Woodman's book *Addiction to Perfection*,[2] a psychological study, she writes that "the obese and the anorexic are fighting their battles for consciousness through food—the acceptance or rejection of it. Food in our culture is a catalyst for almost every emotion—a positive way of expressing love, joy, acceptance; or negatively a way of expressing guilt, bribery, fear of rejection. Food and the quality of the food are at the centre of every festival. To share the food is to be part of the festival; to reject it is to be left out of life. . . .

"Fat in our culture is taboo, so the neurosis hits where it hurts most—at the heart of the female ego" (p. 22).

Stressing that her book is not a condemnation of mothers or fathers, Marion Woodman says it is rather about recognizing the enemy and giving it a name in order to deal creatively with it. "Where the unconscious drive behind the food that involves the girl's relationship to her mother is not understood, it will be acted out destructively ... what consciousness demands is a recognition of the difference between appearance and reality which defines the girl's ambivalent feelings toward the mother. On the one hand she recognizes all the mother has given; on the other she senses the negativity behind the gifts, especially the rejection of herself as a person" (p. 22).

Kim Chernin, in *The Hungry Self: Women, Eating and Identity*,[3] writes that she has discovered in her work as a counselor that "the onset of an eating disorder coincides with an underlying development problem, regardless of a woman's age" (p. 23).

Dealing with mother-daughter bonding, Kim Chernin writes in her profound, penetrating book of the mother who is still able to live vicariously through her child, actively supporting the daughter's development because she sees it as part of her own, as her opportunity to do with her life what she has not yet done. "Problems may arise for the daughter if she chooses to live out her own dreams and finds that these are not what the mother wishes" (p. 84). Chernin goes on to identify "the weak, dependent, unhappy mother who needs to keep her daughter so closely tied to her that no separation or development is possible at all" (p. 84). And

2. Published by Inner City Books, Toronto, Canada, 1982.
3. Published by Harper and Row Perennial, New York, 1986.

Chernin adds: "The daughters of our time are turning against themselves. We have seen the way they break down at the moment they might prosper and develop; we have observed the way they torture themselves with starvation and make their bodies their enemies, the way they attack their female flesh.

"This futile attack on the female body, through which we are attempting to free ourselves from the female role, hides a bitter warfare against the mother. The characteristic traits of an eating disorder speak to us about the guilt we feel and the hidden anger we cannot express" (p. 93).

Agnes Carpenter, a woman with a warm smile and immutable convictions, rejects any suggestion that Karen was needing a physical demonstration of maternal or paternal love. "In our family, you didn't have to do that, not with my mother or father or anybody. We didn't have to say 'I love you.' We knew we were loved."

The tendency of parents to align with one child was evident to most onlookers of the Carpenters unit; although she dutifully phoned her mother every day, Karen was "always Harold's little girl," says one close family friend.

"Agnes always thought Richard was the greatest," says her sister Bernice. By phone from New Haven to Bernice back in Baltimore, Agnes would regale her with stories of Richard's activities in music. "I think Karen felt like her mother favoured Richard. . . . I guess they never dreamed that Karen was going to be just as popular, if not more so, with her beautiful voice," Bernice adds.

Kim Chernin suggests that "the present epidemic of eating disorders must be understood as a profound developmental crisis in a generation of women still deeply confused, after two generations of struggle for female liberation, about what it means to be a woman in the modern world" (p. 17). "Women suffering from eating disorders are telling us, in the only way they know how, that something is going seriously wrong with their lives as they take on the rights and prerogatives of male society" (p. 19).

The crisis of serious, debilitating eating disorders had received a great deal of attention in the national media, Chernin wrote, since the death of Karen Carpenter. "With her life and death, a generation of young women found their exemplar, the representative figure who spoke symbolically to their lives . . ." (p. 12).

The whole Carpenter family were physically nondemonstrative.

"I never saw her mother hug or kiss Karen," says Evelyn Wallace of her twenty-three-year association with the family. "Harold would occasionally give Karen a hug." It did not come naturally to Karen, either, but as she entered into the spirit of show business embraces, Karen did hug occasionally. At one Christmas party at Newville Avenue, she stood at the door welcoming all guests with a kiss, somewhat to their surprise since it was out of character.

It always struck Evelyn as sad that when "the kids" went off on tour, there were no farewell hugs or kisses from their family. Evelyn says she "always grabbed Karen, hugged her, gave her a little kiss, wished her a good trip. And she always hugged me back."

John Bettis remarks that the Carpenter family structure was alien to his and he "had difficulty with it." It was, says Bettis, a straitjacket: "And, bless their hearts, they didn't mean for it to be that way. They were just trying to get the best for their kids. But the truth is it had extremely damaging results."

A much more abrasive interpretation of the Carpenter family chemistry comes from a well-placed insider who describes Karen as "crying for attention and love" from her parents. "From the time it was realized that Richard as a child had a rare gift, the entire family became dedicated to Richard and his career. And that included Karen." Consider the history before their fame: "Agnes, Harold, and Karen dedicated themselves to promoting his genius. At school, Agnes fought his battles. As well as Harold's desire for warmer weather, they had moved to California from the East Coast to promote Richard's career." The focus had been on Richard from their teenage years, particularly since back in New Haven Karen had exhibited no musical talent.

And later, as he wrote the songs and devised the arrangements, Richard held the actual key to the Carpenters' sound and success, so she still felt less important than him by comparison. That role of Richard as the "brain and creator" of their music is emphasized by Bob Messenger, their tenor saxophonist and flautist: "Karen was the paint on Richard's palette."

Was she his puppet? Richard vehemently rejects any such theory. Indeed, anyone who ever encountered Karen would recognize her as difficult to steer. Richard points out that some people polarize the issue of "control" too far the other way, saying their success was *all* due to Karen. "What I did was either write the songs, or pick them, or both, and then arrange and produce them." His intuitive understanding of her range, her voice, her appeal, and the kind of song she could get inside, provided the correct brew, and the importance of such mechanics of song hunting and record production are often ignored. "But Karen sang so well and obviously in a style that I liked, so that I never had to say much to her, other than to give her what parts to sing for the back-up vocals."

Only once did he comment on her lead vocal work. The episode stemmed from their joint admiration of the British ballad singer Matt Monro. When it came to recording, because she loved Monro's pronunciation so much, Karen tended to enunciate the words *you* and *know* more like *yew*. Richard told her this did not sound natural several times when she adopted her "Matt Monro kick" on such words.

Karen became angry at Richard's mild rebukes. "She didn't like me, or anyone else, telling her how to sing. So it's ridiculous for people to say I had my hand in her back when it came to her lead vocals. Who was I to interfere?

"You just let Karen sing a pretty song! I picked out a range for her, and the key, and she was pretty much on her own."

But though their music was harmonious, they were undeniably a brother and sister who both ran into physical problems brought about by addictions.

Another close family friend says angrily of Agnes's dominance: "Richard and Karen were quite capable of dealing with the international landscape but were constantly being told they were suburban kids from Downey." The message from Agnes was: "Stay here where you belong! Come back home! Limit your perspective to mine so that I can keep control!" Conceding that there may be some truth in this view, Richard adds that he was, and remains, a creature of habit so that departing from Downey and all it represented was never in his mind. He was not being "roped in" and stayed close to his parental home through choice.

Yet another frequent visitor to Newville Avenue noticed a curious reaction if Karen was complimented by someone for, as an example, a pretty new dress or a new car. Immediately, Agnes would jump in, apparently as a defence, to point out that Richard, too, had a new car. It was clear that Karen should never be "promoted" higher than her brother, even innocuously. But the reverse was often true: Agnes's nature was protective of Karen's feelings if Richard received a pat on the back.

The core of Karen's life remained her music, and that, importantly, posed no problem. As Maria Galeazzi points out, she was doing exactly what she wanted, even if it was too hard on her during the touring years. Her former hairdresser feels the overriding hurdle was that "her heart was heavy. She had too many worries without the counterpart. You have to have that balance, and she struggled to find it."

Because they are inconclusive, such critical observations neither trouble nor impress Agnes and Richard. Aware of their individual characteristics, they say forcefully that nothing convincingly explains the physical disintegration of Karen. She certainly had a fixation on her weight. Richard believes something was troubling her. But it may have been too deeply embedded in her psyche for anyone to unearth.

"Karen was hefty to the butt like I am," Agnes says, returning to the known territory of her daughter's problem. "And of course she was built real well, a bit heavy in the hips, that's about it. She started to notice it, and I guess she felt everybody was noticing her hips and she wanted smaller and smaller clothing. So she kept on till it was too late to stop.

"Whenever she wanted to buy clothes, she wanted me to go with her. She went from a size fourteen [in 1967] down to a two. And I kept telling her, 'Karen, you're getting too thin.'"

Richard is troubled by the wider issue. "They don't know what causes anorexia nervosa," he says bluntly. "I don't know what the hell this disorder is. This is what upsets me as much as anything. It would be a little easier to live with if she had keeled over from something tangible. It would still be terrible, but at least you could then say: it shouldn't have happened, but I know *why* it happened. But *this*? It's really aggravating, to put it mildly, to have no idea."

He has read many of the theories, "about not being in control of one's world, of the dominant mother factor . . . but even if it is one of those, what the hell is it that puts a person on a self-destructive point of no return? They don't know. And I don't know."

Karen could mask her feelings of depression, in the view of Wes Jacobs, so that made it all the more difficult to spot any looming crisis such as the one that enveloped her. "She was robbed, really, of the opportunity to have a youth, as most people have," Jacobs adds. "By the time she was not even out of high school, her days of leisure were gone." Because of their level of activity, Jacobs said, "scales of normality" did not apply to either Richard or Karen: "I wouldn't consider Richard or Karen 'normal.' They're very gifted, very, very different people from anybody I've ever met."

The desperate appeals by Richard and Mom to Karen to eat to rescue her health were doomed, according to one person who recovered from an addiction problem considered to be similar to Karen's. One of the reasons shouting or screaming could not work was this: if Karen relented and changed her behaviour in response to those pleas, the screaming would obviously stop. "And so would their attention," says the observer. "The moment Karen responded to those demands, what she was seeking would be over. What she *knew* from Richard and Agnes's screaming was that she was succeeding in being noticed. She was the centre of attention! She certainly would not do as they wished, because their pleading meant, to Karen, 'Hey, I know you're there'—which is precisely what she wanted."

Cajoling, pleading, shouting, and threatening therefore may have even strengthened Karen's resolve. Like many anorexics, when she looked in the mirror she saw something entirely different from the view of others: she saw a woman getting thinner by the day and maintaining that slimness, which is exactly what she aimed for.

"We all have broad shoulders in this family," Richard says, "and Karen had the classic womanly figure, the hourglass—thin waist, broad shoulders, and some hips.

"Look through history and people's ideas of the perfect woman's shape differ from period to period. And of course for the past twenty years or so we've been going through this 'thin is in' thing. And some women don't have hips to speak of. Well, Karen wanted to be up and down. And there was no possible way she could have been because hips are bones, and if she'd got down to sixty pounds, relatively, she would still have had broad shoulders, a thin waist, and hips—that hourglass figure.

"I yelled my brains out at Karen at times. I got SO MAD with her." During his own problems he recalls saying and doing things that "must have driven Karen to pull out her hair." As she continued her spiral, the hot-tempered brother blew his top. "She'd say certain things that would just touch a button in me, and I'd go through the roof. Like 'Oh, I just ate the table,' or 'I ate every-thing in the refrigerator.' I knew she was lying through her teeth about eating anything, in the same way I lied to her about my con-dition." It was insidious, he says, because she really did not think she was obsessed.

For manager Weintraub it was a personal nightmare. "I saw these two people disintegrating in front of my very eyes. I couldn't do anything about it. I truthfully don't think anybody could have.

"I did suggest the Menninger clinic, and I did get Levenkron, but nothing seemed to work for Karen. This thing was falling apart at the seams, getting worse day by day."

"We'd yell at her," says Tony Peluso, recalling the touring years. "We were like her brothers, don't forget. When she got down to about eighty pounds, that wasn't skinny, it was emaciated. Strangers, fans, would look at her on stage and say, 'My God, what's *wrong* with that girl?'"

In hotels, the band tried both persuasiveness and bullying. "Karen, what are you doing? Why don't you eat? Get out of your room." The musicians even joined together once to go to her room, insisted on her getting dressed, and took her down to the hotel restaurant.

"You eat this food, goddamn it, right now," Peluso said to her. "OK, all right," she said.

Peluso, Strawn, Messenger, Sims, and O'Brien had no way of interpreting her problem as a serious disorder. "If we had realized her life was in danger, we would have tried to have done more, although if she didn't want to help herself, nobody was going to be able to make her. At that point, I'm sure she was spiralling end-lessly down this road of starving herself," Peluso says.

Puzzled, they discussed the situation with Richard—and in 1975 Sherwin Bash asked the band if they had any ideas on how to solve the problem. "Each one of us cared so much for her in our own way that we thought: What can *I* do? Maybe I'm the one who can tell her how to get over this," adds Peluso.

Pursuing his friendship with Karen, Peluso took her for dinner to Les Prennes, a French restaurant in Santa Monica. Perhaps, just perhaps, he thought, he as a buddy could get through to her. She ordered seafood but fiddled around with it, eating little. He nudged her. "Come on, Karen, you gotta eat." Then he pulled away. They were pals out for a good conversation, and he didn't want to sour the evening. He went home as worried and as power-less as ever. "There was a lot of frustration," he ruminates. "Some-where inside there, you knew she was unhappy. Why else would she be doing this to herself? I just don't know what caused her day-to-day unhappiness, her lack of satisfaction, or lack of self-esteem."

Everyone who knew her spelled out explicit warnings. On a visit to New Haven, she and her father dropped in on a former neighbor friend. "When I gave her a hug, all I could feel were bones," says Marion Connellan. "Yet she was full of pop, and she didn't think she had a problem." Harold repeated to his daughter the real concern of Marion: "If you don't take care of yourself," he told her, "you won't be around very much longer." Nothing could divert people's stare from her sunken cheeks, the dark rings under her eyes, the skin-and-bone of her fingers.

"The more people told her about her slimming too much, the stronger she got into it, maybe the more she wanted to lose," says her hairdresser Sandy Holland. Some of the band quickly went to Sandy, as the "new girl," asking if she could persuade Karen to eat more. She tried but soon realized she faced a boss as decisive about her eating routine as she was about her nails and hair, which had to be left looking as natural as possible.

And so, getting Karen to confront her crisis was impossible. To Karen, her family and friends, she was "watching her weight" rather than encountering something called anorexia nervosa. So the preferred in-patient treatment recommended by Professor Arthur Crisp and his colleagues in London was never properly debated—and consequently she decided on the outpatient therapy programme in New York.

Of his methods, Professor Crisp says: "The therapeutic propo-sition is that she is being asked to trade in her anorexia nervosa—essentially her avoidance stance—for the ultimate prospect of a full recovery. She is invited to surrender her spurious and only current freedom, namely to sustain her anorexia nervosa, in return for the potential freedom inherent in gaining weight and thereby rediscov-ering her mature self and ultimately expressing it in a healthier manner."

Both she and those around her would need to experience this goal as acceptable and sufficiently fulfilling. At the point of discus-

sion of inpatient care, she would need to know that others antici-
pated that she would have "great emotional problems in this
respect for some while, often several years"—and that the potential
for redeveloping the problem would be all too readily available to
her.

"The most difficult task, sometimes it seems impossible, is to
help the anorexic make this conceptual switch," says Professor
Crisp. Transference problems are at the heart of it.

Treatment involves handing over control concerning weight to
the medical team. Target weight is the matched population mean
weight related to the age at onset of the condition.

Thus the target weight for a twenty-four-year-old, five-foot-tall
anorexic who fell ill at sixteen years of age would be not 124
pounds but 118 pounds. "Since the age of sixteen when she
'derailed' in terms of maturation, she has, to our minds, been stuck
at a regressed and certainly prepubertal age. At the time she could
not cope with being sixteen. How can she now anticipate being
able or expected to cope as a twenty-four-year-old? She needs to
know that this is not expected of her but that she will have to
grapple with adolescent tasks. It is an essential element in the therapeutic alliance both with her and her parents."

In the full-time care programme, the patient would go to bed
full-time and eat three thousand calories a day. Her fear, of course,
would be that she would lose control over her weight/"fatness"/
shape. "She needs to know that she will be protected against over-
shooting her target weight. We reassure her." With this treatment
approach, Professor Crisp states that "it has never been necessary to
tube-feed or intravenously feed an anorexic."

PART FIVE

BI-COASTAL BLUES

Doing something out of the family was important, a show of strength, of independence.

—OLIVIA NEWTON-JOHN ON KAREN'S PLAN TO MAKE A SOLO ALBUM

It's not treachery. Why should her career wait on you? When you're ready to do a great album, she'll be there.

—THEIR LAWYER, WERNER WOLFEN, TO RICHARD

Karen was at Los Angeles airport on May 1, 1979, awaiting a flight to New York. Although she was an experienced traveler and not nervous, she had superstitions and had told road manager David Alley to ensure that she was never booked on a DC10 ever again.

The travel agent had assured Alley that Karen's chosen flight would not be a DC10.

But as she and Alley neared the departure gate and she saw the plane was an L-1011, she "went nuclear," with David Alley. She would fly only on a 747, she declared.

With a lot of persuasion, she finally relented, and with a hug and a kiss to her former boyfriend, she boarded the flight.

Karen had every reason to be jittery, and it had nothing to do with flying. She was going to New York . . . to make her solo album.

With Richard recuperating from his clinic experience amid talk of their declining record sales, people around the Carpenters were getting edgy. It was a classic example of "great expectations." For nine years they had been high on A&M's table of bankers, and a hiccup in such a dollar-generating machine raised many an eyebrow.

Karen was taking the general downward trend of their sales very badly. She thought it was the fault of someone at the record company, or a lack of promotion—anything but a natural fallout of their record-buying audience, which, Weintraub persistently explained to her, happened to any artist after scaling such peaks.

Karen and Richard had always been keen students of sales barometers. "A lot of people would say once you'd had a couple of hits, the radio stations would play anything we recorded and the people will buy it," Karen said to me. "Baloney! You have to watch everything you put out, and with each hit you get you have to work five million times harder for the next." Criticizing artists who released similar sounds, record after record, she said: "It's their own dumb fault [that they failed]. Anybody who treats the business that way doesn't deserve to be in it. Because this isn't a game. It's a highly respected, smart business. Very few records are automatic, out-and-out smashes, and if you get one in your entire career, you're damned lucky."

Hit to hit, Karen said she and Richard prayed for the next one. "Every time a record comes out, we watch every radio station that picks up on it, day by day, reports, charting, numbers, sales. Because that's our business. There's not a day goes by when we're not buried in the charts of the music papers. Also, we keep watching what we're up against. The competition is unbelievable."

Although by that stage in their careers income did not matter to them so much as achievements, Richard was concerned, too. "It was in our blood," he says of their hit-making routine, "and any financial reward was the icing on top of the cake. Where a movie star is judged on the latest picture, record people judge you on your last three minutes, meaning your last single."

Although their sales graph was not so rosy as in previous years and worried him, he was even more aware than Karen of the vagaries of the record industry. Better able to rationalize about peaks and troughs, he tried to reassure his sister:

"Karen, we've been going strongly and successfully for seven years. That's longer than most anybody has in this field. It's incredible and it's been great. Let's just be grateful." There were still years of music ahead, and they would probably enjoy it better without the frenzy. It was time, he said, to review their schedule. There was no need to make an album every year. He remembered how Herb Alpert was virtually a musical father to them, insisting that they be relaxed in the studio, not feeling the pressure to produce so frenetically as in their early days, and saying to Richard: "Are you *sure* you're happy with this album, and the schedule? Let me know . . ."

They were lucky to have a creative and compassionate boss.

But Karen's insecurity was surfacing. She did not want to say good-bye to a level of limelight she had relished. For the drummer girl who had become the star singer, here came the downside. Fewer people wanted to buy their records, and she was less equipped to handle that reality than her brother. ... just as she was less able than he to deal with a major physical threat.

And so the seed for Karen's solo break was planted as Richard rested at the home of Gary Sims in Long Beach. Alpert told Moss that Richard was not in good shape and needed time off, and the A&M chiefs both went to Weintraub with the idea for the solo project.

"Rich is not going to like it," Karen said immediately to Werner Wolfen, who supported A&M and Weintraub's plans. "Too bad," the lawyer replied pithily. "If he's let you wither on the vine for a long time, the best thing that could happen is that you make a great album. Then he'll make a greater one."

According to Derek Green in London, Karen had been encouraged to make the solo album for a pragmatic reason: "It would be good news for any of us who were making money out of it." This was a straight business scenario: they were less impactful as a selling act. The songs were not really working. "Our business turns on the excitement of tomorrow's new works," Green points out. "So the argument would have run: Do we really *need* Richard? Karen's got this magical voice. Wouldn't we do better with her alone?

"And there's no damage on the downside. If her solo album did well, it would strengthen the Carpenters' return together."

To Karen and other onlookers, there was a less cynical benefit. Her identity crisis would be confronted. Her reliance on Richard as her navigator might be eclipsed as she stretched into different pastures of music. And a solo outing, if successful, could give them that physical break from each other to later rejuvenate their career together.

Still, she was petrified. It might seem a good idea for the troubled Carpenters name, she told friends, but for ten years she had lived and breathed every note through her genius brother. They'd been joined at the hip professionally and personally. A solo album was almost an act of *treason*.

Richard was indeed livid about the idea at first. In conversations with Wolfen, "he thought it was treachery of a sort," the lawyer recalls. Wolfen repeated the potential value of the separation as he had expressed it to Karen, adding to Richard: "It's not treachery. Why should her career wait on you? When you're ready to do a great album, she'll be there."

Olivia Newton-John, who spoke to Karen on the eve of her flight to New York, says she was excited but apprehensive about her first splinter from Richard. "That was difficult for her. She had such a feeling of loyalty to him. Doing something out of the family was important, a show of strength, of independence. But she and Richard had great friendship and commitment to each other. As far as she was concerned, nobody wrote more beautiful arrangements or was more of a perfectionist."

Ironically, Richard had earlier had a long conversation with Karen in which he urged her to seek some kind of solo activity. "You're a lot more at ease in doing certain things than I am. . .in front of a camera, with lines to learn, and so on.

"You pick up those dance steps so quickly when they work you for the TV specials. Why don't you take an acting class or a dancing class?" Many of her friends had echoed the fact that Karen learned quickly and might expand her interests theatrically, but she always answered firmly that it wasn't of interest. More important to her was when Richard told her what a marvellous, natural singer she was.

How bizarre it was to consider that the solo album gamble would have been unthinkable if Richard had not needed to go for treatment in the clinic, followed by a prolonged period of rest! She was reluctant to go through with the plan and worried endlessly about breaking the bond with her brother. Werner Wolfen put to her bluntly what so many thought but dared not say: "Who knows what's going to happen with Richard? How do you know you're still going to have a career?"

Herb Alpert's choice of producer was as provocative as the decision itself. Phil Ramone was as hot as a pistol, the producer of recent winning albums by Paul Simon, Billy Joel, and Bob Dylan. With an abrasive, contemporary approach, he ploughed deeply into character analysis of his recording artists to help them assert fresh and individualistic slants to their work.

He had met Karen and Richard in 1970 when they opened a

concert at the Westbury Music Fair for Burt Bacharach, whom Ramone was coproducing. As their career moved on and he saw them occasionally at the A&M studios in Los Angeles, he believed they were cocooned and pampered: "Herb and Jerry were extreme fans of Karen and Richard. They treated them like their children. You couldn't go near the Carpenters' rooms or their studios when they were in; they were sheltered and coddled."

Nearly ten years later, he was about to form the opinion that Karen was alarmingly unchanged in her outlook; she had not grown one iota, he felt.[1]

In New York Karen moved at first into a sumptuous suite complete with grand piano at the UN Plaza Hotel. After two weeks Ramone and his wife, Itchy, suggested she would enjoy life better by moving into their home at Poundridge, Connecticut. "The hotel life is not going to work," he told Karen. "It's just another road trip for you." She enjoyed integrating with the Ramone family unit and began their daily forty-three-mile commute by car into the Manhattan studios. As they drove, they auditioned tapes of hundreds of songs.

Ramone wanted to steer her toward a stylistic change, but he hit his central problem, what he perceived as her immaturity. It was time, he believed, for Karen to stop making "cutesy-pie" records, and at twenty-nine she should have been able to draw on some life experiences which would make her singing resonate. "Singing with passion about a subject matter you know nothing about is extremely difficult," he told her. In trying to pull her into a fresh territory of song and style, he felt himself coming up against Karen's difficulty: both she and Richard had gone straight from college into show business and he believes they had "never been scruffy teenagers." Neither physically nor mentally had they allowed themselves to leave their parents' nest.

Richard and Phil were diametrically different in their approach to producing Karen. Whereas Richard relied on his and Karen's

---

1. Rebutting Ramone's comments, Richard points out that Jerry Moss was not a major fan of their music. To the statement that they were treated like Herb and Jerry's children, Richard says that in fact he and Karen were little more than children when they began (she was nineteen, he was twenty-two). As for studio privacy: "That's traditional for artists—but in fact we didn't get it! One of our working problems was that everyone kept walking into the studios when we were there, making it hard to get anything done."

intrinsic musicality allied to strong melodic songs, Ramone sought something beyond that, an infusion of "real life" as he saw it.

Dismissing any theory that Karen might have been handicapped by lack of life experience when she sang, Richard hits back forcefully. "Karen had the uncanny ability to sing lyrics about which she had no experience and make them sound like she'd lived every damned experience! She was only twenty-one years old when she sang 'Rainy Days and Mondays,' and she sounds way beyond her years. She sounds like she believed and lived every damned thing she's singing. That's part of her magic.

"Phil Ramone says singing with passion about a subject matter you know nothing about is difficult? Not to Karen, it wasn't! She sang 'Superstar'—but she never dated any rock 'n' roll guitarist like the song says. But you might have guessed she did from the way she sang it."

Ramone detected "a little girl in a glass house," fantasizing pretentiously; he theorized that her innocent voice carried little discernment. Her meticulousness gave her away, in his view— "Even her jeans were pressed the right way"—and he teased her for her well-matched satin shoes and satin jacket.

"You're terrible," she would respond, embarrassed. "Well," Ramone said testily, "we're not in L.A. We're in New York, and I don't want you to dress like that."

Attempting to reshape Karen in any new direction, and trying to reinvent her perception of herself, was as inadvisable as it was to prove fruitless. She was strongly her own woman facing another "value judgment" on her self-perception, while she was three thousand miles from her home.

Trying to get her to unwind, shed a skin or two, Ramone says the unsolvable problem remained Karen's cultural background, or rather the lack of it—what he described as the "all-American cheeseburger" life-style that had conditioned her. Because of its constraints, he felt Karen had not grown as a person, so that her music had not developed beyond its basic purity, outstanding and natural though that was.

He was torn. Like many who encountered Karen, he found her "cute and adorable," and he felt a responsibility for her while she was away from home. "Like her uncle! If she went out, would she be home by midnight? And it was none of my damned business!" he says.

As friends, he and Itchy were strong and true to her, but as her producer, he was far too much of a maverick. He found songs that went well beyond the melancholic love ballads at which she excelled. With titles like "Remember When Lovin' Took All Night," "My Body Keeps Changing My Mind," and "If I Had You," these called for expansive sensuality. And Karen's reading of them didn't sit right.

Condemning most of Ramone's choice of songs as wholly inappropriate for Karen, Richard says: "Phil's idea of maturity was to have her singing explicit lyrics, things with a double entendre. I don't consider that necessarily mature. I consider it in the same way as when a comic has to go out and swear to get a laugh, whereas a Jack Benny or a Steve Martin got and get just as many laughs without that. Paul Williams wrote fine lyrics for 'Rainy Days and Mondays' and 'We've Only Just Begun' without any gratuitous reference to sex. Ramone had her singing 'My Body Keeps Changing My Mind.' Is that supposed to be *mature?*"

In the studio for one session, Ramone brought Karen to tears. He criticized her singing of the word *love*—she was probably emulating Matt Monro too closely once again, and the criticism might have reminded her of Richard's presence at such moments. "It's phony as hell," Ramone rebuked her. "You have to *immerse* yourself in that word. You can't be Karen Carpenter of the Carpenters singing that. It doesn't work.

"No one's asking you your personal life in the studio, but when you give it up to a record and you say, 'I wanna spend the night with you,' you can't have this vague veil in front of you. If you want to withhold it from your audience, that's up to you, but I can't have you do that for me."

Richard interjects: "I just let Karen sing and that worked very well. She didn't need anyone to tell her how to interpret lyrics. Karen never held anything back when she sang."

Karen was upset by this full frontal criticism, but on the next "take" she cried because she felt she had released something from within herself.

After a few weeks, she returned home to California for one of several visits during the sessions. On her return, what Ramone construed as the "Downey conflict" had surfaced, and she "would not be the same human being for days on end," Ramone remembers. "She wouldn't get into the fun of it again or realize that we were doing her *solo* album."

Early in the trip, Karen developed a nasal infection. When he took her to his doctor, Phil Ramone voiced his concern about her weight. "She's working with me," he told the doctor. "Is this something we should be concerned about?" The doctor replied, "I don't like what I see." But since Karen had a regular doctor back in California who knew of her difficulties, he did not think he should interfere.

When Karen next developed an ear infection, a crisis erupted in the recording of the album. She entered the hospital briefly for treatment, but when she returned she had only about 60 percent of normal hearing in her troubled left ear. Putting on her headset, she began singing out of tune, something unthinkable for Karen. "She was distraught, very frightened," Ramone recalls. She even panicked by asking whether it was serious enough to threaten her career.

The next day Ramone told her to abandon the headset, and he set up two speakers in front of her for her "playbacks." She now had to learn to listen out of two ears since she had been working with an ear and half in listening ability for so long. "She started to sing with the aid of the speakers (instead of the headset). Hearing takes a long time to readjust, but thank God it started to work." Several days later she was able to return to the headset and had no major hearing difficulties after that.

But Karen soon had a medical crisis of another sort. One night at his home, Phil Ramone heard a thump from the kitchen. Running in, he found Karen passed out, slumped on the floor. He phoned 911. Worried that her skinniness might have led to her breaking bones, he carried her carefully to the couch. When the paramedics arrived, she had recovered but was woozy. She refused to be taken to the hospital.

Questioning her about her medication, the ambulance men discovered she had been taking Quaaludes. "My darling little girl," said Ramone, "do you know what these things are? This is the pill Richard used to take." Karen said she just took half a tablet if she could not sleep. He pointed out that half a tablet inside her frame was possibly equivalent to about a bottle of whiskey in anyone else's. Then she admitted that she'd very recently had a glass of water and passed out when the pill hit. "She was scared because I had to cover it up. I begged the ambulance people not to release her identity; they knew who she was."

After that incident, as Phil and Itchy Ramone noted her predictable visit to the bathroom as soon as a meal had ended, Ramone became more assertive about her physical condition. He blew up when they watched a video of her appearance on an Olivia Newton-John TV special. "Look how heavy I am!" Karen said. Angrily, Ramone froze the picture on the screen to argue with her. "Do you see what I am seeing?" he said, pointing to Karen's thin body. Karen repeated that she looked fat.

"This was a woman with no breasts," Ramone says. "She was totally without femininity." But she was not hearing him. In the comfort of a friend's Connecticut home, she was as consistently "deaf" to the truth as she had been "on the road" or back home in California.

With these negative observations about her appearance, Karen must have been surprised to get a totally different reaction from another quarter. At the studio Karen met another celebrated female singer whom she had first encountered in California years earlier. Phoebe Snow, who at that time had her own eating disorder, hugged Karen, noting that she had almost no muscle—but her thin physique was riveting: "I really got excited and wanted to talk to her about this great diet she was on." Snow sought the secret of Karen's food intake, and what followed was a long telephone conversation.

Karen was guarded. After four years of being berated for not eating, hearing congratulations on her appearance was weird. After recovering from learning that Snow wanted a conversation about diet as much as about music, Karen loosened up and said, "Well, you know, two gals talking about diets ... what could be bad here?" She spoke openly about her daily food intake, her ritualistic weighing of herself, her current weight (seventy-nine pounds, she said), and she admitted that she had taken thyroid medication, which sped up her metabolism.

Moving on to discuss music, the two singers found plenty to empathize about, and Karen was excited about her solo project. Pondering how Karen managed to sing without showing a trace of her illness, Snow suggests: "She was never a belter. She was organically natural. And as she knew how to rigidly conserve food portions, she may well have known how to conserve her vocal cords."

* * *

In what became a watershed experience for Karen, the feisty Ramone hammered away at her need for growth, maturity, the break with the past that he felt an adult young woman artist had to make. She accepted his word but battled with her inborn naïveté and her resistance to change. At his home, Ramone observed that she was on the phone to California for hours, and from Karen's remarks and demeanour after such calls, he got the impression that "Mom was ruling across the wires." He sensed that Karen was lonely.

She also felt a pressure to come up with a winning album and believed Ramone's theory that she should become more adult in her approach. But by then, he realized the raw material there was in Karen and had planned and executed the album accordingly. Listening in the car as they drove into Manhattan, Karen was taken with a song that called for an explicitly sexual interpretation—and to her surprise, Ramone rejected the song.

"No. What are you gonna do? You're gonna have to talk about going to bed with a guy, ruffling his hair, the first time you meet him? Are you going to be believable? Are you going to take off your white dress and say that deep down you're this scarlet, crazy woman?" He had concluded by then that her personality in her work was impossible to change.

"Well," Karen replied, "that's what I would really like to sing."

"It's not important you make that statement," Ramone told her finally. "What are you trying to do here? Are you going through a catharsis, or are we gonna make a record?"

It wasn't all work. Phil and Itchy took her to Mexico upon completion of the album for a holiday, where they worried endlessly about her failure to eat. And the trio went to a New York baseball game between the Mets and the Dodgers. When she arrived at Shea Stadium, the huge scoreboard flashed up: "Welcome Karen Carpenter" to the tune of "We've Only Just Begun." Modest though Karen was, she loved such moments. Ramone remembers another side of the "funny little girl": when entering a store, "if somebody didn't really recognize her, she'd handle something at the counter and sing a line from one of her hits."

Karen had invested about $400,000 of her own money in the album's production costs, adding to A&M's commitment of

$100,000. By the time she had completed it in early 1980, Richard was fit. The customary "playback" for senior A&M executives was set up. New pictures of Karen had been taken for the cover. A promotion campaign was being arranged. It was projected as one of A&M's prime releases for spring 1980, and everyone inside the company was being "talked up" for a blockbuster.

Derek Green was by then senior vice president of A&M internationally as well as the boss in the United Kingdom. Trusting Green's ears, Jerry Moss asked him to fly in to New York to hear the initial playback of the songs in the studio. The general response, Phil Ramone declares, was "fantastic"; as the champagne flowed and Karen jumped around ecstatically, "everybody said it was great."

But Green remembered it differently. "Jerry Moss and I used to communicate almost telepathically. We looked at each other, and we knew we had a dog from a commercial sense." With Ramone present and the atmosphere jubilant, they could hardly condemn it, but once outside—"we knew we had a problem: the record was not good enough." Ramone says, however, that Green praised the record in conversation with him.

Flying on to Los Angeles, Green faced an attempt to soften him up with a playback of tracks that had been doctored and refined. "Phil Ramone, being experienced, caught the drift, and I was invited by Quincy Jones to go to his house when Phil Ramone happened to be present. Then I had to listen to the whole album again, which was further mixed and further produced, with Quincy telling me how fabulous it sounded.

"They were trying to hype me up. I just couldn't share the view. The record represented a very poor choice of songs, the wrong way forward. I was very disappointed. I thought she was capable of making the most stunning record. And this was not it. Jerry and Herb certainly shared that opinion. To everybody's credit, the record was stopped. The responsibility to the greatest extent, with an artist like that, would rest with the producer. And it was a mismatch."

Karen loved the record, Green says, but he, Moss, and Alpert were unanimous: it had to be cancelled. Breaking that news to her was going to be tough, even though she had voiced certain fears to intimate friends. "She was afraid Richard wasn't going to like it," says her pal Debbie Vaiuso's husband, C. J. Cuticello. "She knew he didn't like the fact that she was doing it; she was afraid he wouldn't like the sound because it was different from what they'd done together."

"She told us that several times," confirms Debbie Cuticello. "When we went to the studio to listen to it, she looked at us several times for a response, and we said 'Beautiful.' It really was some of her best work." But at dinner, Karen expressed her concern about Richard's attitude; she said, "He's not taking this well at all."

Her concern encompassed Richard's response to the texture of the sound and to the principle of her being named as soloist. Would she and Richard ever be able to reunite? She seemed defensive and protective of him and could not bear to think of him being swept aside. And she knew in her heart that Richard would react against the fundamental tone of the record, with its trendy disco-and-dance flavour clashing with his love of strong melodies and lyrics.

Angry and hurt when Alpert and Moss told her of the concensus, she went home to her apartment to think through her formal response. Then she returned to A&M with a surprise. She said she wanted to continue the idea of a solo album, and asked if they would pick some new songs for her. It was typical of her makeup to try to turn a negative situation around. But it was not to happen.

Moss hoped it would be "an amazing record" but says they were all disappointed by the quality of the songs. Ramone could not be blamed "because he was trying to do something different, and we weren't throwing him a lot of songs, either." Another record executive who described the album as "horrible" said it made him appreciate Richard's work with Karen: "He had been able to produce her *voice*." And Jerry Weintraub felt in retrospect that the album was "that last-ditch effort every artist makes when they have to get a hit. Every pop artist who stops selling records has to try something new, so most of them go to Nashville and make a country album, or they make a live album at Carnegie Hall, or they switch producers. Phil Ramone was an old, dear friend of mine and a very talented man. But he couldn't make the album with Karen that Richard could make because the communication, the bond they had, didn't exist. He was a great producer. She was a great singer. But that's not necessarily what makes great albums."

Karen played some of the tracks to Mike Curb, who says: "She never felt the magic that she felt when she recorded with Richard. There was a magic in their harmonies, in the simplicity of their arrangements; in New York I know she was feeling uncomfortable."

When he heard the music for the first time, Richard's worst fears were realized. "Of course," he says now, "they did disco. And I had only said to Karen she shouldn't do it because I strongly believe that she was never *meant* to do disco."

He still feels Ramone was misreading Karen if he considered that she could not interpret songs with maturity. "Karen sang plenty of mature songs. I made mistakes, and I'm the first to admit it. Looking back, especially now without having her around, I feel them badly. At the time, we thought we had the rest of our lives to be recording. Had I known she was going to die at thirty-two, I wouldn't have been recording songs with her like 'Beechwood 4-5789' or 'Please Mr. Postman.' I regret doing those things, now. We should have been doing a lot more songs of the calibre of 'I Get Along without You Very Well.' But we did quite a few mature and timeless songs, from the aspect of melody and lyrics, and I don't know what Phil Ramone is driving at on that point unless he is referring to the minority of our output such as 'Postman' and 'Sing.'"

He feels Ramone's attempt to make Karen sound tough was "as phony as hell. He had her sounding like she was from New York, and to me that didn't sound natural. It just wasn't right for Karen to be singing that stuff."

Werner Wolfen was slightly suspicious of the rejection. Had it been vetoed for wholly artistic and creative reasons, or because Richard did not like the basic principle? Was the dismissal of the solo album in itself a method of kick-starting their renewed partnership? That level of scepticism probably mistook the degree to which Karen admired Richard. Ignoring the fact that they were brother and sister, she knew that nobody on earth could get close to his intuitive understanding of what made her voice work so well inside her natural style.

When it was clear the album would not be released, the debt for its production was charged against Carpenters royalties. Karen was furious. "I gotta get my money back—go in and get my money back," she harried Wolfen. But with no new Carpenters product yet, they had no leverage with A&M to reclaim it. Their sales had slid, and with no new album yet imminent, there was nothing against which A&M could offset the solo record's expenditure. Karen had a big heart, but when it came to spending money, and earned business money at that, she always displayed economical thinking instilled in her by her parents. When A&M finally insisted the debt would have to be set against future royalties, she was not amused. The loss of more than $400,000, plus a dumped album, together with a relationship with Richard that had been nearly fractured and was now in need of rekindling, was a heavy price to pay for a stab at independence.

Karen played her solo tapes to her friend Olivia Newton-John. Richard was present, and a comment he made shocked both women. Olivia recalls:

"He said to Karen, 'You've stolen the Carpenters sound.' And I always remember that because—well, she IS the Carpenters sound! Even though he might have thought up the harmonies and everything else, it was her voice that made that sound." With all her admiration for Richard, Karen was, Olivia remembers, "very, very confused" about that implied criticism of her solo work.

What Richard actually meant was that "they had done all this overdubbing with all that four-part harmony, and that didn't sit well with me. I figured they were supposed to have made an album that was so different from anything we had done—and then I hear all the Carpenteresque vocal sounds!"

Was Karen the whole of the Carpenters sound? No! "Nor was I," Richard states categorically. Disagreeing with Olivia, he says today: "People will fight this from now until Doomsday. I say that Karen was the major part of the Carpenters sound—but she wasn't all of it.

"Part of the Carpenters sound, which I devised at the beginning, was all the overdubbed vocals, with Karen taking the lead, plus many other ingredients like the use of piano and oboe, for example.

"Olivia is of course entitled to her opinion. But when I spoke of the Carpenters sound on the Ramone production, I meant all the vocal overdubs and tight harmonies. I was *not* happy when I heard that."

Intervention in the Karen-Richard relationship was always going to be impossible. They wanted a perfect partnership that went well beyond the sibling tie. It meant making music together for life. Ramone once challenged Richard about the possibly stultifying effect of being "The Carpenters" for ten years to the exclusion of everything else. However brilliant and successful they were, artists needed to stretch, Ramone told him. "Why don't you go write a movie? Why don't you get an agent for solo work? Why don't you donate your life or time to a project? She'll do a solo album, you'll find yourself." In Richard, Ramone perceived the same refusal to grow that he felt dogged his progress with Karen in the studio.

Richard is predictably sanguine about the Carpenters as a unit in explaining why he never felt the need to "break free." "I felt Karen and I were something unique. The two of us were really meant to work together. And as far as finding myself—I really had! The two of us were put here to make music together, and that's what I wanted to do for the rest of my life. We had something very special, and that's what we would have been doing still: making records and doing occasional tours. I don't consider that a refusal to grow."

With the solo album jettisoned, Ramone says he was "destroyed at the fact that we never had a chance to exploit something we believed in. It certainly would never have hurt the Carpenters in a million years." Richard agrees.

Although she was short of "life experience," the sweet little girl behind Karen had a cutting edge, a determination, an obstinacy that Ramone had recognized. That was what he had tried to invest in her record. He had wanted her to say with that album: "I'm grown up. Please allow me to show you."

Once recovered from the decision that the album was killed, Ramone reflected that there was "a tremendous paternal feeling from the label toward the Carpenters. Maybe we had taken their little daughter into too many risky areas. But all we did was let her out to play because her brother was off in a land that couldn't be dealt with."

By the time the album was complete, Richard was cured from his pill addiction. "Now it was time to get their business together and go back to work," Ramone says. "I said to myself: 'You stupid boy. Why didn't you see that happening all along'" (meaning that Karen or Richard or both were perhaps viewing the solo project as an exercise that would in some way give them a psychological thrust to reunite.)

Richard, however, denies that it was a ploy. "Once Karen made up her mind, she was committed to whatever it was.

"So she would never have done this lightly. Once she threw herself into that project, you couldn't have had a more willing partner." But the solo project "without a doubt" was never intended to signal the end of the Carpenters.

At A&M, the sales team had been whipped up into a state of fervor, the album had been designated a catalog number, and artwork was being prepared with fine new photographs. Now the die was cast, Karen sent a politically deft memo to everyone concerned with the project.

As Richard had "wanted to take some time off," she wrote, she had been recording a solo album with Phil Ramone "and I'm not totally happy with it, and now Richard's back in action I'm really excited that we're gonna work on a new album together again."

Richard believed that though the album was a technical success, it lacked "gut appeal." "It was extremely well done. It was produced well, of course she sings well, with very intricate arrangements all very well executed. But I had three complaints. One, they went and took the Carpenters overdub sound, whereas it should have been different with her. Two, Phil at times had her singing beyond her comfortable range, too high. Three, it did not have strong enough material.

"For artists like us, a top-five sell-through hit single is required before album sales go nuts. That is the primary reason why "Hush" and "Passage" did not sell well. And I'm convinced there wasn't a hit single on her solo album with the possible exception of 'If I Had You.'" He believes the album would have fared no better in sales than their releases around that time.[2]

John Bettis, who agrees there was no hit on the album, says a shrewd move by Richard would have been to press A&M to

---

2. After Karen's death, at the request of fans, Richard included some of the Ramone-produced tracks on fresh releases. These included "If I Had You," "Remember When Lovin' Took All Night," "If We Try," and "Lovelines" on the album of that title. Included on the "From The Top" collection was Karen's version of "Still Crazy After All These Years." For this song, at Karen's request, Paul Simon had rewritten one word. In place of his original phrase, "Four in the morning, crapped out, yawning," he substituted "tapped-out, yawning." She felt the original was too crude for a female voice. On this, Richard declares, "So don't put the so-called failure to spread Karen's wings on me entirely—because after all this talk of her apparent need for maturity, she didn't even want to sing 'crapped out'!"

release it. "It wouldn't have met with much success—and then it would have been a case of: OK now, *next!*" Richard feels that if he had done that, and A&M would have accepted, Karen would have had to fly between Los Angeles and New York several times while new material was recorded, because A&M was set against releasing it as it stood. The extra workload would have cost her yet more money. And anyway, she was in no physical condition to undertake a rerun of those bicoastal recording sessions. "She looked truly terrible during the making of the solo album and after it. Besides that, I had no business in offering an opinion to A&M regarding this."

"From an emotional point of view," Richard reflects, "I wanted the album released. I had been tired of everyone saying, since we had not got those recent hits: 'We need another producer. Richard's not doing his job.' I hadn't tried to talk Karen out of doing this. Karen's solo could have come out while we were recording what became *Made in America*. (released in 1981.)

He adamantly rejects the implication of his critics, including Ramone, that he pulled any strings to get the album dumped because he was ready to return to work with her. "Herb and Jerry did not want it released and that was the bottom line."

The more he thinks about it, the more he considers that he should have "turned her loose, if in fact she wanted to be turned loose. Maybe I should have said, 'Look, Karen, I don't want to be in the Carpenters any more.' Karen might well have been concerned about her identity, in that it was Carpenters rather than Karen Carpenter." Their mother says, though, that Karen never wanted to split from Richard. And he insists that "nobody understood her voice better than I."

As for Ramone's contention that Karen went downhill physically after Richard and Agnes allegedly talked her out of putting out her solo album, her brother states: "You only have to look at pictures of Karen taken during the making of the album. She looks like death. And that had nothing to do with the decision later not to release the album."

*She wanted a wedding and a family and a white
picket fence. . . . She was searching for something,
and she never found it.*

—MANAGER JERRY WEINTRAUB

Back in California during a break from the New York project in October 1979, Karen enjoyed the job of finding her friend Elizabeth Van Ness a gynaecologist. And when Elizabeth gave birth to Sarah, Karen's maternal instinct seemed at a peak; she was predictably warm and generous. But Elizabeth noted that while she seemed on top of the world in so many respects, "Karen was lonely, wanted to meet a terrific guy, get married, and have kids." Since she was becoming almost neurotic about not meeting men, Elizabeth arranged a date for her with actor Tony Danza. It remained just that, leaving Elizabeth to ponder Karen's solitariness.

"People say she sang from the heart, but I feel it was from her soul, some sort of soul that she wasn't even in touch with. She was a very smart girl but not particularly intellectual. Yet when she sang there was an intelligence, a message that borders on profundity, so well thought out and expressive that it came from something beyond her."

A deep emotional vacuum, as many saw it, contrasted sharply with whackier facets of her makeup. On one of her daily calls to Elizabeth, she said she had a great new recipe: "Hamburger slosh! Mash it up with vegetables." And that, says Elizabeth, was another side of the enigma. "She didn't want to sit down and analyse."

Scarred by the album rejection, Karen's return might have become morose, but her life was often exhilarating. Olivia Newton-John suggested a break, and the two drove to San Diego for a few days at the Golden Door health farm. This seemed an incongruous trip since Karen was so painfully thin, but after the tension of Richard's cure and her solo crisis she wanted a break. During the journey Karen spelled out to Olivia what she wanted in her perfect man: "Someone of about thirty, successful in his own right so he could cope with my success." Olivia replied that it sounded terrific, "but in reality to find all these things in one man, you'll be very lucky." Karen felt she might, if she looked as pretty as Olivia.

On her return from San Diego, Karen was keen to plunge into her new album with Richard, but he refused. He told her she looked like "a rail" and obviously did not have the strength. "It may do some damage to you," he continued. "I'm not going to make an album until you see someone and *just start eating*."

Grudgingly, Karen agreed to see an internist in Beverly Hills who was treating family friend Beverly Nogawski, who was trying to lose weight. The plan was that Karen would stay at her parents' home and provide real evidence of her improvement, joining everyone at normal dining times, drinking milk shakes, and eating lunch and dinner with no absences or excuses. The Beverly Hills specialist helped her, and she gained weight to about 106 pounds. "For a short time she looked great," Richard says, "and got some colour back in her cheeks."

Then, the anorexic's panic must have taken control. She quit the visits to the specialist and "seemed to think she could lick it by herself," Beverly says. The specialist had been disappointed by Karen's non-attendance. He told Beverly that Karen had an illness and it was imperative that she go for treatment, even if it was not to him.

According to Richard, there had been two problems with that specialist: he was star-struck—and she had somehow got him to tell both her and her family that she did not have anorexia nervosa. "Whatever unsettling experience an anorexic goes through, she dreaded putting this weight on, and she had this doctor tied up. Karen could be very persuasive." Feeling vindicated when he said she did not have the disorder, Karen said to her family: "There, see, he said it. And this guy is supposed to know! I don't need to be doing all this."

It had been another cover-up. She had gained a little weight and silenced those around her for a while. For those brief shining few weeks, she looked and sounded confident and insisted to Richard that she was raring to go for their new album.

Romance, too, was in the air as she felt much more confident in her appearance. As quickly as she gained her composure, though, she seemed to lose it and returned to her old ways, eating little and confiding to some friends that she was troubled.

At a Christmas Eve party in 1979 at the home of Jerry Weintraub, Karen saw Mike Curb, by then married to Linda Dunphy, whose father was the noted Los Angeles television newscaster Jerry Dunphy. Talking to them both animatedly about children, Karen seemed to have entered a new phase, and Mike sensed she was ready for marriage. The Carpenters career was in perspective, and a new life was on her agenda, Mike recalls. "The way she talked about my baby daughter, the way she was relating to my wife . . . she was talking about family things, not about records."

Karen renewed a casual dating spell with Steve Poe, but this old friendship, and any observations Mike Curb might have made about Karen's new outlook, were quickly overtaken by plans to return to the studio to record an album with Richard. Several boyfriends confirm that she never had a second thought about canceling a date if a sudden requirement to work overtook her social plans. "Sorry, gotta go to the studio" became a ritualistic phrase from Karen, expected by many of her friends.

To all of them, though, she gave out signals that she needed warmth and attention. She gave an abundance of both in return. These factors meant she acquired a dedicated coterie whose love of her went well beyond traditional levels of friendship.

It was, indeed, a clan, led by Mike Curb and his sister Carol, who were both deeply embedded in the social, political, and show business framework of Beverly Hills. Mike was by then lieutenant governor of California, and his slender and attractive sister, who worked alongside him in his thriving record company, became one of Karen's major confidantes. They spoke by phone most days and met often for lunch or dinner, making a quartet with their respective brothers.

The singing Osmond Brothers, who were signed to Curb Records, were managed by Ed Leffler, who, with Frenda, had also become a mainstay of Karen's life from the moment in 1976 when she bought her condominium.

Meeting Carol for lunch at the Beverly Hills Hotel, Karen spelled out her problem to such a close friend who had survived a bout of anorexia. "It's like being haunted," Karen said to Carol.

"It's the worst thing in the world." Carol believes she "wanted someone to deliver her from that awful feeling, that she was scared to death to eat."

When Carol went to Karen's apartment, the anorexic's obsession with precision was clearly visible. In the closet, all her clothes were immaculately hung on the same type of hanger, perfectly arranged. "This was something to behold," Carol says. And as they spoke, it transpired that a new routine had developed. Someone had told her that adding weight could be avoided if she did all her eating before 5:00 P.M.

As Carol pointed out to her, that would make dating difficult.

All the men who knew Karen socially found her lively, unaffected by fame or success but enjoying both, witty, unpretentious, and open. In spite of her diet, she was energetic and sincere in her interest in others. Women had a different perspective. They could see that she was unhappy in love.

She asked Werner Wolfen occasionally if he had a "nice young lawyer" for her to meet. But the man she was to marry came into her life unexpectedly.

Through her brother's political activities, Carol Curb met the handsome Tom Burris and was impressed by his winning personality and philanthropic acts. She considered him "gallant, charming, suave," a man of apparent substance who offered rides on his own plane and was involved in charitable causes.

He was not part of the show business crowd and, in fact, was unfamiliar with the Carpenters, a factor that Carol felt might even weigh in his favour with Karen.

"I think I have someone for you to meet," Carol told Karen on the phone one evening in the spring of 1980. It was the first time Carol had ventured anything of this nature. Karen valued her friend's taste but was initially dubious about going on a "blind date." Such uncertainty went against all her principles; she preferred to plan her social life like her professional diary, with considerable attention to detail.

But she went along with it because she reasoned that any evening fixed by Carol and her husband, Tony Scotti, probably carried little risk. It became, in fact, quite the reverse. The dinner date for four went so well that within days, Karen and Tom Burris were dating, and after a whirlwind romance of two months they were engaged. Three months after their visit to the health farm, Olivia's phone rang. "Are you sitting down? Well, I'm engaged!" Then Karen asked her mother: "Should I marry him?"

"Karen, that's all up to you," Agnes replied. "You're old enough to know what you're doing." Agnes felt Karen was worrying about "marrying a businessman dressed in a suit." But the momentum continued.

At Karen's wedding shower at the exclusive Hillcrest Country Club in Beverly Hills, a hundred women welcomed a glowing Karen, neatly dressed in a yellow suit and hat.

"Hi, Agnes, how are you?" a cheerful Maria Galeazzi inquired. "Oh, I'm OK, but you should see Richard, what that poor kid's been through," Agnes replied. Maria was astonished to hear of his pill-taking cure of the previous year. "When we toured, he took one, I took one, and we went to sleep," she said.

Meeting her with Tom, Olivia believed Karen had found her dream guy with all the qualities required. "She was the happiest I'd seen her. Their period of courtship was so good for her. She'd put on a bit of weight and looked healthy."

Everyone considered them a fine match, and although Richard thought Tom "just fine," there were a couple of rocky moments between them. Richard and Karen had worked as a team for so long that when he said she was needed somewhere, she was expected to be available without question. At Martoni's restaurant in Hollywood one such night, when Richard announced a business meeting for them, Tom Burris accused him of being "a dictator." Incensed, Richard stormed out.

But all was sweetness as plans were made for the wedding.

Carol's theory about the speed of decision is that Karen realized she had let several good men slip through her fingers— "because of her youth, and not knowing how to value a relationship. Tom made a terrific impression on her, and she did not want to make that mistake again. She wanted children very badly. At heart, she wanted a family and a white picket fence."

Until 1980, all her focus had been on her career and her body. Now it was to be marriage and children. She also believed that getting married could form a major part of her therapy in combatting her anorexic hurdle.

Four hundred and fifty guests were at Karen Carpenter's wedding to blond, blue-eyed Tom Burris. Her show business friends, including Olivia Newton-John, Dionne Warwick, Herb Alpert, and Burt Bacharach, heard the service begin with Richard Carpenter at the piano to accompany a forty-piece choir. The magnificent decor of the Crystal Room of the Beverly Hills Hotel was specially designed to simulate a 1930s wedding in an Old English garden setting: every window and pillar in the huge room was covered with silver foil-backed trellises, interwoven with white orchids, gardenias, violets, and lemon leaves. Huge baskets of orchids were suspended from the ceiling, and another trellis heavily laden with purple stocks, to simulate wisteria, and lemon leaves, hung over the custom-built altar, framing the bridal party. There were ten bridesmaids.

As Karen and Tom walked down the aisle, and the choir ended their medley of Carpenters hit songs, Karen's voice boomed out from a recording of a beautiful song, which her brother and John Bettis had composed especially for the great day: "Because We Are in Love." Peter Knight had flown in from London to assist with the speedy work essential to complete this masterpiece in time.

The bridal path was lined with custom-built white gardenia topiary trees and large woven baskets of pink chrysanthemums. Top designer Bill Belew's gown creation for Karen was modelled after an eighteenth-century riding ensemble. Made of white mousseline de soie, the long-sleeved jacketed gown with a long train featured a floral design of seashells and sequins. Fifteen yards of material had been used for this work of art. The bride's silk veil cascaded from a white chiffon detachable brimmed picture hat, fashioned with a juliet cap crown embroided with sequin-studded flowers. Karen chose lilies of the valley for her bouquet, interwoven with wired loops and streamers of tiny white pikake petals to give a lace effect.

After Richard sang "The Wedding Prayer" and the couple exchanged marriage vows and rings, Karen and Tom walked down the aisle and out into the Maisonette Room for a press conference. Then it was on to the wedding luncheon for what the local glitterati considered the society wedding of the year. Guests feasted on limestone lettuce salad with shrimps (Karen's favourite), chicken chasseur under glass, broccoli polonaise, rice pilaf, strawberries with bisquit fans, and Chablis wine. A toast to the bride and groom was proposed by Mike Curb. Like his sister Carol, Mike was thrilled to see his cherished friend so serenely happy, so visually gorgeous, and with a great new life ahead of her.

But even amid the gaiety, others in the room took a sober, cynical view. As Karen and Tom led off the dancing to the accompaniment of a dance band playing "We've Only Just Begun," at least one former boyfriend of Karen was choking back the tears.

David Alley still truly loved her. The Carpenters' personal assistant he remained, even if there was no "road" to organize any more; still he had dutifully made the couple's honeymoon travel plans. Watching the revelry, their air tickets in his pocket, he nursed his inner sadness: "It was like a knife through my heart."

Karen's family, too, held their peace while suspecting that this fairy-tale, whirlwind wedding was not all it appeared to be. It was surely unconventional, to say the least, for besotted newlyweds to invite, as Karen had done, members of her family including her Aunt Bernice, to go on the honeymoon with them. When they tactfully declined, Tom's brother and his wife accepted the invitation.

The destination was the Tahitian island of Bora Bora. Karen immediately disliked it, describing it as "boring, boring" in phone calls to her parents and to Richard. She always preferred top-range hotels rather than anything vaguely bucolic. The spartan nature of their life in Bora Bora, with few creature comforts and not even radio and television in their room, was so dull for her. She ended the honeymoon early.

Back in California, Karen and Tom planned a future with homes in Bel Air, Newport Beach, and even one in Mexico. Significantly, Karen kept her private condominium on Avenue of the Stars and flitted between the homes as she and Richard returned to their career with gusto. After a robbery at the Bel Air house in which their maid was held up at gunpoint during their absence, Karen said she would never return there again.

She told her lawyer, in whom she confided personal as well as professional matters, that she wanted to become pregnant. "I asked her how she could possibly do that, given her physical state. She pooh-poohed that and said this was what she wanted; she and Tom wanted children," Werner Wolfen says.

Richard was among the sceptics about the marriage. Tom certainly had met the requirements of Karen's "checklist." He was fair, handsome, and appeared financially secure. But Richard pondered that love did not work that way, and he believed that choosing a partner for marriage was hardly like going shopping with a checklist for an automobile.

The conundrum of Karen reached its zenith in matters of the heart. She could be mature beyond her years, as her singing demonstrated, but in dealing with herself she became almost petulant and childlike in her stubbornness.

As she returned from her honeymoon, gnawing away at Richard was the deep conviction that "there was something seriously ailing Karen and it was in full force when Tom was married to her." Many other friends, relatives, and musicians who saw her from various perspectives believed that beyond that day of smiles and splendour at the Beverly Hills Hotel, the marriage, in her brother's words, "didn't have a snowball's chance in hell of working."

While Karen was away on her honeymoon, Richard prepared material for their reunion album. Richard had been urged by Jerry Moss to return to their more trusted formula of "bread-and-butter stuff, nice ballads," which had been so successful in the early 1970s. This advice bemused him slightly, but, bouncing back with vigour from his own difficulties, he was hungry, like Karen, for a hit collection.

In fine fettle when she flew home to Newport Beach with Tom, Karen even started to develop a tan to disguise those sunken cheeks.

For a while, she seemed to eat more sensibly, consulted a nutritionist, and lived life as a happily married woman. Was her greatest dream coming true? Tom had entered her life when she was at her most vulnerable. Perhaps, just perhaps, for a few months toward the end of 1980, contentment bordering on happiness was in Karen's destiny.

The mood of that "comeback" album, *Made in America*, released in 1981, was symbolized by the joyful cover art and inside photographs. Karen and Richard look at a physical and mental peak, smiling as if to bury the sadnesses of the past two years. Only on close inspection is Karen's face seen to be thin.

When she heard the playback of one of the album's most enduring tracks, "Those Good Old Dreams," Karen's first love came to the fore. She enthused repeatedly about the drumming work of Ron Tutt, ignoring her own vocal on lyrics that seemed yet again to echo significant signposts of her life:

As a child I was known for make-believing
All alone I created fantasies

As I grew people called it self deceiving
But my heart helped me hold the memories.

As I walk through the world I find around me
Something new yet familiar's in the air
I feel it everywhere

Like a child's eyes on a Christmas night
I'm looking at you now finding answers to my prayers

It's a new day for those good old dreams
One by one it seems they're coming true
Here's the morning that my heart had seen
Here's the morning that just had to come through.

The introspection of the album's mood captured perfectly
what was to be Karen and Richard's twilight time together. The
mature, ambitious arrangements should have presaged a golden
future. Heard now, songs like "Strength of a Woman"—"It's
gonna take the strength of this woman/to keep fightin' for the
lovin' of her man"—and talk of suffering and pain in "When It's
Gone (It's Just Gone)" evoke the bleakness of the Carpenters'
broken dream.

As she did so often in her work, Karen sounds alone, solitary,
yearning, singing to, and for, similarly fractured kindred spirits.

Made in America was a remarkably powerful album, its lyrics of
often searing self-examination showing the maturing of a brother
and sister whose personal and professional journey was entering a
new phase. Both had sustained some severe knocks, but they
appeared to be coming out of the fire. And it showed.

Two songs in particular—"Somebody's Been Lyin'" and
"Because We Are in Love (the Wedding Song)"—stood out as

commentaries on Karen's love life, past and present. "Somebody's Been Lyin'," written by Carole Bayer Sager and Burt Bacharach, sounded as if it was aimed by Karen straight at a former, significant lover, an almost regretful look over her shoulder at something that might have been:

> Somebody's been callin' me tellin' me he still loves me
> But not the way I thought it would be
> He's making fun of me and laughing at my dreams
> And I know that he keeps saying not to worry.
>
> He's tellin' me to just hold on
> But he's not here to lean on
> And words won't warm my bed now he's gone
> It isn't easy letting go of what we had
> And I guess I'm just scared
>
> And I still believe him though
> I'd be wiser to go on my way
> Somebody's been lyin'
> And I know you're telling me the only things you want to
>
> I guess I lie as much as you do
> It seems so funny letting go of yesterday
> Guess we're much too afraid and we're much too alone
>
> Were we just too much in love.

If those words were an unwitting reminder of her past, there was a resounding commentary on her existing marriage on "Because We Are in Love (The Wedding Song)." Richard and John Bettis had toiled throughout the night at Lubec Street completing the song before inviting Peter Knight to fly in to score it in time for the wedding. The choir on the album track was directed by Frank Pooler, their former university tutor now established as a special friend.

The extraordinary, uncanny symbiosis between the songwriters reached a peak with this direct hit on Karen's emotions allied to a gorgeous, multi-layered arrangement. All her sentiments were here: "Children, it was more fun to be children ... we just took life as it happened, run through the days, don't look behind," she sang.

As the song progressed, there was her excitement at finding herself, together with mention of her mother: "I didn't sleep at all last night/Mom, I've come to you like yesterday about today/Mom, I'm afraid/Hon, come and sit by my side/Listen to me/words come so hard, but what my heart says I will give you."

She sang of imagination and losing concentration when the name of her partner was mentioned: "Because we are in love/we reach for our tomorrows/And know we won't be lonely/In laughter and in sorrow where love abides/There is the place we'll keep our home together/You and I."

For all its majestic beauty, the lines sung by the choir with interjections by Karen may have pinpointed her psyche at the time it was recorded: "Same little girl who's frightened (Karen sang)/ But I love him so/Same little girl who's sure (Karen sang)/ That she loves him so/Sees with a woman's vision, knows what a woman knows."[1]

In his fourteen-year-long partnership with Richard, Bettis had frequently written masterpieces extolling the pleasures of pure love, and Karen had found the themes both warming and hopeful in a personal sense. Sometimes, the story line carried a tinge of uncertainty, of questioning. In "Because We Are In Love," Bettis brilliantly spoke for the inner woman's mood at the time, one of brooding celebration.

Karen's marriage had been her fairy tale. But even as that song, which had been her wedding day anthem a year earlier, "went public" on the *Made in America* album, her relationship with Tom was becoming rocky.

"She claimed to be in love," says her lawyer, Werner Wolfen, but he became aware of indications that made him wonder if all was well. When he asked her if she was happy, she said yes; but she was not the best candidate for marriage in terms of health and outlook in 1980. By the time *Made in America* was released a year later, an energetic Richard wanted to return to touring, but she was clearly not fit enough.

"She wanted a wedding and a family and a white picket fence around her house. And she wanted everything to be Disneyland," says Jerry Weintraub. "That's why Mickey Mouse was always in her life. She was searching for something, and she never found it."

And Richard says: "I will go so far as to say that Karen could never have been happily married to anybody going about it the way she did."

If there were already signs that, after only one year, her marriage was not made in heaven, Karen at least gained confidence and pleasure from the artistic renaissance of *Made in America*. Their tenth studio album, and the last she made with Richard, it was a robust pointer to what might have followed, an imaginative enough departure from their existing work but still carrying the essential Carpenters resonance.

Powered by a hit single, "Touch Me When We're Dancing," it should have sold more copies than it did, but it ran into the Carpenters' "image" problem. Some radio programme staffers told A&M's promotion team that no matter what record they turned out, the Carpenters would not be played because to do so would damage the public's perception of their station. Karen and Richard were simply not hip.

That factor is why "Touch Me When We're Dancing" rose to only number sixteen on the charts, Richard believes. But he notes that "it was a top-twenty hit so we were starting to return. It would only have been a matter of time before we picked the right song, something that was irresistible for radio. And we would have got back into the top five."

Even with that disappointment, *Made in America* joined the long list of records that were very profitable, both for A&M and for the Carpenters.

Their return to the fold was, of course, heartening news in both personal and professional terms for Herb Alpert, who with

Jerry Moss hosted a "welcome back" party attended by two hundred guests on the lawns of the Bel Air Hotel.

Shortly afterward, Jerry and Jane Weintraub threw a party at their new Malibu home. Surprisingly, not all the guests found Karen in a buoyant mood; Justin Hayward of the Moody Blues began talking to Karen, whose singing he greatly admired, but he thought she seemed "distracted, very nervous, sad, maybe tragic. There was something about her that wasn't quite right. ... she didn't have the confidence of a normal person." He registered that she was "talking to me from a little bit of a haven and what she really wanted to do was go home."

In August 1981, Karen and Tom, with Olivia Newton-John and her husband, Matt Lattanzi, decided to take a trip on Tom's boat to Catalina Island. When they arrived, the men went diving while the women sunbathed. By 4:00 P.M., the ocean had become choppy so they decided to return home early, but ten miles out of Catalina while battling the forceful current, the drive shaft snapped. Tom steered the boat back to harbour, and they stayed overnight on the island, returning the next day. "It makes life interesting," Tom said nonchalantly.

The next week, Tom and Karen left for an anniversary vacation in safer transport, his four-wheel drive Ram Charger. They headed for Durango, Colorado, from where they went on a scenic tour of Canada.

Then it was back to work to promote the album. Karen seemed in fine fettle, eating normally as she and Richard headed for Europe, first stop Paris, where they guested on a television show with Julio Iglesias, who joined them as they performed "Sing."

Richard and Karen were feted, taken down the River Seine and to the Moulin Rouge, and as they flew on to Britain, their enjoyment of working together recalled the tempo and pleasure of ten years earlier.

Visiting London to promote *Made in America,* Karen and Richard went on October 25, 1981, for dinner with Peter and Babs Knight to the Bedford Arms, an award-winning restaurant at Chenies, near Rickmansworth.

Karen ate a gourmet meal enthusiastically, Babs recalls, "and she did not disappear after the meal to do what some anorexics do." Nor did she appear to be quite so thin as the Knights remembered her previously with some concern. But within weeks, on her return to California, Karen's condition must have worried her as much as others, for she was making plans to go to New York for that year of therapy.

Her physical stress was compounded by a rapidly disintegrating marriage. A clear sign that it was doomed came when, after an awkward atmosphere during a birthday dinner for Harold Carpenter in a Downey restaurant on November 9, 1981, Tom Burris later walked downstairs from Karen's room at her parents' home. She remained upstairs as he announced to her flummoxed parents and brother, "You can keep her." That said, he drove away.

Karen regarded this as the final moment of decision in the marriage, which had by then lasted fifteen months. Her cousin Joanie went upstairs to comfort her. By then aware that anorexia might be a psychological problem, Joanie hugged her, telling her how much she cared for her and loved her. "We are not terribly demonstrative in our family. I hadn't hugged her a lot, and I had begun hearing that this was one of the things the doctor was saying we should display more: feeling and affection. She was very gracious and glad I told her all that, and responded that she loved me too." The cousin with the uncanny facial resemblance to Karen adds with a tinge of personal regret: "She could have used that support more. She needed to be told that more often."

When Thanksgiving came, though, Karen was upbeat. The infectious smile had returned, and the old warrior in her was never far away. She chastised family members who had not "dressed up" for dinner, and she even ate a little turkey. Her mood was "jolly," Agnes recalls, and that continued into Christmas, which she always enjoyed.

By then she was making plans to relocate to New York for the next year. She would never see Tom again.

I have to lick this before it licks me.

—KAREN TO HER CLOSE FRIEND DEBBIE CUTICELLO

You *can do anything if that's how you feel.*

—DEBBIE'S REPLY

By nature, Karen was guileless, outward, quick to smile and joke, and had a wide-eyed innocence that belied her mature age. Yet in her anorexic life she was a skilled, wily veteran who employed every trick in the obsessive dieter's textbook to lose weight—while assuring everyone that she knew the problem must be conquered. But she was a woman who invariably "followed through" and did as she said or planned. So when she finally told all those she knew of her plan to go to New York to deal with her difficulties, they believed she must have meant it. Karen never did anything lightly.

But the woman who arrived at Steven Levenkron's office turned out to be "in big, big trouble, loaded on Dulcolax laxative tablets, hurting her system," her therapist recalls. An even more explosive discovery awaited him on one particular evening in the second week of her daily visits.

As Karen sat down on the brown leather sofa opposite him, wearing only a short-sleeved shirt and casual pants, she was perspiring unnaturally. Outside, the weather was just cool, and his office had an even temperature that should not have induced perspiration.

"Anorexics are colder than the rest of us," Levenkron points out. "They don't run 98.6 temperatures, but 97 or lower, because as the body starves it takes steps to protect itself from the famine that exists. So the heart and blood pressure slow down, and the temperature drops to burn fewer calories. And here is Karen sitting dripping with perspiration." Anorexics should not sweat because the body has metabolically "shut down" to conserve energy.

Levenkron fixed her with his customary eye-to-eye stare and challenged her. "Why are you perspiring? It's cool in here ... this makes no sense to me. You're emaciated; you're supposed to be cold." Anorexics usually turn blue in a cold room and Levenkron felt cool.

"I just feel warm," Karen shrugged.

"What are you taking?" Levenkron persisted. "You must tell me everything." Karen would not volunteer anything, he says, but she would lie by omission. "If you didn't ask her, she wouldn't tell you, but if you asked her, she wouldn't lie."

"Well, I'm taking eighty or ninety Dulcolax a night" (these laxative tablets are available at pharmacies). "I'm not taking anything else except thyroid."

Levenkron was baffled and shocked. "*Thyroid!* Why are you taking thyroid?"

A doctor had prescribed them, she replied.

"How many a day are you taking?" Levenkron asked quickly.

"Ten."

Levenkron continues the story. "I said, 'Do you have no thyroid gland?' She said, 'No, I have a normal thyroid.' I said, 'You have a normal thyroid and you're taking *ten a day!* Do you have the bottle with you?' She said no, it was back at the hotel. I said, 'I want the bottle tomorrow.' And she looked at me like a kid caught with something."

The next day, Karen took in her bottle. The prescription was dated August 17, 1981, three months before she went to Levenkron. Written out in her married name of Karen Burris, the prescription stipulated one tablet per day, which would represent .1 milligrams. Levenkron was told later by a physician that the pharmacy label had a typographical error, wrongly denoting one milligram and missing the decimal point which should have preceded it. "Not being a physician," Levenkron says, "I didn't catch that. She told me she was taking ten a day." It was still ten times the normal dose.

Levenkron, a non-medical psychotherapist with a Master of Science Degree in counselling, says: "At that point I had been treating anorexia for twelve years and I had never known anyone to toy with thyroid as a metabolic accelerator, to race her heart to burn more calories. This was a new one on me." Inquiring with physicians of the significance of someone with a normal thyroid taking ten tablets a day, he says he met a "shocked and horrified" response. "I spoke to two physicians, and I heard each of them sigh deeply and say she'd never get to the bottom of that bottle alive. She would either put herself into a thyroid storm or harm herself in some other way." Richard and her parents knew nothing of her use of thyroid tablets.

Why was she ingesting thyroid tablets in such quantities? It is one of many questions nagging away unanswered in the puzzling life and death of Karen Carpenter. Anorexia suffers are notoriously cunning, but this tactic was unknown, even to an expert like Levenkron. "They do lots of terrible things to themselves, but this was unique." It would, he states, speed up her metabolic rate so that the heart was beating 120 to 150 beats a minute. "You run the heart at that rate while you're emaciated, and you wear out that little muscle. So now I had somebody who had been emaciated for six or seven years, worked very hard doing singing tours, and had taken enormous quantities of laxatives and God knows how many bottles of thyroid, all of which cause enormous cardiac stress. So she had pushed herself to the physical limits."

Levenkron says that her use of thyroid tablets ceased, to his knowledge, after his discovery. The vial remains to this day in his office, eerie evidence of the convoluted self-hurt practised by a woman who certainly could not have realised how much damage she was inflicting. Of the 250 tablets that were prescribed, 107 remain. The damage done by those she took (and perhaps by previous prescriptions of the same drug) cause Levenkron to theorise that she might well have arrived at his office too late.

"We don't know when she started taking them," says Levenkron, commenting on Karen's statement that she took ten a day, a figure that hardly tallies with the date of the prescription and the amount left. "We truly have an information gap here." She could have started taking them a month after she got the bottle; she might have stepped up her intake to ten a day.

"And since frankly we assumed that no one would perish, right up to the time she left for California, I never saw fit to investigate this. We thought we had caught this in the nick of time." Karen had built up an enormous tolerance to toxins through her doses of laxative tablets, but he believes that the interaction of the thyroid tablets with laxatives created an arhythmic heartbeat which "probably took its toll over the years. It's very sad. Because of her surreptitious behavior, by the time we all started intervening, we were too late. This is an alert. Here was a lovely person who didn't want to die but was unstoppable." The lesson is in the deadliness of the disorder if unchecked.

Karen always insisted that, like all the Carpenter family, she had an iron constitution, but Levenkron believes it was weaker than she thought. "She had broken capillaries in her legs, which indicated that her vascular system wasn't terribly strong. She reported to me that she'd had a very slight stroke in her midtwenties. So we're dealing with someone who's physically a rather fragile person. She took a fragile constitution and then punished and exhausted it repeatedly."[1]

As she began treatment with Levenkron, Karen phoned Cherry Boone O'Neill. Surprised that Karen had flown to New York rather than heed her advice to visit Seattle for therapy with Dr. Ray Vath, who had treated her so successfully, Cherry was worried by Karen's attitude. "She had this time limit she was creating, a goal of being well in six months. She was limiting this recovery process to an arbitary period. I encouraged her to be more open-ended about it, but she was determined to be able to get back to the old grind of her career by a certain time. I told her in no uncertain terms that limiting the recovery process was certainly not realistic and may be counterproductive."

To a fellow traveller like Cherry, it was easy for Karen to open up about her personal habits. Cherry told her about her self-induced vomiting as part of her bulimia; Karen replied that she could not do that and relied on laxatives.

After about six weeks, Levenkron had established a good rapport with Karen. "I don't know how you do it," she told him with her customary warmth, "but you really make a person feel good about themselves." Levenkron's aim was partly to persuade Karen to analyze herself. "You have to relate to someone in such a way that whatever level or depth they are relating to feels better and offsets their compulsion to play with numbers, to play with their bodies, to hurt themselves.

---

1. Although she had certainly worn herself down by the time she reached New York, Karen's stamina had been constant since childhood. In the Carpenters' early days she joined in with the rest of the band in the loading of their equipment. And even as the years brought punishing touring schedules, she suffered no more than an occasional cough or cold. Members of the band confirm Karen's extraordinary strength.

"Anorexia, bulimia, obsessive compulsive disorders—they're all interrelated, what I call failed dependency illnesses. But something just isn't clicking, doesn't quite work. There's a degree or connection of trust that is withheld. And it isn't that Karen mistrusted everyone around her, but whatever her personal sensitivity barrier was, it put her in enough conflict."

Following his formula, Levenkron developed a relationship with his patient that went beyond mere treatment for dieting. "There was a whole fabulous entourage of people who loved Karen in New York. You could not dislike her because she was as genuine and sweet and as extremely shy as she looked. She was who she appeared to be. She would sit here and say: 'Why do I have this horrible illness? I do love my life, I love my career, I love my family—why do I have this?' And we had to do a lot of work around that problem together."

A typical daily session began with Levenkron asking how many laxatives she had taken since the previous day. "I was astounded that she could ingest as many as ninety to a hundred of these pills at once. But she'd always own up to it." He had no illusion that after admitting taking the laxatives, she would stop using them. He knew she would return to her hotel and continue to take them, "but it becomes different once she's admitted it. She takes them in conflict."

His plan of communication had several stages: first, to become friends and make a connection; second, to instill trust and dependence on him; third, to get Karen to emotionally accept him as one who could supervise her and to want that supervision; and fourth, to change her behaviour. Levenkron's early inquiries by phone to California about his new patient had given him ominous forecasts.

"We think Karen is dying. We really hope you can stop her," a psychiatrist whom she had consulted told Levenkron. "She's not a very good bet," said another. "She really resists every kind of treatment. We think this is a very poor prognosis." The last internist to see her said: "Good luck, Steve. This is not a treatable person."

"You have to get inside their mind," Levenkron says, explaining his process with anorexics. "To connect with them in a way that's just as important as their connection to the anorexic ideas. Most people who have anorexia feel a nagging sense of emptiness inside."

During their first sessions, he honed in on a central characteristic of Karen exhibited by many anorexics: "They're usually quite good at nurturing other people but quite impossible or inaccessible at nurturing themselves." It was a truism of Karen's behaviour that she enjoyed organizing the lives of her friends and, where possible, her relations, but she was difficult to influence.

She first weighed in with him at seventy-eight pounds. He addressed her with quiet dominance: "You are actually going to have to receive some care from me, and this is not in your constitution or character. That's how we are going to make this illness go away. If I can't get you to accept care from me, I can't repair your illness at all."

Karen pulled a face showing disapproval, as only Karen could.

"I don't need any care," she said, interrupting him. "I'm successful like this."

"But you *do* need care," Levenkron retorted, "because you are incompetent." Karen looked at him in horror. Her family and friends had warned her, but no stranger had hit her with such harsh tones.

"You're incompetent," Levenkron continued, "because you can't keep yourself alive. There's food aplenty, and you can't eat. You have the physical ability and the means at hand to keep yourself—and you can't. That's a major incompetence."

She was deeply stung by this, but with logic Levenkron had broken through the initial barrier of proving to her that she needed outside assistance to win.

This central thesis of the treatment was a struggle. Anorexics are adept at diverting attention from themselves, and Karen attempted to steer the conversation to all manner of topics: she would bring up her career, sing a new song, say how she'd been delighted to have been recognized on the street en route to his office; and she would inject her impish sense of humour to lighten the atmosphere. The resulting admonition from Levenkron became a standing joke as he told her so often: "Thank you very much, but the five minutes of taking care of *me* are now up. We now have fifty-five minutes of taking care of *you*." She enjoyed such banter, and the turnaround worked.

Karen adored Richard, he discovered. Emulating her mother's possessiveness, Karen was rather possessive about her brother. But somehow what never worked for Karen was that "in the midst of all these dynamics, Karen never got to *feel* cared for. And I'm not saying she wasn't cared for; but she was so busy controlling and manipulating herself that there was never a moment when she could feel that she could be a *recipient* of care. That creates enormous tension, loneliness, and separateness in the most congenial and outgoing personalities."

Richard and Karen were "parentified," Levenkron decided, because they saw their parents as emotionally needy. In his sessions he did not sense Karen was angry with her mother over her priority of Richard. "I got a sense of Karen meeting her mother's needs."

He believed there had been "a premature crossover of dependency of role" as Karen and Richard became rich and famous at young ages. "Most children earn more money than their parents perhaps in their thirties. What happens when two kids barely out of their teens are earning more money than their parents ever dreamed of is that there's an enormous transfer of strength and dependency. Parents of many stars have to worry about that."

With most female anorexics, he believes, "you have a starving girl and at least a starving mother there, emotionally, no exceptions. I've very, very rarely found an emotionally non-needy mother."

Continuing his theme of parent-child dependency, he asserts: "It affects the family structure enormously when suddenly, the parents of a seventeen-year-old are dependent on her for money. First, they buy the folks a big house, and the folks discover that they are now dependent on their children for income. And that affects things emotionally."

And children, conversely, become frightened if they assume too much power. "They wonder if there's anyone there to support *them*." Suddenly, the situation whereby a parent might say, "Stop that, honey; I'm in charge of your life" no longer exists. The power axis has shifted.

Richard insists that there was no change in relationships between him and Karen and their parents as a result of their fame. "Our father was still our dad, whether the money was coming from us or our parents. There was no personality change in any of us," a view shared by the Carpenter family's wide circle of friends. Their parents were interested in all aspects of their lives, not merely their finances, Richard avers. He believes any change in relationship with them was as normal and natural as any other son's or daughter's: "It related to age rather than to finance. Karen and I were growing up and wanting to assert ourselves more." Independence mattered to them more than a million dollars. And Agnes and Harold were never avaricious.

Although Karen felt emotionally alone in New York, she was never short of company or invitations from friends.

One visitor from California was John Bettis, whom Karen adored both as an ex-college friend and as her brother's lyricist on so many Carpenters hits. Their encounter bemused him. After an evening at dinner, he dropped her back at her hotel expecting to continue their conversation in her suite. "But she shooed me out of the door at ten o'clock." Such abruptness, particularly between close friends, perplexed Bettis. Only later did he realize that Karen, as an anorexic, had the need, immediately after dinner, to begin the routine of visiting the bathroom to expel the food. What Bettis had interpreted as antisocial behavior was to Karen an important physical routine.

This prolonged stay in New York brought some compensations socially. Most Friday evenings she would take off for a weekend, staying with her surrogate sister, Debbie Cuticello, at her New Haven home. Debbie's husband, C.J., would drive the ninety miles to knock on the door of Karen's hotel suite in Manhattan and return her to the rolling green of the Connecticut of her childhood. In the darkness of night, Karen became edgy about the safety of the countryside, which contrasted with the bright lights of New York and Los Angeles.

But she found security among her dearest friends. With some needlepoint for baby Jamie Cuticello and at least two suitcases overloaded with clothes, Karen enjoyed the drives there, talking animatedly about her week, inquiring about baby Jamie's health and progress, and confirming her faith and trust in Steven Levenkron's treatment. "You'd never know," says C. J. Cuticello, "that here was a patient undergoing treatment for this kind of illness." At Karen's suggestion, Levenkron phoned the Cuticellos' to complete his study of her characteristics and take note of their observations.

These were natural, therapeutic weekends in a house Karen considered a second home: she went shopping in Macy's department store in New Haven, enjoyed being recognized and challenged by assistants and bank tellers by the name on her credit card; cooked and washed dishes and helped to clean the house; babysat while Debbie and C.J. went to church. Certain television shows were mandatory viewing over a glass of Mimosa and a dish of strawberries: "Saturday Night Live" and "Dallas," and if the trio dressed up and went out for dinner when these shows were broadcast, they would have to be taped. Karen was addicted particularly to the prime time soaps.

"I have to lick this before it licks me," Karen said with typical directness to Debbie one night when they touched on her problem. Debbie replied as one who knew Karen from childhood: "You know, *you* can do anything if that's how you feel." Karen went on to say that her therapist was thrilled with her progress: "It usually takes a year, and the doctor is so thrilled that I'm doing this in six months or could even do it in four." This was self-deluding camouflage. Levenkron says he would never tell a patient that recovery could be achieved in such a short span.

Karen told Levenkron how much she loved her music and her work, but in one illuminating flash of candour, she revealed her lack of self-esteem. "When the lights go off after the performance, often I feel like nothing."

In therapy, a "quick fix" for such a confession is clearly impossible. His method was aligned more to reflecting on the personality of the patient over a given period, identifying her "wonderful traits," building trust.

"People with anorexia suffer emptiness of spirit and identity," Levenkron states. "They really don't know who they are. That's why they are monkeying with their bodies. I try to help them build a sense of identity."

After seven years of punishment of her body, Karen was among the estimated 65 percent of anorexia sufferers considered by specialists in the disorder to be in a chronic condition. The success rate for total recovery for such people after seven years is considered "negligible."

For Levenkron, the prospects were especially bleak. "I thought, grandiosely enough, that I'd talk her out of this disease. I still think I did. It's one of those obnoxious situations where I think I succeeded—and she died."

Visiting Manhattan from California, Dennis Heath went with Karen for a long walk near the East River before taking her to see the hit movie *E.T.* As he stood in line at the theater, Karen had an urge for some iced tea and, wearing giant sunglasses, walked around the corner. When she returned, she told Dennis Heath that a cop had warned her never to take out such a huge wad of dollar bills in a public place in New York.

After crying during the emotional movie, the two old friends from school years went to a restaurant. Heath was shocked: she picked away at two shrimps, a piece of lettuce, and sipped a glass of water.

On some weekends, Karen would fly alone to Baltimore to stay with her aunt, Agnes's sister Bernice. To avoid having to talk to strangers, Karen would book two first-class seats to ensure that she sat next to one empty. Cheerful and animated, Bernice had tried to lift Karen from her problem, taking her to great seafood restaurants and cooking the local speciality, crab, which Karen had enjoyed so much in past years.

Like everyone who dined with her, Bernice saw the tricks: giving everyone in her company a forkful of food from her plate; saving the lettuce leaf so she could end her meal by pushing food underneath it, hopefully out of sight.

Big hips were Karen's problem. "She took after her mother, Agnes, and our mother," Bernice says. "Where Richard got the slender hips and broad shoulders, Karen was hippy like her grandmother."

One night with her, Karen's guard on her emotions collapsed. At Bernice's home she always slept in her cousin's pretty bedroom, which had a long mirror on the back of the door. Stepping out of the shower, Karen slumped into a chair in her aunt's bedroom next door—and wept. She had caught sight of her pathetic frame in that mirror and realised just how thin she had become.

Normally, Karen could contain her emotions, but this was no situation for pretense toward an aunt who was particularly close to her. "She was really broken up and cried and cried and cried her heart out that night," Bernice says. "And she had me crying with her … it was so sad to see her like that. So young, so pretty, so much to live for, a gorgeous voice, a millionairess."

Bernice tried to hold her—but that only emphasized the tragedy of her protruding bones.

Karen's progress under the wing of Steven Levenkron was
not good enough for some who monitored her condition
from afar.

Her therapist's credentials as an authority on her problem had
attracted Karen, and she felt secure with his methods. But in California, as the weeks and months passed with no tangible result that
he could detect, Richard concluded that his sister was pulling a
confidence trick on him.

What she needed, as he had told her and everyone who would
listen, was an inpatient hospital programme. "If a person goes in to
get themselves off a drug or alcohol or whatever, in this case a disorder, they don't do it by checking themselves into a luxury hotel
and then see a psychologist or a therapist or a counsellor for fifty
minutes a day—then go back to the hotel for the rest of the day
and evening, and then take a weekend off.

"They check into a place where other people suffering the
same thing reside, and they have a programme, an itinerary, and
it's day after day. Not the Regency Hotel!

"As the months went by, if anything she was getting thinner,
and I got madder and madder. I got the feeling I was being bull-
shitted by Karen that she was in treatment seriously to get better."

Responding to Richard's argument, Levenkron says that before
going into therapy with him, Karen had consulted four people in
California, both physicians and psychiatrists. "Why was this [inpa-
tient treatment] not done in any of those four cases? The reason is
that they all tried desperately to get Karen to go into a hospital, a
center, and in that sense, she was untreatable. She would not listen

to anyone. And when she came to New York I said the same thing, and she wouldn't listen to me."

He does not disagree with Richard; he says he would have put her in an inpatient unit immediately. "She just about laughed at the notion." So the option to his treatment of her as it occurred was "to send her packing back to Los Angeles because she wouldn't do it the correct way."

What Richard's contention overlooks, says Levenkron, is the difficulty of treating this disorder—"of treating an adult woman who says, 'I'll do this and I won't do that.' I remember Karen describing her internist chasing her around the room with a hyperdermic needle. She really pushed away all medical and psychiatric care. She was enormously resistant to this.

"My dilemma, then, was to work with this woman who had moved to New York to be in treatment with me. And how rigidly I can have her under my control is really still up to her. And then, if she doesn't do everything the way I want her to do it, do I simply send her packing, when I know there's nobody to send her back to?" (Levenkron is referring here to his statement that "everyone in California had given up on her.")

So he settled for what he considered "a less-than-perfect treatment modality. I would still reflect that the modality didn't really matter. In the end, what killed her was all her behaviour previous to coming to New York." Richard accepts this.

The theory that Karen should have been an inpatient is supported by one of the world's leading authorities on anorexia nervosa. Professor Arthur Crisp says, "From what I have heard I would have thought that any chance she had of recovery would have required breaking the patterns of behavior." Describing anorexia as "a very sinister, very lethal" condition, Professor Crisp says that between 13 and 20 percent of those who suffered it at the degree that Karen did would die as a result of its effects within twenty years. With intervention, that mortality rate could be reduced to 4 percent. As a specialist who has treated many hundreds of anorexia victims in the past thirty years, he adds that he would never treat anorexics without also treating their families. Sessions always involve them.

Conversely, Levenkron had been surprised that there was so little contact with him from Karen's family, "no curiosity about her care or treatment. I do not believe I got one telephone call in the year that Karen was here, asking about her condition." Agnes and Harold visited once; Richard accompanied Karen to Levenkron's office once, but that had been a social rather than therapeutic visit to his sister. "There was no interest shown to me," Levenkron says. "They apparently expected her to be repaired as a package and mailed out.

"So this was a no-win situation, I'm afraid. It was no-win in the endeavour, no-win during it, and it's no-win in the aftermath." She remains his only fatality in twenty-seven years of practice. He says they had made significant progress and that he had fulfilled his challenge: "I had someone who came in abusing herself. She left not abusing herself."

Richard retorts: "With the exception of that one time when she got me so upset I didn't call her, we dealt with Karen; we didn't deal with Levenkron. It's not that we weren't interested. My Lord, my parents were back there any time she wanted; I went to visit her, and I called her far more times than I didn't. We were dealing with *Karen* during this period in New York, not with him. It was not like she went back there and we forgot all about her!" Since Richard did not care for Levenkron, he says he was "hardly going to call him to get his opinion of how things were going." He states that Levenkron conversely did not call him to discuss Karen's progress; "I got no phone calls at all."

While Richard accepts Levenkron's statement that Karen *would* have said, "It's going to be this treatment or nothing," her brother was furious with her for taking what he believed to be an inade-quate method of treatment. For a period, Richard ostracized her; in an act he now considers cruel and always regrets, he did not phone her for several weeks.

This temporary non-communication deeply upset Karen, according to Itchy Ramone. "She really depended on him, thought he was the most gorgeous man in the world. And to have your brother, to whom you're close, cutting you off, is not good." It depressed her.

Richard was irked, too, by a passing remark to him by Lev-enkron during their first and only meeting. The therapist said that when Karen emerged from this treatment successfully, the change in her might be so profound that she might never want to sing again. "Sure, that sounds like Karen," Richard said to himself with heavy sarcasm. The comment ensured that Richard would never regard Levenkron as Karen's saviour since it was apparent to her brother that such a remark did not identify what really made her tick. Music had always been her life.

There was anger, too, from Jerry Weintraub. Within three months of Karen's treatment, he complained by phone from California to Levenkron that the treatment was not working. As the instigator of her journey to New York, he felt responsible. And as well as being the Carpenters' manager, Weintraub spoke with the emotional concern and love of a father figure. He was furious that Karen, still skinny, was not feeling fit enough to attend a Billy Joel concert that Weintraub was promoting in New York.

Levenkron says he told Weintraub that with "seven years of history behind her with this problem, it was going to be a long haul—but he was yelling and cursing at me, telling me this was all bullshit. He was genuinely frightened and upset because he loved her and was worried about her. And I knew that what he wanted done couldn't be done as fast as he wanted. I said: 'I really think you're underestimating the tenacity of this illness and what goes on. I'm sorry you're unhappy with my work but this is where we are now.'"

To Debbie Cuticello in New Haven, Connecticut, the decline was both visual and tangible: for the months she was in New York, Karen asked Debbie to take care of some of her jewellery. Included was a Rolex watch. The reality of this hit Debbie hard: looking at the strap, she realized Karen's wrist would be far too thin to wear it safely. Karen's appearance and outlook shocked the whole Vaiuso family, who had known her since her birth in New Haven.

Debbie's mother fondly remembered how the younger Karen enjoyed popping into her home for meatballs, macaroni, and rigatoni. "I can't *believe* you won't eat, Karen!" Theresa reprimanded the woman who had been almost part of her family. Karen replied that she had an intestinal disorder, but she did eat. "You don't look right to me," Theresa countered.

It was on a Saturday visit to her daughter Debbie's house that the full force of Karen's problem struck Theresa Vaiuso. Karen, taking a shower, opened the bathroom door and called out, "Would you mind making me a hot cup of tea?"

Delivering it and knocking on the bathroom door, Theresa was aghast at the sight that opened it. "There was a mirror behind her. I could have cried as she stood there. I could see her full figure, and I could see every bone in it, like a row of golf balls down her back. And they were huge—because she had no muscle, no flesh. She weighed about eighty-six pounds, and she was about five feet four.

"I thought, 'Oh God, she is *sick*.' After the shower she came into the family room and lay down on the couch. And she shook like a person who had a temperature of 105. I took an Afghan and covered her, then a coat, then a blanket. And she just kept shaking.

"And I said: 'My God, Karen, this is *it*. Something's wrong. I don't know if you're going to the right place. Maybe you should see someone else.'" Karen answered as persuasively as ever: "Oh no, no, no. I'll be all right. I'm sure to get over this intestinal thing." She went to her giant jar, which she carried everywhere on her travels, a jar stacked with pretty coloured vitamin pills, and took a handful. Slowly, she pulled herself out of that crisis, but Theresa says, "It was pathetic." The incident was probably a result of her use of thyroid tablets.

Gregarious and self-critical, Karen became friendly with three other anorexics whom she met in Levenkron's waiting room. Known to them as K.C., she phoned the girls regularly to check on their progress. "Stop hurting yourself," she would say to them. Although it was hollow advice from a fellow sufferer, her celebrity status carried some clout.

Though Karen was always an extrovert in her nature, such a switch of the spotlight from herself to other girls might have been part of her ploy to convince others that she had now taken herself in hand.

Writing of the anorexic's "terrified manipulation of others," Professor Crisp states that the vast majority of patients are teenage girls from middle-class families. "Effective psychotherapy must be accompanied by a restoration of normal body weight," he continues. "A behavioural approach to gain in weight may be possible." Fundamental treatment requires "an initial unravelling of the developmental psychopathological state," with the initial goal to enable the anorexic to recognize the possibilities of an alternative life-style. "Suicide is the most common cause of death," writes Professor Crisp.[1]

---

1. Reproduced from Professor Crisp's article in the *British Medical Journal*, September 24, 1983.

Richard states adamantly that there is no way that intentional suicide would have been on Karen's mind. "She had no death wish," states Levenkron firmly. "Zero." Anorexia is, he says, an addiction to an *idea,* and it took control. "She really hated it; she was angry at the part of herself that succumbed to it."

The baffling question is why that happened; why, after a ten-year scale to the peak of her profession did a woman with so much to live for allow herself to be drawn into a life-threatening disorder?

Was it not a psychological problem at all but merely a passionate desire to slim? Dr. Joel Yager states that no distinction can be drawn. "To have a straightforward desire to slim that becomes such an overriding obsession that you are putting yourself at death's door seems to me to be pretty psychological. That can be an obsessional problem. The question then is: Are obsessional problems a biological issue? What's the basis of them?"

Pointing out that more than 70 percent of women want to slim, Dr. Yager asks: "Why should 3 percent of those become anorexic, or even 1 percent? Something else is going on that adds to the likelihood that a ubiquitous desire to slim suddenly gets challenged and transformed into a life-threatening obsessional thought and compulsive attitude."

To embark on the anorexic route, he declares, takes willpower, drive, and determination, which could be virtues. And the thinner some people get, the more compulsive they become: "It's as if the brain becomes more boxed in, in some ways, when it's malnourished. I work with some patients whose level of obsessional thinking is highly weight-motivated. At a 110 pounds, for example, somebody can think they're fine. At 106, it could become much more obsessional."

Anorexia nervosa is not, according to Dr. Yager, something that can afflict anyone. "I'd say it starts out with being a temperamental vulnerability; certain people are born with a greater likelihood of being vulnerable to it in the right environment." And there has to be a "fit" of temperament and environment to make anorexia possible. A person may lack self-confidence but feel the need to excel.

Many families value performance greatly but include children who do not excel—and there is no pressure on them to do so. In Karen's case, she *did* excel. Yet despite being continually praised by

Richard and scores of her contemporaries for her natural talent, despite the multimillion record sales and the multitude of awards that lined her walls, none of this seemed to do anything for her self-esteem.

According to Dr. Yager, that might be too simplistic a rationale. "Using Plato and Aristotle as her yardstick, she has a form of perfection [in mind]. We're saying 'It's good enough'—and she's saying 'No.'"

At Manhattan's Regency Hotel, Karen demonstrated patterns of behaviour that would not cause alarm or suspicion among her friends. Her days with Itchy Ramone moved with precisionlike routine. They shopped at Bloomingdales and at Saks and meandered down Madison Avenue. Karen bought so many greetings cards that it became a standing joke that she was keeping the Hallmark company in business; all her life she had been a compulsive sender of letters and gifts to friends and relations, and the New York trip found her with time to accelerate this habit.

She and Itchy chose the restaurant for dinner with immense care. The table was reserved for 6:00 P.M. since anorexics believe that to eat early adds less weight (and the Carpenter family normally eats dinner at this time). Surprisingly, Karen took a keen interest in the venue, veering toward fish restaurants. Dinner over, it was back to the hotel to watch television, with "Dallas" essential viewing.

On some days, Karen would drop in to the recording studio where Itchy's husband, Phil, was producing (she once guested on an Art Garfunkel session and was proud at his compliments); but such visits often left her dejected. She realized what music making she was missing during this year of therapy.

In April 1982, Karen flew home for a two-week intermission in her treatment. Levenkron says that, having gone to him at about seventy-eight pounds, then picked up to about eighty-nine pounds, Karen had dropped back down around this time through increased use of laxatives.

Though she told her family she was improving, responding to Levenkron's methods, the sight of Karen shook them all. "She looked like hell," Richard declares, "worse than she did when she went to New York. Then I really got mad at her." Richard repeated his firm belief to her that "the world's foremost authority on anorexia could not cure this by meeting you five days a week for fifty minutes a day and then sending you back to the hotel."

When she returned to New York after recording successfully during that California trip, Richard and Roger Young flew in to Manhattan. With a view to recording some more with Karen while she was there, he and Roger viewed some studios. But somehow the prospect did not feel right, away from their natural base.

Dr. Joel Yager, stressing that he did not know enough about the specifics of her treatment, says that if she was not eating adequately as an outpatient in psychotherapy and her weight was continuing to fall, "most people would say at a certain point that it would be better to have her hospitalized and contained, so that her treatment would have included behavioural intervention at an early stage."

However, many people who are treated in the hospital resent it, are not psychologically prepared to gain the weight. "It can go both ways," says Yager. Some people leave the hospital feeling better and grateful; others believe they are being coerced into eating: "You're stuffing me like a goose and as soon as I get out of here I'll do what the hell I want." It can be counterproductive.

Even though she was down below eighty pounds, Karen pronounced herself fit enough to record when she returned to her family in what would be her last spring. She looked drawn, and yet, as she had shown in the past seven troubled years when battling a devastation of her body, she always found an inner strength to keep her universally loved voice intact.

The song "Now," which would be the last song she ever recorded, found Karen with a resonance that seemed rooted in her self-expression of sadness. At her most potent with rich, sentimental story lines, she seemed touched by the magic of this song about a triumphant relationship—maybe because it allowed her to live out, in song, a fantasy of something that had eluded her. She sang these words as if they were an autobiographical desire:

> NOW, now when it rains I don't feel cold
> Now that I have your hand to hold
> The winds might blow through me but I don't care
> There's no harm in thunder if you are there

And now, now when we touch my feelings fly
Now when I'm smiling I know why
You light up my world like the morning sun
You're so deep within me we're almost one

And now, now when I wake there's someone home
I'll never face the nights alone
You gave me the courage I need to win
To open my heart and to let you in
And I never really knew how, until now.

Music by Roger Nichols. Lyrics by Dean Pitchford. © 1982 Almo Music
Corp & Three Eagles Music (ASCAP) & Warner-Tamerlane Publishing
Corp. & Body Electric Music (BMI). All rights reserved. International copy-
right secured. Used by permission, courtesy of Rondor Music International.

Back in New York, Itchy Ramone had begun to subtly pull away
from accompanying Karen to and from every appointment,
although they still met most days. The test was to see if Karen
would still reach her sessions with Levenkron on time. She did.
Besides, Karen said, she was becoming very bored with her own
company in a hotel room every day and needed to stretch out
independently.

Like Richard and the folks back home in California, Itchy was
distressed at Karen's poor physical progress. Karen told her she was
determined to win and had stopped taking laxatives. "Please, for
yourself, come out of this," Itchy pleaded with her, weeping and
hugging her at her home. "No more laxatives. Try to keep something in your system! I really love you . . . I can't stand to watch
you dying."

As always, Karen mollified Itchy's tears and fears. Richard was
also giving her a hard time, she said, but she would prove them all
wrong and get better.

Shortly after that harrowing exchange between the two
women, Itchy was dumbfounded to find laxatives hidden around
her house and back in Karen's room at the hotel: behind a fruit
bowl, in her pillowcase, in her luggage, behind cabinets, even in
her shoes.

Hiding was an accepted ploy by anorexics, but Itchy was angry that Karen had lied to her. "Do you want to explain all these?" she said, showing her the evidence. "I thought you'd told me you stopped this stuff?"

Karen assured her she was no longer using laxatives. "I just need it there for my security, to know it's there but not to use it," she replied sheepishly.

The pressure now hit Itchy hard. "There were very emotional scenes, outright yellings."

Just after the discovery by Itchy of those laxatives, Karen returned to her old habit of visiting the bathroom immediately after eating a fairly normal entrée.

After one bathroom visit, she was greeted by a distraught Itchy waving her Visa credit card bill for $1,200. Most of the charges were for restaurant dinners with Karen.

"I threw down the bill at her. 'THIS has just literally gone down the toilet,' I shouted. 'I should have just taken the $1,200, ripped them up, and thrown them out of the window.'" Tearfully, the two women embraced, pouring out their sorrow.

Two months passed. Karen continued to double the treatment with her social round. Joe Layton, the Broadway producer who had restructured the Carpenters' last stage show, was another New York visitor. For her dinner dates with Joe, who would be professionally watching her visual appearance, Karen dressed to the nines. She "looked gorgeous always and was very up," he recalls, and elected to go to Chinese restaurants. And she ate enthusiastically. But there was a Cinderalla-like ritual attached to the ending of their pleasant, regular evenings.

Karen said she had to be back at her hotel by 9:40 P.M. so that she could "call Steven" at the prescribed time of 10:00 P.M. The conversation would assure her guru that she had consumed a hearty meal.

There were other, more troublesome, phone calls: to her mother and to her husband, Tom, back in California.

If her attempt to recover from anorexia nervosa was not tough enough, she also had to attend to a collapsing marriage. She had been wed two years earlier. Knowing the marriage was on the rocks, she wept into the phone when she and Tom spoke. Agnes, visiting her, urged her to hang up to avoid such distress. Karen told her she was upset by what she considered Tom's unreasonable demands, and she had decided irrevocably to divorce.

Levenkron was privy to her feelings. "I remember the day she took off her wedding ring in this office and started crying and said she was going to call her attorney and begin divorce proceedings. And she did.

"She said: 'I want to be a married woman. I don't want to be a divorced woman, but I can't stay married to this man.'" In other sessions with her therapist, Karen wept bitterly and told him: "I'm just afraid that I'm gonna miss it all." Levenkron asked just what she meant. "I'm gonna miss being married and I'm gonna miss being a mother ... I'm just afraid I'm gonna somehow live my life and never do those things."

As her self-imposed deadline of six months in therapy passed, she became agitated, but events took a frightening twist when, in September, she realized her condition was critical. She called Levenkron. "I can't walk. I'm dizzy. I'm upset. My heart's beating funny." Alarm bells rang for him as he recalled the pessimism of people in California whom he had spoken to at the start of her treatment. "We think Karen is dying . . . she's not a very good bet . . . she really resists every kind of treatment." Now, if Karen said she needed urgent admission, the situation was threatening.

He called a doctor to have her admitted to Lenox Hill Hospital, Manhattan. Meeting her at the admissions office, Levenkron found her "very embarrassed" at her plight. She registered under her married name of Burris, but it did not work. "Aren't you that Carpenter singer lady?" inquired a receptionist.

All her life, Karen had feared and loathed hospitals, but with her weight now down to what Levenkron recalls as "seventy-seven pounds of dehydrated skeleton," and a blood potassium level at a critical 1.8, there was "a real sense that it would be touch and go."

Getting nutrition into her, the first urgent task, proved problematic. Her digestive tract was so damaged that she had to be fed by the hyperalimentation process in which nutrition is passed through a wide tube directly into the bloodstream.

There was an early complication. When the tube was inserted into her chest, it accidentally punctured one of Karen's lungs. The news angered Richard and Agnes, but this wound soon healed and Karen responded to the injection of calories. When, after a few days, she gained her first twelve pounds in weight from the bottle that hung from a stand with casters, she was able to walk around. "See, I look better," she said as she saw herself in a mirror. "Unlike many anorexics, she was pleased with her return," Levenkron says. "She was being deflowered and really feeling better about it." As the weeks passed, she gained thirty pounds from the intravenous feeding.[2]

When Richard Carpenter flew in to see her on October 25, he immediately became choked up at the sight. Three years earlier he had survived his own dice with death through overdosing with sleeping pills. Now here was his sister, his best friend, his favourite singer hooked up to an intravenous drip. For too many years, he pondered, she had been either walking away from her problem or simply fencing with it—and now, was she really any closer to conquering it?

As he sat by the bed, he reflected on their roller coaster to fame. "My God, look what we've done to ourselves. It's not too good. We're world famous; we have all this talent. I'm better, thankfully, but here's Karen in a hospital bed, and we're going through our seventh year of this crap."

He took her a video of a favorite movie, *Camelot*. "Don't I look great, Richard? Can't you see how great I look?" Always, in every aspect of her life, Karen craved Richard's approval. She would mother him and berate him, but none of his peccadilloes diminished her aura of him.

"I'm getting better. Richard, you see how much better I look?" Richard intimated that she was improved, but he was reluctant to say how sad he really felt. Something still wasn't convincing about either her appearance or the method Karen had chosen to get herself right. And he thought to himself: instead of doing what they both really wanted—touring and making records—she was still battling for her life. He flew back to California after that hospital visit knowing that their career would have to remain "on hold" for longer than Karen thought.

---

2. Although it was clearly heartening that Karen had elected to go to the hospital, the hyperalimentation that was considered necessary is a topic of various medical opinions. "The problem with her gaining of thirty pounds is that she had nothing to do with the weight gain," says Dr. Joel Yager. "That is, psychologically it didn't become part of her own repertoire." Hyperalimentation does not teach the patient to eat.

Visiting New York from London, Babs Knight, wife of the musical arranger Peter and by now a firm friend of the Carpenters, visited Karen in the hospital during this period. Surrounded by toys sent by friends and often showing visitors the pasta brought in by her friend Christina De Lorean, wife of the industrialist, Karen seemed confident.

Although she was waiflike, Babs remembers her as "still beautiful. She hadn't lost her cheery disposition, even though she was obviously ill, and I'm sure she never realised how ill she was. She said to me in that bed, 'They're ever so pleased with me in here … I weigh eighty-four pounds.'" Babs could not but wonder how Karen considered such a weight as anything to be happy about. "She was just skeletal."

Returning to Manhattan after his bizarre, speedy farewell from Karen at her hotel a few months earlier, her friend John Bettis wanted her to enjoy a Broadway show, *42nd Street*, with him and singer Donna Summer. Calls to the Regency Hotel met no response, but eventually Karen phoned him back: "I heard you've been trying to get hold of me. . . . I just wasn't seeing anybody. . . . I could see you . . . you have to keep this really secret."

Stunned to hear she was in the hospital, Bettis sped there in a cab, a Mickey Mouse pen in his hand to cheer her. Shocked to find her on an intravenous drip, he kissed her as she pointed to her arm. "Don't pay any attention to this. That's like food. Lots of calories they're putting in me so I gain weight. They're trying to fatten me up so they can give me a running start on this anorexia thing." Bettis felt sore as he told her of his plans to visit the theatre with Donna Summer—he would have liked Karen to go, too—but Karen was typically practical as time passed, reminding him he ought to be leaving to get to Broadway. Choking back some sadness at what he'd seen, Bettis walked away, smiling bravely to her. The man who wrote the words to some Carpenters anthems, notably "Only Yesterday," "Top of the World," "Goodbye to Love," "Yesterday Once More," and "I Need to Be in Love," would never see her again.

When Levenkron told his wife that Karen had few visitors, Abby asked apprehensively if she should go to see her in the hospital. "I didn't want to mess up any of the transferential relationship." Steven thought it would be beneficial.

It was a slightly awkward visit on both sides, but it began with laughter. Abby took her paperbacks, including one of the Cathy cartoon character: an apposite subject in which the woman jokes about herself as a classic unwed, thirtyish female trying to unravel the foibles of dating. As Abby and Karen took the books out of the bag, they burst into laughter. One cover had a joke about bingeing on chocolate cake as a result of being upset. "Oh my God," Abby said. "All these eating jokes are everywhere. I'm sorry; I didn't notice." Karen smiled. "It doesn't matter; I don't care."

Karen overcame her initial shyness about meeting her therapist's wife. She had gained weight to about ninety pounds but still looked terribly thin, Abby Levenkron says. "She'd put on twelve or fourteen pounds. I remember thinking, God, I wouldn't have liked to have seen her ten pounds ago because she still looks pretty emaciated."

In her eight-week stay in Lenox Hill Hospital, Karen gained not merely weight but panache. As she improved and her release became imminent, she was told that she would not be able to go marching around Manhattan again so athletically—and she would need a nurse. Karen was appalled at this news as she left the hospital on November 8, 1982.

The nurse assigned to her was pregnant so walked slowly, and Karen said she would "go nuts" holding back to that pace for long. Though she grumbled, she complied as she returned to the comfort of the Regency Hotel.

After a few days there she called Levenkron. "I can't stand being here any more," she told him. Her family, friends, and career were in California, she continued, and she felt homesick. Within a couple of weeks she announced that she would return in time for Thanksgiving, 1982. To Abby Levenkron, she joked, "Well, your husband's a real sweet guy, but I have to go back to California and get one of my own," a wry aside on her creaking marriage.

She seemed in a hurry to go, too. "I'll have spent a year here," she told her therapist, "twice as long as I originally planned."

Levenkron informed her, as he had done at the outset, that such treatment needed three years, but Karen wasn't listening. "I'm thirty-two years old . . . you've been a great help . . . but I have to leave you." Karen's resolution was, as usual, unswerving.

He offered the name of a therapist for her to continue treatment in Los Angeles, but she demurred. "No, no, no. I'm not starting with anyone else. I'll call you. I'll be your patient on the phone, and I promise I won't take any more laxatives. And I promise I won't lose any more weight."

Her parting gift to him was touching evidence of the boring hours spent in her hotel suite. Embossed in green on a board and framed, Karen's needlepoint message included four words which showed her love of ironic wordplay: "YOU WIN—I GAIN." On the back, she handwrote: "Dear Steve, love to you. It's been different! K.C."

That memento, dated November 16, 1982, hangs in his office, an upbeat contrast with the somewhat macabre bottle of thyroid tablets prescribed to Karen, which remains in his drawer.

That endless season
When time was all we had
We saw forever/and caught it in our hands
Life was a charm/our hearts were filled with music
And laughter
When time was all we had.

—RICHARD'S SONG OF DEDICATION

Soon after her return from New York, two separate incidents in restaurants caused Agnes and Richard to arrive independently at the conclusion that all was far from well with Karen.

As she often did, Karen slipped out to lunch with her mother. When they went to a Howard Johnson's at Cerritos, not far from Downey, Karen disappeared into the bathroom for about half an hour. Agnes was naturally perturbed.

"When she returned, she upset me, really scared me, because she acted like a drunk," Agnes recalls. "She was out of it, and her speech was slurred." Agnes tried to soothe her, but because they were friendly with the waitress and did not want to attract attention, both she and Karen preferred to let the incident pass quietly.

Karen told her mother she had been to the bathroom to take tablets prescribed for her colon problem. She was clearly embarrassed. Agnes told her she would drive home, and though Karen resisted this, her mother insisted she did so for their safety.

When they arrived back at Newville, Agnes phoned Richard. Later, Karen explained to her concerned brother that she had taken "stomach medicine," which had a bad effect on her sometimes. (Later, it transpired that this would have been Butalbital, which appeared on the autopsy report.)

When Agnes asked Karen why she was carrying no less than five prescriptions for medicine inside her bag, Karen explained that these had been given to her by a doctor in New York "to hold me over until I got out here."

Now, back in California, she went to see a doctor. The episode bothered Agnes, who asked if she could accompany her, but Karen said no; and the doctor refused to reveal to Agnes the reason her daughter had visited him.

A similarly perplexing experience awaited Richard when, with one of their former college friends, he went to meet Karen for dinner on January 14, 1983.

The look of sheer terror and pain on Karen's face was frightening to behold. She was sitting opposite Richard and Dennis Heath in the Hollywood restaurant St. Germain.

Suddenly, she put down her knife and fork—and her face froze. Horrified, Richard asked, "What *is* it?"

"Something, something . . ." she spluttered. Karen couldn't or wouldn't go beyond those words. Slowly she stood up and managed to walk to the ladies' room.

Returning to the two men after what seemed an eternity, she said the problem had subsided. She was now OK to do what they had planned to do after dinner—to drive to A&M's studios and hear some playbacks of the tracks she and Richard had cut in April 1982 during her break from treatment in New York.

When they reached the studios, Richard's concern increased. Normally Karen would stand behind the control board, or sit next to him at the board, and react animatedly to what she heard. That night, she could neither stand nor sit near it. But on a couch she listened quietly to the music and went back with Richard to Downey to stay at Newville, pronouncing herself "all right."

Richard found the experience that night "really upsetting." Her datebook for the next day records one word: *Rest.*

Relating to Werner Wolfen what had happened, Richard repeated his concern that Karen was not well. And he reiterated his unshakable conviction that she needed inpatient care to cure anorexia nervosa.

So many times, Richard had pointed out to Wolfen and their inner circle that they had helped to persuade *him* to enter a clinic to solve his problem. Karen's own solution, that year in New York, had never satisfied him. Now she was back in California, he felt vindicated. Experiences like that in the restaurant demonstrated that she was still far from right.

The friction between Richard and Karen over this worry had reached Wolfen often. Repeatedly, after judging the look of her eyes, Richard would say, "She's not well," while Karen would vent her annoyance to their lawyer that her brother was commenting on her behind her back.

When Wolfen expressed Richard's real anxiety about the restaurant episode to Karen, she erupted with anger. First, she told him, she was feeling bad because she got her period back. Next, she demanded a meeting with Richard in Wolfen's office—immediately. Taken aback, Wolfen asked if it could wait a day or so. No, Karen answered, there was to be a meeting with the three of them right now. Wolfen summoned a perplexed Richard.

Just then, Steven Levenkron phoned Wolfen. Told of the scenario and the meeting about to take place, he offered to fly in to be present if they delayed it. No, Wolfen said, he'd handled similar crises before. But neither he nor Richard was prepared for the force of Karen's speech to her brother in her lawyer's office.

Seething with anger, she was at the most articulate and peremptory Richard had ever heard her.

"Now listen to me. I've been through a lot, and you have, too. I stuck by you when you came home, behaving weird [meaning not returning to Lubec Street] after you'd been to the clinic with your problem. I said nothing about your behaviour at that time. And now I've come home from my treatment, you're gonna have to stick by me. And I *have* put weight on. And I *am* better."

Her cogency and emotive power got through to Richard, and Wolfen felt it was the healthiest thing to happen, their unloading both of their grievances in front of a friend. But she reckoned without his conviction of the grim truth.

He replied: "Karen, when I came home from the clinic I might have acted strange; it was a trying experience. But I was in good health. I was cured. You are *not* in good health. And I'm only telling you this, Karen, because I love you. And I'm worried."

Karen repeated that she was angry with him for spreading alarm about her health among their family and friends. Richard countered that it was natural that he should vent his real concern.

When she recovered from her agitated state, they were both clearly relieved. As they hugged to call a truce, Richard said he would remain worried and couldn't help that; Karen repeated that she had her problem under control. But the air had been cleared, and later both Wolfen and Richard would reflect that it was a valuable day's therapy for them both, and if it had not happened, Richard would always regret it.

A few days later, Karen told a girlfriend that she was seeing spots before her eyes—"but don't tell Mom." She said she would tell Agnes herself. But she never did.

Nagging doubts about her health continued to be a subject of conversation among those around her. Beverly Nogawski remembers Karen talking, during a dinner with her and Agnes and Harold shortly after returning from New York, about her concern about her thumping heart.

When Beverly saw her again in Downey on Saturday, January 29, she was struck by the fact that Karen used precisely the same words to describe her heart pounding—this time in talking about her problem with the plumbing under the sink at her apartment. "She'd been down there trying to fix it," Beverly says, "and she said the same remark: 'I finally got it fixed, but my heart was beating so hard I thought it was going to come out of my chest.'"

Since returning from New York, Karen had astonished and worried those close to her with her displays of energy. It irritated her mother that she may have jeopardised her health even more by running errands for friends, even to the point of getting them pizzas from restaurants to take to their home when she visited. Werner Wolfen's wife Mimi was appalled that she was running around as much as before she went to New York. As if to prove she was cured, she was more active than any normally healthy person might be. It was as if she wanted to pre-empt the kind of criticism and observation that had come from Richard: that she might not be as well as she claimed to be.

Bubbly and energetic, Karen behaved in the week before she died in a way that seemed normal to many of her business friends. By day at least, she would propel herself around town with her old élan; but when evening came, she needed to rest on the couch. Too often, Florine Elie, the Carpenters' housekeeper, noticed Karen resting on the floor of the living room at her condominium.

Mentally, though, she was lively, and she had been cheered by the outstanding "comeback" she and Richard had enjoyed with their last album. After a creative hiatus, their continuity together was now ensured, and on Tuesday, February 1, they met for dinner at Scandia on Sunset Boulevard. Their stage producer Joe Layton joined them to discuss their return to concert work. She ate quite heartily, an appetizer and a chicken entrée.

Like everyone who worked with Karen, Layton had developed

deep affection for "the little waif, such a gamine little thing." As the three of them split from Scandia, he reflected that though she was still overrun with sweaters to hide her hips, and though she would rarely wear a belt that might emphasize them, they all had every reason to be confident. Her mood was up.

Richard drove back to Downey, Joe to West Hollywood, Karen to her apartment in Century City. They would never see her again.

On the evening of February 3, 1983, she phoned Phil Ramone from Downey to New York. She said she had had a chance to relisten to her solo album.

Apprehensively she asked, "Can I use the f--- word?"

"Yeah."

"That album's fucking great."

The next morning, she was dead.

A feeling of palpable love, grief, anger, and bewilderment swept over the funeral on February 8, 1983. Five hundred people crammed into Downey Methodist Church and another five hundred were outside, many of them locals who knew Karen as the simple, home-loving girl who had never really left this town.

After an emotional, tearful embrace of Richard, Herb Alpert led the six pallbearers: Werner Wolfen, David Alley, Gary Sims, Roger Young, and Ed Sulzer.

Olivia Newton-John, Dionne Warwick, and Burt Bacharach were among those who heard the service begin with a pianist playing Carpenters hits. The Reverend Charles A. Neal, who officiated, recalled his years as their pastor at Park Methodist Church, New Haven: "evenings spent in the basement of their home with Ping-Pong sets, hi-fi, baseballs, and more records than I had ever seen. … our two girls finding in Karen a friend, baby-sitter, and confidante." He spoke of the "spontaneous outpouring of love and grief for one of God's truly talented and gifted daughters who has died so young." Suddenly, he reflected, in the midst of the rock era, the world had been graced with a new song.

"Ave Maria," one of Karen's favourite songs, was sung by the choir of California State University featuring her old friend Dennis Heath. A distraught Terry Ellis held a weeping Carol Curb's hand throughout the service. A notable absentee from the funeral was Jerry Weintraub. Too broken up to attend, he flew away from California to expunge the reality of that day.

A few days before the service, Tom Burris had thrown into Karen's casket his wedding ring.

From the church, Karen's coffin was taken to a marble crypt in the mausoleum of Forest Lawn Cemetery in Cypress, California. Lustrous gold letters on the crypt read: "Karen 1950–1983. A star on earth. A star in heaven."

Karen Carpenter died with a broken heart, emotionally and physically. The strain of a collapsed marriage had been preceded by another traumatic reality of lost love.

Soon after returning to California from making her solo album, Karen was telephoned by Itchy Ramone. As they often did, they spoke of Karen's need for a man in her life. Itchy said she had heard Terry Ellis had become engaged.

Karen was dumbfounded. She had deeply regretted their split four years earlier. Despite prodding from Itchy, she had not gathered enough courage to phone him.

There followed weeks of hesitation and soul searching. Karen tried hatching a variety of plans to lure him back, since he was not yet married. Itchy said she should call and invite him to lunch, since they had not parted on bad terms.

Karen made the call with great trepidation. "I'm really sorry," she said to Terry Ellis of their split. "I've had treatment, and I'm living on my own at my own apartment. And I'd like to see if we could start again." (Her optimism about her physique is not shared by Richard, who describes her as "a rail" at that point.)

That crie de couer from Karen met a reply that "destroyed" her, according to Itchy Ramone.

"Well, unfortunately," Terry Ellis said, "it's too late. I'm engaged to someone I love very much, and we are going to get married."

Always, there seemed to be evidence that Karen was never really consumed with Hollywood or show business glitz, so it was appropriate that the two significant events to celebrate her life took place in her two true homes.

At a tribute to Karen concert at the First Congregational Church, Long Beach on June 25, 1983, Richard, John Bettis, and Dennis Heath, three men at the core of her life, were the performers, while the choir was under the direction of Frank Pooler.

In New Haven on March 5, 1983, Debbie Cuticello and her husband with Frank Bonito organized a memorial service at Yale University Divinity School. In her eulogy, Debbie spoke movingly of their weekly phone calls and Karen's visits to her "home away from home" during her New York year. From Debbie's address and that of Bonito, both packed with anecdotes of Karen's letters, taped messages, and tales of needlepoint through the mail, it was clear that the singer had never truly left either New Haven or Downey.

A year before she died, Karen had rewritten her will. She left all her assets, estimated at between five and ten million dollars, to her family.

One of Karen's financial investments, appropriately in view of her love of children, was in the Strolee of California company, which makes baby strollers, swings, high chairs, car seats, and playpens. In September 1983 Richard attended the dedication ceremony of the firm's Karen Carpenter Plant at its new building in Church Hill, Tennessee.

Shortly after Karen's death, memorials were established by Richard and his family to help sufferers from eating disorders. They launched the Karen A. Carpenter Memorial Foundation, from which money continues to help research; and they launched a scholarship for student musicians at her old university at Long Beach.

At the University of California in Los Angeles, Dr. Joel Yager supervises research assistants funded by the foundation. Among subjects studied is the question of what helps certain people recover from anorexia nervosa and bulimia, as against those who have difficulty recovering. "I wish Karen Carpenter's death had never occurred and the money had never been there," says Dr. Yager sagely, "but the money is being spent on exactly the kind of problems that Karen had—and had we known more about them, [such research] might have saved her."

One of show business's most coveted accolades, a star on the Hollywood Walk of Fame, was designated to the Carpenters on October 12, 1983. Richard attended the inauguration of the star, which is located at 6931 Hollywood Boulevard near the corner of Orange Avenue.

On May 19, 1984, the Carpenters band returned to Downey

to join Richard's extended family and friends for his wedding to Mary Rudolph. The service was at the town's Methodist Church, the wellspring of so much of Richard's early life. As the years passed and their children were born, friends observed a stable and well-matched partnership, Mary's warm, outward nature contrasting with Richard's caution and punctiliousness. They have three daughters: Kristi Lynn, born on August 17, 1987; Traci Tatum, born on July 25, 1989; and Mindi Karen, born on July 7, 1992.

A week before she died, Karen had bounced into Herb Alpert's office. "Hey, look at me!" she exclaimed. Pointing to her weight gain, she was as infectiously lovable as ever. She told Herb she was better after the New York visit and enthusiastically looked ahead to recording sessions and concerts.

"She'd always been this little girl reaching out to be a woman," Alpert says. He was always trying to "get her to realise that there's more to life than bullets on the charts." It was sad that, having given millions joy with Carpenters music, Karen had not fully reaped the personal benefit, although "she was on the right road" in her search for contentment.

Like Henry Mancini, Alpert believes her introspection might well have contributed to her greatness. "A common trait in all great performers, instrumentalists or singers, is that great quality that tugs at your heart. It doesn't come from that bubbly, 'up' side of their personality. It always comes from their undercurrent of reality."

Alpert loved her "like a sister." On the day of her death he wept . . . then went alone to the piano and composed "Song for Karen." He dedicated his 1983 album *Come Blow Your Horn* to the woman whose voice he championed and whose sincerity touched him.

Deep affection for Karen and protection of her memory remains among everyone who knew her, from New Haven to Downey, from New York to London; from her band to her hairdressers, from her lawyer to her schoolmates, from her therapist to her special girlfriends, to the thousands of celebrities who admire her work.

"She won the game she was playing," says John Bettis, "but the price she paid was amazingly high."

"Being a star was not enough for her," says Jerry Weintraub, pinpointing her central dilemma. "I miss her a lot and still get tears in my eyes when I hear her voice on the radio." Mike Curb says that when he drives near Downey, he gets a lump in his throat.

"It was the saddest thing," says Maria Galeazzi Cooper. "The one thing she wanted most was to be in love, have children, and make a home. We used to enjoy making cookies together."

To Werner Wolfen, she was a young woman "very warm, with a twinkle in her eye, and a very, very cute sense of humor." For her lawyer's office, she had needlepointed a sign: TANSTAAFL (which translated into: There Ain't No Such Thing As A Free Lunch). As with all the professionals around her, his affection was countered with personal concern for the star who was "festooned and inundated with problems."

"There's a kind of loneliness in her voice," observes Olivia Newton-John. "There's a warmth there, but also a kind of longing in it."

Former President Richard Nixon wrote to Richard a handwritten letter of sympathy on February 22, 1983, recalling their appearance at the White House ten years earlier. "I remember how impressed I was with her vivacious and captivating warmth. The two of you were a great team and provided a sharp contrast to some of the groups in the Seventies who professed to be musical artists. I know how much you and her family will miss her but just remember that for millions of her fans she left only pleasant memories."

Singer Phoebe Snow, describing Karen as "a wonderful talent and a fine, unpretentious woman," adds: "I'm enraged beyond words that she didn't make it. She soldiered and she fought, just to be killed."

Richard is sometimes asked if, having seen his sister wasting away, he feels a degree of guilt at failing to stop her. No, he replies, he and his family had tried everything: cajoling, pleading, shouting, threats. "There is nothing more I could have done. Being human, I feel a certain amount of guilt, which any of us would feel at the loss of a loved one. Instead of remembering the good times, you recall when you lost your temper; you recall hollering and wish you'd never done that.

"I tried every approach, the gamut that people go through if they're dealing with an eating disorder victim or an alcoholic: you try heart to heart, yelling, and screaming. I went through all that.

"I don't feel guilty. I feel terribly saddened. Being musicians at heart I keep thinking of all the great music the two of us could have made, how the world was robbed of such a terrific talent and a very nice person. Not a day goes by without my thinking of Karen."

And to the question by some of whether he might team up permanently with another female singer to somehow try to re-create that golden sound, he shakes his head. "No. When you've worked with the best . . ."

Such emotions ran deeply in the months following her death, but Richard returned to the studio after a few weeks to formulate an album he was sure Karen would have wanted released.

Her face in close-up stared, alone and sad eyed, from the cover of the collection touchingly called *Voice of the Heart,* released in the autumn of 1983.

In a moving tribute, Richard introduced it by saying that though he and his family would never get over losing her at such an early age, "we can take comfort in the marvellous legacy she left us all. . . . Karen's voice touched and will continue to touch the lives of millions. . . . I am proud of her. She is greatly missed."

Containing some tracks recorded by Karen in mid-1982 when she returned to California during her New York therapy sessions, the mood of most of the songs was eerily soul searching.

On "Your Baby Doesn't Love You Anymore," the lyrics were full of pathos:

> Just take some loneliness
> Then add a tear or two
> Throw in some emptiness
> Mix till you're bluer than blue
> Keep it all under cover
> Next to your broken dreams
> And when you're through
> Then you'll know how I
> Sit alone and cry
> As the nights go by
> Makes you wanna die

Apart from the majestic "Now," mentioned earlier, two other doleful songs marked the album. "Ordinary Fool," written by Paul Williams, was sadly reflective, talking of "a lesson to be learned, a page I should have turned." And the finale, "Look to Your Dreams," was a jewel-like Carpenter-Bettis composition.[1] Hearing the voice of a woman who had just passed away, the words allied to a melody of simple beauty painted a truly poignant farewell:

Look to your dreams
Don't they still seem worthwhile?
Don't they still seem in style?
Aren't you glad they're still there?

Look to your dreams
There's a need for them now
When the world has us down
Aren't you glad they're around?

Once conceived, once believed fantasy's reality's childhood
And like a seed, visions need constant care
    like a child would, we should

Look to our dreams
We can still make the stars
We can still break the bars
We have built here on earth

1. This song is evidence of Karen's keen ear for a memorable song and of her sentimentality. It dates back to 1974 when she asked Richard and John Bettis to write her "a cross between a standard and a show tune." It was finally recorded in 1978, but Richard kept postponing its inclusion on an album during Karen's lifetime. Though it was clearly a quality performance stamped by a strong Peter Knight arrangement, Richard was concerned that it was not contemporary enough. But Karen never forgot it.

Look to your dreams
And tomorrow may be better for you and me
The future may say
Blame blind yesterday for taking dreams away
They could mean more than they seem

In the aftermath of the tragedy, Richard felt desolate. At first, there had been a natural insulation from the reality of it; there was so much practicality required as well as support for his bewildered parents.

Gradually it registered even more deeply that he had lost not just his sister but an irreplaceable artistic partner. "Karen's passing was a blow I can't even put into words," he reflects. "One of the emotions I was feeling was that everything was over, in just about every sense." He needed to get back to the recording studio.

Importantly to Richard, Alpert and Moss reassured him that A&M was still his creative home, and in 1985 he surfaced for work on a solo album. *Time,* released two years later, was a highly creditable, melodically strong collection.

"When Time Was All We Had," a rich and tearful paen in dedication to Karen and their work together, would move all but the stonehearted. Herb Alpert contributed an eloquent solo on flugelhorn, which evoked both the sadness and celebration of the song; Richard's solo vocal, sung a capella, hit the right mood of despair and gratitude for their magnificent days together:

That endless season
When time was all we had
We saw forever/and caught it in our hands
Life was a charm/our hearts were filled with music
And laughter
When time was all we had.

I never will forget your face in silhouette
Your voice will be the sweetest sound
I'll ever hear, and yet
We knew somehow the song would never end
When time was all we had to spend.

Since two songs needed female vocals, Richard recruited Dusty
Springfield for "Something in Your Eyes," which became a radio
hit, and Dionne Warwick for "In Love Alone," both powerful ballads in Karen's style. But while the technique of making such an
album came easily to him, and the women sang imaginatively,
there was an underlying sadness in Studio D. "I couldn't help
thinking, wouldn't it be nice if Karen was here, singing this?"

Though Richard was bashful about his singing, the performances of some excellent songs, notably "I'm Still Not Over You"
and "Calling Your Name Again," were strong, and the album sold
moderately well.

In 1989 he returned to the studios to produce *Lovelines,* a pot-
pourri which celebrated the Carpenters' twentieth year with A&M.
This collection included tracks for which there had been no space
on previous albums. Three fine ballads, "The Uninvited Guest,"
"Where Do I Go from Here," and the standard "When I Fall in
Love," redeemed an average batch. Responding to many requests
from fans, Richard included four songs prepared for the aborted
Phil Ramone-produced album. Substituting a contrived sexuality
for Karen's normally understated discretion, these inferior tracks
proved the wisdom of the earlier decision to stop the album.
Where Richard always had her singing songs about love and relationships, Ramone pointed her toward physically explicit lyrics that
did not suit her. The songs served only to underscore her real
magic and the value of Richard's stewardship.

Since Karen's death, many collections have been produced by
Richard for the United States, Japan, and Britain. These have been
highly successful commercially and requests for new variations of
their work continue to this day.

*   *   *

Public awareness of anorexia nervosa and other eating disorders has grown since Karen's death. She was not a martyr, for she would certainly have chosen life, but one result of her tragic loss is the attention it has focused on the problem of eating disorders.

By 1992 Karen remained the only celebrity to die after her battle, and nine years after her death had been *People* magazine's cover story, the publication returned to the subject on February 17, 1992, to report on "Eating Disorders: A Hollywood History."

The TV actress Tracey Gold spoke of her problems with anorexia, and model Christine Alt told *People:* "I remember looking at Karen Carpenter's picture in *People* and thinking: 'God, how lucky she was because she died thin.' I was very envious. I remember saying: 'How can I get to that point—being really thin without dying?' That's a sick mind. Karen Carpenter was a skeleton."

Karen's decline was debilitating for her and also for her family. In the midst of it, some personalities added to their agony by making cheap jokes about the singer's anorexia. Among them were Bette Midler and Joan Rivers.

In September 1990, Bette Midler apologised for her tasteless remarks. Interviewed by the magazine *Redbook,* she said she regretted making "all those Karen Carpenter anorexia jokes. I *cannot* tell you how much I apologize. From the bottom of my soul I apologize to her family." When Midler and her husband drove near Downey on their way to their home in Orange County, she always thought of Karen. "She had tremendous talent, and I was a jerk for saying those things. I was young and stupid and crazy and thought I was doing profound and enduring stuff. But I wasn't. I was adding to the ugliness in the world."

In the United States, the National Association of Anorexia Nervosa and Associated Disorders, founded in 1976, is the oldest and largest organization of its kind.

It estimates that of the eight million victims in the United States alone, seven million are women, one million men, and 6 percent of serious cases are fatal. The peak age is between eighteen and the midtwenties in women.

A nonprofit organization, ANAD says anorexia and bulimia, once thought to affect privileged white females, now strikes every segment of society: rich and poor, old and young, every race and ethnic group.

Advocating additional study, ANAD's president, Vivian Meehan, says: "Our youth have a serious image problem, and it shows up in their use and abuse of dietary products and the ever more frequent development of eating disorders. We must adopt a comprehensive public programme to re-educate our youth and our public in general to overcome our mistaken and dangerous fascination with thinness as an ultimate ideal and to focus upon the real values in life and health."

ANAD operates as a clearinghouse with more than two thousand therapists, hospitals, and clinics in the United States, Canada, and other countries. It also offers hotline counseling. (In the immediate aftermath of Karen's death, calls from sufferers increased by thousands a week. Richard is currently a member of its honorary board.) The organization's resource and advice services are free. To contact the ANAD, write to Box 7, Highland Park, Illinois 60035, or phone 708-831-3438.

In Britain, the Eating Disorders Association states: "While on the surface eating disorders appear to be about food, they are fundamentally the outward expression of deep psychological and emotional turmoil." Pointing out that anorexia nervosa literally means "loss of appetite for nervous reasons," the association says the name is misleading because sufferers have not lost their appetite but their ability to allow themselves to satisfy it. Eating disorders are fundamentally NOT disorders of eating; they indicate and express a disturbed perception of self.

Anorexics and bulimics have very low self-esteem and little confidence. Sufferers are not trying to starve to death but are trying to cope with living, the association adds. "Anorexia is not merely a silly obsession with slimming or a misguided wish to be slim and beautiful. Rather, it is a desperate bid for psychological survival."

In Britain there are sixty thousand known sufferers. The true figure is probably nearer 150,000 to 200,000.

The Eating Disorders Association charges a small membership fee with free access available to those with severe financial problems. Its address is Sackville Place, 44 Magdalen Street, Norwich, Norfolk, NR3 1JU; phone, 0603-621414.

*   *   *

Connecticut, June 19, 1991. Beside the carousel in Lighthouse Point, New Haven, where Richard and Karen went for picnics as children, the students of his old elementary school have gathered on a hot midsummer evening. It's Graduation Day.

The Carpenters have always been a roots-conscious family, and Richard and Karen returned often to the territory of their childhood memories. This particular homecoming was deeply emotional for him and the teachers and students of Nathan Hale School, which he and Karen attended until they were twelve. He (and posthumously Karen) was there to receive the school's Hall of Fame award.

Addressing the graduates, Richard had a message drawn from years that had included, he said, "joy and pain." In the thirty-one years since he and Karen had been at Nathan Hale, there had been countless innovations, ranging from video to computers to microwaves. But nothing could replace the need for good health and strong education. They would be aware, he said, of the "drug problem"—and as one who had been through it to some degree, he had a pithy message which seemed to echo his life's experiences, both personally and professionally: "However much you want to be in with the crowd—don't. And had Karen been here she would have joined me in wishing you a very happy, healthy, and successful life."

As the mortarboard-wearing school chorale launched into "For All We Know," "Top of the World," and finally, inevitably, "We've Only Just Begun," New Haven reclaimed the Carpenters on an evening of moving nostalgia.

Burbank, California, September 15, 1990. It's exactly twenty years since they hit the top with "Close to You," but Richard is still working on their music tonight, in Enterprise studios.

His self-imposed task is to refine and renew the sound of some of their best-known songs. The project is a four-package Carpenters retrospective Compact Disc collection featuring sixty-seven selections, with forty remixed and twenty previously unreleased, including home recordings, demos, jingles, and interviews.

As in the halycon days, Richard works from noon until 1:00 A.M. with engineer Roger Young, listening repeatedly to that extraordinary voice which, as Herb Alpert says, feels like it's right there with you in the room.

His focus is as meticulous and as exhaustive as ever as he works on polishing the sounds for the album set, which will be called *From the Top,* a chronological anthology.

It's difficult to comprehend how he can face the emotional turmoil that must be awakened by listening, hour after hour, to every note, every word, sentence, and nuance of Karen's delivery until he is satisfied that the production cannot be improved.

Just occasionally, as he lights up another More cigarette and works repeatedly on one of his favourite tracks, the scientific, microscopic attention to detail seems to be overtaken by an unspoken sadness. The song is "Let Me Be the One."

AUTHOR'S NOTE

Their sound is glorious, timeless, incomparable. The Carpenters' contribution to popular music will stand forever. Great love songs never go out of style, and Karen and Richard's work surely strikes a chord in all who cherish beautifully honed compositions set amid rich melodies and lush arrangements.

And there will always be that stunning voice. Unique and instantly recognisable, the finest female singer in her genre provided the Carpenters with the bedrock of music that will always transcend trends and fads. Its beauty is its simplicity, directness, and melodic power.

Increasingly, their records are played on the radio, while their Compact Discs generate interest among new listeners. That's not just because of the paucity of memorable new material in this field. Richard and Karen were precision workers who proudly set the highest standards in their craft. And they developed music built to last.

What motivated and drove the Carpenters, from Richard's early obsession with pop songs in their New Haven birthplace, through Karen's adoption of the drums in California, and their remarkable battles for recognition and eventual triumph, was the foundation of this biography.

Sadly, this is a finite story, but since their music endures, so should the history of its evolution, for it continues to touch millions. As an admirer of their work from their early years, I wanted to know what shaped them, their origins, the characteristics that contributed to the art. This proved to be a tale of organic talent, great resilience and dedication, and that crucial ingredient of luck, which every artist needs.

It was impossible not to be touched by sadness during the preparation of this extraordinary denouement. Their journey to the heights was marred by years of illness followed by the loss of the woman who—as well as being loved by all whom she touched—gave us a voice to treasure. Karen had that rare ability to make you feel she was singing just for you; her talent was natural, unschooled, and particularly precious because it is unrepeatable.

Perhaps, just perhaps (as several people theorised during our conversations), Karen sang the way she did *because* of an underlying restlessness. She was certainly not merely "singing the notes."

If that was so, she paid a terrible price for delivering magnificent music which gives so much pleasure. The beauty of its texture, contrasting with the ugliness of what happened, reached everyone who spoke to me. But none more so than Richard and his mother, Agnes, who knew the special nature of Karen's gift but were rendered powerless as they witnessed her decline.

Attempting to dissect what went on in Karen's anorexic world proved to be a minefield, an obstacle course that even specialists have found difficulty in explaining with assurance. It was about "being scared to grow up." It was "an expression of conflict about dependence, autonomy, and control." It was simply "the pursuit of thinness through self-starvation." It was "family induced, a response to peer pressure, or a cry for attention." Richard, who saw it happen, says we shall never fully understand Karen's personal difficulties, which caused her to be in the grip of the disorder. And after three years of looking for clues, I agree with him.

"Anorexia nervosa is inhabited by a secret society," one confidante told me at the outset of my research. "It's a disorder full of components which even people inside it will not discuss." That, together with the individual facets of the Carpenters story, caused more than one insider to warn me: "Don't even *attempt* that book. It will drive you crazy trying to get even close to the truth." Well, it probably did. But I did have the best shepherds.

Richard's positive outlook in helping me assemble this biography was reflected in his response to the tragic aspect of its story. "We had some really great times, too," he said. "And as much as I'm still puzzled and angered by Karen's passing, she did give me and millions of people countless hours of pleasure." He rightly prefers to dwell on that rather than on the still-saddening loss.

The pendulum of this story swung between glory and darkness, rich creativity and human despair. Richard and Karen displayed both toughness and vulnerability that can be measured in the sensitivity of their songbook and their volume of output.

As entertainers, they offered a sharp contrast with many of their contemporaries. Show business folk are expected to be temperamental, some even narcissistic, but neither of these features plagued Karen or Richard. Despite being consumed by success from the ages of nineteen (Karen) and twenty-two (Richard), they remained pretty down to earth. They faced up to their human faults but were untainted by show business excess.

During my research for this portrait of them, I found a universal respect for their integrity quite unlike that usually encountered on the highways of the entertainment world.

There was also deep fury, bafflement, and many tears at the loss of Karen.

In trying to recapture the golden years, as well as attempting to fit the jigsaw of her problem, I needed the help of scores of Richard and Karen's friends, relatives, and professional colleagues. For many of them the memories were painful as well as joyful. For while Karen and Richard's music is the epitome of sophistication, their offstage lives have naturally been dotted with peccadilloes and contradictions.

Some of the opinions expressed in this book have been tough for Richard and his mother Agnes to hear, but their support and encouragement have been paramount as they eased my path, providing vital signposts and introductions. Without such cooperation, this would have been a fruitless pursuit, and I thank them, together with Richard's wife, Mary, for their valued friendship and help in my work in California and Connecticut.

My lawyer, James Mulholland in Los Angeles, has been an inspirational supporter as well as a practical ally whose guidance along some difficult terrain has been unstinting and rock-solid. Cynthia Barrett, my astute and intuitive editor at HarperCollins in New York, recognised the strengths of this story from its inception, and I thank her for such patience and insight, as well as practical suggestions. Thanks also to Ari Hoogenboom, and to Vicki Haire, a meticulous copy editor, for her observations to improve the manuscript. My energetic literary agent, Alan Nevins at Renaissance in Los Angeles, gave unflagging support to this project, and I thank him warmly for such tenacity.

Exploring the rise to fame of the Carpenters as an act, and the complex disaster that enveloped Karen, I sought the observations of scores of their associates, friends, relatives, and medical experts in the United States and in Britain. For many hours of stimulating conversations, road maps (literally and figuratively), hospitality, thoughtfulness, and laughter, and above all enlightenment, my deepest thanks to:

In California: David Alley, Jim Allgood, Dave Alpert, Derek Alpert, Herb Alpert, Tom Bahler, Randy Bash, Sherwin Bash, John Bettis, Clare Baren, Ken Black, Paul Bloch, Maria Luisa Galeazzi Cooper, Carol Curb, Mike Curb, Gil Friesen, Bruce Gifford, Doug Haverty, Leslie Johnston, Joe Layton, Henry Mancini, Bob Messenger, Jerry Moss, Olivia Newton-John, Beverly Nogawski, Cubby O'Brien, Barbara Orbison, Tony Peluso, Brent Pierce, Frank Pooler, Gary Sims, Doug Strawn, Lee Vail, Elizabeth Van Ness, Evelyn Wallace, Jerry Weintraub, Werner Wolfen, Ken Welch, Mitzie Welch, Paul Williams, Dr. Joel Yager at UCLA, Roger Young.

In New York: Terry Ellis, Abby Levenkron, Steven Levenkron, Karen Ramone, Phil Ramone, Marisa Sabounghi, Phoebe Snow, Susan Weiner.

In New Haven, Connecticut: Frank Bonito, Rudy Canelli, Debra Cuticello, C.J. Cuticello, Marion Connellan, Jim Squeglia, Carl Vaiuso, Joe Vaiuso, Theresa Vaiuso, Henry Will, Rosemarie Will.

In England: John Adrian, Leslie Bricusse, Nicky Chinn, Professor Arthur Crisp, John Deacon, Derek Green, Justin Hayward, Babs Knight, Peter Knight, Jr., Michael McCartney, Paul McCartney, Brian Southall, Dr. J. Allister Vale at the National Poisons Information Service, Birmingham; Joanna Vincent at the Eating Disorders Association, Norwich; Dave Price and Sally Hine at the BBC Sound Archive; Michael Alcock and Kate Hill at the publishers Boxtree.

In other locations: Bernice Rudolph (Baltimore, Maryland), Joan Pennisi (Phoenix, Arizona), Vivian Meehan and Pat Haden at ANAD (National Association of Anorexia and Associated Disorders in Chicago); Joe Osborn (Shreveport, Louisiana), Paul White (Toledo, Ohio); Cherry Boone O'Neill (Seattle, Washington); Norman Weiss (Salt Lake City, Utah); Sandy Holland (Las Vegas, Nevada); Don Murphy (Topeka, Kansas); Dennis Heath (Munich, Germany); Wes Jacobs (Detroit, Michigan); Roger Nichols (Montana).

Finally (as befits the bill-topping position), my gratitude goes to my family—my wife, Pamela, and our sons, Miles and Mark—for being there and for again tolerating the intolerable.

Ray Coleman
Richmond, England
Autumn 1993

THE CARPENTERS ON RECORD

T his list sets out to detail Richard and Karen's recording career as they planned it, chronologically year by year. It does not, therefore, include the many Compact Disc compilations and reissues which continue through public demand. It is a record of their single A-sides and album tracks, providing an at-a-glance listing of their studio work.

SINGLES

1969
Ticket to Ride
1970
Close to You. We've Only Just Begun. Merry Christmas Darling. For All We Know.
1971
Rainy Days and Mondays. Superstar. Hurting Each Other.
1972
It's Going to Take Some Time. Goodbye to Love.
1973
Sing. Yesterday Once More. Top of the World.
1974
I Won't Last a Day without You. Please Mr. Postman. Santa Claus Is Coming to Town.
1975
Only Yesterday. Solitaire.
1976
There's a Kind of Hush. I Need to Be in Love. Goofus.

1977
All You Get from Love Is a Love Song. Calling Occupants of Interplanetary Craft. Sweet, Sweet Smile.
1978
I Believe You
1981
Touch Me When We're Dancing. (Want You) Back in My Life Again. Those Good Old Dreams. Beechwood 4-5789.
1983
Make Believe It's Your First Time. Your Baby Doesn't Love You Anymore.
1987
Something in Your Eyes (Richard Carpenter solo)
1989
If I Had You (Karen Carpenter solo)
1990
You're the One

ALBUMS

1969: OFFERING/TICKET TO RIDE
Invocation/Your Wonderful Parade/Someday/Get Together/All of My Life/Turn Away/Ticket to Ride/Don't Be Afraid/What's the Use/All I Can Do/Eve/Nowadays Clancy Can't Even Sing/Benediction.
1970: CLOSE TO YOU
We've Only Just Begun/Love Is Surrender/Maybe It's You/Reason to Believe/Help/(They Long to Be) Close to You/Baby It's You/I'll Never Fall in Love Again/Crescent Noon/Mr. Guder/I Kept on Loving You/Another Song.
1971: CARPENTERS
Rainy Days and Mondays/Saturday/Let Me Be the One/(A Place to) Hideaway/For All We Know/Superstar/Druscilla Penny/One Love/Bacharach-David Medley: Knowing When to Leave/Make It Easy on Yourself/(There's) Always Something There to Remind Me/I'll Never Fall in Love Again/Walk on By/Do You Know the Way to San Jose/Sometimes.
1972: A SONG FOR YOU
A Song for You/Top of the World/Hurting Each Other/It's Going to Take Some Time/Goodbye to Love/Intermission/Bless

the Beasts and Children/Flat Baroque/Piano Picker/I Won't Last
a Day without You/Crystal Lullaby/Road One/A Song for You
(reprise).

1973: NOW AND THEN

Sing/This Masquerade/Heather/Jambalaya (On the Bayou)/I
Can't Make Music/Yesterday Once More/Medley: Fun Fun
Fun/The End of the World/Da Doo Ron Ron/Deadman's
Curve/Johnny Angel/The Night Has a Thousand Eyes/Our Day
Will Come/One Fine Day/Yesterday Once More (reprise).

1975: HORIZON

Aurora/Only Yesterday/Desperado/Please Mr. Postman/I
Can Dream, Can't I/Solitaire/Happy/(I'm Caught between)
Goodbye and I Love You/Love Me for What I Am/Eventide.

1976: A KIND OF HUSH

There's a Kind of Hush/You/Sandy/Goofus/Can't Smile
without You/I Need to Be in Love/One More Time/Boat to
Sail/I Have You/Breaking Up Is Hard to Do.

1977: PASSAGE

B'wana She No Home/All You Get from Love Is a Love Song/I
Just Fall in Love Again/Don't Cry for Me Argentina/Sweet, Sweet
Smile/Two Sides/Man Smart, Woman Smarter/Calling Occupants
of Interplanetary Craft.

1978: CHRISTMAS PORTRAIT

O Come O Come Imanuel/Overture: Deck the Halls; I Saw
Three Ships; Have Yourself a Merry Little Christmas; God Rest Ye
Merry Gentlemen; Away in a Manger; What Child Is This; Carol of
the Bells; O Come All Ye Faithful; Adeste Fideles/Christmas
Waltz/Sleigh Ride/Medley: It's Christmas Time; Sleep Well Little
Children; Have Yourself a Merry Little Christmas; Santa Claus Is
Coming to Town; The Christmas Song (Chestnuts Roasting on an
Open Fire)/Jingle Bells/First Snowfall/Let it Snow/Carol of the
Bells/Merry Christmas Darling/I'll Be Home for Christmas/Christ
Is Born/Medley: Winter Wonderland; Silver Bells; White Christmas;
Ave Maria.

1981: MADE IN AMERICA

Those Good Old Dreams/Strength of a Woman/(Want You)
Back in My Life Again/When You've Got What It Takes/Some-
body's Been Lyin'/I Believe You/Touch Me When We're Danc-
ing/When It's Gone (It's Just Gone)/Beechwood 4-5789/Because
We Are in Love (The Wedding Song).

1983: VOICE OF THE HEART

Now/Sailing on the Tide/You're Enough/Make Believe It's Your First Time/Two Lives/At the End of a Song/; Ordinary Fool/Prime Time Love/Your Baby Doesn't Love You Anymore/Look to Your Dreams.

1984: AN OLD FASHIONED CHRISTMAS

It Came upon a Midnight Clear/Overture: Happy Holiday; The First Noel; March of the Toys; Little Jesus; I Saw Mommy Kissing Santa Claus; O Little Town of Bethlehem; In Dulce Jubilo; Gesu Bambino; Angels We Have Heard on High/An Old Fashioned Christmas/O Holy Night/Home for the Holidays/Medley: Here Comes Santa Claus; Frosty the Snowman; Rudolph the Red Nosed Reindeer; Good King Wenceslas/Little Altar Boy/Do You Hear What I Hear/My Favorite Things/He Came Here for Me/Santa Claus Is Coming to Town/What Are You Doing New Year's Eve/Selections from *Nutcracker:* A: Overture Miniature; B: Dance of the Sugar Plum Fairies; C: Tretak: D: Valse Des Fleurs/I Heard the Bells on Christmas Day.

1989: LOVELINES

Lovelines/Where Do I Go from Here/The Uninvited Guest/If We Try/When I Fall in Love/Kiss Me the Way You Did Last Night/Remember When Lovin' Took All Night/You're the One/Honolulu City Lights/Slow Dance/If I Had You/Little Girl Blue.

1991: FROM THE TOP

This is not a repackaging but sixty-seven selections including twenty titles previously unreleased, and forty remixed. Presented by Richard as a chronological history of Carpenters music, including home recordings, demonstrations, and jingles, it was the ultimate collector's item, tracing their story in words and music from 1965 to 1982.

Caravan/The Parting of Our Ways/Looking for Love/I'll Be Yours/Iced Tea/You'll Love Me/All I Can Do/Don't Be Afraid/Invocation/Your Wonderful Parade/Goodnight/All of My Life/Eve/Ticket to Ride/Get Together/Interview/Maybe It's You/(They Long to Be) Close to You/We've Only Just Begun/Merry Christmas Darling/For All We Know/Superstar/Rainy Days and Mondays/Let Me Be the One/Bless the Beasts and Children/Hurting Each Other/Top of the World/Goodbye to Love/Santa Claus Is Coming to Town/This Masquerade/Canta-Sing/

Yesterday Once More/Oldies Medley/Radio Contest "outtakes"/ Please Mr. Postman/Only Yesterday/Solitaire/Good Friends Are for Keeps/Ordinary Fool/I Need to Be in Love/From This Moment On/Suntory Pop Jingles/All You Get from Love Is a Love Song/Calling Occupants of Interplanetary Craft/Christ Is Born/ White Christmas/Little Altar Boy/Ave Maria/Where Do I Go from Here/Little Girl Blue/If I Had You/My Body Keeps Changing My Mind/Still Crazy After All These Years/Touch Me When We're Dancing/When It's Gone/Because We Are in Love (The Wedding Song)/Now.

INDEX

Danza Tony, 278
Daugherty, Jack, 73, 76, 81, 97,
    106, 107, 120–22, 124
David, Hal, 76, 83
Davis, Skeeter, 129
Deacon, John, 313
Denver, John, 215
"Desperado" (song), 181, 210
Diamond, Neil, 85
Disneyland, 65–66, 141, 173
"Don't Cry for Me Argentina"
    (song), 230, 231
Downey, (CA), 15–18, 49–50,
    205–7, 245, 320, 323–24
Downey High School, 50–52, 54,
    63, 68
Downey Methodist Church, 50, 55n,
    68–69
Dunphy, Linda, 280

Eagles, The, 85
Eating Disorders Association, 331
Edelman, Randy, 129
Elie, Florine, 20, 320
Ellis, Terry, 174–80, 186–93, 196,
    198, 215, 321
    Karen's break-up with, 191–93,
    322
    Richard's relationship with, 179–80
    as temporary manager, 190, 191,
    211
Emetine poisoning, 21–23
Emmons, Buddy, 133

Fans, 95, 113, 127–28, 149, 171,
    173, 208–10
    newsletter of, 188–89
Feather Leonard, 60
Fiedler, Arthur, 173
Fifth Dimension, 74
Findley, Chuck, 84
Fink, Seymour, 41
Firings, 89–90, 103, 145–47, 180
    of Bash, 189–90
    of Sedaka, 188–89
First Edition, 73
"For All We Know" (song), 100,
    105, 107
Ford, Mary, 39

Ford Motor Company, 72, 77
Freed, Alan, 39
Friberg, Dan, 57, 58
Friesen, Gil, 91, 94, 132
From the Top (compct disc
    collection), 333

Galeazzi, Maria. *See* Cooper, Maria
    Galeazzi
Garfunkel, Art, 308
Gerhardt, Ray, 121
Germany, 197–98, 220–21, 224
Gifford, Bruce, 51, 52, 54
"Girl from Ipanema, The" (song),
    60
Gold, Tracey, 330
*Golden Cage, The: The Enigma of
    Anorexia Nervosa* (Bruch), 249
"Going Thing, The" (commercials),
    72, 77
"Goodbye to Love" (song), 120,
    124–28, 131, 135, 180, 183,
    193
Grammy Awards, 95, 99, 108, 128
Great Britain, 161–66, 198, 290,
    331
    Carpenters' music in, ix–x, 95–96,
    128, 130, 131, 133, 135n,
    161–64, 173, 177, 191, 210,
    216, 221–22, 226, 236,
    240–41, 329
    eating disorders in, ix, 331
Green, Derek, 96, 176–78, 263, 271
    "Softly" and, 197–201
Guder, Vic, 65

Hardin, Tim, 94
Harmon, Mark, 168
Haverty, Doug, 162
Hayes, Vance, 50, 55n, 63
Hayward, Justin, 290
Heath, Chris, 162n
Heath, Dennis, 54–55, 300–301,
    318, 321, 322
Hobbies, 173, 208–10
Hoerburger, Rob, 162n
Holland, Sandy, 157, 186, 211, 247,
    257
Hollywood Reporter, 122